J. Henry Shorthouse,
"The Author of John Inglesant"
(with reference to T. S. Eliot and C. G. Jung)

by
Charles W. Spurgeon

ISBN: 1-58112-183-0

DISSERTATION.COM

Parkland, FL • USA • 2003

J. Henry Shorthouse, "The Author of John Inglesant"
(with reference to T. S. Eliot and C. G. Jung)

Dissertation.com
USA • 2003

ISBN: 1-58112-183-0
www.Dissertation.com/library/1121830a.htm

J. Henry Shorthouse,

"The Author of *John Inglesant*"

(with Reference to T. S. Eliot and C. G. Jung)

Charles Wayman Spurgeon

A Thesis Submitted
for the Research Degree
Doctor of Philosophy in English Literature

Birkbeck College
University of London
1995

Table of Contents

Acknowledgements and Dedication

More than thirty years ago I first read and felt the "mystic" power of *John Inglesant*, which urged me to explore the history of Nicholas Ferrar's Little Gidding. I soon realised that Shorthouse's "philosophical romance" was urging me, as it had Shorthouse, towards "spiritual romance". Though intent on keeping my maturing consciousness in the twentieth century, T. S. Eliot's spiritual autobiography exploded my sense of time and meaning. *Four Quartets* "enspiritualises" personal and collective human experience and redefines philosophical meaning and psychological time and proves, I think, that past and future are gathered and contained in the presence of poetry.

After many visits and pilgrimages to Little Gidding, after much historical searching, literary study, and inner investigation, I find nothing ordinary about Little Gidding, and I humbly dedicate this thesis to the extraordinary **Community of Christ the Sower at Little Gidding**,[1] which lives in conscious awareness of the "familiar compound ghost / Both intimate and unidentifiable", to the worldwide charitable trust, **Friends of Little Gidding**, and to Valerie Peters, "Poet of Little Gidding".

As words may suffice in compelling recognition of "a double part", I acknowledge personal and professional debts: Thanks to my supervisor, Andrew Sanders, and to Birkbeck College for its unique educational opportunities; to the British University International Summer Schools programme, especially to Edwina Porter of the London University summer programme; to Regent's College for the opportunity to teach and study in London; to "The Librarians" and the many libraries in Britain and in the United States that carefully preserve and eagerly share the treasures of our heritage; to Sir John and Lady Sophie Laws for their kindness and hospitality, to Adelheid Birch for her enduring support, to Maureen Jupp, my spiritual friend at Westminster Abbey, and to my friends and colleagues at the Henry E. Huntington Library and at Marymount College, Palos Verdes, California.

---

[1] Since this thesis was completed in October 1995, the Community of Christ the Sower has moved away from Little Gidding, and the properties surrounding the Church of St John the Divine are administered by The Little Gidding Trust, Clermont House, Little Cressingham, Thetford, Norfolk IP25 6LY.

Introduction

By the time Joseph Henry Shorthouse began writing *John Inglesant* in 1866, the English novel had developed a considerable tradition of religious controversy. As many as 40,000 novels were written between 1837 and 1901 to persuade atheists to believe, agnostics to reconsider, and believers to accept specific doctrines or dogmas. As the studies of Baker, Drummond, Maison, Chapman, and Wolff have demonstrated, religious novelists attempted to inculcate faith in their readers and to challenge readers to theological correctness.[1] As defined by Woolf, the major religious controversies of the Victorian church provide, in retrospect, six classifications:

> Catholic and anti-Catholic
> High Church (Tractarian / anti-Tractarian)
> Low Church (Evangelical / anti-Evangelical)
> Broad Church
> Nonconformist (Dissenting)
> Varieties of Doubters[2]

However "ambiguous" Anglo-Catholicism may be today, as Pickering contends,[3] and however debatable its origins in Catholic and High Church traditions, Anglo-Catholicism is a dynamic and powerful force in the national religious life of England that owes many of its greatest achievements and much of its theological tradition to the Oxford Movement.[4]

Launched by a daring and ardent sermon preached by John Keble before His Majesty's Judges of Assize at Oxford, Sunday, 14 July 1833, in St. Mary's Church, the Oxford Movement's political and religious ardour had effectively transformed the religious life of England before it reached its highest achievement in fictional form, *John Inglesant* (1880). As with other movements in the religious life of England and in the world-wide Anglican communion, Anglo-Catholicism finds its strengths in historical tradition, and in the Victorian Church, Anglo-Catholicism represents the "high serious" and "high earnest" aspirations towards a strongly united national life. Pickering's analogy expresses the relationship between the Oxford Movement and Anglo-Catholicism as that of "mother and daughter"[5] as literary critics think of the relationship between major and minor authors or between specific genre and literary offshoots. The Oxford Movement still lives in its aspirations, and modern "interfaith dialogue" may lead to an "intercommunion eucharist" between the Anglican and Roman churches.[6] Although there appears to be little difference between Anglo-Catholic and Roman Catholic services and places of worship, now or in the recent past, the deeply rooted conflicts of the Victorian Church have by no means been resolved, though the fires of controversy have been generally quelled in the twentieth century, especially in the post-World War II, Vatican II era, by the modern ecumenical movement.[7] However deeply rooted in the human psyche or in cultural traditions, the essential differences between Anglican and Roman religious convictions may be simplified to metaphoric terms. Patristic and matristic spiritual values conflict against each other as patriotic and nationalistic values conflict against international ones; so too spontaneity and emotional worship conflict against formalized liturgy and ritual as Protestant local authority conflicts against Papal or Roman authority. Religious hierarchy, religious orders, and questions of authority differentiate the Roman from the English church, even though within the Anglo-Catholics or "Anglican-Catholics" or "Catholic-Anglicans" "great variation is to be found...from the moderates to the extremists."[8] Although infighting is inherent in all churches, the "vast amount of infighting" within Anglo-Catholicism "is virtually incomprehensible to the outsider [and] has much weakened the movement."[9] Study of the "insider" religious literary and critical work of J. Henry Shorthouse and T. S. Eliot clarifies Anglo-Catholicism and provides philosophical and psychological grounding for appreciating their respective "minor" and "major" contributions to Victorian and modern literature. As their artistic achievements and personal commitments to the religious life of England and to the vitality of the Church of England help clarify the causes of infighting and strengthen the spirituality of Anglo-Catholicism, the analytical or depth psychology of Individuation developed by Carl Gustav Jung provides a critical basis for assessing how their literary achievements define, resolve and strengthen Anglo-Catholicism.

The primary concern of the present study is the "enspiritualised" literary achievement of Shorthouse and the relationship of his Broad and liberal churchmanship to the High and conservative religious convictions of Eliot. The literary and critical work of both authors will be considered in some detail to illustrate their religious sensibilities, to show how their Anglo-Catholic ideals inform their respective spiritual visions, and to demonstrate how Jung's psychology of Individuation provides an important theoretical and critical basis for appreciating religious literature. Analytical study of the interrelations and interconnectedness of religion, philosophy, and psychology in literature risks reduction and oversimplification of "the spirit in man, art, and literature".[10] Study of *spirit* usually complicates, confounds, or simply denies the empirical value of formal methodology,[11] but the psychology of Individuation translates the "rhetoric of the soul" into a psychological frame of reference through "the empirical method". As Jung defines the psychology of the empirical method itself, process becomes more significant than causal analysis. Cause and effect categories which are acceptable to the methodologies of the materialistic sciences become unacceptable in the study of acausal or synchronous relationships. The dynamics of consciousness and the psychodynamics of the unconscious require an acausal theory. To address the proverbial "chicken or the egg" and "cart before the horse" problems of deterministic methodology, Jung proposed the acausal theory of synchronicity which, at least, makes the problems of the *spirit* susceptible to psychological theory. Analogously, the "rhetoric of the soul" or the "poetics of the Self" provides a frame of reference for the study of the "dynamics of the spirit" in religious literature. Shorthouse and Eliot assumed and defined critical values from their own creative practices and consciously chose the language and imagination of Anglo-Catholic Christianity to give historical continuity and validity to their spiritual visions. Eliot's pre-Christian work contrasts against his Christian writings and does not reflect the lifelong religious sensibility and continuity of Shorthouse's work. Shorthouse's transition from the Society of Friends to the Anglican Church evoked philosophical considerations, whereas Eliot's conversion transformed the philosophical rhetoric of his Unitarianism into the psychological and spiritual vision of Catholic Anglicanism. As artists of religious experience, both accepted the literary logic of Christ and Christianity, the necessity of paradox, irony, and symbolic imagery as the only means of communicating "sacramental vision" in industrialized and commercialized, secularized and materialized culture. As Jung had to observe, study, and assess the perceptual patterns and unconscious attitudes of his own personality before he could define the objectivity of empirical psychology, Shorthouse and Eliot defined their own natures and assessed their artistic preferences and prejudices through the practice of literary criticism. Jung had to assume great indifference, detachment, wonder, and objectivity towards his own personality, which by all accounts was neither an easy endeavour, nor was his a simple personality. After his conversion, Eliot had to redefine and defend religion itself to readers who had shared the agnostic stance and modernism of his pre-Christian poetry. Never as self-conscious as Eliot and certainly not as intellectual, Shorthouse never had to struggle for objectivity or to win the sympathies of non-religious readers. Rather, he felt his way towards critical theory and romanced his religious convictions into his literary practice. His influence today is that of a "minor Victorian" writer, and his work is known to only a small audience, though his influence has been compared with that of Malcolm MacMillan's *Dagonet the Jester* (1886), Richard Blackmore's *Lorna Doone* (1869), Thomas A. Pinkerton's *The Spanish Poniard* (1890)[12], Walter Pater's *Marius the Epicurean* (1885)[13] and his influence has been detected in Margaret Irwin's *Royal Flush* (1932), Rose Macaulay's *They Were Defeated* (1932), Charles Morgan's *The Fountain* (1932), and David Garnett's *Pocahontas* (1933), and his experimentation with philosophical and spiritual romance and with musical rhythms ultimately makes him a predecessor of such diverse writers as Hermann Hesse, Andre Gide, and Virginia Woolf.[14]

However minor his role as church apologist, essayist, novelist, and public literary figure among late Victorian authors, Shorthouse's religious sensibility bears intellectual sympathy with Eliot's Anglo-Catholic values in poetry, drama, critical essays and lectures and prefigures Eliot's work, as Jung's psychology of Individuation gives value to Eliot's "mythical method". In his 1923 essay on "Ulysses, Order, and Myth", Eliot credited James Joyce with having invented the "mythical method", which Eliot celebrated as having "the importance of a scientific discovery". By "manipulating a continuous parallel between contemporaneity and antiquity", Joyce advanced "a step toward making the modern world possible for art"[15] As poetry expresses "the most ancient and most modern" mode of religious thought, so the alternating philosophical and lyrical qualities of *John Inglesant* suggest a dialectical rhythm of mental time play between historical imagination and the contemporaneity of stream of consciousness. Writing in secrecy and privacy, Shorthouse did not, however, think of himself as a "conscious artist", as an author aware of his niche in English literature, during the years he worked on *John Inglesant*, and, indeed, he did not see the need to make art "possible for the modern world"; rather he saw the need to make religion and religious life an art.

The central symbols and themes of Shorthouse's "Broad Church Sacramentalism", as he described his own religious persuasion, and his personal tendencies towards Platonic mysticism disclose parallels with Eliot's struggles as churchman, apologist, and Christian poet-dramatist. Eliot's *Four Quartets*, in particular, owes much to Shorthouse's revival of interest in seventeenth-century Anglicanism and his recreation of Nicholas Ferrar's holy community at Little Gidding. By romanticizing Little Gidding, Shorthouse created a literary symbol that is at once spiritual epiphany and psychological vision, and he transformed historical interest in Little Gidding into a myth of Anglo-Catholic ecumenism. Eliot, inheriting the myth, combined historical interest in Nicholas Ferrar's community and the Church of St. John the Evangelist at Little Gidding, into an intense, poetically conceived universal, "the world's end", and made the "end" a place "where prayer has been valid".[16] As *John Inglesant* inspired Emma Marshall's *A Haunt of Ancient Peace* (1897) and Elsie K. Seth-Smith's *The Way of Little Gidding* (1920?), so it prepared the way for Eliot's fourth quartet, "Little Gidding" (1942). Today a vital ecumenical community flourishes at Little Gidding and acknowledges both Shorthouse and Eliot inside the Church of St. John.

As the work of Elizabeth Drew, Joseph Henderson, and other

critics has shown, Jungian theory validates the archetypal qualities of Eliot's poetry and dramas and, in fact, Eliot's literary work exemplifies the stages of growth and development of Individuation psychology.[17] Jungian theory also validates the archetypal nature of Shorthouse's work, but neither Shorthouse's life nor his work conform to the accepted pattern of Individuation. When Eliot first expressed awareness of the "agony of the artist" and the "pain of the poet", he did so in a bold and brash fashion. The Eliot of 1917, as he self-reflectively described himself in 1961, was immature, brash, and presumptuous in his literary pronouncements and had assumed an authority of certitude and conviction that made his criticism controversial, popular and quotable.[18] Shorthouse's youthful and mid-life enthusiasms also gives his work a sense of urgency and authority, but his more mature work claims authority almost too dogmatically. The older he became the more he reacted against the Church of Rome, although he never experienced "the agony of the artist" to "escape from emotion... [or] from personality".[19]   In "Tradition and the Individual Talent" Eliot defines "historical perspective" as necessary to sound criticism and argues that the artist must be separated or divided from his medium in order to make possible the "Impersonal theory of poetry". Only an impersonal theory, he asserts, can "save" poetry, and poetry must be saved because only "poetry is capable of saving us", as I. A. Richards declared, from the pernicious "onslaughts" of that "most dangerous of the sciences...the whole subject which includes Psychoanalysis and Behaviourism."[20] Eliot shared the belief of theorists like Owen Barfield and Rudolf Steiner that romanticism had failed to give the Victorian age a new basis for truth[21] and had not resolved the "dissociation of sensibility" within English poetry. When Eliot defined "the historical sense" as "the pastness of the past" and "perception of its presence",[22] he was not a Christian, and, in retrospect, the "dissociation of sensibility" reflects his search for the historical continuity of religious emotion as it prefigures his later struggle for an Anglo-Catholic interpretation of English history, especially of the Reformation. Shorthouse, on the other hand, celebrates romanticism as revelation of spiritual truth and reaffirmation of "providential aesthetic".[23]

After dissociation from his immediate past and reintegration of personal experience into ancestral perspective, Eliot found a new basis for truth itself in "the historical sense". "Ash-Wednesday", "Marina", *Four Quartets*, and each of his dramas reflect Eliot's maturing. His philosophic and intellectual attempts to understand history develop into profound struggles to comprehend time, meaning, and consciousness, as his experiencing of moral order transforms the perception of the past's presence into moments of potential transcendence and symbols of divine providence. In *Four Quartets* he posits "the still point of the turning world"[24] and attempts to make the strictly personal moments of life (like the "evening with the photograph album")[25] into impersonal patterns of experience; then he expands generalizations into theory: "for history is a pattern / of timeless moments".[26] The transforming of "personal and private agonies" through knowledge and experience into universals and absolutes is, in fact, the dominant theme, the poetic action, and the great achievement of the *Four Quartets*. In essence, resolution of the struggle illustrates the "progress of the poet" through what Jung called "symbols of transformation" towards unitary culmination: the point of perception when "[we] arrive where we started / And know the place for the first time" and at which "the fire and the rose are one."[27] Shorthouse's correspondence and friendship with Lady Victoria Welby, a pioneer of semantics and "significs", and Jung's pioneering of the "word association test" point towards what Eliot called "the intolerable wrestle with words and meaning",[28] the wrestle to give words figurative and associational implications, to deepen metaphor through contextual development into literary symbol, to create the dynamic qualities of literary archetypes.

To qualify, "art never improves", Eliot asserts, "but the material of art is never quite the same."[29] In Eliot's view, the material of art is transformed or "reordered" whenever an artist creates the "truly new", a process that requires the poet to separate in himself his personality and personal life from "the mind which creates": "The more perfect the artist, the more completely separate in him will be the man who suffers and the mind which creates." The "suffering" of the artist confronts him with his "business" as a craftsman: "The business of the poet is not to find new emotions, but to use the ordinary ones and, in working them up into poetry, to express feelings which are not actual emotion at all." Thus, only by recognizing that "the poet has, not a 'personality' to express, but a particular medium" can a poet effect the necessary internal separation.[30]

Although Eliot regarded "Tradition and the Individual Talent" as "perhaps the most juvenile" of his essays, he did not repudiate his early views about "depersonalization", which enabled him to define the "Dissociation of Sensibility". "What I see, in the history of English poetry", he asserted, "is...the splitting up of personality."[31] His acute personal and artistic struggle to "possess integrated or undissociated sensibility...to embody thought and feeling together, fused in a single indissoluble expression"[32] presents his reworking of the dilemma he first defined in "Tradition and the Individual Talent" and which later becomes part of his argument in favour of an Anglo-Catholic view of history. He redefines the problem in "Shakespeare and the Stoicism of Seneca", an essay that "smacks of Old Possum"[33] and, according to Virginia Woolf, of the "damned egotistical self".[34] He asserts "that which alone constitutes life for a poet" is the struggle "to transmute the personal and private agonies into something rich and strange, something universal and impersonal."[35] As the "poet makes poetry, the metaphysician makes metaphysics", so "Tradition and the Individual Talent" "proposes to halt at the frontiers of metaphysics of mysticism". Had Eliot rewritten the tradition essay or redefined his position, as he qualified "Milton, I" (1936) in "Milton, II" (1947), he may have restated his assertion that "this essay proposes to halt", and he may have re-introduced the "I" into his essay. Only five years after he wrote "Tradition and the Individual Talent" he underwent psychological treatment.[36] No essay halts itself unless produced by "automatic writing", a process of composition that Eliot specifically repudiated.[37] Eliot never incorporated Jungian terminology into his critical works, yet a transition from Freudian to Jungian orientation is as clear in Eliot's development as is his pre-Christian to Anglo-Catholic conversion, and his dramas are decidedly Jungian, not Freudian.[38] Applied to Eliot's mature poetry or dramas, Freudian interpretations, which prescriptively assume the sublimation of libido or subconscious neuroses as the "cause of creativity", are quite misleading.[39] No "King Bolo" or "Sweeney Erect" appears in Eliot's post-conversion poetry, and after the poet's private life encounters *The Rock* in 1934, the persona of "Sweeney Agonistes" disappears abruptly and never reappears.[40] None of Eliot's pre-Christian work affords comparison with Shorthouse's work.

As Shorthouse's public reputation grew from 1881 until his death in 1903, he became more rigid and authoritarian in his convictions, especially those regarding the Church of England and his literary tastes. As Eliot's public reputation grew, he became self-conscious about his earlier judgments and pronouncements. Particularly in public lectures, he defined his qualifications and limited his critical authority. Most notably, as the "elder statesman" of poetry, he re-evaluated his career as a poet-critic in his 1961 lecture "To Criticize the Critic" and explained his declaration that he was "a classicist in literature, a royalist in politics, and an Anglo-Catholic in religion". He made the original declaration of his conservative nature in the 1926 "Preface" to a collection of essays entitled *For Lancelot Andrewes*.[41] (In the first edition "anglo-catholic" appears; Eliot never explained the change from small case to capital letters.) Ironically, Eliot explained that "the sentence in question was provoked by a personal experience". He had made the declaration of allegiances because he had "felt obliged to acquaint" Irving Babbit, under whom he studied at Harvard University, with the fact that he "really had been baptized and confirmed into the Church of England." Certainly, he also had his Harvard professor in mind when he published "The Humanism of Irving Babbitt" in 1928. Announcing his convictions in print, Eliot commented that "what must have been a greater shock to Babbitt was the 'defection' of Paul Elmer More from Humanism to

Christianity".

Interestingly, it was Paul Elmer More who declared *John Inglesant* to be "the one great religious novel of the English language".[42] Eliot refers not only to More but also to Edmund Gosse, who became a personal friend of Shorthouse in 1883, two years after the first public publication of *John Inglesant*. Gosse, of all of Shorthouse's reviewers and critics, described the "author of *John Inglesant*" as a man of postures and covers, not unlike Eliot's own usage of pseudonyms and his Old Possum persona.[43] Yet, Eliot never mentions Shorthouse or *John Inglesant* in any of published essays, reviews, or letters. When he taught English literature in 1916 at the University of London, Eliot demanded a great deal of reading from tutorial students, as the course syllabus suggests, but he skipped over Shorthouse completely, including Disraeli, Peacock, Reade, and Trollope as "minor novelists".[44] Of course, 1916 was a decade before Eliot's conversion. Yet, within three years of his conversion, Eliot composed "Arnold and Pater" (1930) as a study of the "fluctuating relations between religion and culture" and as a valuation of Pater's role in developing "aesthetic religion" in *Marius the Epicurean* (1885), the novel that shares critical comparison with *John Inglesant*. Again, and this time as a Christian, Eliot ignores "the greatest Anglo-Catholic novel of the Victorian age".[45]

Eliot's ignoring of Shorthouse's achievement is a literary mystery in itself, especially in light of Eliot's own pilgrimage to Little Gidding and his personal interest and involvement in creating the trust society, Friends of Little Gidding. His neglect of Shorthouse has led more than one critic to bafflement, among them, Dame Helen Gardner, who, during her lifetime, was an acknowledged authority on Eliot scholarship:

> I find it difficult to believe that this book, so famous in its day, was not known to the Eliot family, with their passionate interest in religious discussions, and that Eliot had not read it as a boy.

"But, even if he had not read it when young," she argued, "it seems likely he would have done so in later life." Noting More's "distinguished book" on Anglicanism, Gardner adds,

> And even if More's praise of it as the finest of religious novels had not stimulated his interest, it seems likely that Smyth's praise of it would have done so.[46]

Eliot's ignoring of Shorthouse remains a mystery which continues to provoke speculation and research. Eliot formed several connections of varying sorts with many persons interested in Little Gidding. Among them were Canon George Tibbats, Canon Charles Smyth, critic and reviewer Bernard Blackstone, and Alan Maycock, librarian at Magdalene College,

Cambridge. When Eliot gave the Clark Lectures in January--March 1926, he concentrated attention on "The Metaphysical Poets of the Seventeenth Century", which gave him scholarly responsibility for assessing George Herbert and Richard Crashaw, both of whom were directly connected with Nicholas Ferrar and the Little Gidding community. Assessing the Anglican divine and the Catholic poet, Eliot, though not yet formally a convert to the Church of England, defined the principle of "dissociation of sensibility" that occurred while the Ferrars were at Little Gidding. Discussing how a poet's mind "is constantly amalgamating disparate experience" and asserting that "the greatest two masters of diction are also the greatest two psychologists, the most curious explorers of the soul", Eliot argues that to understand why "English poetry has remained so incomplete" since Milton and Dryden, "One must look into a good deal more than the heart. One must look into the cerebral cortex, the nervous system, and the digestive tracts."[47] Thankfully, it is not possible to look into the "digestive tract" of Eliot, except in Francis Bacon's metaphorical sense,[48] which leaves one with another Shorthouse mystery. Edmund Gosse excluded his friend and correspondent from his four-volume study of English literature, which was published after Shorthouse's death, published by Shorthouse's publisher, Macmillan, and published at a time when tributes and assessments of Shorthouse were being offered in abundance to the public.[49]

A decade after giving the Clark Lectures, Eliot made his one and only visit to Little Gidding in May 1936.[50] At the time he was editor of *The Criterion*, which two and a half years later published reviews of both Blackstone's and Maycock's books on Little Gidding.[52] Shorthouse, according to Maycock, created "the myth of Little Gidding", and it strains credulity to believe that Eliot did not know about *John Inglesant* or Shorthouse's role in resurrecting interest in Little Gidding and Nicholas Ferrar's community. As *John Inglesant* transforms historical interest in Little Gidding to "spiritual romance", so Eliot's "Little Gidding" creates the ideal of ultimate pilgrimage: "the world's end... [where] the intersection of the timeless moment is England and nowhere. Never and always," where history can be seen as "a pattern / Of timeless moments".[53] Shorthouse redeemed Little Gidding from the neglect of history by transforming history and vitalizing it as myth; Eliot transformed the myth into an absolute reality, a symbol of permanence, where modern man may "kneel / Where prayer has been valid" and listen to "the communication / Of the dead", which, he declares, "is tongued with fire beyond the language of the living".[54]

After privately printing 100 copies of *John Inglesant*, Shorthouse added a preface to the first public edition published by Macmillan in 1881. Regretting that James Hinton's *The Mystery of Pain* had not been "thrown...into the form of story" which would have given the book a greater

12

audience, Shorthouse asks, "Do you not think that for one sorrowful home which has been lightened by his singular genius, there would have been hundreds?" Yet, not until friends urged public publication, and, in fact, not until Alexander Macmillan wrote to Shorthouse saying he thought *John Inglesant* "a work of real genius"[54] and offered to publish the novel at his own expense.[55] The preface stands as the boldest declaration of the power of romance that Shorthouse ever made. His reference to *The Mystery of Pain* merely hinted at what he believed throughout his life to be the real efficacy and power of storytelling:

> "But," you say, "it is only a Romance."
>
> True. It is only human life in the 'highways and hedges' and in 'the streets and lanes of the city' with the ceaseless throbbing of its quivering heart; it is only daily life from the workshop, from the court, from the market, and from the stage; it is only kindliness and neighbourhood and childlife, and the fresh wind of heaven, and the waste of sea and forest, and the sunbreak upon the stainless peaks, and contempt of wrong and pain and death, and the passionate yearning for the face of God, and woman's tears, and woman's self-sacrifice and devotion, and woman's love. Yet, it is only a Romance. It is only the ivory gates falling back at the fairy touch. It is only the leaden sky breaking for a moment above the bowed head, revealing the fathomless Infinite through the gloom. It is only a romance.[56]

Shorthouse proclaims romance as revelation of the transcendental and supernatural seen through the realities of daily life. His argument, however, betrays his sense of audience and glorifies the suffering of women and their need for romantic stories. Throughout his life he always read his work aloud, almost on a daily basis, to his wife Sarah. Though he never thought of the novel as an art form "for women", he most assuredly appreciated women readers; his letters to Lady Victoria Welby and to his female cousins are among his most insightful and revealing, and his sense of the feminine in audience and of the masculine in narrative style are vital to *John Inglesant*'s speaking "immediately to human intuition... without regard to the reader's own faith or philosophy".[57]

Because *John Inglesant* so directly penetrates through readers' individual prejudices and preferences, through conscious values and beliefs and, more subtly, through subconscious or unconscious attitudes, it cannot properly be called a "religious novel", as it often has been.[58] A more appropriate appraisal must consider the psychological and intuitive dynamics of "philosophical romance", especially non-religious readers, and such analysis leads to the essential differences between Jungian and archetypal criticism.

Eliot's reputation as a literary critic and his firmly established stature as a dramatist and great poet need no argument here. Indeed, the number of scholarly works and critical appreciations, appraisals and re-examinations of Eliot's work still claims much attention in international criticism and in the popular media. The publication of his letters, begun in 1988 to mark the centenary of his birth, public readings, presentations, performances, videos and recordings of his poetry and drama testify not just to his popularity but to the serious questions and challenges his work commands. Shorthouse's reputation, however, is another matter altogether, and his last claim to popular attention was in 1961 with the republication of *John Inglesant* and the inclusion of a special preface by the Archbishop of Canterbury. Rather ironically, the republication contained only those episodes that take place in England, though most of Shorthouse's critics agree his best writing occurs in the Italian sections of the novel. His vehement attack on the Church of Rome was, in the interests of Anglo-Roman reunification efforts, not published. His novels and essays still have, though, a significant number of admirers, and critical studies have maintained a steady, if trickling, attention to his achievements, though sadly the attention comes more from the United States, Canada, and Germany than from England. Unlike the critical "touchstones" Eliot has given to literary scholarship (concepts and principles like "auditory imagination", "objective correlative", "the dissociation of sensibility", and the revaluation of the Elizabethan and Metaphysical dramatists and poets), Shorthouse's critical ideas are neither applicable nor specifically useful in studies outside of romance literature and religious novels, and very few of his ideas afford serious intellectual challenge to modern literary criticism and its highly specialized terminology. Indeed, by modern standards, Shorthouse's critical work seems amateurish, lacks intellectual sophistication, and reads like ardent enthusiasm for the simple sake of enthusiasm, but such a judgment is shortsighted and incomplete, and it overlooks his interpretation of the history and achievement of the English novel and his advancement of the genre towards the lyrical and intuitive "great musical novel" that he believed would be "a revelation to mankind". Much of Shorthouse's early essay writing is highly polished in style and exhibits wide reading, zealous interest in history and landscape, and in art, music, and nature as realisations of God as the "Divine Principle" of daily life.

From his youthful membership in the Friends Essay Society in Birmingham through his public career as "the author of *John Inglesant*", Shorthouse developed critical ideas from rather voracious reading and from close attention to his own nature. Probably none of his critical essays will ever appear in a general critical anthology, but it must be remembered that

Shorthouse wrote to please a small circle of friends, that he had no public literary ambitions until after the publication of *John Inglesant*, which forced reputation upon him, and that he never sought to earn his livelihood as author, critic, or literary spokesman. Certainly, he never entertained any sense of himself as an academic. Literary scholarship as we know it today simply did not exist in his day. During Eliot's lifetime, on the other hand, academic literary scholarship and the study of language and literature became institutionalized. As Bradbrook asserts, Eliot's critical method in "Homage to John Dryden" (1924) and *The Sacred Wood* (1920) were "canonized in the Cambridge of the time".[59] In Shorthouse's defence, it should be remembered, too, that Eliot himself regarded two of his famous touchstones, the "objective correlative" and "the dissociation of sensibility" as little more than "conceptual symbols for emotional preferences".[60] Shorthouse's emotional preferences, critical tastes, and convictions continue to represent "significant curiosities" of historical, religious, philosophical, psychological, and musical interest in the English novel. He laboured with a genuine mission to transform and redirect England's literary tradition towards a new art form, one that could inform historical fiction with philosophical dilemmas and subtly resolve them into ideals, then into spiritual realities, through the power of romance and the appeal of musical rhythms. "Enspiritualising" history and daily life into a lyrical aesthetic, he hoped to unite "the godlike and the beautiful in one". "What we want", he wrote Canon Boyd Carpenter in 1884, "is to apply [spiritual aesthetic] to real life. We all understand that art should be religious, but it is more difficult to understand how religion may be an art."[61] Shorthouse's aesthetic is deeply rooted in his romantic zeal and self-dedication to Platonism, his lifelong admiration for Wordsworth and Tennyson, especially for Wordsworth's "The Excursion", and his goal of going beyond Matthew Arnold's Hellenism versus Hebraism and Literature versus Dogma, to create a new understanding of "humour" in literature. Believing that "All history is nothing but the relation of this great effort--the struggle of the divine principle to enter into human life", Shorthouse sought repeatedly to inculcate "fundamental reality" in his novels and tales: "...we have nothing but what *is* real life" and writers, especially poets, must "enter into the struggle" to make the reader engage himself in "mental fight" to hear, or as his Quaker background had taught him, to listen to the Inner Voice.[62]

To establish Eliot's literary kinship with Shorthouse it is not sufficient to talk of "the music of Inglesant's life" as having a "kinship with Eliot's personal music", nor does it suffice to argue that Shorthouse's English Civil War theme "finds expression in words that anticipate Eliot's in 'Little Gidding'", as Max Sutton has done.[63] However minor Shorthouse's critical and artistic achievement now is in the broader valuations of English literature, his overall contributions to the late Victorian era and his success as a novelist cannot be questioned, and his work is of special interest in understanding the continuity and transition from Victorian to modern literature. One approach to understanding the continuity between authors has its roots in Shorthouse's era and virtually spans Eliot's lifetime and was introduced into English literary criticism in 1934, the year of Shorthouse's centenary. Applying Jung's theory of Individuation to the study of literary imagination, Maud Bodkin identified *a priori* "determinants of individual experience" in *Archetypal Patterns in Poetry: Psychological Studies of Imagination*. Individuation theory describes the psychodynamics of how consciousness itself evolves and centres within the Ego and how the Ego interrelates with its unconscious "principle of order", the archetype of the Self. As a literary artist struggles to create an "integrated text", a unified and coherent whole, so all psychologically alive personalities must work to integrate the autonomous and objective contents of the collective unconscious into personal consciousness. As Individuation theory provides literary criticism with descriptive metaphors of the creative process, it grounds psychological interpretation of literature in the texts themselves, not in the biography or psychology of the artists, and in the psychodynamic processes of critical reading. Bodkin, viewing the archetypes as unconscious potentialities of experience, defines literary taste as "readiness to assimilate...themes, patterns of images and emotional associations". The patterns themselves are various "pre-text" orientations, "pre-existing configurations" of "ordering tendencies" which lead readers to "an organized, living unity". According to Individuation theory, archetypal potentialities of experience make possible "the city of God within" because they are activated and actualized by "that within each individual human mind which imposes these patterns, the organizer, the logic of the human mind".[64]

"What, then, occurs", Bodkin asks, "in the mind of a student/critic who attempts to trace through analysis and synthesis the successive movements of these archetypes, of literary 'plots' or themes?" "In effect," she argues, "the imaginative thinking of the student will discern patterns of emotional forces that operate within his own imaginative activity." By tracing and analyzing the motivations of literary characters, the student synthesizes and objectifies "the lineaments of his own personality." Such traits of personality "are consciously observable [and have] cause-effect relationships...centered in Ego, in that dimension of mind which sees the self, the individual, as source and recipient of the data under study". The dynamics of the process suggest that the writer may unconsciously or very deliberately project, displace, or transfer his own "self" into or upon the text as "at once the subject and object" of study. Paradoxically, the reader "finds these cause-effect, pleasure-pain 'realities' to be valueless", which forces the imaginative reader's mind "to find another energy with which to discover order." The processes of analysis and synthesis do not, in themselves, "impose order on the literary texts". "Herein", Bodkin states, "begins the active process of creation; Ego ceases to be an efficient frame of reference and a new, active, seemingly beyond-imagination 'frame' is created: the archetypal Self actualizes."[65]

Theories, however, are "the very devil": "It is true that we need certain points of view for orienting an heuristic value, but they should always be regarded as mere auxiliary concepts that can be laid aside at any time."[66] The imposition of theory upon texts or "determinism in criticism" fails to achieve a "critical attitude for criticism" and merely substitutes "one of a miscellany of frameworks outside literature", as one of Bodkin's critical heirs, Northrop Frye, has insistently pointed out. "If criticism exists, it must be an examination of literature in terms of a conceptual framework derivable from an inductive survey of the literary field", or criticism cannot properly be said to exist.[67] The imposition of Bodkin's theorizing would dictate that critics read the creative works of Shorthouse and Eliot as psychological, fictive autobiography and would suggest that students and critics alike are paradoxically seeking "self-knowledge" when they study Shorthouse or Eliot. Eliot's declaration that a new work of art radically effects a reordering and revaluing of all previous works of art confines his critical view to the literary field, but it also literally "sets him up" by self-imposing a theoretical ideal, the creation of the "new". "Tradition and the Individual Talent" holds the same place in Eliot's artistic achievement as the "Preface" to *John Inglesant* does in Shorthouse's, and these two early critical declarations align both authors in the quest for "ideal order". Having defined their artistic goals in such ideal and visionary terms, both men had to confront in private and in public the intense psychological, religious, and spiritual anxieties of their self-chosen literary tasks. One thinks immediately of the great task of justification Milton set himself in *Paradise Lost* and of the self-study of imagination Wordsworth undertook in *The Prelude*, but neither Shorthouse or Eliot could invoke Milton's "heavenly Muse" nor could they "stand and wait"[68] for inspiration. Wordsworth, perhaps more than any other writer, had prepared the way for Shorthouse, and Eliot, too, found more than impersonal "historical perspective" in Wordsworth's "general Truths... Elements and Agents, Underpowers, Subordinate helpers of the living mind".[69]

Eliot's profound personal disruption has been read out of "The Waste Land" by numerous critics and the reordering of his personality, which can be dated outwardly and publicly, at least, from 29 June 1927 with his baptism at Finstock Church in the Cotswolds, has been read out of *Four*

17

Quartets. Shorthouse never experienced such personal stress, but he, too, sensed the "great work to be done" early in his life and often contemplated what his family and friends called "Henry's book" long before he began writing *John Inglesant.* His religious struggles and transition from the Society of Friends to the Church of England in August 1861 provide the background and motivation for composing his philosophical romance and afford comparison with Eliot's conversion from Unitarianism to Anglo-Catholic Christianity. Indeed, both artists accepted the heritage of the Oxford Movement and confronted the religious struggles of their respective eras with serious "mental fight", though they certainly did not evolve personal myths of meaning or share the more Protestant vision of Blake's "Jerusalem". "The intolerable wrestle with words and meanings" was certainly more than the "mug's game"[70] of poetry to Eliot, for it directed his mind towards historical and traditional catholicity, as the perception of historical parallels led Shorthouse to modernize and recreate Christian mythology rather than evolve or express personal myth.

Although meaning may be myth that informs literature with autobiographical representations,[71] Shorthouse and Eliot were too orthodox to seek truth in the "individual and local" and sought it instead in the "general and operative".[72] Had they expressed only their own personal psychologies, they should have reduced their creative work to autobiographical metaphor and not have achieved the qualities that distinguish metaphor from literary symbol. The critic and the biographer reduce the symbol to metaphor, not the artist who creates the symbol. "The artist is not a person endowed with free will who seeks his own ends, but one who allows art to realize its purpose through him."[73] Literary symbols express the unknown and the unknowable, that which is mysterious, mystical, and ineffable. Through critical analysis, comparison, contrast, and assimilation, the critical mind translates and reduces symbol to metaphor. Metaphor is "essentially a way of knowing...the unknown through the known", a psychological and linguistic process that supplies the connection between "a wholly new sensational or emotional experience" and "another experience already placed, ordered, and incorporated".[74] Thus a symbol may be felt and experienced but cannot be consciously understood, even though it may seem to have specific biographical reference, unless it is reduced and assimilated through metaphor. Nonetheless, it is not necessary to translate Shorthouse or Eliot out of the conventions, figures of speech, and literary rhetoric of their day to appreciate the value of their work in contemporary critical theory. Modern critical terminology does not superannuate Shakespeare by imposing more modern "dress of the day". "The difference between the present and the past", as Eliot realised, whether in art, criticism, or the art of criticism, "is that the conscious present is an awareness between the present and the past in a way and to an extent which the past's awareness of itself cannot show." When someone argued, "The dead writers are remote from us because we *know* so much more than they did", Eliot countered, "Precisely, and they are that which we know."[75] Jung, too, developed his "primary intuitions" about language into a clear warning: "Not for a moment dare we succumb to the illusion" that we can actually and finally explain anything of symbolic power: "Even the best attempts at explanation are only more or less successful translations into another metaphorical language. (Indeed, language itself is only a metaphor.) The most we can do is *to dream the myth onwards* and give it a modern dress."[76] Maud Bodkin, Herbert Read, Wingfield Digby, Leslie Fiedler, Theodora Ward, Walter Abell, James Olney, and Northrop Frye are among critics who have demonstrated the essential metaphoric and symbolic distinctions that make archetypal theory one of the modern dressings of literary criticism.[77]

Eliot's "intolerable wrestle" is the "perpetual vexation of the intellect" towards some "Ideal Order".[78] As though he were experiencing *a priori* determinants, Eliot argued that the "existing monuments [of literature] form an ideal order among themselves".[79] Eliot was not as concerned with identifying such *a priori* determinants as he was with defining "the historical sense...[which] compels a man to write not merely with his own generation in his bones, but with a feeling that the whole of the literature of Europe from Homer and within it the whole of the literature of his own country has a simultaneous existence and composes a simultaneous order".[80] Just as the "new (the really new) work of art" modifies and alters "the relations, proportions, values of each work of art toward the whole", so anything new within the poet's personality affects "the individual as a whole"--be it dream, vision, fantasy, or active life experience--and activates the "metaphors of Self" process in distinguishable stages:

> ...expression in symbolic language; the attempt to reduce
> the direct experience to a rational sequence, giving
> personal and impersonal origins; and the hope of assimi-
> lating the experience to the now revised whole of the
> personality.[81]

As Jung, "made his own soul" and gave "the face of humanity a new aspect",[82] artists of moral experience may represent the search for Ideal Order as analogous to psychological Individuation. After completing *John Inglesant*, his most complete metaphor of Self, Shorthouse dissolved his personal, masculine persona, experimented with feminine personae, and actively sought a public literary audience for the "now revised whole" of his personality, even as Eliot ended his writing of "impersonal poems" in *Four Quartets* and thereafter wrote poetic dramas which are personal enough to invite autobiographical interpretation. The "many voices" of the impersonal figures and "personages" of "The Waste Land" abandon their allusive, hidden, and obscure qualities and take on identities as dramatic personae and characters in his plays. "Old Possum" baited critics and sent scholars "into temptation" with the "Notes" to "The Waste Land". *The Elder Statesman* deliberately "spiked" the dedication of his last drama to spur readers into autobiographical digging and interpretation. As if he were answering the critics who had accused him of plagiarism in his impersonal poems,[83] Eliot offered *The Elder Statesman*, "To My Wife":

> ...to return as best I can
> With words a little part
>   of what you have given me.
> The words mean what they say, but some have   a
> further meaning
> For you and me only.[84]

Indeed, as the impersonal, creative voices of Eliot tease and activate imaginal experience, his personal, critical voices provoke sophisticated readers and tempt them to re-examine his creative works.

"Occupied with the frontiers of consciousness beyond which words fail, though meanings still exist",[85] Shorthouse and Eliot captured and contained intuitive ideas in *John Inglesant* and *Four Quartets* "lie beyond the bourn of our understanding" and cannot be "formulated in any other or better way [because] no verbal concept yet exists".[86] The texts, therefore, invite analysis grounded in Jung's intuitive vision of "the spirit in man, art, and literature". To Jung, the mysterious, ineffable, transcendent "something of the spirit" can only be expressed symbolically as a "metaphor of Self". However grounded in the psychology of an author's personality, symbolical or visionary literature cannot be reduced to personal causes or interpreted as some *alter* of the author's *Ego*. Jung denigrated psychologists and literary critics who presumed a "psychology of literature" without studying the relations between "psychology *and* literature", and he warned that reducing literature to psychology was a blatant denial of "the spirit in man, art, and literature" that would ultimately reduce itself to an illogical pseudoscience that worships its own rationalism.[87] Jung insisted that true symbols, like the archetypes of the collective unconscious, defy rational reduction to specific signification. He asserted that the Self "cannot be distinguished from the God-image, the God-concept, the God-theory"[88] and that translating symbols into metaphors cannot proceed upon any definitive, prescriptive means or methodology of interpretation. As Tagore observed, "We may imagine that our mind is a mirror", that it can more or less accurately decode and translate symbols from subjective experience to objective meaning. "On the contrary, our mind itself is the principal element of creation. The world [and the literary text], while I am perceiving it, is being incessantly created

20

for myself in time and space."[89] Thus, to effect a contemporary interpretation is to make a "forward step in culture...an extension of consciousness...that can take place only through discrimination."[90] Words might fail, as Eliot noted, to extend the frontiers of consciousness, but only in words can one successfully posit the essential meanings and differences between psychological literature and visionary literature. As dreams may be interpreted, psychological literature may be understood; the fictive disguises of metaphoric imagery may be decoded and translated into representations of the psychodynamics of personality, but "visionary literature" creates true symbols in the mind, thus expresses irrationality, which, as Jung said, ultimately "mocks all our rationalistic undertakings".[91] Though literary critics may apprehend and interpret the psychological aspects of art works, no critical discourse can finally or absolutely reduce the mythic and mystical effects of visionary literature, and both *John Inglesant* and *Four Quartets* extend the psychological mode of literary creation into the visionary mode. The critic may seek "a magic lantern" to "throw the nerves in patterns on a screen", but, when dealing with visionary material, the critic may ultimately share J. Alfred Prufrock's frustration: "It is impossible to say just what I mean!"[92] and may decide it is only possible to let art speak for itself in its own terms.[93] As Virginia Woolf admonished her listeners in her talk "How Should One Read a Book?", "Do not dictate to your author; try to become him. Be his fellow-worker and accomplice".[94]

To advance culture, to extend the "frontiers of consciousness", to develop one's own literary sensibility and taste, it is necessary, of course, to be intellectually critical. A strictly historical, biographical, or "placing" evaluation of art that invites other methods of investigation cannot suffice as adequate criticism for the modern mind, though modern attempts to assess the achievements of minor authors like Shorthouse and to define the continuity of English literature that minor authors create and maintain must locate perspectives within the continuity of tradition.[95] Application of psychological theory in the practice of literary criticism may describe and attempt to explain how meaning is created within a given text and may help a sensitive reader discover new meaning, but reducing artistic experience to sublimation or transference of neuroses misdirects criticism towards the psychology of the artist. The theory of Individuation, however, does not attempt to reduce art to probable causes; rather it amplifies artistic responses through "active imagination". Amplification or "willful imagining" is a therapeutic technique used by Jungian analysts to enable their patients to dialogue with repressed psychic and emotional material, and to a student of literature the process enhances understanding of the emotional and imaginal grounding of sub-texts, images, and concepts like Eliot's "objective correlative" and "dissociation of sensibility".

Throughout *John Inglesant*, Shorthouse juxtaposes emotional and imaginal episodes against philosophical and reflective scenes to form a rhythmic, musical dialectic. Analytical, reflective narrative alternates with dramatic action; philosophical self-reflection and religious pondering define paradoxical, moral conflicts of duty and obedience to authority; moments of self-knowledge satirize modes of self-knowing. Shorthouse's published works and his unpublished and private letters reveal his continuity and development as an artist and suggest that he counterpointed his seemingly uneventful life by idealizing the musical potentialities of prose. Although he was reared in the Society of Friends, his soul did not quake in religious ecstasies, nor did his mind indulge religious doubts. Convinced of *a priori* truths, he understood religious and literary traditions as expressions of such truths, and in his certain faith, he experienced nothing like Eliot's "dark night of the soul" or Jung's "confrontation with the unconscious". His most criticized writing, the rather abrupt and defensive ending of *John Inglesant*, is a direct result of his attempt to make John Inglesant's apology for the Church of England into a rationalistic undertaking rather than leaving it irrational and mystic or visionary. Yet, it is from the final chapter of his first novel that Shorthouse learned the limitations of philosophical romance and began to compose spiritual romance. In the context of his complete works, impassioned rationalism and intense irrationality form the extremes of his sacramental vision, and in his quest for musical harmony and providential aesthetic, he juxtaposed the philosophical, rationalistic ending of *John Inglesant* against the spiritual, irrational ending of *Blanche, Lady Falaise*.

During the ten years which Shorthouse gave to the composition of *John Inglesant*, his mind embraced an aesthetic that resolved religious conflicts and church in-fighting into a liberal, greater comprehensiveness. To Shorthouse, the sacramentalism of daily life establishes the catholicity of the Church of England, and he testifies to the spiritual efficacy of the Church's orders and its sacraments, by expressing the religion of John Inglesant as a culminating and comprehensive symbol, as "that which the limited human mind creates in order to express an unfathomable and ineffable experience".[96] Eliot's more conservative nature and more conservative Anglo-Catholicism embrace and create "catholic Christianity" with little direct reference to the Church of England. *Four Quartets* creates a universally embracing Christian vision without localizing or defending the Church of England. *John Inglesant*, however, argues passionately on behalf of the specific national church. Nonetheless, Shorthouse's liberalism and Eliot's conservatism meet on ecumenical grounds as valid in the seventeenth century as they are today. Personalities and preferences aside, the hearts and minds of Shorthouse and Eliot meet at Little Gidding and transform the real, physical place and its historical continuity into a perfected symbol of

Christian community.

Although it cannot be proved that *John Inglesant* directly influenced Eliot or had any part in his visit to Little Gidding and the completion of *Four Quartets*,[97] Shorthouse's Broad Church Sacramentalism and Eliot's Anglo-Catholicism and the numerous parallels and links between their literary careers and their personal lives provide ample grounds for valuing their contributions to Anglo-Catholic literature and for revaluing Shorthouse's minor literary achievement in the light of Eliot's greater achievement. Great attention has already been and is rather constantly being given to Eliot's achievement, but little consideration has been given to establishing and maintaining Shorthouse's individual talent and his specific contributions to the Anglo-Catholic tradition of the English novel. As the psychology of Individuation provides a "poetics of Self",[98] an archetypal basis for literary criticism, so the pioneering achievement of Shorthouse's philosophical and spiritual romances provides a remarkable *via media* for understanding Anglican and Roman religious sensibilities and for the unifying "enfolding" of "the tongues of flame" of the English "rose" into "the crowned knot of fire" that Eliot achieved at the end of *Four Quartets*.

After a chronological consideration of Shorthouse's literary background and development and close examination of his works, this thesis will offer an interpretation and assessment of Shorthouse's achievement. Grounding the criteria of value in Jung's psychology of Individuation, this thesis will also explore Shorthouse's contribution to the continuity of English literature and to the achievement of T. S. Eliot. Shorthouse, of course, did not have the opportunity of exploring his Broad Church sacramentalism in the light of modern, international ecumenism, nor could he have examined his religious attitudes in terms of modern psychological perspective and theory, but he would surely have rejoiced in the struggles and achievements of Eliot and Jung. Shorthouse wanted to arouse mankind "to a sympathetic perception of their daily life, and at the same time perceive on such perception, as on a stage, the divine excellence at work". "Theologians", he argued, "have endeavoured the reverse of this; they have *started* with revelation, and tried to drag mankind 'neck and crop' into it, but with how little purpose..." He yearned for "such a disciple of Christ as...Plato would have been could he have known Him".[99] Readers of Shorthouse today will discern a mind and a spirit that would have yearned to be a disciple of Jung and a literary brother of Eliot could he have known them.

23

Notes to the Introduction

[1]Five major studies provide a comprehensive overview of the history of the novel with special reference to religious themes: Joseph Ellis Baker, *The Novel and the Oxford Movement* (Princeton University Press, 1932); Andrew Landale Drummond, *The Churches in English Fiction* (Leicester: Edgar Backus, 1950); Margaret Maison, *Search Your Soul, Eustace: Victorian Religious Novels* (London: Sheed and Ward, 1961); Raymond Chapman, *Faith and Revolt: Studies in the Literary Influence of the Oxford Movement* (London: Weidenfeld and Nicolson,1970); and Robert Lee Wolff, *Gains and Losses: Novels of Faith and Doubt in Victorian England* (New York: John Murray, 1977).

[2]Robert Lee Wolff, *Gains and Losses: Novels of Faith and Doubt in Victorian England* (New York: John Murray, 1977) is the comprehensive introduction to 121 novels selected by Garland Publishing Company, New York, for reprinting as a set.

[3]Arguing that "all religions contain elements of ambiguity", W.S.F. Pickering asserts that "of all the major Christian denominations the Church of England is the most ambiguous". In *Anglo-Catholicism: A Study in Religious Ambiguity* (London: Routledge, 1989), 3-10, he defines ambiguity as "'a lower order' of thinking" than paradox. "Paradox immediately conjures up the unlikelihood of resolution" between "elements of conflict or elements which seem totally opposed to one another" but which contain "a hiddenness--a something which is not immediately clear". Ambiguity, he argues, is "a more neutral term", one that lacks "the emotional accompaniment which is often associated with paradox". The resolution of paradox involves discovery of the hidden likeness between two elements that express "seeming contradiction", whereas the understanding of ambiguity involves an interpretation in which "one of the components is accepted in all its fullness and the other played down or even discarded". Thus, Anglo-Catholicism may be interpreted as the ambiguous movement within the Church of England that accepts Catholicism "in all its fullness" while downplaying Anglican theology. By "downplaying" Pickering means that both "the Oxford Fathers" and modern Church of England theologians find "the basis of Anglican Catholicity...amongst the Caroline divines" to whom the Church of England "was not just a Protestant church which had emerged at the time of the Reformation, but was basically Catholic--part of the Catholic church--and had not cut itself from its progenitor" (17).

[4]Pickering's *Anglo-Catholicism: A Study in Religious Ambiguity* explores his own early "affectionate attitude towards Anglo-Catholicism", the "distance" he experienced from it during World War II and during his theological study, and how he is "back in it once more. But with a difference..." ("Preface", XII). He concludes, "Thus the movement has given something to the Church of England, which has become part of it. It has deposited itself and transformed the Church, making it indeed comprehensive" (268).

[5]Pickering 23.

[6]This view derives from interviews with Anglo-Catholic priests in London, Oxford, Cambridge, Birmingham, and Edgbaston. (See also Pickering 28.)

[7]Pickering, "What is Anglo-Catholicism?" 15-24.

[8]Pickering 32.

[9]Pickering 40.

[10]Carl Gustav Jung's essays on art and literature, *The Spirit in Man, Art, and Literature*, volume 15, *Collected Works* (Bollingen Series XX: Princeton University Press, 1966). "Spirit and Life" was also published in *Contributions to Analytical Psychology* (London: Kegan Paul, Trench, Trubner and Co., 1928) 77-98.

[11]James Olney, *Metaphors of Self: The Meaning of Auto-biography* (Princeton University Press, 1973): "It isn't that Jung was less than a scientist; he was more. He was a man of a full and rich life who, in his work and writings, discovered metaphors adequate to the experience of that life." (104)

> Jung considered his lifework a "personal confession" and recognized that psychology cannot be "defined altogether as a science". He addressed scientific problems of Individuation in *Psychology and Religion, Collected Works*, vol. 11, and in his autobiography, *Memories, Dreams, and Reflections* (New York: Pantheon Books, 1961). For a summary of the argument, see June Singer's *Boundaries of the Soul: The Practice of Jung's Psychology* (Garden City, New York: Anchor Press, 1973), 371-373.

[12]Paul Nissley Landis, *The Development of Nineteenth Century English Historical Fiction Dealing with British History from 1640-1688*. Diss. University of Illinois, 1923.

[13]James A. Durham, *Marius the Epicurean and John Inglesant*. London: Hatchards, 1905.

[14]R. Ellis Roberts, "*John Inglesant*: Centenary of Henry Shorthouse", *Observer* (Birmingham), 8 February 1934.

[15]Elizabeth Drew's *T. S. Eliot: The Design of his Poetry* (London: Eyre and Spottiswoode, 1950) is the first, and probably still the best, Jungian exploration of Eliot's "mythical method" and "mythical vision".

[16]T. S. Eliot, "Little Gidding", Part I, *The Complete Poems and Plays* (London: Faber and Faber, 1969), rep. 1987, 192. (Cited as *Complete* hereafter.)

[17]Drew's study influenced Joseph Henderson's work on Eliot (see note 35). Mark Stephen Shearer's dissertation, "The Poetics of Self", is a meticulous "Study of the Process of Individuation in T. S. Eliot's *Four Quartets*" (University of South Carolina, 1985).

[18]Eliot explains the "deeper impression" of his early work upon "references, quotations, and reprints in anthologies" than that of his later work in "To Criticize the Critic". He attributes his influence to two causes: the "dogmatism of youth...When...we are confident in our opinions" and to the fact that "I was implicitly defending the sort of poetry that I and my friends wrote, which gave my essays...urgency, the warmth of appeal of the advocate..." *To Criticize the Critic and Other Essays* (London: Faber and Faber, 1965), rep. 1988, 15-16.

[19]Eliot, "Tradition and the Individual Talent," *Selected Essays, 1917-1932* (New York: Harcourt, Brace, 1932), 10.

[20]Eliot quotes Richards in "The Modern Mind," *The Use of Poetry and the Use of Criticism* (London: Faber and Faber, 1933), rep. 1987, 124.

[21]Owen Barfield, *Romanticism Comes of Age* (London: Anthroposophical Publishing Company,

1944). Barfield's studies, *History in English Words* (London: Methuen, 1926) and *Poetic Diction: A Study in Meaning* (London: Faber and Gwyer, 1928) also explore the failures of Romanticism and help clarify Eliot's anti-Romantic, pro-Classical stance.

[22]Eliot, "Tradition and the Individual Talent," *Selected Essays, 1917-1932* (London: Faber and Faber, 1932), 4.

[23]Thomas Vargish's *The Providential Aesthetic in Victorian Literature* (Charlottesville: University of Virginia, 1985). "In a thoroughgoing providential worldview no event can be fully apprehended without some acknowledgement of its potential spiritual or moral content. No circumstance can be assumed to exist and no event to occur simply for its own sake. All being and action are susceptible to meaning beyond themselves. The fall of a sparrow may have significance" (3).

[24]T. S. Eliot, "Burnt Norton", *Complete* 173.

[25]Eliot, "East Coker", *Complete* 183.

[26]Eliot, "Little Gidding", *Complete* 197.

[27]Eliot, "Little Gidding", *Complete* 198.

[28]Eliot, "East Coker", *Complete* 179.

[29]Eliot, "Tradition and the Individual Talent", *Complete* 6.

[30]Eliot, "Tradition and the Individual Talent", *Selected Essays* 9. Eliot emphasized the maturing of the poet as "wholeness" or "unity" which the poet achieves through the virtual "extinction of his personality" as a sacrifice to his medium, the language he is capable of using.

[31]Eliot, *The Use of Poetry and the Use of Criticism* (London: Faber and Faber, 1933), rep. with preface, 1964, 84.

[32]Harold F. Brooks, *T. S. Eliot as Literary Critic* (London: Cecil Woolf, 1987), 34.

[33]"Old Possum" is commonly assumed to be a nickname given Eliot by Ezra Pound and refers to the persona of *Old Possum's Book of Practical Cats* (London: Faber and Faber, 1939).

[34]Virginia Woolf, *The Diary of Virginia Woolf*, Vol. II, 1920-1924 (New York: Harcourt Brace Jovanovich, 1978), 14. Virginia Woolf's entry for 26 January 1920 discusses the "danger" of writing "from oneself without its becoming... narrowing and restricting".

[35]T. S. Eliot, "Shakespeare and the Stoicism of Seneca", *Selected Essays*, third enlarged edition. (London: Faber and Faber, 1951), rep. 1986, 137.

[36]Eliot's psychological life, especially the treatment he received at the time he was at work on "The Waste Land", has received much critical attention. A. Alvarez quotes Eliot's poetry and criticism sparingly but suggestively in *The Savage God: A Study of Suicide* (London: Weidenfeld and Nicolson, 1971): "Eliot wrote 'The Waste Land' in Zurich, when convalescing from some kind of breakdown and, possibly, while under psychotherapy." (257)

      Peter Ackroyd's *T. S. Eliot* (London: Hamish Hamilton, 1984) details Eliot's "nervous breakdown" and treatment with Dr. Roger Vitto in Lausanne, 1921, during the composition of "The Waste Land".

In details of "The Waste Land Traversed", *Eliot's Early Years* (Oxford University Press, 1971, 86-119), Lyndall Gordon treats Eliot's therapy with the flavour of Sherlock Holmes; then she confesses the composition of the poem "remains, as yet, unresolved...one can do no more at present than weigh one body of circumstantial evidence against the other." The solution to the mystery lies, "Probably somewhere in Eliot's unpublished manuscripts" (146).

Mrs. Valerie Eliot brought the riddle to a seeming end with the publication of *"The Waste Land": A Facsimile and Transcript of the Original Drafts, Including the Annotations of Ezra Pound* (London: Faber and Faber, 1971) and *The Letters of T. S. Eliot, Vol. I: 1898-1922* (London: Faber and Faber, 1988). Eliot insisted, "Honest criticism and sensitive appreciation is directed not upon the poet but upon the poetry." ("Tradition and the Individual Talent", *Selected Essays, 1917-1932*, 7.) He limited his self-examination in *To Criticize the Critic and Other Writings* to his "literary criticism *qua* literary" (26).

[37]Eliot, "Conclusion", *The Use of Poetry and the Use of Criticism* 144.

[38]Joseph L. Henderson, "Stages of Psychological Development Exemplified in the Poetical Works of T. S. Eliot", *Journal of Analytical Psychology*, Vol. I (May 1926) and Vol. II, no. 1 (January 1957).

[39]Jung attacked Freud's "constant point of departure...the neurotically degenerate psyche" and the theory of sublimation because Freud applied the assumptions of his psychoanalytic theory to uncover and decode works of art in direct relation to the psychodynamics of the artist's personality. See "In Memory of Sigmund Freud" and "Sigmund Freud in his Historical Setting" (*The Spirit in Man, Art, and Literature* 33-48).

[40]King Bolo refers to a rather ribald narrative that Eliot wrote in correspondences with Conrad Aiken, 1913-1914, now in the Aiken Collection, Henry E. Huntington Library, San Marino, California. Selected excerpts and references have been included in Vol. I of *The Letters of T. S. Eliot* (40, 42, 86, 125, 206, 455, 505, 568). Careful examination of the Aiken Collection proves Mrs. Eliot did not censor the correspondence in her publication, a possibility that concerned Peter Ackroyd in his biographical work on Eliot.

[41]Eliot, "Conclusion", *Use*. Eliot defined different kinds of critics: the Professional Critic or Super-Reviewer, the Critic with Gusto, and the Academic or Theoretical, then added the Critic as Moralist to include F. R. Leavis. The essay on Andrews shows Eliot's transition from Academic-Theoretical critic to moralist and church apologist.

[42]Paul Elmer More, "J. Henry Shorthouse", *Shelburne Essays*, Third series (Boston: Houghton Mifflin, 1905), 227.

[43]Edmund Gosse, "The Author of *John Inglesant*", *Portraits and Sketches* (London: William Heinemann, 1912), rep. 1924, 151-162. I. A. Richards discussed Eliot as a man of many roles in *The Mysterious Mr. Eliot*. Video. CRM Films, 109969-7 and 109970-0.

[44]T. S. Eliot, "Syllabus for a Tutorial Class in Modern English Literature" (University of London Press, 1916-1918).

[45]More, *Shelburne Essays* 227.

[46]Helen Gardner, *The Composition of "Four Quartets"* (London: Faber and Faber, 1978), 61.

[47]Eliot, "The Metaphysical Poets", *Selected Essays*, Third Edition, (London: Faber and Faber, 1951), rep. 1986, 281-291.

[48]Francis Bacon's "Of Studies" (1625) employs the metaphor: "Some books are to be tasted, others to be swallowed, and some...to be chewed and digested..."

[49]Edmund Gosse and Richard Garnett, *English Literature: An Illustrated Record* (New York: Macmillan, 1904).

[50]T. S. Eliot signed the visitors' guest book at Little Gidding in May 1936. Provocatively, Bernard Blackstone's signature is next to Eliot's, but there is no evidence that Blackstone and Eliot were ever there at the same time.

[51]Bernard Blackstone's review of Alan L. Maycock's *Nicholas Ferrar of Little Gidding* (London: Society for Promoting Christian Knowledge, 1938) appeared in *The Criterion*, Vol. XVIII, no. LXX, October 1938, 154-157. Canon Charles Smyth's review of Blackstone's *The Ferrar Papers* (Cambridge University Press, 1938) appeared in *The Criterion*, Vol. XVIII, no. LXXI, January 1939, 366-371.

[52]T. S. Eliot, "Little Gidding", *Complete* 192.

[53]T. S. Eliot, "Little Gidding", *Complete* 192.

[54]C. L. Graves, *Life and Letters of Alexander Macmillan* (London: Macmillan, 1910), 359.

[55]Sarah Shorthouse, *Life, Letters, and Literary Remains of J. Henry Shorthouse* (London: Macmillan, 1905), 106. [Cited as *LLLR* hereafter.]

[56]Shorthouse added the preface to the first Macmillan edition, which was published in two-volume format in June 1881.

[57]Joseph Ellis Baker, *The Novel and the Oxford Movement* (Princeton University Press, 1932), 199.

[58]J. W. Dawson, "Religion in Fiction", *The Makers of English Fiction* (London: Hodder and Stoughton, 1905), 253-272. Dawson's limits the religious novel to works "in which the faculty of creative imagination is definitely devoted and subordinated to the exposition of religious ideas" (255). Excluding Thackeray, Dickens, Kingsley, Charlotte Bronte, George Eliot, and Defoe, Dawson extols George Macdonald, Shorthouse, Mrs. Humphry Ward, Olive Schreiner, and Mark Rutherford.

        Baker's attitude (cf. note 52) is more useful: "For a Modern of entirely secular culture, there would be few more attractive introductions to religion than *John Inglesant*." The attraction in Shorthouse's novels is their literary merit as works of historical imagination which recreate the religious and spiritual sensibilities of their respective settings, not the religious ideas they present.

[59]M. C. Bradbrook, "Eliot's Critical Method", *T. S. Eliot: A Study of his Writings by Several Hands* (London: Dennis Dobson, Ltd., 1947), 119-128.

[60]T. S. Eliot, "To Criticize the Critic", *To Criticize the Critic and Other Writings* (London: Faber and Faber, 1965), rep. 1978, 19.

[61]Sarah Shorthouse, *LLLR*, Vol. I, 221.

[62]Shorthouse's letter to Arnold: See *LLLR*, Vol. I, 83-89.

[63]Max Keith Sutton, "*John Inglesant* and 'Little Gidding'". *Yeats Eliot Review*, Vol. 8, Nos. 1 and 2, 1986, 119-122.

[64]Maud Bodkin, *Archetypal Patterns in Poetry: Psychological Studies in Imagination* (London: Oxford University Press, 1934). Individuation theory is discussed in all studies of Jung. Perhaps the most useful is Joseph Goldbrunner's *Individuation: A Study of the Depth Psychology of Carl Gustav Jung* (Indiana: University of Notre Dame, 1964).

[65]Bodkin, *Archetypal Patterns in Poetry* 22-25.

[66]Jung, *The Development of Personality, Collected Works*, Vol. 17, 1954, 7.

[67]Northrop Frye, *The Anatomy of Criticism: Four Essays*. (Princeton University Press, 1957), rep. 1973, 6-7.

[68]Milton invokes the "heavenly Muse" to aid his "adventurous song...to soar" in Book I of *Paradise Lost*; and in the sonnet "On His Blindness", he concludes: "They also serve who only stand and wait."

[69]Eliot believed that any poet who had ever been "visited by the Muse is thenceforth haunted". Yet, Wordsworth, he asserts, "had no ghastly shadows at his back, no Eumenides to pursue him". See "Wordsworth and Coleridge" in *The Use of Poetry and the Use of Criticism* 69. The quotation is from Wordsworth's Book I, *The Prelude* 150-153.

[70]Eliot, *Use*: "As things are, and as fundamentally they must always be, poetry is not a career, but a mug's game. No honest poet can ever feel quite sure of the permanent value of what he has written: he may have wasted his time and messed up his life for nothing" (154).

[71]Aniela Jaffe, *The Myth of Meaning: Jung and the Evolution of Consciousness*. (Zurich: Daimon, 1970). Jaffe's book is an exceptionally clear and authoritative statement of Jung's ideas about myth, meaning, and consciousness.

[72]T. S. Eliot, "Wordsworth and Coleridge", *The Use of Poetry and the Use of Criticism* 74-75.

[73]C. G. Jung quoted by Morris Philipson, *Outline of a Jungian Aesthetics* (Chicago: Northwestern University Press, 1963), 126-127.

[74]James Olney, *Metaphors of Self: The Meaning of Autobiography* (Princeton University Press, 1972), 31.

[75]T. S. Eliot, "Tradition and the Individual Talent", *Selected Essays* 16.

[76]Morris Philipson, *Outline of a Jungian Aesthetics*. (Chicago: Northwestern University Press, 1963), 61-62. [Philipson, *Outline* hereafter.]

[77]Philipson's *Outline* discusses a few of the direct applications of Jung's psychology made by literary scholars and critics. Jos van Meurs, however, has published the most comprehensive and useful of all studies of "Jungian Literary Criticism": "A Survey of Jungian Literary Criticism in English", *C. G. Jung and the Humanities*, Karin Barnaby and Pellegrino D'Acierno, eds. (Princeton University Press, 1990), 238-250.

[78]Jung, quoted by Philipson, *Outline* 61.

[79]Eliot, "Tradition", *Selected Essays* 15.

[80]Eliot, "Tradition", *Selected Essays* 14.

[81]Philipson, *Outline* 9.

[82]Olney, *Metaphors of Self* 150.

[83]Eliot, "The Frontiers of Criticism", *On Poetry and Poets*. (New York: Farrar, Straus and Cudahy, 1957), 121.

[84]Eliot, *Complete* 522.

[85]Eliot, "The Music of Poetry", *On Poetry and Poets* 22-23,

[86]Jung, "On the Relation of Analytical Psychology to Poetry", *Collected Works*, Vol. 15, par. 105, p. 70.

[87]Jung insisted upon the proper relations between psychology and literature in a lecture entitled "On the Relation of Analytical Psychology to Poetry", which he delivered to the Society for German Language and Literature in Zurich, May 1922. In 1930 he reiterated his essential argument in "Psychology and Literature". Both essays are in Vol. 15 of his *Collected Works*, 65-83 and 84-105 respectively.

[88]Jung defines the Self as a "psychic fact of direct experience" in "Spirit and Life", *Contributions to Analytical Psychology* (London: Kegan Paul, Trench, Trubner, and Co., 1928), rep. 1942, 87, and as a "God-image" in *Aion*, Vol IX, part 2, par. 42, of his *Collected Works*. He states that the Self can be only conceptually distinguished from "God" in *Mysterium Coniunctionis*, Vol. X, par. 330, of *Collected Works*.

       In the first English translations of Jung's work, *Self* was capitalized to denote the archetype. Unfortunately, in the *Collected Works* published by the Bollingen Foundation, Princeton University Press, and by Routledge and Kegan Paul in London, the distinction is no longer observed, which confuses the archetype with "ego", "I", and personal awareness of identity. Throughout this thesis, Self and Ego are capitalized to denote archetypes; self and ego refer to functions of personality: self-esteem, ego-consciousness, etc.

[89]Rabindranath Tagore, *Personality*. (London: Macmillan, 1917), 47.

[90]At the Oxford University International Summer School in 1986, lecturers presented one critical stance that shocked many of the students. Students were told to "stop reading fiction and literature" and to devote themselves "to where it's really at: critical theory and modern psycholinguistics". (Professor Valentine Cunningham, "Straddling the Unknown: Reading

Modern Fiction", Gulbenkian Lecture Theatre, 1 July 1986.) Students were also given the distinct impression that Christian writers connected with Oxford--C. S. Lewis, J. R. R. Tolkien, Charles Williams, and Eliot himself--were somehow not appropriate authors to study.

[91]C. G. Jung, "On Psychical Energy", *Contributions to Analytical Psychology*. (London: Kegan Paul, Trench, Trubner, and Co., 1928), rep. 1942, 68.

[92]Eliot, "The Love Song of J. Alfred Prufrock", *Complete* 16.

[93]Jung made his clearest distinctions in the "Appendices" of *Two Essays on Analytical Psychology*, Vol. VII of *Collected Works*. Publishers and scholars alike confuse readers by introducing terms like *persona* and *anima* first in italics and then dropping the italics in subsequent usages. Most publishers of Jungian texts or studies do not capitalize, bold face, or italicize the names of archetypes, but throughout this study the names of archetypes will be underscored to avoid the suggestion that archetypes are common literary terms.

[94]Virginia Woolf, "How Should One Read a Book?" *The Common Reader*, Second Series. (London: Hogarth Press, 1935), 258-270.

[95]Eliot, "The Classics and the Man of Letters", *To Criticize the Critic and Other Writings*. (New York: Farrar, Straus and Giroux, 1965), 147: "...secondary writers provide collectively, and individually in varying degrees...the continuity of a literature...It is very largely the function of secondary writers to preserve this continuity, and to provide a body of writings which is not necessarily read by posterity, but which plays a great part in forming the link between those writers who continue to be read."

[96]Jung, "The Meaning of Psychology for Modern Man", *Collected Works*, Vol. 10, par. 330.

[97]Valerie Eliot confirmed in a letter to me (6 October 1989) that Eliot owned a copy of *John Inglesant*, that Eliot did indeed visit Little Gidding only once, and that she does not know if Eliot ever read Shorthouse.

[98]The concept of a "poetics of the Self" derives from numerous sources, specifically from Shearer (see note 11) and from Barfield, Philipson, and Olney.

[99]J. Henry Shorthouse, Letter to Matthew Arnold, (23 October 1971), *LLLR*, Vol. 1. As a Platonist, Shorthouse would have been interested in the comparisons modern scholars draw between Jung and Plato. At least three scholars have noted similarities between Jung's archetypes of the collective unconscious and Plato's realm of ideas and between Jung's typology and Plato's "aspects of soul": P. W. Martin, *Experiment in Depth* (London: Routledge and Kegan Paul, 1955), James Olney, *Metaphors of Self* (Princeton University Press, 1972), and Andrew Samuels, *Jung and the Post-Jungians* (London: Routledge and Kegan Paul, 1985).

Chapter One: Historical and Biographical Background of Joseph Henry Shorthouse

Only three weeks after Shorthouse's death on 4 March 1903, Lady Victoria Welby suggested to Sarah Shorthouse that she collect her late husband's many letters, essays, tales, and stories as a memorial, and to assist her, Lady Welby offered to lend letters of "the deepest interest"[1] she had received from "the author of *John Inglesant*". When Sarah Shorthouse began to make enquiries of her husband's correspondents, she promptly received several offers of advice and assistance, and when George Macmillan agreed to publish her tribute, she set to work immediately. To avoid confusion, she decided to accept her publisher's advice in all matters of detail with the same implicit trust and confidence that typified Shorthouse's working relations with the Macmillans. She kindly rejected, however, the offer of assistance from the famed critic Edmund Gosse, who had often stayed with the Shorthouses at 60 Wellington Road in Edgbaston when he was on lecture tours at the Midland Institute in Birmingham. Although Gosse had been a close friend of Shorthouse for twenty years and had dedicated *Questions at Issue* to him,[2] Mrs. Shorthouse published only eight of her husband's forty-six letters to Gosse and none of Gosse's letters to her husband. Why she rejected Gosse's assistance we shall never know, but she felt concern about how Gosse would have handled the memorial, and, after publication of her husband's biography, she was very upset by Gosse's descriptions of her husband's manner of dress and religion in his review of *LLLR*. In particular, she was upset by Gosse's accusation that her husband "not only went through life as a 'masque' but even in his religion played the same part".[3] Before asking George Macmillan for advice about how to respond to Gosse's review, Mrs. Shorthouse discussed the matter with her brother-in-law, John William Shorthouse, who had been their next-door neighbour since 1881 when he bought The Woodlands villa. John explained that "these literary people must have a standpoint of their own" and that Gosse's viewpoint was similar to George Macmillan's own description of Shorthouse's "literary pose"[4] Mrs. Shorthouse wrote Macmillan on 22 May 1905 and received an immediate reply that calmed her, as she acknowledged to Macmillan on the 24th.[5] Macmillan advised her, as she stated, "to keep my own identity",[6] and apparently, he hoped she would not adopt a literary pose of her own. She took the advice literally and presented Macmillan with a personal, loving tribute to her late husband, precisely the kind of biography that Gosse objected to, "the feeble waxworks produced by pious Victorian biographers". Gosse knew only too well "that the characters that interest us are those whose weaknesses we recognize in ourselves and in our friends, the victims not the heroes", and he despised the "goody-good lives of good men".[7] What Mrs. Shorthouse compiled is, indeed, the work of a devoted, loyal, Victorian wife, and despite unevenness of narrative, frequent gaps and oversights, it remains the best biography of Birmingham's most famous novelist [8] and the only publication of twenty-three of his "Early Essays" and five of his "Later Essays". In fact, most of what we know about Shorthouse as a person and as an author is contained in the 1905 tribute, *Life, Letters, and Literary Remains of J. Henry Shorthouse,* and though her appreciations are thoroughly one-sided, "domestic rather than public, and uncritical",[9] and often sentimental, *LLLR* remains the essential record of Shorthouse's outwardly uneventful life, the developmental influences that informed his personal views, and his creative and critical literary activity. Because "It is his art", as Jung argued, "that explains the artist and not the insufficiencies and conflicts of his personal life",[10] we need not criticize the "goody-good" in Mrs. Shorthouse's tribute to his husband, and despite gaps in her chronology, *LLLR* is an accurate presentation of Shorthouse's life and art.

Perhaps the most apt observations for understanding Shorthouse's background were contributed to the memorial by his cousin, Margaret (Southall) Evans and concern a century of "daily life" as observed by his aunt, Sarah (Shorthouse) Southall. The following memories were published by the family to commemorate Sarah's one-hundredth birthday (12 September 1901):

> In the century during which she lived, the greatest changes have taken place in the shortest time. For long after her birth Englishmen and Englishwomen owned slaves...It was deemed right that a man should be hanged if he stole property worth 5\-. The prisons were crowded...Little boys of eight and nine were sent up chimneys to sweep them, and many died in the flues of suffocation...Man-traps, spring-guns and gins were set in gardens and woods to catch poachers. The Mail coaches all had guards who carried firearms to protect the mails against highwaymen...Criminals were executed in public...and their bodies left on the gibbet for years; no laws protected dumb animals from cruelty...Bulls were baited;... gentlemen patronized cock-fighting, and the clergy badger-baited on Sunday evenings after church...Little boys addressed their fathers as 'Sir'...little girls were taught to sit upright and turn out their toes...It cost 1\- to send a letter from Birmingham to London...Ladies wore muslin made in India and linen

33

made in France and Ireland. Goods were taken about the country in stage wagons or on packhorses. People travelled by stage coaches well padded inside, as they were often upset. There were a few steam coaches before 1840, that travelled between London and Birmingham and had a funnel at the back...and there were velocipedes made of wood ...Many people stayed at home...In the principal streets [of Birmingham] many of the houses were thatched...There were no policemen, only parish constables and night watchmen who called the hour. The town was lit by oil-lamps...water was sold in Birmingham streets from carts, as milk is...There was a cherry orchard in the middle of the town where Cherry Street now is, and corn was reaped just to the west of St. Philip's Churchyard...Birmingham always had a bad name for coining and coiners...Bad money used to be much more common than it is now...There was no British Empire...Large parts of India were in the hands of the East India Company... Part of Canada belonged to England...Nelson died on board the 'Victory' when [she] was four years old... Australia was discovered by the Dutch and called 'New Holland'. The English government formed a penal settlement to which to transport its criminals.

Following the catalogue, Mrs. Evans recorded her aunt's belief, "The world has moved quickly since [she] was born. It has moved chiefly in one direction--it has found the value of a human life.[11] Of course, this cataloguing of personal memories overlooks and excludes much that may be thought necessary to describe the intellectual environment of Shorthouse's era adequately, but because they are so personal, they are appropriate to Shorthouse's declared aim, to display "only daily life", or "human life in the 'highways and hedges' and in 'the streets and lanes of the city', with the ceaseless throbbing of its quivering heart".[12] Although he rejected his grandmother's Quaker religion and gave little attention to her extroverted observations of social change, he accepted her conclusion that the Victorian age had discovered the value of individual life.

Joseph Shorthouse and Mary Ann Hawker-Shorthouse were 37 and 32, respectively, when Joseph Henry was born 9 September 1834. As a child of four years, Henry, as he was called throughout his life, though his two younger brothers, Edmund and John called him "Harry", became so intensely excited while his parents read Bunyan's *Pilgrim's Progress* aloud that they were "obliged to stop" their reading.[13] Concerned about their son's excitable temperament and delicate health, they moved from Great Charles Street, Birmingham, to 30 Calthorpe Street, Edgbaston, and sent their four-year-old son to a Friends' school in Frederick Street run by Miss Harris. Though nothing certain about his experience has been recorded, it is clear that he began to stammer severely while attending Miss Harris's school and that his parents removed him from the school and hired tutors to work with him at home. His health remained a constant concern. When Henry was eight, he suffered a severe attack of typhus fever, and his parents removed him further from the city to stay with his paternal grandmother at Moseley. During his convalescence, he developed his lifelong love of books, which his family generously indulged. "It is not easy to speak adequately", wrote his widow, about his delight during his convalescence at Moseley. "He seemed only to retain the most vivid memories of pleasure", and the period of convalescence at Moseley "sealed his life with glimpses of the gardens below" his grandmother's spare bedroom and views of "the distant woods".[14]

Throughout his childhood, his mother read aloud to him, his father regaled him with imaginative and vivid accounts of business travels in Italy, and four cousins, Anna Mary, Ellen, Margaret, and Isabel, met with him regularly at Rebecca Shorthouse's home and encouraged his literary imagination. He composed his first work, the "Moseley Pieces", for a female audience in the quiet security of a Quaker family, and he gathered memories. Years later, when reading exceptionally vivid and remarkably accurate descriptions of Italy, of countryside, courtly homes, art museums, monuments, and libraries, his father felt amazed and proud that Henry could so vividly recall and recreate the scenes he had described to his eight-year-old convalescing son. Henry never travelled in Europe, but the minute attention to detail in his descriptions convinced many readers that he had made lengthy travels, and many assumed he had had the benefit of early literary training.[15]

During childhood Henry absorbed children's stories, especially "Infant's Progress" and "The History of the Fairchild Family" by Mary Martha Sherwood, and "My Own Story" and "Peter Parley's Evenings at Home" by Mary Howitt, and he became fascinated with the classical world in Mary Russell Mitford's writings. Before he was sixteen, he discovered spiritual pilgrimage in Bunyan's *The Pilgrim's Progress*, excited his natural introversion with the gothic, antiquarian flavour of Hawthorne's *Twice Told Tales*, gloried in Tennyson's heroic narrative poems about Ulysses, especially "The Lotus Eaters", and devoted himself to *In Memoriam*. At 16 he entered Grove House, Tottenham as a pupil, but after only five months, his stammer became so severe that he had to return home again. In 1850, while studying French, Italian, and drawing at home with private tutors, he entered the family business, began attending the Friends Essay Society, and took his first holiday adventure. Exploring Yorkshire, he was enamoured by the gothic enchantment of Rievaulx Abbey, where he and his cousins read and re-read Tennyson and Matthew Arnold. Two years later, he made a second journey, again with his cousins, to Scotland and to Cumberland, where they again "read and re-read Tennyson" with constant enthusiasm, read James Hogg's Scottish poetry, and climbed Westdale Head to see the view by moonlight. The view of Duddon "under a sun on a hazy afternoon" and "the everlasting dream of peace" he felt in the old church at Seathwaite confirmed his natural disposition for romanticism.

"From a child his own self-culture had been going on", his cousin explained, and "The love of books was an absorbing passion with him at an age when other children [were] satisfied with their toys."[16] He preferred Hawthorne's *The House of Seven Gables* and *The Scarlet Letter*, Michelet's *Life of Luther*, Chaucer's *Canterbury Tales*, and Spenser's *The Fairie Queen*. Macaulay's essay on Lord Nugent's *Life of Hampden* awakened his desire for biography and for educational histories. He began to attend public lectures and to become consciously critical. Of Macaulay, for instance, he wrote,

> *The Life of Hampden* which is the foolishest [of Macaulay's essays]...contradicts itself; the more I read of his works, the more I consider him to be shallow and unworthy of the great reputation he has gained.[17]

His reading was always tinged and tingling with excitement, if not exultation, and with, too, an odd touch of guilt: "There always seems to be something awful and almost wicked," he confessed after a visit to a local bookseller's, "in buying such splendid thoughts and words...for money."[18] Though he later conquered this rather mild Puritanical element in himself by portraying the Puritans as unnatural and antihuman in *John Inglesant*, he was often gripped with a sense of guilt whenever he bought "noble books", though he knew Grandmother Rebecca had worked hard to save her pocket money to buy a first edition of Wordsworth's *Lyrical Ballads*. He could accept, "that men should get the means for providing for the commonest and vulgarest wants of life, and worse still, for its vilest and most sordid passions, by buying and selling, and trading" but "bargaining over the most sublime thoughts, feelings, and aspirations" contained in books seemed to him "like trafficking in men's souls".[19] Nonetheless, he visited his favourite local bookseller "well-nigh daily for nearly twenty-five years" and collected an extensive, distinguished personal library.[20]

Illness, of course, was not uncommon in Victorian life or in Victorian fiction, nor was it uncommon in Shorthouse's family. His mother, Mary Ann Shorthouse, was afflicted with rheumatic arthritis, went blind in

1858, only one year after Henry and Sarah's marriage, and spent the last three years of her life "on a waterbed, helpless, blind, and suffering in every joint".[21] Following her remarkable example of patient suffering, Shorthouse thought it "impossible to think of what would be if things were different from what the providence of God has ordered that they *should* be". "I can recognize a still clear *blessing*...[and] I never should have been what I am without it", he wrote to Lady Victoria Welby in 1883, about his lifelong convulsive stammering. Descriptions of Shorthouse usually include reactions to his lifelong uncontrollable stammer, a speech disability which he accepted as a divine blessing. He explained to Lady Welby:

> This might at first sight seem a terrible misfortune, but I am convinced that I never should have been what I am without it...in spite of the example of St. Paul, I cannot quite look upon my stammering as a "messenger of Satan", whatever my unfortunate friends may be inclined to do. It seems impossible to think of what *would* be if things were different from what the providence of God has ordered that they *should* be.[22]

When he was ten years old, Shorthouse was sent by his parents to Dr. John Bishop (1797-1873), famous in London for his "magnetic" personal influence and for having "only a 1 percent failure rate" in his cures.[23] Indeed, in Doctor Bishop's presence young Henry could not stammer at all. Another Victorian doctor who claimed almost miraculous results was Dr. John Hunt, who treated novelists Charles Kingsley and Charles Dodgson, but they, like Shorthouse, "stuttered to the end" of their lives.[24] "At any rate", Shorthouse declared, without the stammer "*John Inglesant* would never have been written or conceived, and much which is very dear to me in philosophy would have been unknown."[25] With sincere gratitude grounded in faith, he regarded attitudes towards suffering and affliction as conscious, philosophical choices, and characteristically, he related them to choices in writing and made them part of his personal philosophy: "If Fiction...is allowed to select and to condense from life, surely Philosophy may do so too."

> If we may view life from an artistic, or dramatic, or picturesque standpoint, using such incidents and characters only as meet one or other of the requirements, surely we may select incidents and characters with a philosophic intent.[26]

As Wordsworth autobiographically studied "the growth of a poet's mind" in *The Prelude* and fancied how his own character might have become in the circumstances described in *The Excursion*, and as Thomas

Browne composed *Religio Medici* at "leisurable hours for private exercise and satisfaction",[27] the "author of *John Inglesant*" chose characters and plot incidents from his own life experiences and from his reading with deliberate "philosophic intent". Sarah Shorthouse verifies that the teachings of the "wind voices" and the "reed voices" at his father's pool at Thimble Mill were "recorded in his own beautiful language in *A Teacher of the Violin*", his father's descriptions of Italian journeys became vivid metaphors of "business" and "secret mission" in the travel scenes of *John Inglesant*, the gardens at William and Rebecca Shorthouse's home at Moseley informed the spirituality of the gardens in *The Countess Eve*, the "blue door" in the Moseley garden wall became the symbolic divider between spiritual innocence and worldly corruption in *Sir Percival*, and neighbouring villages and churches near Torquay gave definition to the religious sensibility of *Blanche, Lady Falaise*.[28] As a general rule, however, he did not derive material for his early literary work from the social and political concerns of his day but from the interests of the Friends Essay Society, and, in fact, the themes, metaphors, and style of much of his later writings derive from his literary apprenticeship with this Quaker reading, writing, and discussion group.

As early as 1829 a group of Quakers in Birmingham founded the Friends Reading Society to study "sound and useful literature within the reach of all connected with the Society of Friends". Concerned with "the moral dangers threatening the growing number of young men attracted from all over the country to work in Birmingham",[29] they shared "intimate concern for the spiritual welfare of the younger Friends"; thus they excluded study of novels, romances, and political works.[30] Shorthouse's grandfather, his father, and his uncles were original members of the Reading Society in the days when the Society was restricted to men. By 1840 the group acknowledged the literary interests and educational needs of Quaker women, and Rebecca Shorthouse, Henry's grandmother, became a member. According to an anonymous letter in Volume 16 of the *Essays of the Friends Essay Society*, the Essay Society itself grew out of the Reading Society and must have begun not later than 1835.[31] Shorthouse's "Early Essays" included women in his audience, and, as Wager notes, the Essay Society was "almost a family compact", for it included Shorthouse's two brothers, his three Southall cousins, his future wife, Sarah Scott, and her brother and sister.[32] As dating and chronology present problems, so does ascertaining authorship. Several essays in Shorthouse's handwriting seem to reflect his voice, style, and content, but even his widow and relatives could not identify exactly which essays he composed. Papers to be read at the monthly meetings were "anonymously laid on the table" after presentation by a selected member, though never by the author; copies were made in longhand for circulation and further discussion, and for some years Shorthouse served as copyist. Author, copyist, and reader were not necessarily the same person, so nothing can be properly inferred from pencilled notes on the essays. Wagner guessed "about sixty" of the papers may be Shorthouse's "apprentice pieces", and he added a cautionary note:

> Only sheer perversity could induce one to make a doubtful point about Shorthouse's development during his literary apprenticeship in the Friends Essay Society unless not only the number but also the chronological order of the essays could be firmly established.[33]

Indeed, much about Shorthouse's early work remains unknowable, though the existing evidence suggests Shorthouse composed his first contributions when he was twenty. Except for those essays identified by Sarah, there is no certain way to identify Henry's essays, and it was not until fifty years after these Essay Society meetings that Sarah Shorthouse began compiling her husband's early work. Writing in 1904, Sarah told George Macmillan of her difficulty in identifying and dating the early writings. Though she recognized her husband's "distinctive genius" and argued it made "the charm of his contributions so great and so unique", especially "as no other member of the Essay Meeting... [had] published a *John Inglesant*", she followed Macmillan's advice in selecting the essays for inclusion in her biographical memoir. Many of the "Early Essays" have never been published, but they are not as distinctive as Sarah thought them. Some she thought "most characteristic of my dear husband's views and ideas when he was 19 or 20 years of age" were not selected for publication, because George Macmillan thought them "too jocular". "Confessions of George Wellsbourne" and "I've Been Haunted" were published only after Sarah erased the more jocular passages. She urged inclusion of a few early letters "to his cousins and one or two to Mr. Levett [which] are full of fun as well as graver thoughts", and Macmillan complied.[34]

A more difficult decision for both of them involved whether to retain the "plain language" and rhetorical style of the Quakers. Frustrated by his stammer and believing that "To write or speak attractively is the rarest and most precious gift of a beneficent God",[35] Shorthouse rejected the "plain speaking" of the Quakers. Considering Shorthouse's determination in his later writings to capture the "spirit of the age", it seems rather ironic that Mrs. Shorthouse changed the earlier "thee", "thy", and "thou" of Quaker idiom. "They all used it in that day but very few retain it now", she explained and added, "My husband did not like any of the peculiarities of Quakerism."[36] Sarah Shorthouse and her cousin Elsie Ball copied twenty-one "Early Essays" out of the bound volumes of the Friends Essay Society, six other essays and two stories that were not included in the Friends collection, and numerous letters which they offered to George Macmillan for publication. Though most of the letters were dated, most of the essays were not. "I can give the dates approximately but not absolutely accurately," Mrs. Shorthouse explained to Macmillan, "for it was only an after thought to bind the Essays of years into 9 or 10 great volumes and the dates are hardly affixed to a single Essay, as it was not the custom to date them at the time they were read".[37] Wagner studied the handwritten documents assiduously and suggested the following chronology and pagination:[38]

Volume I: None.
Volume II, 1854-1855:
> "Recollections of a London Church", 21-25
> "Twenty Miles", 291-298
> "My Fever", 335-344
> "The Last of the Rabbis", 509-514
> "The Autumn Walk", 593-602
> "The Ringing of the Bells", 683-697

Volume III, 1856-1857:
> "An Essay Which is No Essay", 51-55
>
> "The Little Graveyard", 413

Volume IV, 1858-1864:
> "Bede", 219-236
> "The 'Morte D'Arthur' and 'Idylls of the King'", 411-416
> "Sunday at the Seaside", 633-638

Volume V: None
Volume VI, 1865-1869:
> "The 'Paradise Lost'", 173-188
> "Literature", 273-282
> "Religio Historici", 449-470
> "Vestiga", 559-586

Volume VII, ends 25 February 1870:
> "Fragilia", 59-63

Volume VIII, possibly 1870-1872:
> "Ars Vitae", 251-254

LLLR contains the first publication of two stories, "A Midsummer Night's Dream" and "The Fordhams of Severnstoke". The six essays not included in the Friends volumes were paginated in volume II of *LLLR*:
> "Books Versus Books", 16-21

"Chivalry", 22-30
"Suggestions of 'Epitaphs'", 44-52
"The Successor of Monsieur Le Sage", 61-84
"George Burrow and his Works", 85-86
[an insertion, not a complete essay]
"Nature's Homily", 184-192

LLLR reprints four other essays in the chronology of their original publication, which suggests that Mrs. Shorthouse may have tried to present all of the *LLLR* essays in order, but there is no internal evidence in the essays or in the folio bindings to make dating of composition certain. These four essays, however, were composed after *John Inglesant*, so will be examined after analysis of the philosophical romance.

Because the Essay Society's social pleasures afforded "attractions when the intellectual [had] been forgotten or overlooked" and because the intellectual interests of the group had been "narrowed to one phase, and that a somewhat peculiar one,"[39] Henry left the Essay Society to concentrate his energies in private to the composition of *John Inglesant* in much the same manner he left the Society of Friends to commune with the Church of England, quietly. He was not quiet, however, in his enthusiasm for a wide-ranging and voracious appetite for literature, and his Early Essays demonstrate his seriousness in wanting to awaken his own audience through their "natural interests" to become "thinking human beings in whose common nature author, subject, and reader are united". Author and reader should be united "absolutely"; subject and reader, "either absolutely or relatively, as the case may be". To achieve such unity the writer

> must know an immense deal more than he absolutely writes: he must not only have mastered the subject on which he writes, but he must have mastered every other subject which in the remotest way relates to or has any influence upon it--mastered it, that is, as far as it is necessary to understand its influence on his more particular subject.[40]

Writing his essay on "Literature" in the late 1860's, probably during the time he was composing *John Inglesant*, Shorthouse affirmed ideas and values that accord with most of Eliot's views in "Tradition and the Individual Talent". Mastering what Eliot called the "historical sense" and becoming personally responsible as an artist are the major lessons Shorthouse learned in his work as a member of the Friends Essay Society. What he failed to learn, perhaps because of his participation in the group, was how to involve political and social issues in his work.

To regard the development of the English novel during the early, middle, and late phases of the Victorian period as social and political documentary is critical commonplace. Indeed, the history of the novel during the Victorian period outlines a broad range of social and political controversies and suggests that Victorian novelists were actively involved in their resolutions, when such resolutions were achieved in Parliamentary legislation, or were instrumental in social actions aimed at guaranteeing individual and group freedoms and rights, especially in relation to the established Church of England.[41] Allen, Baker, Maison, and Wolff, among others, have contributed to the understanding of the Victorian novel as a vehicle for religious controversy and have demonstrated how the search for Christian faith contributed directly to social, political, and religious reforms.[42] To a great extent the novels of Shorthouse have been overlooked, even ignored, by most modern critics because of his seeming lack of social and political concerns. "You speak too harshly of these things," and he remonstrated against the accusation that he was uncaring of social or political issues in the twenty-eighth chapter of *John Inglesant*:

> I see in them nothing but the instinct of humanity, differing in its outward aspect in different ages...My imagination follows humanity through all the paths by which it has reached the present moment, and the more memorials I can gather of its devious footsteps, the more enlarged my view becomes of what its trials, its struggles, and its virtues were.

Wagner's study (1979) set out to repair Shorthouse's reputation and to give his work the recognition accorded to other Victorian minor novelists, notably William Hale White (Mark Rutherford), George MacDonald, and Mrs. Humphry Ward. Where Wagner's study fails, and he is certainly not alone in this failure, is in his acceptance of Shorthouse as *homo unius liber*, the "author of one book". The assumption derives from the general success of *John Inglesant* and from Victorian publishing and marketing, which advertised and promoted the later novels as "by the author of *John Inglesant*". Doris Dalglish, whose religious quest lead her from her predominantly Anglo-Catholic background to her spiritual home in the Society of Friends, was the first critic to reject the stereotyping of Shorthouse as "the author of one great novel" and to suggest that Shorthouse should be studied as the author who developed his art "from the philosophical into the spiritual".[43] She did not, however, develop her critical observation into argument.

Though he was quite conscious of social and political unrest, though the success of *John Inglesant* gave him national attention and took him to 10 Downing Street as the guest of Prime Minister Gladstone, and although he was "lionized in London",[44] Shorthouse seldom expressed interest or concern for the social issues of his day. "There are audible no clinkings", in his novels, "of the economic chains which were being forged or broken; there is not expression of either joy or distress about working conditions in the mines and factories, nor any recognition of what Elizabeth Barrett called 'The Cry of the Children'".[45] He did not share in the deep concerns of most Victorian novelists or in their "ideological"[46] battles, and, in his self-identification as a Broad Church sacramentalist, he never thought of himself as engaged in the "Battle of the Churches".[47] A lifelong optimist and hardworking businessman actively involved in the manufacturing and commercial life of Birmingham, Shorthouse believed social and political issues were matters for others whose special gifts made them capable, worthy, and fit for public leadership. As a matter of taste and manners, he preferred the "mystic", his favourite word, according to his friend Hunter Smith,[48] the philosophic, the Platonic, the romantic, and the "spiritual", and he avoided social and political issues as he avoided religious controversies. According to Smith, Shorthouse was "not much in harmony" with the political or religious habits of "the majority of his fellow-citizens" and was rather an anomaly, with his "blend of freedom of thought with scrupulous attention to religious observances, which was the chief note to outward observers of Shorthouse's character."[49] He shunned religious dissent and believed that elegance in taste and manners forbid a gentleman from engaging in public controversy. Indeed, inner freedom and outward conformity distinguished Shorthouse throughout his life as did his dedication to a "higher calling".

Although he did not know George Gordon, an early professor of English literature at Oxford, Shorthouse would certainly have rejected Gordon's description of the condition of England and of the Victorian Church, and although he would partially have sympathized with Gordon's view of the purpose of literature, he would also have rejected Gordon's relating literature to political motives. Writing about the time Shorthouse's novels were published, Gordon declared:

> England is sick, and...English literature must save. The Churches (as I understand) having failed, and social remedies being slow, English literature now has a triple function: still, I suppose, to delight and instruct us, but also, and above all, to save our souls and heal the State.[50]

The "author of *John Inglesant*" believed the greater work of literature was not to save souls or heal the State but to awaken readers to "the enthusiasm of humanity". According to Shorthouse, man should be "studied in the circumstances of his existence, and indeed *because* of such circumstances" an author could absorb "the various fortunes, sorrows, failings, and littleness of mankind" into "an infinitely varied drama". The drama of human life should be studied not for what "man *might be* but by what he *is*". Such study would awaken the "the enthusiasm of humanity", an enthusiasm "so far from wishing to *alter* its circumstances that [the student of human life] would scarcely wish it *improved*". Enthusiasm for "what is", he believed, is sufficient to make "the contentions of mankind appear so needless that religious animosity, or indeed any rancorous feeling, becomes impossible."[51] The Great Work of an author was to arouse men to this enthusiasm, and the natural result of this enthusiasm could only be compassion. In compassion for human life as it is, he theorized, an author would invariably arouse readers "to a sympathetic perception of their daily life" and enable them "at the same time [to] perceive on such perception, as on a stage, the divine excellence at work."[52] No matter how miserable the plight of the masses, the horrors of poverty, or the evils of social and political injustice, the Great Work of an author was clear to Shorthouse, to show God in action, to make readers conscious of the "divine principle" at work in their daily lives. "The enthusiasm of our sacramental hours is at work in every one of us", he believed, "constantly endeavouring to permeate our daily life."[53]

Once his literary career was established in the minds of the reading public and he realised he had a national voice, Shorthouse dedicated his energies to writing imaginative stories, tales, and essays that allowed him to participate in the Great Work by resisting materialism and dissent and their accompanying "realism" in literature. While composing *John Inglesant*, he grounded his intuitive understanding of the problems of his era by drawing parallels between the past and Victorian England. Later, he redefined his Anglo-Catholic sensibility with an expansive, European outlook, and chose settings for his stories to complement the Church of England's missionary work and to explore the roots of English Protestantism.

John Inglesant (1880) metaphorically draws historical and religious parallels between the 17th century and the Victorian era by dividing the action of the novel into halves. The first part traces the Inglesant family history from the time of Henry VIII through the execution of Charles I; the second part takes place mostly in Italy, offers a "grand tour" based loosely on a combination of the travels of John Evelyn and young Nicholas Ferrar, and returns Inglesant to England during the Restoration. *The Little Schoolmaster Mark* (Part I, 1883; Part II, 1884) explores religious sensibility in 18th century Germany. *Sir Percival: A Story of the Past and of the Present* (1886), set somewhat vaguely in 19th century England, closes with a scene in Africa that unites past and present by dramatising the living power of the Arthurian legend and modernizing myth into contemporary Christian analogue. *The Countess Eve* (1888) studies 18th century Burgundy, and *Blanche, Lady Falaise* (1891), his final novel, takes place mostly in England, but reaches an intense climax in the Austrian alps. His major tales also take Continental settings, explore the roots of Protestantism, and reveal the universality of spirituality: "The Marquis Jeanne Hyacinthe de St. Palaye" (1882) is set in 18th century France, "The Baroness Helena von Saarfeld" (1882) in 18th century Germany, and "A Teacher of the Violin" (1888) in 18th century Bavaria.   Because Shorthouse's works "enspiritualise" daily life, they do not fit into the mainstream of secularization that Eliot outlined in "Religion and Literature".   By 1935, Eliot voiced an insistently religious point of view: "What I want is a litera-ture which should be unconsciously, rather than deliberately and defiantly, Christian."   Eliot then outlined three phases in the "secularization of the novel":

> In the first, the novel took the Faith, in its contemporary
> version, for granted, and omitted it from its picture of life.
> Fielding, Dickens, and Thackeray belong to this phase.
> In the second, it doubted, worried about, or contested the
> Faith. To this belong George Eliot, George Meredith and
> Thomas Hardy. To the third phase, in which we are
> living, belong nearly all contemporary novelists except
> Mr. James Joyce. It is the phase of those who have never
> heard the Christian Faith spoken of as anything but an
> anachronism.[54]

Had he considered Shorthouse, Eliot would have needed to define another phase between his second and third, a phase of "enspiritualising the novel", though he might have considered Shorthouse's achievement too "minor", too unsuccessful in preventing the novel's gradual secularization, or simply too consciously Christian.

Many Victorian novelists were more concerned with using their novels to advance religious ideas and to engage in the "Battle of the Churches" than they were committed to the development of the novel. Self-criticism is, of course, a well-established tradition of English authors, and, indeed, it may be true, as Eliot argued, that the best criticism has been written by authors who used their critical writing as a kind of self-improving workshop, seeing and placing, understanding and comparing their own efforts with reference to conventions and traditions.[55] As their earlier counterparts had done, Victorian novelists frequently defined and defended their innovations in prefaces and introductory essays. Shorthouse was no exception.   The "Preface" to *John Inglesant* proclaims the novel as something new in the history of the art, and of Shorthouse's novels, only *John Inglesant* significantly explores and creates an advance within the English novel.   The other novels, though they are fine works within themselves, were largely neglected by critics of his day, and they are neglected by critics today because they failed to advance the art of the novel.

Although Shorthouse never consciously placed himself within the context of the Oxford Movement, his religious ideas and ideals are within "the mind of the Oxford Movement", as Owen Chadwick has delineated it, and derive generally from historical roots in the time of Henry VIII (1509-1547) and, more specifically, from the Elizabethan era of Archbishop William Laud (1573-1645). *John Inglesant* begins in June 1537 during the dissolution or suppression of the monasteries. *John Inglesant's* success in capturing "the spirit of the age" has led more than one critic to dig for Shorthouse's historical sources and to find some inaccuracies and some fascinating discoveries. Certainly, more than one critic has approached the novel as a source of highly imaginative mental gymnastics, not unlike the critical reactions to the famous "Notes" Eliot appended to "The Waste Land". In 1925, twenty-two years after Shorthouse's death and in the midst of critical attacks and investigations into "The Waste Land", William Kaye Fleming boasted he had uncovered the secrets of Shorthouse's visual imagination, historical authenticity, and rhetorical style as a literary fraud, an ingenious invention, a virtual patchwork of inserted passages taken from sources with no citations of reference. Fleming's attack, "Some Truths About *John Inglesant*", appeared in the *Quarterly Review*[56] and quickly drew the attention of J. Brodrick, who scornfully denigrated "the author of *John Inglesant*" in the Roman Catholic *Month* as "the Prince of Plagiarists".[57] Six years later an academic in Holland tried to seal Shorthouse's literary fate by publishing a passionate dissertation on *The Historical, Philosophical, and Religious Aspects of "John Inglesant"*.[58] Meijer Polak's personal and heated invective strains his argument, which utterly fails to convince, for he, rather ironically, fell into the same problem as Brodrick. Neither critic advanced Fleming's argument with new discoveries or examples of Shorthouse's supposed "plagiarisms"; both merely referred their readers to Fleming's study as if Fleming had presented the convincing, comprehensive analysis. Fleming, Brodrick, and Polak did not investigate the history of the composition of *John Inglesant* or its publication, and they did not discuss, even remotely, the complex problems which surround plagiarism,[59] and they certainly ignored the motives and purpose of Shorthouse's technique of composition.

Shorthouse wrote *John Inglesant* as a personal and private study of the religious spirit of the 17th century to entertain himself, his wife, and a few intimate, like-minded friends. Indeed, he may have composed *John Inglesant* to explain or justify why he and his wife resigned from the Society of Friends, and he may well have had unconscious motives. His personal honesty and sincerity, however, have never been doubted by even his most ardent and suspicious critics, and as the invective of Fleming, Brodrick, and

Polak weakens their argument, the work of Paull and Mallon on the history of plagiarism absolves Shorthouse of charges of plagiarism.[60]

An interesting approach to Shorthouse's motives for composing *John Inglesant* probes the diversity of philosophical speculations and the intensity of religious emotions and experience he contained within the novel. One of his three themes, the conflict between Culture and Fanaticism, directly involved Shorthouse in literary forms and modes, myth and ritual, lyricism and musical rhythms, which oppose Puritanism and against the "plain speaking" of the Quakers. Puritanical absolutism reduces the symbolism of sacred mysteries, which, like irrational aspects of human behaviour, cannot be stated in direct language and can only, at best, be approximated in metaphor. Ineffable sacred mystery necessitates the intensity and indirectness of poetry,[61] and poetic states of mind invite cryptomnesia, or "concealed recollection". "There are many reasons", Jung explains, "why we forget things that we have noticed or experienced and there are just as many ways in which they may be recalled to mind":

> An author may be writing steadily to a preconceived plan, working out an argument or developing the line of a story, when he suddenly runs off at a tangent. Perhaps a fresh idea has occurred to him, or a different image, or a whole new sub-plot. If you ask him what prompted the digression, he will not be able to tell you. He may not even have noticed the change, though he has not produced material that is entirely fresh and apparently unknown to him before. Yet it can sometimes be shown convincingly that what he has written bears a striking similarity to the work of another author--a work that he believes he has never seen.[62]

Cryptomnesia may explain some instances of Shorthouse's inclusion of passages from sixteenth- and seventeenth-century authors, but Shorthouse's family and friends simply did not object to such borrowings to recreate "the spirit of the age". Shorthouse's incorporating selected passages from other writers without specific attribution to sources was quite in keeping with the practice of many authors, especially those of the Tudor and Stuart eras, whom he so admired.[63] Shorthouse never claimed academic attributes, scholarly titles, or theological qualifications, and regarded himself simply as a lover of books whose enthusiasm enabled him to see their descriptive power of spiritual vision. Believing poets to be the most capable of showing men "God at work in their midst", Shorthouse informed *John Inglesant* with the descriptive and imaginative qualities of poetry, and, if he did not cite references for his borrowings, he did, indeed, make appropriate attributions to his sources: he utilized sixteenth- and seventeenth-century conventions and ingeniously imitated them in his narrative; more importantly, he personified his sources by as characters in the novel.

Believing that Truth had once and for all been made absolute in Christianity, Shorthouse studied the Early Oxford Movement and discovered that the conflicts and aspirations of the sixteenth and seventeenth centuries mirrored those of the nineteenth. He accepted the parallels between Tudor, Stuart, and Victorian England as proof of timeless Truth. Any representation of Truth must, therefore, borrow or plagiarize, and the best that any author can achieve is the truth of art in the rhetorical form or literary "dress" of his or her own cultural era. It is "an obvious fact that art never improves", as Eliot argued.[64] "A common inheritance and a common cause unite artists consciously or unconsciously"[65]; thus "Immature poets imitate, mature poets steal",[66] and in view of Plato's world of ideas it is not difficult to understand Emerson's comment that "An author is considered original in proportion to the amount he steals from Plato."[67] Shorthouse's "thefts" are his means of giving vividness and spirit to his historical parallels and, perhaps, his borrowings form part of the satire in *John Inglesant*.[68] In the "Preface" to the 1881 edition he defined his conscious intention to be original: "To blend together these three aims in one philosophy--the memory of the dead--the life of thought--the life of each one of us alone." Then he qualified his attempt as "the tangled web of a life's story" with three distinct threads: "the conflict between Culture and Fanaticism --the analysis and character of Sin--the subjective influence of the Christian mythos". Victorian and modern critics have largely ignored his aims and have focused instead on generalizations about his "outwardly uneventful life".[69]

A well-to-do middle class gentleman and a manufacturer of chemicals, Shorthouse was "confined unobtrusively to Birmingham" with the "occasional family holiday at Llandudno, in Wales".[70] Most reviewers of *John Inglesant* found the novel "worthy of notice on many grounds", as did the first reviewer, because it came from "one of our great industrial towns", and most critics have expressed surprise that a manufacturer of chemicals could present a "defence of the Church of England [as] an ideally conceived...halfwayhouse and meeting place of the religious and rational-ising instincts in man, against the great mother Church of Rome".[71] The anonymous reviewer was later revealed as Mrs. Hymphry Ward, without whom the novel probably would never have gone beyond private publication and limited circulation. Mrs. Ward took a copy of the private edition to Alexander Macmillan and recommended publication. Her courtesy on Shorthouse's behalf attracted interest in *John Inglesant's* reception,[72] and, later, her personal involvement must have occasioned private curiosity among Shorthouse's friends. When she published *Robert Elsmere* (1888), the most popular of Victorian novels of doubt, Shorthouse refused to read her novel. As he wrote Dr. Talbot, Warden of Kebel College, Oxford:

> I do not think that I shall read *Robert Elsmere*. I have no sympathy with what I understand to be its tendency. To say that God exists wherever a good action is performed seems to me to be *simply bosh*. Any good action can only be performed *because God exists*.[73]

Despite his stern refusal to read *Robert Elsmere*, Shorthouse generously acknowledge his debt to Mrs. Ward, as did his widow Sarah when she published her husband's *Life, Letters, and Literary Remains* in 1905. Shorthouse's refusal to read Mrs. Ward's novel demonstrates an intolerant side of his character, though it also demonstrates his lifelong consistency of literary and religious tastes, preferences, and sensibilities. Despite his Broad Church sympathies and liberal views, he was self-confirmed within his ways and did not respond to challenges or "dissent". Assertive in private, Shorthouse seems to have followed Polonius's advice to Laertes: "Beware \ Of entrance into a quarrel, but being in, \ Bear't that th' opposed may beware of thee."[74] Unfortunately, for the most part, he made "the opposed" aware of his convictions only through private correspondence, and we have limited knowledge of how Shorthouse responded to his critics. His intolerance appears ironic in contrast with the free-thinking of *John Inglesant*, but, like his most famous protagonist, he regarded argument as distasteful and unbecoming to a gentleman, and as a Broad Churchman, he belonged to a movement that is "perhaps better considered a network of liberal friends and relations" who opposed dogmatism and "did not acknowledge that they belonged to any party at all" within the Church.[75] By composing a religious novel that speaks "immediately to human intuition in terms that are acceptable without regard to the reader's own faith or philosophy", Shorthouse "revived the very cadence of the subjective, mystical seventeenth century"[76] and won respect for the historical tradition of Anglican "comprehensive-ness" as descriptive of a religious attitude that typified Broad Church sentiment and served the unity of Low and High Church "catholicity". Aware of the bi-polar tension inherent in Anglo-Catholicism,[77] Shorthouse worked towards a *via media* within the Anglican *via media*, a Broad Church grounded in liberal-minded sacramentalism.

Shorthouse's sacramentalism does not separate and preserve "emotions without the beliefs with which their history has been involved".[78] Describing, analyzing, and associating emotions with beliefs in all of his novels, he achieved an intellectual synthesis of what he defined as "Revelation and Humour". The Oxford Movement had ironically set itself "against enthusiasm with considerable zeal",[79] and, as if her were satirizing the zeal, Shorthouse dramatically intensifies religious sensibility and studies the abuses of enthusiasm, especially in *Sir Percival, The Countess Eve* and *Blanche, Lady Falaise.* Platonism and the quietism of the Society of Friends, however, tempered his romantic and mystical philosophic reasoning with contemplative, self-reflective detachment, and he directed his religious aestheticism into metaphors. Transforming his graphic and vividly intense descriptions of nature, cities, churches, ideas, and states of mind into philosophic analogues, he drew intimate portraits of refined characters from the higher social classes. His descriptions of aristocratic manners and of refined sensibilities earned him his earliest and most lasting critical praise, though it also earned him a reputation as a religious aesthete. His interest in the refinement of feeling, tone, and sensibility began, as discussed earlier, in childhood during periods of physical illness and confinement when he could live in dreams. Indeed, he echoes Prospero's belief that "We are such stuff / As dreams are made on"[80] and often foreshadows events in his characters lives through dreams, self-reflective dreaminess, intense, soul-searching confusion and hallucination.

Although he was himself a dreamer, he never conceived of religion as less than the art of living consciously. Near their wedding anniversary, Henry and Sarah were baptized by the Reverend Francis Morse at St. John's, Ladywood, in August 1857. Moving from the Quaker neighbourhood of Francis Street to 6 Beauford Road, the Shorthouses lived "within a stone's throw" of Cardinal Newman and were within eyesight of Newman's Oratory. Although they shared the "same intimacy" with Dr. Robert Coane Jordan, Newman's personal physician, they never met the Cardinal. Shorthouse must certainly have read Newman's *Apologia Pro Vita Sua,* and writing to his cousin Arthur Galton, an Anglican Church apologist who had once been a Roman priest, he contrasted his own easy transition from the Society of Friends into the Anglican Communion against Newman's intense conversion from the Church of England to the Church of Rome:

> What agonies poor Newman went through when he
> found himself and all his exalted ideals, and the whole
> *Romanist* Church in England, crushed beneath the more
> than brutish hoofs of ignorant Italian priestbishops.[81]

From Sarah's point of view, her husband's conversion to the Church of England required no more explanation than that it suited "his tastes and sympathies" and that he found "the idea of an historic and national church peculiarly attractive to him".[82] His conversion represents, however, what Jung called a personal "cultural process".

Jung likened the cultural process within an individual to psychological Individuation. "Whenever the cultural process is moving forward, whether in separate individuals or in groups, the disintegration of collective convictions is to be found,"[83] Jung stated, and his observation suggests the fundamental truth about Shorthouse's transition from Quakerism and Eliot's conversion from Unitarianism. Drawn towards Anglo-Catholicism through their respective historical imaginations, their love of England, of English church history, and of English culture, both authors responded more to the cultural aspirations of the Oxford Movement than they did to the Movement's theology. As the Quaker convictions of Shorthouse "disintegrated" from the collective austerity of the Society of Friends and advanced towards the cultural life of the Church of England, Eliot's Unitarianism "dissolved", and he found the rational, responsible and loving solution to England's modern problems in the cultural comprehensiveness, the *via media* created by Elizabethan Anglicanism.[84] Shorthouse's transition from Quaker simplicity to High Church ritual and sacramentalism is a personal cultural advance, not a fundamental change in his religious convictions. To make a cultural advance, an individual must "first return to the fundamental facts of his own being, quite irrespective of all authority and tradition" and find "a new way through hitherto untrodden country", and then he must become "conscious of his uniqueness and the distinctiveness of his consciousness... Insofar as an individual succeeds in giving collective validity to his widened consciousness", Jung noted, "he creates a tension of the opposites that provides the stimulation needed by culture for its further advance."[85] However philosophical or religious, *John Inglesant* is fundamentally a cultural novel that dramatises the tension of the opposites and specifically supports England's national cultural life. Shorthouse composed *John Inglesant* in response to private needs, but more significantly, he wrote to save his chosen church from threats to its cultural vitality. The historical controversies that Shorthouse dramatises in the life of John Inglesant have by no means ended, and the novel continues to excite "the tension of the opposites". By grounding Victorian conflicts in historical parallels and by colouring religious conflicts with philosophical reasoning, Shorthouse helped Anglican readers to understand the heritage and authority of the Church of England. Blending the three themes he declared in the "Preface", "the memory of the dead--the life of thought--the life of each one of us alone [into] one philosophy" and into the life of one "English-saint", he sought a unifying perspective to support the national, cultural life.

Unlike his fellow Victorians who shaped and clothed their arguments around social and political issues, Shorthouse grounded his fiction in what seemed to him deeper and "more real" issues. He believed all men are guided from within. As the "Inner Light" and the "Inner Voice" of Quaker tradition inform his sacramental vision, the imaginative, intuitive qualities of *John Inglesant* contribute philosophical quest to the English historical novel and move the historical fiction towards the modern psychological novel. By composing "the one great novel that speaks immediately to human intuition... without regard to the reader's own faith or philosophy",[86] Shorthouse contributed to the experiments with historical imagination, lyricism, and irrational and visionary states of mind of his Victorian contemporaries and to the psychological symbolism and the search for unifying intuition of the modern novel. Appealing to the Platonic and archetypal aspects of Christianity, *John Inglesant*'s argument evokes the national symbolism and mythology, "the cultural dress" of the Church of England, on behalf of the intuitive grounding of Christianity itself. The thrust of Shorthouse's achievement is ultimately more similar to Jung's than to Eliot's, for Shorthouse and Jung composed apologies of the religious nature of the human psyche.

Although Shorthouse's later novels never rivaled the popular achievement of *John Inglesant*, they did extend the limits of philosophical romance into studies of spirituality toward, if not beyond, "the frontiers of consciousness". Despite Gosse's implication that Shorthouse lived the literary life as though he were wearing a mask or acting in a masque, "The sincerity of the man and his spiritual fervour are self-evident," and "the author of *John Inglesant*" did not hide anything about himself behind a literary pose or psychological mask; *John Inglesant* is "his own life and quest for truth put in a romantic dress".[87] When a man has created "the nearest approach in English to a religious novel of universal significance"[88] and "the greatest Anglo-Catholic novel of the Victorian age",[89] surely his development from philosophical thought to spiritual vision merits careful study. Here, analogy with Eliot's artistic development deserves attention.

Acclaimed as both "the greatest poem of the twentieth century" and as a "literary hoax",[90] "The Waste Land" represents a critical turning point in Eliot's artistic journey from the detached philosophical agnosticism of his impersonal poetry to the ardent Christianity of his autobiographical poetry and dramas. Struggling in his insecurity and paranoia between his ego and "his" impersonal truth, J. Alfred Prufrock proclaims, "It is impossible to say just what I mean!" though he senses his meaning "as if a magic lantern" had thrown his "nerves in patterns on a screen".[91] The struggle within Prufrock continues in the "Sweeney" poems, and in "Sweeney Agonistes" the persona blames language itself for his inability to communicate, and in his desperation, he exclaims, "I've gotta use words when I talk to you / But if you understand of if you don't / That's nothing to me and nothing to you".[92] By the time of *Four Quartets*, however, the struggle "to say what you mean and mean what you say"[93] has been resolved. The personality behind "Little Gidding", "best [stands] the test of saying exactly what it [means]", as Eliot told Helen Gardner, and it is the autobiographical nature of *Four Quartets* that gave Eliot his realisation, "I stand or fall on *Four Quartets*".[94] When

Eliot confronts the "familiar compound ghost" of "Little Gidding", he defines Prufrock's urge to squeeze "the universe into a ball / To roll it towards some overwhelming question"[95] in words that restate Shorthouse's fundamental struggle: "...how to rescue ordinary life from its worthless banality" and prove that "the eternal pierces the familiar facades of ordinary life".[96] To answer Prufrock's overwhelming question, Eliot had, as Gordon says, to "join the immortals",[97] which, metaphorically, absorbs J. Henry Shorthouse into the "familiar compound ghost / Both intimate and unidentifiable".[98]

Unlike Jung and Eliot, who often began their essays and public lectures with disclaimers about the limited value of their opinions and by drawing attention to problems of language, Shorthouse did little in his "Early Essays" to define critical terms or limit the subjectivity of his enthusiasm. He did not, of course, write the "Early Essays" for an impersonal or even public audience but for Friends who shared his own interests and frames of reference. Though "the rays perceptible in Shorthouse's early essays are brought into focus in *John Inglesant*, then are dispersed in the succeeding novels with decreasing intensity",[99] and because "what he was anxious to say it seems he said many times over with but slight variation in his essays and novels",[100] the thought quality of the "Early Essays" is repetitive, immature, and simplistic. They are, however, in the judgment of one critic, "on the whole, better work than the more elaborate essays, such as that on 'The Platonism of Wordsworth', which followed the production of his masterpiece....[because] there is a certain freshness in his immature presentation of that idea which was lost after it once received the stamp of definitive expression."[101] Although the tone and urgency of his youthful voice suggests he was resisting the social function and restriction of his Quaker audience, Shorthouse did not see himself as any kind of social rebel or religious dissenter.

Years later, after he had begun correspondence with Lady Welby,[102] he began to qualify his terminology for a more general audience, but he never became as self-conscious as Eliot or as scholarly as Jung in defining terms with specific frames of reference for specific audiences. Eliot, for instance, knew he must "avoid the word *spiritual* because it can mean almost anything".[103] In contrast to both Eliot and Jung, Shorthouse used language casually and, for the most part, assumed his audience's sympathies, yet he would readily have understood Eliot's famous note about the meaning of the "personages" in "The Waste Land".

Eliot defined the role of Tiresias in the "Notes to 'The Waste Land'" in collective and unitive terms: "Tiresias, although a mere spectator and not indeed a 'character', is yet the most important personage in the poem, uniting all the rest". Eliot intended that none of the personages be "wholly distinct". Thus, all the female personages are "one woman, and the two sexes meet in Tiresias."[104] James Olney explains the impulse behind the idea: A writer's life and personality must not be seen as "a formal nor as an historical matter", which thereby separates the subject of study from the interest in the writer's real life as a human being somehow endowed with "meaning", but must be viewed intellectually "in relation to the vital impulse to order that has always caused man to create and that, in the end, determines both the nature and the form of what he creates."[105] As Shorthouse assumes the certain and absolute reality of God, Olney assumes the *a priori* "vital impulse to order", which owes much to his understanding of Jung's theory of Individuation. Seemingly, the Individuation process dissolves distinctions and resolves differences as readily as Eliot dissolved his many male and female personages into the complex singularity of Tiresias, but with a difference.

To regard Shorthouse as "the author of only one book" is, pardon the word play, to shortsightedly house the Birmingham author's literary achievements within the confines of *John Inglesant*, to mistake the "vital impulse to order" for a fragment of the order. Olney's theory of autobiography combines elements of Gestalt psychology within a Jungian perspective: All the characters in the literary works of Shorthouse form a map, as it were, of his total personality, a gestalt or whole which comprises the interactions and dynamics of the contents of his unconscious as they impinge upon and interrelate with the consciousness represented by Ego and *persona*. Thus, Shorthouse's "Early Essays" and tales may be read psychologically as illustrations of the struggles of his individuating ego in confrontation and wonder at the mystery of the unconscious. His attaining an authorial voice, both in his critical essays and in his early creative fiction, represents a unique synthesis of creative and critical faculties into "philosophical romance". The *persona* in Jungian understanding represents a psychological mask, a social role with its attendant expectations and demands for emotional and intellectual identification. Shorthouse's transition from Quaker to Anglican, like Eliot's from Unitarian to Anglican, necessarily involves him in dramatising changes in the *persona*, thus his frequent usage of masques represents adaptations and explorations of the "mysteries of identity",[106] and it suggests that Gosse may have understood Shorthouse's literary persona better than Mrs. Shorthouse did. Just as "No poet, no artist of any art, has his complete meaning alone" but takes "his significance, his appreciation" in "his relation...to the timeless as well as of the temporal and of the timeless and of the temporal together",[107] so Shorthouse's master work can only be justly appreciated within the context of his total achievement. Elements of romance, Platonic idealism, Aristotelian irony, spiritual imagination, and intuitive reasoning combine in

Shorthouse's work, and, although he uses traditional Christian language, he explores a specific interpretation of Christianity in his novels that places his work within and among the larger religious categories that derive from the Oxford Movement: Tractarian, Broad Church, Anglo-Catholic. Investigating the "varieties of religious experience"[108] in an intellectual world that was internationalizing its perspectives, he consciously addressed the problems of language as they were known to him, problems which Eliot stated simply: "...last year's words belong to last year's language / And next year's words await another voice."[109] The necessity of using "this year's words" presents problems that confront all writers, and Shorthouse, Eliot, and Jung each confronted the problems with keen sensitivity to etymology and historical sense. Eliot, for instance, noted a major shift in general usage of the word *tradition*: "You can hardly make this word agreeable to English ears without...comfortable reference to the reassuring science of archaeology."[110] Jung tried to modernize traditional mythological, astrological, alchemical, and philosophical perspectives into scientific terminology, and he was forever struggling to prove that his terms were scientific, not just philosophy "in modern dress". Shorthouse's linguistic dilemma was as subtle and as difficult as Eliot's and Jung's, but, rather than dispute terms or "split hairs", he delineated his meanings and his arguments by dramatising them in his fiction through characterization, ironies of plot, and subtleties of allegory, unconscious symbolism, and historical parallels.

However desirable it might be to make literary criticism more scientific, to do so would destroy the very aspects and elements of under-standing that transform intellectual problems into the artistic qualities of literature. Bronowski defined the problem succinctly:

"Science, like art, is not a copy of nature but a re-creation
of her. We re-make nature by the act of discovery, in the
poem or in the deep theorem. And the great poem and
the deep theorem are new to every reader, and yet are his
own experiences, because he himself re-creates them.
They are the marks of unity in variety."[111]

Neither science nor literature represents facts that somehow add themselves up into meaning or even "educated taste". "The good critic--and we should all try to be critics", Eliot argued in "Religion and Literature", "joins wide and increasingly discriminating reading" to "a keen and abiding sensibility", and the good critic realises that "Wide reading is not valuable as a kind of hoarding, an accumulation of knowledge, or what sometimes is meant by the term 'a well-stocked mind'." The facts of literary tradition, like the facts of the sciences, are

"valuable because in the process of being affected by one

powerful personality after another, we cease to be dominated by any one, or by any small number. The very different views of life, cohabiting in our minds, affect each other, and our personality asserts itself and gives each a place in some arrangement peculiar to ourself."[112]

Because of the "peculiarity" of the individual and the uniqueness of his "vital impulse to order", tradition "cannot be inherited" but can only be acquired by "great labour".[113] Eliot's "Animula" dramatises how the "simple soul" becomes a "growing soul" only when it realises its own "heavy burden," which

> Perplexes and offends more, day by day;
> Week by week, offends and perplexes more
> With the imperatives of 'is and seems'
> And may and may not, desire and control.[114]

Eliot seems to be updating Wordsworth's stages of growth in the "Ode: Intimations of Immortality from Recollections of Early Childhood" into his own modern and anti-romantic vision. The "vision splendid" that fades "into the light of common day" as one matures in Wordsworth's view becomes "The pain of living and the drug of dreams" which "Curl up the small soul in the window seat / Behind the *Encyclopaedia Britannica*". "Unable to fare forward or retreat," the "Animula" hides behind the great collection of facts and opinions rather than develop his own experiences and self into an integrated and "particular mind".[115]

As a collective and unitary "metaphor of Self", Shorthouse's mind reveals itself and his search for order and meaning into fictive representations, the disguises of his characters. After *John Inglesant* and the many personal and professional changes that its success brought him, Shorthouse spent the rest of his life trying to reformulate the intuitive synthesis, the vision of order and meaning he had found and formulated in *John Inglesant*. He discovered that the historical development of the Church of England had, in fact, already satisfied his spiritual needs, but that to retain his intuitive vision he needed an intellectual grasp of philosophy and theology, a personal romance of Self. He discovered, as Eliot did sixty-eight years later, that to defend his vision he had to defend the Church of England. His sacramental vision is at once a testimony of the sacredness of the individual psyche and the spiritual validity of the Church Catholic in England. The Anglican communion satisfied the most frequent complaint in his "Early Essays" against the social nature of the Friends Essays Society, an informality which conflicted against its purported intellectual intent. To compose an essay "at once first-class and still exactly suited to the idea of the Essay Meeting," he believed, was "the most difficult of attainments".[116]

The limitations of his audience restricted his intellectual enthusiasm and confined his voice to that of "Young Henry". His audience was well prepared to receive his romantic notions and his sentimental compliments, but they were not willing, perhaps not able, to nurture his intellectual needs. It may well be that the limitations of the Essay Society and the seriousness of his desire to write caused him to change his outward religious form, but it is impossible to trace the origins of the impulse to write *John Inglesant* to any specific experience.

"It is easy to suppose," Jung explained, "that an intimate personal experience underlies...art," but, as he clarified, such a supposition derives from "the influence of Freudian psychology" which reduces personal experience to "something unreal and unauthentic--a mere substitute...nothing but a symptom...of psychic disturbance."[117] Nothing we know about Shorthouse suggests any psychic disturbance or even imbalance, and he, like Eliot and Jung, believed that the goal of criticism was to interpret the art, not the private life and psychology of the artist. To Eliot "criticism is as inevitable as breathing" and "honest criticism and sensitive appreciation is directed not upon the poet but upon the poetry,[118] and, though comparison and analysis are the "chief tools of the critic," the highest critical activity "finds... its true fulfillment in a kind of union with creation in the labour of the artist."[119] Eliot insisted that in the interpretation of any artistic endeavour one cannot readily distinguish between the "creative" and "critical" faculties, and he criticized Matthew Arnold, among others, as being "with the weaker brethren" of critics because Arnold distinguished "far too bluntly" between the two activities.[120] Indeed, the "labour of sifting, combining, constructing, expunging, correcting, testing: this frightful toil is as much critical as creative."[121] The success of *John Inglesant* owes much to Shorthouse's urgency to create an artistic form, philosophical romance, that unifies creative sensibility with the critical faculty.

The struggle for voice and style in any writer represents an urgency for individuated self-recognition, a process that involves more than the kind of self-knowledge acquired from ego-consciousness, that knowledge which derives from self-analytical awareness of one's physical senses and body image. Examined psychologically, voice and style express more than ego-consciousness; they express the degree of a writer's escape from "the participation mystique". Jung borrowed the concept and principle of "participation mystique" from the French philosopher Lucien Levy-Bruhl (1857-1939) and defined it as "a state of identity in a common unconsciousness"[122] which begins as "the primitive unconscious identity of the child with its parents"[123] and develops into unconscious identity with "the tribe, society, the church, or the nation". "As a result of puberty", Jung continues, "the possibility of a new *participation mystique* comes into existence, and therewith also the possibility of replacing that part of the personality that was lost in the identification with the parents."[124] Should a child does not experience the "constellation of a new archetype", and, therefore, the possibility of a new identity, he remains forever a child, infantile, and irresponsible for his social and cultural world. The new archetype, the *anima* which predominates in men and the *animus* which acts as the counterpart in women, performs what may be the most vital and important function in the human psyche, that of establishing relatedness and healthy relationship to others. Thus, these two key archetypes control and regulate the quality of relationships between the sexes, and more importantly, within individuals in their emotional, instinctual, and psychological lives. The *anima* and the *animus* express themselves as contrasexual symbolic images and serve as "guides to the soul" by regulating the relationship between the Ego and the Unconscious. During Shorthouse's "psychological puberty", he broke with the Society of Friends, which activated the energies of both new archetypes, the *anima* and the *animus*. Throughout his maturity he worked with and through these two archetypes, which, in effect, constellated as the philosophical, or critical faculty, and the spiritual, or creative faculty. The philosophical derives from Ego and *shadow* projections. The *shadow* as an archetype represents the "unpleasant and immoral aspects of our selves which we would like to pretend do not exist or have no effect on our lives--our inferiorities, our unacceptable impulses, our shameful actions and wishes".[125] One of the most difficult tasks of the Ego is to raise the *shadow* to consciousness, which "drags all the *shadow*'s long-hidden impulses and fantasies into the realm of moral choice".[126] The *shadow*, for instance, is responsible for the paranoia of Eliot's J. Alfred Prufrock, and, as this thesis will show, Shorthouse personifies the *shadow* in all of his novels. The *shadow* archetype is especially useful in explaining Shorthouse's male narrators and characters, and though speculation may suggest the shadowy characters are autobiographical self-representations, there is too little knowledge about Shorthouse's personal psychology to justify the speculations. Likewise, philosophical and religious doubts express the *shadow*'s affect. Because spirituality derives from the Ego's encounters and relationships with the *anima*, Shorthouse's female characters, and particularly his female narrators, express his deepest self-knowledge. As the *anima* and *animus* archetypes are the agents of Ego/Self integration, both serve the maturation and reordering of personality around a new self, the archetypal Self, which Shorthouse's characters experience as profound love "of the idea of the Christ".

Indeed, in Christianity these archetypes are of fundamental importance, as Jung repeatedly pointed out. "Thou shalt love the Lord thy

God with all thy heart, and with all thy soul, and with all thy mind" is the "greatest commandment in the law," according to Jesus, and the second most important commandment is "Thou shalt love thy neighbour as thyself."[127] The teachings of Jesus urge that a man's relationships with his fellow men [and, of course, with women] are within the responsibility of his free will and that a man must "first be reconciled to his brother" before offering any gifts to God.[128]

If it is true, as Baker affirmed, that *John Inglesant*'s greatness lies in its direct appeal to human intuition regardless of a reader's religious bias or orientation, then it follows that a close examination of the psychological aspects of the novel may reveal psychic patterns which stimulate or create intuition. Analysis of *John Inglesant* does not reveal an "objective correlative" of intuition, nor does it disclose a formula or technique for "opening the doors of perception",[129] but such analysis does illustrate a central idea of Jung's about the nature of art and the relationship between artist and art work.

To provoke intuitive responses in a reader, a work of art must "draw its strength from the life of mankind", not from the life of the artist. As Eliot defined the effects of a "new work of art" and argued that such a work radically changes the accepted values of the traditional canon of literature, so Jung asserted that great art "becomes a living experience" and affects "the conscious outlook of an age". Such art represents an "event" of importance "for the whole epoch" of the artist and "a message to generations of men".[130] Thus, *John Inglesant* expresses Shorthouse's recognition of the need for unified vision, for synthesis of psychological faculties, for unity of thought and imagination. Shorthouse was well aware of the historical conditions of religious life that provided him with the novel's setting and from which he drew his Victorian parallels. As many as forty-six religious sects fought against each other during the reign of Charles I and throughout the Commonwealth, sects paradoxically united "in their love of God and their hatred of the other forty-five."[131] In Shorthouse's Victorian era, the fundamental challenge to all religions and religious sects came from the emerging sciences, from Darwinism, materialism, and their accompanying social and political theories which fostered religious doubt and agnosticism. Shorthouse saw that unity and peace could not come to his era through intellectual or scientific debate, but through some new synthesis, some new intuition of "the law of life we feel within".[132] To Shorthouse in his pre-psychology era, the collective unconscious meant the world of ideas, and the great work of any religious artist was to serve the idea of the Platonic Christ, not a person nor a personality, but divine wisdom itself, which he defined on the last page of *John Inglesant* as the "law of life we feel within...in harmony with that law of gradual development which the Divine Wisdom has planned". To discover the essence of unity between Christ and Plato, to see the divine principle at work in daily life, Shorthouse practiced and adhered to the Quaker doctrine of Inner Light, of listening to the Inner Voice, and he dramatised the process by making *John Inglesant* itself a conscious study of the dynamic processes which Jung called Individuation. A work of art is "not a human being, but is something suprapersonal. It is a thing and not a personality."[133] As a "thing" or text, it may be consciously analyzed as an artifact of the collective unconscious. Joseph Henderson, a Jungian analyst, has identified the pattern of "stages of psychological development" in the poetry and dramas of Eliot,[134] and has suggested that such developmental patterns may be found in anyone undergoing psychoanalysis, projecting self-analysis in creative activity, or unconsciously transferring the dynamics into a literary text. Because the pattern represents "something suprapersonal", it may be applied with reasonable objectivity to Shorthouse's literary work to illustrate how he reflected upon his personal growth and integrated his personal psychology into a suprapersonal symbol. That which connects personal with suprapersonal, that which enables the Ego to "marry" the Self, that which empowers an individual talent to transform tradition has been called by many names: In metaphor appropriate to Shorthouse, the Inner Light of sacramental vision; to Eliot, Christian dogma united with the mystical philosophy of "the still point of the turning world"[135]; and to Jung, symbols of transformation which express archetypal dynamics of Individuation.

As the integrity of Shorthouse's Quaker-Anglican transition cannot be doubted from his works, the significance of Eliot's conversion from philosophic, moralistic Unitarianism to Anglo-Catholicism cannot be under-stated in any evaluation of his complete work. "Ash-Wednesday", *Murder in the Cathedral*, and *Four Quartets* force reinterpretation of "The Waste Land" and "The Hollow Men". Similarly, the spiritual romances, *Sir Percival*, *The Countess Eve*, and *Blanche, Lady Falaise*, force re-interpretation of *John Inglesant* as philosophical romance and re-consideration of Shorthouse as "the author of one great book". Development need not imply progressive improvement, and the judgments against Shorthouse are grounded in the public success of *John Inglesant* and his subsequent failure of his later novels to attract and win the diverse and large audience that responded so enthusiastically and critically to *John Inglesant*. Although the later works claim merits which cannot be attributed to *John Inglesant*, it was only in his first novel that Shorthouse was able to express a dramatic vision of the suprapersonal unity of the Church of England. Only *John Inglesant* creates a national myth of an "English-saint" and offers a rational means of apprehending "the religion of *John Inglesant*".

Notes to Chapter One

[1]Sarah Shorthouse, Letter to George Macmillan (25 March 1903), British Library MS. 54934.

[2]Edmund Gosse, *Questions at Issue* (London: Heinemann, 1893).

[3]Sarah Shorthouse, Letter to George Macmillan (22 May 1905), British Library MS. 54934. Commenting on several letters and some reviews she had received from Macmillan, Mrs. Shorthouse complained: "The only one that has really given pain to my Brother John Shorthouse and myself was sent to me from Durrant's Press Cutting Firm. And to my great surprise I found that it was signed by 'Edmund Gosse'. Mr. Gosse wrote a most kind letter to me after receiving my Book and I enclose it because of its most strange contrast with his description of my dear one's person, and of his whole life--It seems to us that while all *literary* criticism, whether true or false--kind or unkind, must be accepted in silence by Authors--*personal* descriptions stand on a different footing and to say that a man of transparently high and genuine character not only went through life as a 'masque', but even in his religion played the same part, does not seem to be justifiable." She asked Macmillan whether she should ignore Gosse's "accusation" or respond in print. He advised her to ignore it and to try to understand its "literary" nature.

[4]Sarah Shorthouse, Letter to George Macmillan (24 May 1905), British Library MS. 54934. "My Brother's first remark to me after reading Mr. Gosse's article was, 'these literary people must have a standpoint of their own' and this is very much like your own explanation of his 'literary pose'."

[5]Sarah Shorthouse, Letter to George Macmillan (22 May 1905), British Library MS. 54934. "It has been a relief to me to consult you about it, for it distressed me so much that I could not forget it."

[6]Sarah Shorthouse, Letter to George Macmillan (30 May 1904), British Museum MS. 54934.

[7]Ann Thwaite, *Edmund Gosse: A Literary Landscape, 1843-1928.* (University of Chicago, 1984), 3.

[8]Birmingham newspapers praised Shorthouse in their obituary notices, revived their praises after *LLLR* was published in the spring of 1905, and celebrated his centenary in 1934. Most commentators extolled him as Birmingham's "leading", "most famous", or "greatest" novelist. One example speaks generally for the others: "We of Birmingham are often told that we are inordinately proud of our city. It may be--there are those who would say emphatically that it will be--one of Birmingham's chief titles to eternal fame that it was the city which produced the author of *John Inglesant*", *Daily Post* (15 April 1905).

[9]F. J. Wagner, *J. H. Shorthouse* (Boston: Twayne, 1979) 181.

[10]Morris Philipson, *Outline of a Jungian Aesthetics* (Chicago: Northwestern University Press, 1963), 91-99. The application of Freudian principles to works of art discloses "the material and efficient causes of the product in the same terms by which a neurosis is explained" (99).
    Philipson quotes from Jung's *Modern Man in Search of a Soul* (New York: Harcourt Brace, 1933): "[It] is conceivable that a work of art...might be traced back to those knots in psychic life we call the complexes...Freud takes the neurosis as a substitute for a direct means of gratification. He therefore regards it as something inappropriate--a mistake, a dodge, an excuse, a

voluntary blindness...And a work of art is brought into questionable proximity with the neurosis when it is taken as something which can be analyzed in terms of the poet's repressions...But should the claim be made that such an analysis *accounts for the work of art itself* [sic], then a categorical denial is called for" (193-194).

[11] *Memorials of the Families of Shorthouse and Robinson and Others Connected with Them, Printed in Commemoration of the One Hundredth Birthday of Sarah Southall, 12 September 1901*. Printed for private circulation (Birmingham, 1902), 94-97.

[12] J. Henry Shorthouse, "Preface" to *John Inglesant* (London: Macmillan, 1881).

[13] Sarah Shorthouse, *Life, Letters, and Literary Remains of J. Henry Shorthouse* (London: Macmillan, 1905), vol. 1, 11. Cited as *LLLR* hereafter.

[14] Sarah Shorthouse, *LLLR*, vol. I, 13.

[15] Sarah Shorthouse, *LLLR*, vol. I, 35.

[16] Margaret Southall contributed her memories to Sarah Shorthouse's *LLLR*, vol. I, 19-35.

[17] J. H. Shorthouse, Letter to Margaret Southall (12 September 1853), *LLLR*, vol. I, 41.

[18] J. H. Shorthouse, Letter to Margaret Southall (12 September 1853), *LLLR*, vol. I, 40.

[19] J. H. Shorthouse, Letter to Margaret Southall (12 September 1853), *LLLR*, vol. I, 40.

[20] Charles Linnel's description of Shorthouse's book buying habits are recorded by Wagner, *J. Henry Shorthouse* 33; Wagner cites *T. P.' Weekly* (13 March 1903), 554, as the source. See also "The Sale of J. H. Shorthouse's Library", *The Times* (18 November 1909), p. 15, col. 4, and (22 December 1909), p. 17, col. 6, for a description of his collection.

[21] *LLLR*, vol. I, 7-9.

[22] J. H. Shorthouse, Letter to Lady Victoria Welby (11 September 1883), *LLLR*, vol. I, 17-18.

[23] Denyse Rockey, *Speech Disorder in Nineteenth Century Britain: The History of Stuttering* (London: Croom Helm, 1980), 243-244. I have been unable to find any studies of literary authorship as compensation for normality of speech, though the problems of stammering or stuttering have attracted much scientific inquiry. The subject is suggestive, and perhaps some day scholars and scientists may be able to relate imagination to speech disorder. Shorthouse, for instance, was always attracted to King Charles I, who also had a speech disorder.

[24] Denyse Rockey, *Speech Disorder* 244.

[25] J. Henry Shorthouse, Letter to Lady Welby, (11 September 1883) *LLLR*, vol. I, 17-18.

[26] J. H. Shorthouse, "Preface" to *John Inglesant* appended to the first public edition: (London: Macmillan, 1881), vii.

[27] William Wordsworth, "The Excursion", *Complete Poetical Works of Wordsworth* (Boston: Houghton Mifflin, 1932), 403-410. See also Thomas Browne's "To the Reader", *Religio Medici*

(London: Macmillan, 1950), 3-5.

[28]*LLLR*, vol. I: 13, 14, 24-25, 70, 72, 74, 76, and 82.

[29]J. D. Hunter, "The Early Years of the Birmingham Friends' Reading Society", *Journal of West Midland Regional Studies*, vol. 2, no. 2968, 44.

[30]F. J. Wagner, *J. H. Shorthouse* 43-44.

[31]F. J. Wagner, *J. H. Shorthouse* 44.

[32]F. J. Wagner, *J. H. Shorthouse* 43.

[33]F. J. Wagner, *J. H. Shorthouse* 45.

[34]Sarah Shorthouse, Letter to George Macmillan (12 August 1904), British Library MS. 54934.

[35]J. Henry Shorthouse, "Literature", *LLLR*, vol. II, 139.

[36]Sarah Shorthouse, Letter to George Macmillan (16 August 1904), British Library MS. 54934.

[37]Sarah Shorthouse, Letter to George Macmillan (2 February 1905), British Library MS. 54934.

[38]Frederick J. Wagner, "J. H. Shorthouse (1834-1903): A Bibliography", *Bulletin of Bibliography and Magazine Notes*, vol. 28, no. 3, July-September 1971, part one, 85. Part two of the bibliography was published in vol. 28, no. 4, October-December 1971.

[39]J. Henry Shorthouse, "Literature", *LLLR*, vol. II, 137-139.

[40]J. Henry Shorthouse, "Literature", *LLLR*, vol. II, 140.

[41]The effects of the English novel on social conditions and Parliamentary legislation and debate have been frequently studied with reference to the work of George Eliot and Charles Dickens. Of obvious interest, too, is the literary work of Prime Minister Benjamin Disraeli, whose collected *Novels and Tales* (Hughenden, ed., 1881) fills eleven volumes, and four-time Prime Minister William Ewart Gladstone, a phenomenal reader and correspondent, whose interest in Shorthouse has been referred to by many critics, though with minimal evidence.

[42]Walter Allen's *The English Novel: A Short Critical History* (1954); E. A. Baker's *The History of the English Novel* (1924-1936); Margaret Mary Maison's *Search Your Soul, Eustace: A Survey of the Religious Novel in the Victorian Age* (1961); and Robert Lee Woolf's *Gains and Losses: Novels of Faith and Doubt in Victorian England* (1977) represent significant achievements in demonstrating the continuity of religious themes within the development of the English novel and the social and political affects of religious novels.

[43]Doris Nellie Dalglish, "The Novels of J. H. Shorthouse", *Friends Quarterly Examiner*, LIX (July 1925), 221-235. In her autobiography, *We Have Been Glad* (Macmillan, 1938), Dalglish shares many of Shorthouse's views; she understood Catholic, Protestant, and Quaker sensibilities, especially their sacramentalism. In her view, Shorthouse was "still a Quaker" despite his membership in the Church of England.

[44] F. J. Wagner, *J. H. Shorthouse* 141.

[45] F. J. Wagner, *J. H. Shorthouse* 20.

[46] Terry Eagleton, *Literary Theory: An Introduction* (Oxford: Basil Blackwell, 1983), 17-53. Shorthouse would never have thought of himself as a propagandist or as a man with a particular ideology; he would have regarded Eagleton's viewpoint about institutionalizing literary study to support political or social ideology as a misunderstanding of the religious nature and function of literature.

[47] Paul Elmer More, "J. Henry Shorthouse", *Shelburne Essays*, Third Series (Boston: Houghton Mifflin, 1905), 228.

[48] J. Hunter Smith provided the introduction to *LLLR*, vol. 1, xiv.

[49] J. Hunter Smith, "Introduction", *LLLR*, vol. 1, xiv.

[50] Eagleton, *Literary Theory: An Introduction* 23.

[51] J. Henry Shorthouse, Letter to Matthew Arnold (23 October 1871), *LLLR*, vol. 1, 85-86.

[52] J. Henry Shorthouse, Letter to Matthew Arnold (23 October 1871), *LLLR*, vol. 1, 88.

[53] J. Henry Shorthouse, Letter to Matthew Arnold (23 October 1871), *LLLR*, vol. 1, 84.

[54] T. S. Eliot, "Religion and Literature", *Selected Essays* (London: Faber and Faber, 1932), third enlarged ed., rep. 1986, 392. All subsequent citations from Eliot's *Selected Essays* are from this edition unless noted otherwise.

[55] T. S. Eliot, "The Function of Criticism", *Selected Essays* 31-33.

[56] William Kaye Fleming, "Some Truths About *John Inglesant*", *The Quarterly Review*, vol. 245, no. 485, July 1925, 130-148.

[57] James Patrick Brodrick, "A Prince of Plagiarists", *The Month*, no. 146 (October 1925), 338-343.

[58] Meijer Polak, *The Historical, Philosophical, and Religious Aspects of "John Inglesant"* (Purmerend: J. Muusses, 1933; rep. Oxford, 1934).

[59] Even the Church has been attacked as plagiarism, and Solomon's famous lament that there is "nothing new under the sun" suggests the complexity of plagiarism as a theoretical, critical issue that extends far beyond borrowing, embedding, "cribbing" or "interlarding" a passage of poetry or prose without specific attribution. Few readers, to be sure, expect or demand textual notes, footnotes, or endnotes in works of fiction, and "larding" or "interlarding" has been admired for its artistic merit.

[60] Two excellent studies of plagiarism absolve Shorthouse of the charges against him: H. M. Paull, *Literary Ethics: A Study in the Growth of Literary Conscience* (London: Thornton Butterworth, 1928) and Thomas Mallon, *Stolen Words: Forays into the Origins and Ravages of Plagiarism* (New York: Ticknor and Fields, 1989). Plagiarism is philosophically and

psychologically more complex than infringement of copyright. Literary "property" did not become a serious legal matter, Mallon and Paull contend, until long after a virtual tradition of "borrowing" had been established.

Mallon cites a conjectural problem about Harold Bloom's *The Anxiety of Influence: Revisionism from Blake to Stevens* (Yale University Press, 1976). When Bloom writes, "Weaker talents idealize; figures of capable imagination appropriate for themselves," Mallon wonders if he were "plagiarizing" Eliot's dictum: "Immature poets imitate; mature poets steal". (Eliot, "Philip Massinger", *Selected Essays* 206).

All critics who have assessed the accusations of Fleming, Brodrick, and Polak against Shorthouse have dismissed the charge of plagiarism with applause for Shorthouse's "ingenuity" in capturing idioms and rhetorical rhythms.

[61]Poetry presents images and emotions immediately, but not directly. When the content is an attempt at "Truth, not just human truth", the poet confronts the limits of what language can communicate. Owen Barfield's *Poetic Diction: A Study in Meaning* (London: Faber and Gwyer, 1928) argues that "meaning itself can never be *conveyed* from one person to another... every individual must intuit meaning for himself" (133).

In *Poetic Truth* (London: Heinemann, 1978) Robin Skelton analyzes Suzanne K. Langer's argument that poetry creates "a virtual 'life' [in] non-discursive symbolic form". "The laws which govern the making of poetry are not those of discursive logic. They are 'laws of thought' as truly as the principles of reasoning are; but *they never apply scientific pseudo-scientific (practical) reasoning*" (77-78). Skelton argues, "The problem of the poet, if he is to produce work which forces his readers to experience real perception, is how to make recognition difficult and perception inevitable" (88). Central to poetic perception is "the relationship of the individual with the idea of God", because that relationship "is also the relationship of the individual with ideas of fundamental unity, complete participation, and universal order" (125).

In *The Poet's Defence* (Cambridge University Press, 1937) Jacob Bronowski declares: "I believe that the mind of man has a steady shape which is the truth...The rules of reasoning... without which the mind cannot be. For formal logics may change, but the rules of reasoning...make an absolute truth, which I think is the truth of poetry" (10).

In *Poetry and Repression: Revisionism from Blake to Stevens* (Yale University Press, 1976), Harold Bloom studies "poetic influence as defensive revisionism" and examines Vico's argument "that if any poet knows too well what causes his poem, then he cannot write it, or at least will write it badly" (5). He acknowledges, "All reading is translation, and all attempts to communicate a reading seem to court reduction, perhaps inevitably" (14).

[62]C. G. Jung, *Man and his Symbols* (London: Aldus Books, 1964; New York: Doubleday, 1964), 37.

[63]For instance, "During the early part of the seventeenth century, there seems to have been no marked change in the way in which the universal practice of plagiarism was regarded", Paul, *Literary Ethics* 103-104.

[64]T. S. Eliot, "Tradition and the Individual Talent", *Selected Essays* 16.

[65]T. S. Eliot, "The Frontiers of Criticism", *Selected Essays* 24.

[66]T. S. Eliot, "Philip Massinger", *Selected Essays* 206.

[67]Cited by Paul, *Literary Ethics* 103.

[68]J. Hunter Smith, "Introduction", *LLLR*, vol. 1, xv. Smith is the only critic to assess *John Inglesant* as "to a large extent a satire, and not altogether a fair one, on the principles and system of the Jesuits..."

[69]Although Wagner published a comprehensive bibliography about Shorthouse (See note 38 above.) "as a left-handed corrective to some hardy errors which have inadvertently been honored with the authority of repetition", his own study repeats the fascination with Shorthouse's "degree and type of cultivation", and, though Wagner's work on Shorthouse is the most scholarly and comprehensive study yet published, Wagner himself left us a curiosity. Wagner did much of his research at the University of London's Senate House Library, but he neglected to give any credit or citation to John Lionel Madden. Madden's meticulous bibliography of Shorthouse's life and publishing career includes a thorough chronological record of critical reviews and is an accurate and valuable guide for any historical or developmental study. One can only wonder why Wagner neglected to give Madden credit. The combination of Wagner's and Madden's work with some corrections and a few additions makes the bibliography to this thesis comprehensive.

[70]F. J. Wagner, *J. H. Shorthouse* 20-21.

[71]Anonymous review in *The Saturday Review of Literature* (9 July 1881). In a letter to Alexander Macmillan (15 July 1881), Shorthouse remarked, "I presume the review in *The Saturday* is by Mrs. Ward. It is beautifully written and a man must be hard to please who is not satisfied with it: where she differs from the author *of course* she is wrong" (British Library MS. 54934).

[72]Charles Linnell, "The True Story of *John Inglesant*", *Athenaeum* (27 July 1901), 127, and (17 August 1901), 222. See also William S. Peterson, "J. H. Shorthouse and Mrs. Humphry Ward: Two New Letters", *Notes and Queries*, 18th series, vol. 216, July 1971, 259-261.

[73]J. H. Shorthouse, Letter to Dr. Talbot, ("Low Sunday, 1888") printed in Sarah Shorthouse's *LLLR*, vol. I, 264-265.

[74]Shakespeare's *Hamlet* (I.iii.65-67).

[75]David J. DeLaura, *Victorian Prose: A Guide to Research* (New York: Modern Language Association of America, 1973), 402.

[76]Joseph Ellis Baker, *The Novel and the Oxford Movement* (Princeton University Press, 1932). Baker quotes Paul Elmer More from *Shelburne Essays*, Third Series, 236.

[77]W.S.F. Pickering, *Anglo-Catholicism: A Study in Religious Ambiguity* (London: Routledge, 1989). The "fond hope" of Anglo-Catholics to "marry" Father Rome and Mother England is more ambiguous than paradoxical, because ambiguity means that "which is open to more than one interpretation", whereas paradox "is that which is contradictory or absurd" (4-6).
    A. L. Drummond, *The Churches in English Fiction* (Leicester: Edgar Backus, 1950) defines the "bi-polar tension [as] asceticism exercising its magnetic influence without preventing an apparently contrary trend towards the sensual" (101).

[78]T. S. Eliot, "The Modern Mind", *The Uses of Poetry and the Uses of Criticism* (London: Faber and Faber, 1933), 135.

[79]R. A. Knox, *Enthusiasm: A Chapter in the History of Religion with Special Reference to the*

XVII and XVIII Centuries (Oxford: Clarendon, 1950).

[80]William Shakespeare, *The Tempest* (IV.i.156-158).

[81]Sarah Shorthouse, *LLLR*, vol. 1, 64-68.

[82]J. H. Shorthouse, Letter to Arthur Galton (17 January 1899), *LLLR* 364-366.

[83]C. G. Jung, "On Psychical Energy", *Contributions to Analytical Psychology* (London: Kegan Paul, Trench, Trubner, and Co., 1928), 68.

[84]Lyndall Gordon, *Eliot's Early Years* (Oxford University Press, 1977), 120-140.

[85]C. G. Jung, "On Psychical Energy", *Contributions to Analytical Psychology* 68.

[86]Joseph Ellis Baker, *The Novel and the Oxford Movement* (Princeton University Press, 1932), 199 and 203.

[87]J. A. Sutherland, *Victorian Novelists and Publishers* (University of Chicago, 1976), 116-117.

[88]Baker 199.

[89]Baker 182.

[90]Numerous studies of "The Waste Land" debate its literary merits. A few summarize the many: Rose Macaulay's "The First Impact of 'The Waste Land'" in *T. S. Eliot: A Symposium for his Seventieth Birthday* (New York: Farrar, Straus, and Cudahy, 1958), explains, "We had been for too long used to the crude and drab simplicities of the Freudian interpretation of the subconscious mind, which tried to reduce all its manifold and intricate complexities to two roots, sex and parent-trouble" (30).

   James E. Miller explored *T. S. Eliot's Personal Waste Land* as an "Exorcism of the Demons" (Pennsylvania State University Press, 1977). Eliot remarked that the poem is "only the relief of a personal and wholly insignificant grouse against life; it is just a piece of rhythmical grumbling", and in a 1959 *Paris Review* interview Eliot stated, "By the time of the *Four Quartets*, I couldn't have written in the style of 'The Waste Land'; I wasn't even bothering whether I understood what I was saying" (9). Miller takes Eliot's famous disclaimers seriously.

   My own view of "The Waste Land" owes much to Helen Gardner's *"The Waste Land": 1922* (University of Manchester, 1972) and to Lyndall Gordon's two studies of *Eliot's Early Years* and *Eliot's New Life* (Oxford University Press, 1977 and 1988). I was fortunate to interview Helen Gardner when she was in California working on *The Composition of Four Quartets* and to discuss the interview with Lyndall Gordon at Oxford in 1986. Both scholars confirmed that "The Waste Land" can no longer be read as it was between 1922 and the time of Eliot's conversion, and that Eliot's own comments on the "purely personal act" of writing "The Waste Land" require more careful evaluation than Miller gave them.

[91]T. S. Eliot, "The Love Song of J. Alfred Prufrock", *The Complete Poems and Plays* (London: Faber and Faber, 1969, rep. 1987), 16.

[92]T. S. Eliot, "Sweeney Agonistes", *Complete* 125.

[93]Lewis Carroll, *Alice's Adventures in Wonderland* (New York: Random House, 1946), 77-78.

At the famous "Mad Tea-Party", Alice argues with the March Hare and the Dormouse about whether to "say what you mean" means the same as to "mean what you say". The Mad Hatter ends the argument abruptly with "It *is* the same thing with you", and the Tea-Party conversation drops into silence.

[94]Lyndall Gordon, *Eliot's New Life* (Oxford University Press, 1988), 143.

[95]T. S. Eliot, "The Love Song of J. Alfred Prufrock", *Complete* 15.

[96]Gordon 140.

[97]Gordon 144.

[98]T. S. Eliot, "Little Gidding", *Complete* 193.

[99]Elfriede Rieger, *Joseph Henry Shorthouse und sein „John Inglesant", Ein Beitrag zur Geschichte des englishchen Romans im 19. Jahrhundert*, Diss., Georg-August 1927 (Göttingen: Göttingen Tageblat, 1927), 29.

[100]F. J. Wagner, *J. H. Shorthouse* 45.

[101]Paul Elmer More, "J. Henry Shorthouse", *Shelburne Essays* 213-214.

[102]Lady Welby, the Honourable Victoria Alexandrina Maria Louisa Stuart-Wortley (Lady Welby-Gregory after her marriage), published two studies that were known to Shorthouse: *Links and Clues* (1881), *The Witness of Science to Linguistic Anarchy* (1898), and her third, *What is Meaning? Studies in the Development of Significance*, was published in 1903, the year of Shorthouse's death.

[103]T. S. Eliot, "Second Thoughts on Humanism", *Selected Essays*, third enlarged edition, (London: Faber and Faber, 1951), 485.

[104]T. S. Eliot, "Notes to 'The Waste Land'", *Complete* 78.

[105]James Olney, *Metaphors of Self: The Meaning of Autobiography* (Princeton University Press, 1972), 3. Jung offers "what one can find in no other writer in English...a psychological theory for autobiography that coincides with an actual autobiography (*Essays* and *Memories, Dreams, Reflections*)". In studies of Jung, Eliot, Darwin, Montaigne, Newman, Mills, and Fox, Olney reads the complete works of each author as an extensive "metaphor of Self".

     Eliot never wrote an essay on Shakespeare, but he refers to Shakespeare more than to any other writer. In "John Ford", *Selected Essays*, he sums up, "The whole of Shakespeare's work is *one* poem...united by one significant, consistent, and developing personality" (203).

[106]Robert Langbaum's "The Mysteries of Identity", *The Modern Spirit: Essays in Nineteenth- and Twentieth-Century Literature* (New York: Oxford University Press, 1977) defines the identity theme in depth but does not examine the psychological nature of autobiography, which is the foundation of Olney's theory.

[107]T. S. Eliot, "Tradition and the Individual Talent", *Selected Essays* 14-15.

[108]William James' *The Varieties of Religious Experience* (Longman, Green, and Co., 1902)

asserts, "The process of remedying inner incompleteness and reducing inner discord is a general psychological process, which may take place with any sort of mental material, and need not necessarily assume the religious form" (172). To Jung, however, the process itself is religious, and spontaneous images created by the psyche are "naturally religious". See *The Undiscovered Self* (Boston: Little, Brown, and Co., 1957), 100.

[109]T. S. Eliot, "Little Gidding", *Complete* 194.

[110]T. S. Eliot, "Tradition and the Individual Talent", *Selected Essays* 13.

[111]Jacob Bronowski, *Science and Human Values* (New York: Harper and Row, 1965), 20. Bronowski addressed similar issues in *The Identity of Man* (Garden City, New York: The American Museum Natural History Press, 1971).

[112]T. S. Eliot, "Religion and Literature", *Selected Essays* 395.

[113]T. S. Eliot, "Tradition and the Individual Talent", *Selected Essays* 14.

[114]T. S. Eliot, "Animula", *Complete* 107-108.

[115]T. S. Eliot, "Animula", *Complete* 107-108.

[116]J. Henry Shorthouse, "Literature", *LLLR*, vol. II, 138.

[117]C. G. Jung, "Psychology and Literature", *The Spirit in Man, Art, and Literature*, vol. 15, *Collected Works*, Bollingen Series XX (Princeton University Press, 1966), 92-93.

[118]T. S. Eliot, "Tradition and the Individual Talent", *Selected Essays* 13, 17.

[119]T. S. Eliot, "The Function of Criticism", *Selected Essays* 31.

[120]T. S. Eliot, "The Function of Criticism", *Selected Essays* 29-30.

[121]T. S. Eliot, "The Function of Criticism", *Selected Essays* 30.

[122]C. G. Jung, "Mind and Earth", *Contributions to Analytical Psychology*, trans. H. G. and Cary F. Baynes, (London: Kegan Paul, Trench, Trubner, and Co., 1928), 125-127.

[123]C. G. Jung, "Analytical Psychology and Education", *Contributions* 374.

[124]C. G. Jung, "Mind and Earth", *Contributions* 127.

[125]Robert H. Hopcke, *A Guided Tour of the Collected Works of C. G. Jung* (Boston: Shambhala, 1989), 81.

[127]The Gospel According to Matthew 22:37-39 (King James Authorised Bible).

[128]The Gospel According to Matthew 5:22-24 (King James Authorised Bible).

[129]William Blake, "The Marriage of Heaven and Hell", *The Complete Poetry and Prose of William Blake* (New York: Doubleday, 1965), 39. Blake believed that "If the doors of perception

were cleansed everything would appear to man as it is, infinite."

[130]C. G. Jung, "Psychology and Literature", *The Spirit in Man, Art, and Literature* 98.

[131]Brailsford, Mabel Richard. *A Quaker from Cromwell's Army* (London: Swarthmore Press, 1927), 13.

[132]J. H. Shorthouse, *John Inglesant* (Birmingham: Cornish Brothers, 1880), 577.

[133]C. G. Jung, "On the Relation of Analytical Psychology to Poetry", *The Spirit in Man, Art, and Literature* 71.

[134]Joseph L. Henderson, "Stages of Psychological Development Exemplified in the Poetical Works of T. S. Eliot", *Journal of Analytical Psychology*, vol. I (May 1956) and vol. II (January 1957).

[135]T. S. Eliot, "Burnt Norton", *Complete* 17.

Chapter Two: Preparation for *John Inglesant*, Shorthouse's Early and Middle Essays

"I have been all my life", Shorthouse declared in "My Fever", "what Nathaniel Hawthorne calls 'a devoted epicure of my own emotions'."[1] Setting out to "express a difference" between how other "people talk and create a world within themselves, and fancy they have made a very grand creation" and how his own mind works, the twenty-one-year-old Henry wrote a fanciful tale that connects his own life and fortunes "to the beautiful lady I met walking in the meadow with the buttercups". The original title, "My Senses", was changed to "My Fever" before its original publication in the second volume of *LLLR* and, if we believe the final paragraph, Shorthouse read "My Fever" to the Friends Essay Society on 18 August 1857, the day before his wedding to Sarah Scott.[2] By imaginatively connecting his recovery from typhus fever at Rebecca Shorthouse's home at Moseley in 1842 with a fall from a pony at Church Stretton in June 1857, "My Fever" prefigures epileptic seizures Shorthouse had in January 1862 and in the autumn of 1864, and it illustrates how Shorthouse projected and integrated his own experiences in *John Inglesant*.

In August and September 1852 when Henry made a journey to Cumberland and Scotland with his cousins, he was "always [in the company of] devout disciples of Wordsworth", though nothing he might have said about Wordsworth impressed itself upon the memory of his cousin who contributed family reminiscences to *LLLR*.[3] However much Henry and his cousins had read and reread Tennyson, "My Fever" owes much to Wordsworth, especially to "Books", Part V of *The Prelude*, the fanciful episode of the "Arab-Quixote". Shorthouse regarded *Don Quixote* as "the masterpiece of philosophic humour...a representation...of the struggles of the divine principle to enter into the everyday details of human life".[4] Asserting that in other people's "dreaming" and in the "beauty of their peculiar worlds [they] themselves remain the chief and ruler as it were over their created kingdoms", he notes, "In my case, on the contrary, *you* [my emphasis] subside, and lose all personal identity, every one of *your* thoughts acting for itself without any exertion of *your* will to call it into being." The subtle switch from *I* to *you* is significant, and the patterns in "My Fever" suggest an interesting lesson he may have learned from his admiring studies of Wordsworth and from changes the poet made in the 1805 thirteen-book version to the 1850 fourteen-book publication of *The Prelude*.

When he wrote the original version of the fifth book of his poetical autobiography, Wordsworth presented the dream material as though it had happened to a friend, most probably Samuel Taylor Coleridge. Yet, in the 1850 edition the poet dropped the third person narrative and acknowledged the dream as his own. The "Arab-Quixote" episode represents what Jung called "a big dream", an event of transformative power that cannot be attributed to daily life and one that contains significant communication from the unconscious through symbolical and archetypal imagery. "Within each one of us," Jung explains, "there is another whom we do not know. He speaks to us in dreams and tells us how different *he* sees us from how *we see* ourselves."[5] Wordsworth's changing *he* and *his* to *I* and *mine* represents an attempt to express this "other" as discoverer of his vocation to be a poet. After lamenting, "Oh, why hath not the mind / some element to stamp her image on / In nature somewhat nearer to her own?", he narrates the dream not seeming to realise it is the "element stamp" of an archetype.

Reading *Don Quixote* at noon in a rocky, seaside cave and musing on "poetry and geometric truth / And their high privilege of lasting life", Wordsworth was "seized" by sleep and "fell into a dream". Seeing nothing but "a boundless plain / Of sandy wilderness, all black and void," the dreamer feels "distress and fear" until "an uncouth shape [who] seemed an Arab of the Bedouin tribes" appears. Mounted on a dromedary, carrying a lance, holding underneath one arm a stone, "and in the opposite hand, a shell / Of surpassing brightness", the Arab-Quixote figure explains that the stone is Euclid's *Elements* and the shell "is something of more worth". Holding the shell to his ears, the dreamer hears

> an unknown tongue,
> Which yet I understood...
> A loud prophetic blast of harmony...which foretold
> Destruction to the children of the earth
> By deluge, now at hand.

Then the Arab-Quixote proclaims his mission; he is racing through "the wasteland" to find a place "to bury those two books":

> The one that held acquaintance with the stars,
> And wedded soul to soul in purest bond
> Of reason, undisturbed by space or time;
> The other that was a god, yea many gods
> Had voices more than all the winds, with power
> To exhilarate the spirit, and to soothe,
> Through every clime, the heart of human kind.

The dreamer saw one reality, heard yet another, but "wondered not...Having a perfect faith in all that passed". He craves "To cleave unto this man...To share his enterprise" and identifies the strange knight as Don Quixote, then realises the figure is the knight "yet not the knight," for he is also "an Arab of the desert". Then union occurs: "Of these [he was] neither, and was both at once." Riding and keeping pace with the Arab-Quixote, the dreamer observes the countenance of his companion has grown more disturbed, and as the two look backwards simultaneously: "mine eyes / Saw over half the wilderness diffused, / A bed of glittering light". Excited, he asks "the cause", and the knight errant tells him, "It is ...the waters of the deep / Gathering upon us":

> ...quickening then the pace
> Of the unwieldy creature he bestrode
> He left me: I called after him aloud;
> He heeded not; but with his twofold charge
> Still in his grasp, before me, full in view,
> Went hurrying o'er the illimitable waste,
> With the fleet waters of a drowning world
> In chase of him.

Instantly, the dreamer "waked in terror" and saw the sea before him, and the book he had been reading at his side."[6]

Wordsworth understood the dream as the discovery of his vocation and purpose and as a revelation of the anxieties and terrors of the "deluge now at hand". The "fleet waters of the drowning world" suggest more than the onslaughts of political and social strife, scientific and educational change, reaction against the French Revolution, warning against the mechanical evils of the coming Industrial Revolution, and the dangerous nationalism of the growing British Empire. To Wordsworth the dream expressed a personal symbolic message: to become a poet he must ground his own identity in his "higher self" and must protect this particular treasure from the "sea of fiction" and from rationalism. Cleaving unto the visionary dream figure and sharing his purpose, he would not "stoop to transitory themes" in his poetry, but would keep a thankful, "uplifted heart" and give proper honour to "all inspired souls...For what we are and what we may become." Shorthouse recognized the Shakespearean and scriptural sources of "For what we are and what we may become" (I John 3:2) and used the scripture as the epigraph to *John Inglesant*.

Believing "There is no absolutely reliable method of dream interpretation and interpretation is to a great extent dependent on the purpose of the interpreter or his expectations, or his demands upon the meaning",[7] Jung recognized dream "as the small hidden door in the deepest and most intimate sanctum of the soul". He defined dream as "the theatre where the dreamer is at once scene, actor, prompter, stage manager, author, audience, and critic", and theorized that "dreams are the visible links in a chain of unconscious events."[8] Because "A dream never expresses itself in a logically abstract way, but always in the language of parable or simile",

73

"One must never forget that one dreams primarily, and, so to speak, exclusively, about oneself and out of oneself."[9] Then Jung cautioned, "He who would interpret a dream must himself be, so to speak, on a level with the dream, for in no single thing can one ever hope to see beyond what one is oneself."[10] By placing himself on the level of the dream experience in "My Fever", Shorthouse used the dream to understand the "stern realities of life" and to see beyond his Quaker background into the Anglo-Catholic tensions of *John Inglesant*.

In "Tintern Abbey" Wordsworth defines the "serene and blessed mood"

> In which the affections gently lead us on,--
> Until, the breath of this corporeal frame
> And even the motion of our human blood
> Almost suspended, we are laid asleep
> In body, and become a living soul:
> While with an eye made quiet by the power of harmony,
>   and the deep power of joy,
> We see into the life of things.[11]

In Wordsworth's mood "the burthen of the mystery...the heavy and weary weight / Of all this unintelligible world, / Is lightened", but Shorthouse's mood "takes place mostly when the body is at rest, and more especially at seasons of ill-health or sickness". He notes the "power to observe or contemplate ...can no longer be called yours", as Wordsworth knew "all the mighty world / Of eye and ear" are "half-created and half-perceived", and that reality is trapped, as it were, between the objective and subjective. "My Fever" dramatises a psychological experience in which the objectivity of the *shadow* is partially integrated into the subjectivity of the Ego through the intervention of the *anima*, and in a "blessed mood" indeed, the *anima* represents the personification of Sarah Scott, soon to become, according to the narrative, Mrs. J. Henry Shorthouse.

Travelling with a "party of young men all reckless and wild from school", young Henry catches a violent cold and separates from his companions to seek care at a friend's home. During the horseback ride, his illness increases and his disordered vision sees "strange things" upon the road. He falls from his horse, unconscious, only to regain the "power of half-observation" when he finds himself "in a large, high-canopied, antique bed, with stars on the top of the canopy, and a large sun with great rays in the midst". From the bed he is just able to see through a large bay window, but he is able to see "over the leafy tops of apple trees into the shady and sunny fields beyond". He notes that he "saw all this... without hardly opening my eyes" and that "it seemed" as if he were "living then in the only possible way any one *could* live", dreamily aware in the present that all past life accumulates and seems to be "faint histories of what occurred a thousand years ago". He begins to see images from "all [he had] ever read of past ages...to wander and die and suffer misery with dead men of the old time" at the very moment that he becomes conscious of "the exquisite luxury of the soft bed". The narrative then shifts to second person, but the *you* is not his listening or reading audience; it is another part of himself "mixed up with what used to be *your* own thoughts, together with the half-seen objects of the material world". As if the Ego has found freedom from the *persona*, he sees the internal meanings of external objects and looks carefully at "the portrait of a gentleman in the costume of a century and a half ago". From this point on, portraiture becomes a technique for Shorthouse that enables him to connect his narratives with the past. The portrait is of "a certain Lord Edward Darrell, who was drowned in the year 1702 in crossing a ford" not far from the house. Beneath the portrait are two verses of a ballad:

> Lord Edward has ridden o'er Lanton Chase
> And down to the banks of the Dee;
> He has ridden hard through the summer heat,
> From his weary thoughts to flee.
>
> O'er Lanton Chase, and down to the Dee
> They have seen Lord Edward ride;
> He entered the ford all fearlessly,--
> But he never came up on the other side.

He records, "As I read these words the chamber and the bed vanished...and I was walking in a beautiful flat meadow all strewn with buttercups and daisies" at the side of a river. There, looking down, he sees the body of the drowned Lord Darrell and thinks him "well buried there in a right beautiful grave...with the lilies intertwined over him [and] his own body for the effigy, and the lilies for the carving". Then, looking up, he sees a projection of the *anima*, "a very beautiful lady [who] came to me and told me I must be quiet and not speak." The lady recounts the tale of the wild and dissipated Lord Darrell, who was betrothed to his cousin though he did not really love her. Riding one rainy April afternoon from London, he drowned while trying to ford the Dee. Henry, speaking in his own voice, thinks it well that Darrell had died then" and prays that he too might die rather than ever "give pain to any one that loved [him]". In his semi-conscious state, he wonders if he is still in the meadows, but the lady tells him his is ill and in bed. Hearing her voice, he instantly sees he is not in the dream but in bed. At that precise moment another lady enters "through the door at the other end of the room...dressed in white in an old fashion, with beautiful golden hair wreathed with strings of violets". The second lady, it turns out, is none other than Lord Darrell's intended. She takes no notice of Henry, but she sits and stares out the window "as a man looks at a beautiful picture which he is quite certain will not fade away". He feels certain he has "come upon a blessed country where all things always [are] the same".

Suddenly, the ghostly past relives itself. The lady starts up with a cry, "A horse, a horse!", and there is "a great noise as of galloping, and the running to and fro of servants and of people being sent out to seek". The body of Lord Darrell is brought in and laid in bed with Henry: "I struggled against the horror of that wet, loathsome thing, but could not shake it off, and its cold, flabby hand fell upon my face, and I fainted away." Quickly, he realises the irony "that when we think we stand, then certainly we fall". In "the most perfect state of bodily pleasure and dreamy happiness", he is also "nearest to that dead body...in all its ghastly horror and deathliness". He ends "My Fever" with an afterthought and a hope:

> And now but one word more. I am now perfectly recovered, and am to-morrow (sic) to be married to the beautiful lady I met walking the meadow with the buttercups; and our love, though begun in a dream, will, I fervently trust, be continued through the stern realities of a life.

In "My Fever" Shorthouse acknowledges indebtedness to Nathaniel Hawthorne, and *LLLR* documents his youthful intent: "If I ever write anything, I intend to make my *debut* as one of his disciples." "My Fever" is the debut, and, although it suggests the mood and substance of one of the *Twice-Told Tales*, it is, more importantly, Shorthouse's first "dream theatre" with Ego, *persona*, *shadow*, and *anima* as *dramatis personae*.

Although Jung insisted he had "no theory about dreams", he asserted,

> On the other hand, I know that if we meditate on a dream sufficiently long and thoroughly--if we take it about with us and turn it over and over--some-thing almost always comes of it...a practical and important hint which shows...in what direction the unconscious is leading.[12]

Jungians, of course, have traced what must, at least, be called a Jungian approach to dream interpretation. James Hall explains:

> For Jung, dreams were a self-representation of the state of the psyche, presented in symbolic form... to compensate the one-sided distortions of the waking-ego; they are therefore in the service of the individuation process, helping the waking-ego to face itself more objectively and consciously.[13]

Shorthouse was a dreamer "whose imagination acted the part to himself of 'guide, philosopher, and friend'".[14] He proclaimed himself one, and he confessed his intolerance of others who did not share his enthusiasm for "the night side of life". Writing to Margaret Southall (16 August 1853), he puzzled over the intimate knowledge "which seems to exist...between myself and the book itself; it seems to me as if...[it] knew me, and knew what part in it I wanted, and opened there".[15] He urged his cousins to read Catherine Crowe's *Night Side of Nature* because,

> She believes in "Ghosts", and by this I mean all kinds of what we call supernatural appearances, dreams, warnings, second sight, clairvoyance, etc., and all this which seems so absurd may be as plain to a "future generation" as steam-engines and railways are to us.[16]

Certainly, as Shorthouse's future generation, we read him as he could never have read himself.

Amplifying the dream in "My Fever" connects Shorthouse's youth and his enthusiasm for reading with the future direction of his life. Had Shorthouse actually read "My Fever" to the Essay Society the night before his marriage to Sarah Scott, a psychoanalytic interpretation might well decode the contents of the dream into manifest anxiety about marriage and latent anxieties about probable changes in Shorthouse's personal life, complete with sexual anxiety and subconscious feelings about husband/wife relations grounded in parental examples. Shorthouse himself, however, urges his audience to allow "My Fever" to speak to them as it did to him, to suspend their more rational modes of thought and to let themselves share the imaginal content without attempting any interpretation. Dream amplification involves extension of natural associations and metaphors and does not insist upon "digging for repressions" or looking for archetypes or symbols. Although "Archetypes in their pure form are the structuring patterns of the mind", they are "without any specific content. One does not 'inherit' an archetypal image, but one has an innate tendency to structure experience in certain ways."[17] Thus, the polarity of Lord Darrell's ancient, woeful tale and Shorthouse's impending happy marriage imposes a structural dynamic upon the tale and suggests an interpretation. The dreamer's curious scrutiny of Lord Darrell's portrait suggests that, as the narrator looks at the representation of a particular *persona*, he sees behind it an image of his *shadow*. In other words, Shorthouse's Ego perceives his narrative persona or "literary pose" and senses the latent power of the *shadow* and projects the self-mirroring vision as the internal structure of "My Fever".

Although Jung's *shadow* archetype shares some similarities with Freud's *Id*, the *shadow* in Jungian literature is not as clearly defined as the *Id* in Freudian or psychoanalytic writings. "In Jungian writings the concept is shrouded in confusion, and the more one reads about it, the more one is left with the impression that 'the Shadow' is a portmanteau term which has been used to accommodate all those aspects of the Self which are not evident in the conscious personality." It appears as a shady character "of dubious integrity, possessing the same sex as the dreamer and displaying characteristics customarily regarded by him as disreputable and 'inferior'."[18] Thus, Lord Darrell's "dissipated life" and his "ghastly body" express dynamics of Shorthouse's *shadow*. The presence of archetypal imagery suggests that in 1854-55 Shorthouse was ready for psychological growth, and, as Hamlet realised, "The readiness is all." Likewise, the antique bed with "gold stars on the top of the canopy, and a large sun with great rays in the midst" suggests that "My Fever" expresses Shorthouse's unconscious condition. Provided he "stays in bed", remains true to the quietism of Quaker worship, he will Individuate. The sun posits the Self as its rays extend the archetype's potentialities for realisation and the gold stars offer promise of success. Neither the ghostly image nor the body of Lord Darrell speak in "My Fever", because their shadowy appearances have not yet attained sufficient psychic reality for speech, but the sun, its rays and stars, speak in archetypal silence. In fact, the only verbal understanding in the dream sequence comes directly from the interaction between Shorthouse's self-image, which is "sick in bed", and that of a double-imaged *anima*, the ghostly form of Lord Darrell's intended and Shorthouse's wife-to-be. In presenting personal aspects of his private self to the public, a public well-known and reasonably intimate, the youthful Shorthouse was performing a necessary task in the process of Individuation. Once contents of the unconscious are made public, they are in the realm of consciousness, and, when they are absorbed into socially-acceptable traditions and rituals, they become "highly developed bodies of symbolic portrayals and protections" of the Ego.[19] "My Fever" established a new "house" for Shorthouse, a symbolic protection for his new married life and his new sense of authorship, and it gave him a glimpse of his future: the sun with its rays and stars suggests the spiritual vision and narrative voices of his future stories and novels.

Another factor in our understanding of his early growth is his use of pronouns. When Shorthouse writes in the 'I-voice', he speaks in a personal, self-conscious voice that, like his stammer, only partly enables him to "go public". Though he seems to be talking directly to his audience when he uses *you*, he literally, however unconsciously, talks to himself and includes himself amongst the audience. Describing how his dreaming differs from that of others, his use of *you* includes himself: "...in my case...you subside...without any exertion of your will...yet you are not so dead asleep but that the knowledge of your own existence is still present with you." Near the end of the essay he connects the *I*-voice with both *you*'s (audience and the objectivity of himself) and uses *we*, a socially inclusive voice that "preaches" as if it had knowledge from a special and private source. Eliot illustrates the same psychological principle in the epigraph to *Four Quartets*. Quoting Herakleitos, and deliberately limiting his audience by quoting him in Greek, Eliot states a theme that guides his readers towards a particular mode of interpretation: "Although the Logos [or Word] is common to all, the majority live as if they had intelligence peculiarly their own."[20] Then he adds a second epigraph that points at paradox: "The journey up and down is one and the same." Applied to Shorthouse's "My Fever", the epigraphs suggest that although all men have access to the Divine Principle, as Shorthouse understood the psychic reality of the unconscious Self, most men live as if they possessed occult, private and hidden, intelligence which sets them apart from "common sense" and that most men regard the *I* as the "way up" towards Ego- Individuation and the *you* as the "way down" into the *persona* aspect of personality.

As "My Fever" expresses Shorthouse's interest in psychological fantasy, his Early Essays serve to define a rhetorical strategy, though not a very original one:

> ...he fixes, through a *persona*, on some object of the past-
> -a person, a manorial hall, a tombstone, some interesting
> incident--and allows his imagination to flit about it to
> form charming pictures, to evoke nostalgic emotion, and
> then to drift toward an instructive conclusion...[as if he
> were] the bright schoolboy armed with the *Encyclopaedia
> Britannica*.[21]

Each of the essays contains a personal experience and a mini-tale, usually with some pious observations on death, but all of the Early Essays are disappointing after "My Fever". "Recollections of a London Church" may derive, for instance, from Shorthouse's youthful experiences when he stayed with Dr. Bishop in London, but the recollections contain no mention of his stammer or medical treatment, thus yield no particular insight into the author. Instead, the essay tells us, quoting Longfellow, that "Every one has a romance in his own heart", then fictionalizes a narrative voice: "My occupation--that of a poor, very poor, author--confining me to my room, I had little other companionship than that old church." An old sexton tells him the story of "Mary, 1721-1734", of her loneliness and poverty and how she used to sit all day at the window facing the church. The writer identifies with her and allows his "imagination to roam at will about her name". He ends his rumination as he listens to the comforting refrain of "that sublime litany which sounded forth, word for word, as she had heard it":

> 'By Thine agony and bloody sweat;
> by Thy cross and passion;

79

by Thy precious death and burial;
by Thy glorious resurrection and ascension;
and by the coming of the Holy Ghost,
Good Lord deliver us'.

The first of his writings to indicate the appeal of the Church of England, "The Recollections" essay ponders why the name of Mary should "haunt me thus", which hints, at least, at Anglo-Catholic devotion to the Virgin.

"The Ringing of the Bells" relates a miracle and moralizes about its lesson. A "few young country louts" bribe a church sexton not to ring the bells on Sunday. The youths are amazed, as are the clergyman and the congregation, when the bells ring by themselves before the church door can be unlocked. When they enter, the church is empty and the bells cease to ring. The clergyman declares, "This is the hand of God...a gracious sign permitted from heaven." The guilty conspirators kneel in prayer, and the essay ends in scripture: "The sacrifices of God are a broken spirit: a broken and a contrite heart, O God, thou wilt not despise." Shorthouse tells the story in his own voice and explains it as a tale he picked up during "a day's tramp in Warwickshire" where he stopped at a wayside ale-house named "The Old Ring of Bells". A pleasant enough account to add charm to an evening of the Friends Essay Society, "The Ringing of the Bells" has little essay content and certainly does not surprise a reader with its originality. It does, however, mention King Charles I hearing church bells before the Battle of Edgehill. Some twelve to fifteen years later Shorthouse wrote about John Inglesant's hearing the local church bells "as he stood amid the confusion and carnage of Naseby". The descriptive power and narrative charm of "The Ringing of the Bells" is minimal, and though the incident is supposedly miraculous, the matter-of-fact narrative tone does not invite imagination or urge the reader to ponder.

The other three essays in Volume II of *LLLR*, "Twenty Miles", "The Autumn Walk", and "The Last of the Rabbis", demonstrate Shorthouse's "flirtation" [Wagner's term] with narrative personae. "Twenty Miles" and "The Autumn Walk" use first person narration and are simple exercises, but "Twenty Miles" does contain one item of special interest. While making a country walk, Shorthouse greets a sudden burst of sunlight: "Welcome, Phoebus Apollo, Lord of Day, or *whatever name thou choosest to be called by*,--thrice welcome here!" The exclamation is the first statement in Shorthouse's writings of a Broad Church attitude towards the many names of God. In "The Autumn Walk", language is central to the essay content. Acknowledging "legends [as] an attempt to find language for nameless sights and voices", Shorthouse gathers passion as he listens to "Nature's language" and declares, "If I had the power of those old legend-makers, what wild stories would I translate for you from what the wind is saying!" He had learned to listen to the wind in 1842 at Moseley while recovering from typhus fever. About thirty-four years later, he translated "what the wind is saying" in *A Teacher of the Violin* (1888). "The Autumn Walk" is, thus, an early, enthusiastic plea to his audience to listen to Nature, and it is also his first declaration of his devotion to Wordsworth's poetry.

Dedicated, as the epigraph states, to Nathaniel Hawthorne without permission, "The Last of the Rabbis" evokes a vivid and poignant moral and is the only one of the Early Essays not written as a personal narrative. Very old and aware that his people are forgetting the ancient customs that make them "a peculiar people", the last of the Rabbis worries about what will happen to his people when they completely forget their "ancient language". Mixing and mingling with "the nations among whom they dwelt" and caught up in the "affairs of life and intercourse with strangers", one by one they lost "the knowledge of their language" and their ability to read "the Law...the sacred book". As the old Rabbi reads to them for the last time, "His voice became firm and high, and rolled forth melodiously through the building and out into the still air beyond, like the fabled death-song of the swan." The Rabbi died; the Law was read no more. Then a stranger "from a Western clime" entered the little synagogue and looked upon the book as an artifact of a dead religion, a religion killed by "man's headlong pursuit after the things of the body" and by "carelessness of the things of his immortal self". Told as a simple, direct story without a narrator, "The Last of the Rabbis" appeals to imagination as an impersonal allegory. Of course, however, it is very personal. Having studied French and Italian and having read and studied many antiquarian books and romantic authors with a serious, absorbing mind, the youthful Shorthouse was ready to do more than collect anecdotal tales from his countryside walks and draw simple moralistic analogues from his reading. Yet he faced a serious problem, his audience, and he was beginning to confront an even greater challenge, how to use the English language in the service of God.

Shorthouse's essays in Volume II of the Friends Essay Society's manuscripts show literary promise, commitment, zeal, energy, and some experimentation. The two most successful ones explore the realm of dream and dream imagery from the "night side of life" and show that he discovered how to appeal to his audience through parable, anecdote, and allegory. The essays in Volumes III, IV, and VI reveal his developing literary powers, and sometime during their composition he began writing as a daily discipline. Whether he kept the work routine described by his wife, who says he "went regularly to business at nine o'clock, came home to dinner in the middle of the day, and returned to town till nearly seven in the evening", then spent his evening hours in "charming conversation during the meal, and for perhaps an hour after it",[22] or whether, as a family friend noted, he "ordinarily [stayed] one day a week at home from business and devoted to writing",[23] does not matter. He was a busy, hard-working man, who felt the very real need for an intellectual life:

> No complaint is more common, amongst us who are engaged in any trade, and who have any tastes and desires other than those of a mere commercial man, than that of want of leisure to follow our favourite pursuits...the tired mind and body are often equally unfit at the termination of the day's labour to start again in fresh pursuit.[24]

At one meeting of the Essay Society he acknowledged rather apologetically, "These things are so generally known and felt that it seems commonplace even to mention them", then he quickly added, "but I think..." and began to discuss the "three occupations of our mortal life", namely, "pleasures or business or book-learning". "We are often surprised at the amount of literary work done by those who, we know, are most occupied in other pursuits...[and] it is to such as these, who think that they have most to complain of, that I would speak." His message is personal and reveals a mind and personality of admirable self-discipline:

> We are placed here for our advancement in learning ...from the busy workshop as from the quiet study... not only to work for the good and improvement of others, but also to learn from that work and from the world in which that work is done.

When he wrote "The End of Learning", Shorthouse was about twenty-four or twenty-five years old, and he believed zealously,

> Life should be regarded as one great university...In the midst of the world's toil and bustle and sorrow ...are the deepest, gravest, noblest truths...If we but learn our station in and relation to the general life of man...

Proclaiming "a good man labouring amid this world's trials and wickedness is a fellow-worker with God",[25] he exhorted the Friends "to participate in and to understand the infinite glories of His heaven". He did not tell them their "station", but their response to "The End of Learning" may have placed him in an awkward situation, for his next contribution was "An Essay Which Is No Essay".

"I shall consider it a personal favour", one member of the Society commented, "if you write [another essay], and so will all, I am sure." Whether the tone implied teasing banter or sincerity, Shorthouse turned to one of his favourite pastimes, reading a topographical book, which, he told the members, he loved "in proportion to its stupidity". "An Essay Which Is No Essay" enables us to see the young writer scurrying off to White and

Pike, the local stationer, for pen and paper and in search of a suitable topic:

> I revolved in my mind things in general and all subjects
> past, present, and to come; but not one did I find but such
> as were unsuitable for the Essay Meeting, or had already
> been written to death there. (53)

This is the first mention by Shorthouse of the suitability of topics, and, as the title of the essay suggests, he was beginning to explore satire to escape the Essay Meeting's lack of serious purpose. In "An Essay Which Is No Essay", he describes how, searching for a subject to write on, he "dipped pen in the ink, and looked--out of the window...from a perfect vacancy...of mind". In that vacancy he discovered an "exquisite stillness, that *silence sweet together*" of the Quakers and, as in "The Ringing of the Bells", he heard "in the midst of that sudden stillness...the ringing of the bells". Their sound sets his mind to excited exploration "of spire, church, shadow, old tombs", and then his mind begins to wander as it wonders. Evoking contrasts "between activity and repose, between the present and the past, between the material and the ideal", he tells a short tale about a young crusader in the Holy Land. Struck with a deadly fever, the crusader lay dying in a small house with Arab women crying beside him. A fishing boat lands and, in the commotion of the fish market their weeping attracts "one who seemed to be a chief, an old man with a beard, whom the rest appeared to reverence". "This man" enters the death room, makes everyone else leave except the crusader's young page, then offers the dying knight a "medicine of such wonderful virtue as would cure immediately", but, which cannot be taken by a Christian. The knight "must own Mahomet and deny Christ". Very ill and with no strength left "to argue with the tempter", the young crusader receives strength "in that supreme moment...to say one word, and that was-- 'NO!'" The old man tries again; this time he offers "every earthy delight that you can conceive", but again the knight "had just sufficient strength to say that one word again--'NO!'" Raising himself with his last energy, the crusader smells the medicine, smiles faintly, then flings the cup across the room "so that every drop of the precious elixir was lost in the sand". Then, of course, he dies, and as was his wont in several pieces, Shorthouse ends "An Essay Which Is No Essay" with "the pious muse of Keble".

"An Essay Which Is No Essay" served him as an exercise in narrative technique and helped him see the possibilities of philosophical romance. The old man, the dying knight, the young page, and the rather magical medicine make the story appealing, and though his mind wanders from topic to topic, his voice has a mildly commanding new confidence in defining knights as crusaders for Christ, not as empire builders. His next contribution tries to provoke his audience of Friends to greater critical awareness by asking them to consider the differences between pre-

Reformation and post-Reformation forms of narrative.

Now about twenty-six years old, Shorthouse proclaims a difference between "the true supernatural creed" and that of "false supernaturalism" and asserts, "Those real traditions and superstitions...however false we may choose to call the narrations, [are] indeed the truest part of history" (145). As if echoing parts of Wordsworth's "Preface" to *Lyrical Ballads*, Shorthouse argues that true forms of supernaturalism have their birth in the "everyday thoughts and necessities" of a people and represent "the aspect and influence of nature [or] the voice of Nature". The false are the "offspring of an affected and superficial learning and civilisation". The poems of Tasso and Ariosto, however beautiful, contain "little else but this false supernaturalism", those of Ariosto being the worse for their "human trees that bleed and human woods that speak". Then he begins what became a life-long complaint against modernism. He detested all forms of literature that "serve as vehicles for...falsifying and slandering some of the most serious and solemn instincts of our nature" (150). He does not define these "instincts", but he probes several possibilities for future study: "It would be an interesting inquiry...", "It would be curious to trace...", and "It would also be very curious to observe..." He offers a catalogue of supernatural forms (fairies in Great Britain, elves in Ireland, alfs in Iceland, trolls and "little men of the mines" in Germany, and dwarfs throughout northern Europe), and wonders why the "spectre huntsmen" of England, Germany, and France are unknown in Spain and Italy and why most of "these legends of the spectral creed" are so concerned with the "awful certainty of and familiarity with death".

"Before the Reformation in England", he believes, "we hear very little of apparitions of the dead", and the fairies, once so universal in England, disappear entirely when the "mind of the people was loosened for its old sure anchorage in the religion of Rome" (148-149). Having rather rapturously proclaimed belief in "all kinds of supernatural appearances" only three or four years earlier,[26] he wonders why the Reformation, which "tossed and confused [the people of England] with religious doubt, graver and more solemn thoughts" should have extinguished the fairies and replaced them with "the spirits of their dead friends". Rather than see beautiful fairy creatures dancing in lonely and romantic spots, post-Reformation seers make contact with "apparitions of the dead...in familiar orchards and rooms". He offers no explanation but notes that this "is one very remarkable instance which is well worthy being traced to its source". Despairing of "such writers [who] never saw or understood the real lessons and teachings", he defines the greatest lesson of supernaturalism as preparation for death: "Intercourse with the spirit-world [will enable] the human soul...to make for itself, as it were, friends of the dwellers of that world", especially "the One, who...at once human and divine...gathered together...all the craving of the whole human race into Himself" (149-150).

He continued to make literary distinctions and began make his own comparative studies. "Bede", written when Shorthouse was about thirty years old, begins with an assertion that the "conditional praise" accorded the *Ecclesiastical History* in the *Encyclopaedia Britannica* proves that the writer of the article was somewhat antiquated or that he had written it before the study of legends became popular. In contrast, Shorthouse finds the work of Bede most admirable: "I know of no book written so long ago that takes a stronger hold on your sympathies--that makes you more akin to a people to distant from you" (151). He compares the work of Bede with that of Geoffrey of Monmouth and Nennius, finds Geoffrey's distasteful and unreal, and asserts that the difference between Bede and the other "monkish historians...may be traced to two distinct kinds of religious legends". One kind derives from the people themselves, folklore; the other legends "are those which ecclesiastics invented in their cells, for the glory of their several orders" (105). The differences he defines in "Bede" demonstrate how logically he can argue when he has definite preferences grounded in his reading rather than in his own experiences. However much he may have believed in or wanted to believe in the "night side of nature", he had no paranormal or extraordinary experiences in his life, so far as we know, at least, none that would excite a parapsychologist. He may exalt "the stuff of which legends are made", but he preferred daily realities. Discussing the life of St. Felix, who was released from prison in Bede's account "by a miracle suspiciously resembling that worked on behalf of St. Peter", he argues that whether a miracle happened or not is unimportant. What matters is "how we see"; the story itself is "the glimpse of a divine truth" (95-96). By seeing "into the life of things", as Wordsworth had urged, "[we understand] that the individual man [in Bede's histories] possessed a cultivation in its manner as complete, and a spiritual life in its way as exalted as our own" (105).

Acceptance of the value of the experience of earlier peoples as equal to that of modern man is fundamental to Shorthouse's historical perspective, as it also is to Jung and Eliot. The "chronological snobbery"[27] of all modern generations distorts their perspectives and prevents their understanding life and art. A "chronological snob" might argue, "The dead writers are remote from us because we *know* so much more than they did." "Precisely", Eliot would retort, "and they are *that* which we know." To Eliot, it is an "obvious fact that art never improves".[28] To Shorthouse, "The noblest things of the world ever are found in the record of the life militant of the righteous man."[29] To Jung this record is the collective unconscious, and the "life militant of the righteous man" is the conscious experiencing of Individuation: "He alone is modern who is fully conscious of the present...

[and] to be wholly of the present means to be fully conscious of one's existence... [with] the most intensive and extensive consciousness [and] a minimum of unconsciousness."[30] As Jung defined:

> ...everything of which I know, but of which I am not at the moment thinking; everything of which I was once conscious but have now forgotten; everything perceived by my senses, but not noted by my conscious mind; everything which, involuntarily and without paying attention to it, I feel, think, remember, want, and do; all the future things that are taking shape in me and will sometime come to consciousness: all this is the content of the unconscious.[31]

Man confronts the unconscious whenever he finds the limits of the field of his consciousness, whenever he "comes up against the *unknown*". Jung explains the *unknown* in terms of "two groups of objects: those which are outside and can be experienced by the senses, and those which are inside and are experienced immediately." Those "unconscious qualities that are not individually acquired but are inherited, e.g., instincts as impulses to carry out actions from necessity, without conscious motivation" and the "archetypes together" form the collective unconscious. The personal unconscious contains psychic materials "made up of individual and more or less unique contents" and are not, therefore, "universal and of regular occurrence."[32] Thus, Shorthouse objects to Geoffrey of Monmouth because Geoffrey derived his histories from the personal dimension of the unconscious, and he praises those of Bede because Bede's histories express the collective. Likewise, Shorthouse's "true supernaturalism" is grounded in the collective, the "false" in the personal.

Most of Shorthouse's Early Essays belong to the "realm of the Ego" because their content expresses his concern with "daily life", with ideas and experiences that can be traced to autobiographical factors. The exception, ironically, is "My Fever", in which the ghostly lady and the horrid corpse of Lord Darrell extend beyond metaphor into representations of *anima* and *shadow* figures. In most of the Early Essays Shorthouse propounds personal preferences in keeping with the standards and agreed purposes of the Friends Essay Society. However, "An Essay Which Is No Essay" and "The End of Learning" disclose his subtle distancing of himself from his audience and his desire to expand his subject matter, which is symptomatic of his readiness for psychological growth. In dealing with legend and myth, Shorthouse attempted to probe beyond the material, beyond the form, to see more than his audience at the Friends Essay Society was prepared to understand. Mildly frustrated that the Essay Meeting was more social entertainment than intellectual discussion, he attempted to introduce critical standards and to compose more thoughtful arguments, and his frustration with the Friends urged him towards the critical stance that he called philosophical romance.

"The 'Morte D'Arthur' and 'Idylls of the King'" represents Shorthouse's first attempt at literary criticism. In his essay on Malory and Tennyson, he states specific criteria and advances his argument to demonstrate them. Because he begins the essay with a survey of published reviews, we know he read "The 'Morte D'Arthur' and 'Idylls of the King'" to the Essay Society sometime after he had formally joined the Church of England. Baptized in August 1861, he resigned from the Society of Friends in 1860 but continued to participate in the Essay Society until at least 1870, and he served as its secretary until November 1867. His name still appears on the "Circulation List" of 23 April 1875 but does not appear on the next list, 25 May 1875.[33] Nothing in the "Middle Essays" suggests sharp conflict against the Friends or any defensive self-justification, and the gradual tempering of his personal opinions suggests he ended his involvement in the Essay Society simply to concentrate on the composition of *John Inglesant*. Unhappy with the reviews of "Idylls of the King", Shorthouse states he has been unable to find any critic or reviewer who troubled himself "to consider the book and its contents as a whole--that is, first, the Arthurian Romances generally, and, secondly, Mr. Tennyson's success or failure in reproducing them". To assess Tennyson's achievement, he states three specific, though subjective, criteria:

> ...either they must preserve faithfully the spirit as well as the exterior form of the legends...; or the age which gave birth to the legends must not be so distant that every trace of the leading idea of that age is lost; or, lastly, the subject of the legends must be simply one of the common wants and fears of humanity, which are alike in all ages, and which the animating spirit of every age, however different, suits and inspires equally (108).

By "spirit of the age" he means "everything that belongs to the spiritual part [or the] sacred meaning", which includes the "work [it] had to do in its day" (114-116). Despite his earlier enthusiasm for Tennyson's poetry, Shorthouse is now blunt in his judgment: "Mr. Tennyson has observed none of these conditions, and it is, as I take it, a natural consequence that he has failed" (108). What Shorthouse specifically objected to was Tennyson's "modernness of thought" which makes the poems "repulsive in the highest degree" (114).

In contrast to Tennyson's work, William Morris's "The Defence of Guinevere" is "the most wonderful reproduction of the tone of thought and feeling of a past age that has ever been achieved" (108). Shorthouse challenges *The Literary Gazette's* reviewer who had found Morris's "Defence" a "mass of rubbish that could not be understood": "The author's most deadly enemy could not have invented a more condemnatory judgment on the book than that...it *could* be understood" (109). He accuses the *Gazette* reviewer of applying modern standards to a literary form that requires "a most careful study of the literature of the age of Chivalry" and which certainly requires "phrases and forms of expression [different from] those to which the present [age has become] accustomed" (109). To preserve "faithfully the spirit as well as the exterior form of the legends", he argues, is only one of the three criteria which represents the "anomaly of writing a romance of Chivalry in a modern popular form". Tennyson's "Idylls" are a "lifeless form of the legends...some sort of galvanised life" which does not preserve "the faintest gleam of that spirit which alone gives to the tales of knight-errantry a vitality and a never-dying truth...the character and ideal of the Christian warrior--the king and the saint" (109-110).

Not realising that the morals of the Arthurian romances are "essentially and inseparably connected with that age and character", Tennyson failed to realise, too, that the "forms of chivalry" simply cannot be reproduced in a modern age "without the spirit which gave them life". The "Idylls" are, therefore, "false in the very groundwork of their conception" (112). Worse, in Shorthouse's eyes, Tennyson had kept the supernatural in subordination "as unsuitable for the present age!" His "modernness of thought and expression...aggravates ...with a continual sense of anachronism... [His] knights might be fox-hunters going to the meet" (114). Tennyson completely omitted the "spiritual essence" of Arthurian romance yet retained "all that is evil and repulsive, and that presented to us in its most sickening and conventional form" (114). Shorthouse declared that the Poet Laureate "has a morbid refinement which is horrified at the mention of sin" (114). Today, one wonders if Shorthouse ever mentioned his views to Tennyson in person or if Tennyson ever knew of Shorthouse's condemnation of the "Idylls". Twenty years after his attack on the poet's modernness, Shorthouse and his wife met Tennyson at a Royal Academy dinner, and later they visited the Tennysons at Farringford. Shorthouse dedicated *Sir Percival* to Hallam Tennyson, and he was invited to be a pallbearer at the Poet Laureate's funeral in 1892,[35] but we have no evidence Shorthouse ever disclosed his criticism to Tennyson.

Although he does not explore Malory's "Morte d'Arthur" in detail, Shorthouse extols its "chiefest quality" as a contrast to the "Idylls". In Malory's work, the "knightly ideal shines out of every page" because every one of Malory's knights believes Chivalry "the worship of the Son of Man in its most perfect form" (113). "Jesus Christ was", Shorthouse declares, "the most perfect knight, the noblest born and best-descended gentleman" (113). Thus, while at work on *John Inglesant*, Shorthouse defined his own task in criticism of Tennyson:

> "If the present age cannot receive nor understand the chivalrous idea in its entirety, let it sleep in peace beneath its stately tomb, and do not trouble its repose by calling it up to an unnatural and spasmodic life" (116).

Many years later, Paul Elmer More discerned the chivalrous idea behind Shorthouse's "native sense of style" and commented that "what other men toil for was [his] by right of birth". The "cadenced rhythms of *John Inglesant* [are] already present...offering to the beholder as it were the sacrament of beauty". "At times", More added, "we seem almost to be reading some lost or discarded chapter of the finished romance." Studying Shorthouse's position in the Victorian "Battle of the Churches", More determined that Shorthouse's resigning from the Society of Friends to join the Church of England was not a conversion but "a transition from the religion of the conscience to that of the imagination, from morality to spiritual vision".[36] Sarah Shorthouse explained her husband's "transition" quite simply in practical terms:

> Though by *birth* a member of the Society of Friends, their special tenets and their peculiarities of dress and language had never been adopted by my husband, from his own conviction. His tastes and sympathies made much that was of value to others uncongenial to him. His wide reading, especially of the older English divines, made the idea of an historic and national church peculiarly attractive to him...At home we were very near to St. John's Church, Ladywood, of which the Reverend Francis Morse was then incumbent. The church was close at hand, the Friends' Meeting-house a mile and a half away, and in the heart of the town, and very much that has given life and interest to the present condition of the Society was absent then...More and more my husband felt that he could only be happy as a baptized member of the Church of England.[37]

Given the distinctions between true and false supernaturalism that Shorthouse made in his Early Essays, we are tempted to probe his rejection of the Quakers further. Fortunately, Mrs. Shorthouse included a letter in *LLLR* "to a lady who was distressed" that helps explain her husband's decision.

Apologizing to the unidentified lady who was "so much troubled about the church" on his account, Shorthouse acknowledges that the Friends had an important truth in their beginnings, the "indwelling of the Divine Word", but such indwelling is to him "only a portion of the *whole* glorious system", which, he asserts, "is to be found in the Church of England". The Friends and "other *so-called* Evangelical Christians [have] misunderstood and limited this great truth" to such an extent that "no man who really holds it can ever be satisfied with his faith". Then he declares, "It is not my fault that I *see* and *know* this and much more which I have neither time nor words to explain...It is not my fault...that *primitive Quakerism* as a distinct sect is dead." To stay with Quakerism, he declares, is "schism, which has been prayed against and dreaded in all ages of Christianity". Underlying his argument is his firm conviction:

> The things which are seen are the symbols of the things which are not seen. The outward kingdom of God in nature and humanity is the symbol of the invisible kingdom of God in reason [and it is most desirable that] an outward visible and *united* Church of Christ on earth [be seen as] a symbol of the Church of Christ in heaven.

The most reliable symbol, he argues, is "the Prayer-book in this country...The Prayer-book is the only human ordinance (if it can be called a human ordinance, being nothing but the religion of the Bible arranged as a manual for daily use) that acknowledges this". The Anglican *Book of Common Prayer* "has preserved over and over again the most vital truths, which were entirely overlooked and forgotten even by those who professed to believe in, and to use it". He ends the letter by urging the upset lady to read F. D. Maurice's *What is Revelation?* Whether the lady was content or whether further correspondence ensued, we do not know, but we do have this letter as testament of his conviction that the Church of England, in spite of its being "distracted and torn with divisions of many kinds [is] the *national*, if you will not call it the *true* church".[38] Believing that he had found a religious philosophy that embraced "the chivalrous idea in its entirety", Shorthouse's outward religious change

> was not a step taken lightly or for social reasons. Shorthouse had become convinced of the catholicity of the established Church, which seemed to possess totally what the sects had only partially.[39]

No argument, however, will convince anyone else who is not already "unconsciously suspicious" of the limitations or psychological preconditions of his or her present standpoint. Shorthouse's argument to the unknown lady suggests he knew her to be patriotic and convinced of the "indwelling spirit" and that he felt the relativity of religious sensibilities to be grounded in the "relativity of personalities", or as Jung named them, "psychological types". "Every judgment made by an individual", asserted Jung, "is conditioned by his personality type [and] every point of view is necessarily relative."[40] As national standpoints have proved "specially attractive to modern Western minds", and as modern mind is both a rhetorical stance and an attitude that never changes very significantly from historical age to historical age,[41] Shorthouse saw catholicity as the indwelling spirit of all ages. While clarifying Malory's success and Tennyson's failure, he began to see the necessity for a modern knight, one who could appeal to "the modern mind" and simultaneously embody the "indwelling spirit" that unifies historical ages. Yet, while composing *John Inglesant*, Shorthouse became aware of the limitations of the form of his argument. However beneficial philosophical romance might be, only a "great musical novel" could harmonize and synthesize personal, cultural, national, and historical spirits and thus become a "revelation to mankind". Sensing his inadequacies as a would-be author and grasping at an intuition of a new "humour for the modern age", Shorthouse wrote to the one man he believed capable of intellectually and artistically synthesizing a new revelation for mankind, Matthew Arnold. "What I want you do to", he pleaded, in a letter dated 23 October 1871, "*at least so far as to point out the possibilities*" is to compose "a synthesis of Revelation and Humour, by which men may be at once aroused to sympathetic perception of their daily life, and at the same time perceive on such perception, as on a stage, the divine excellence at work." Acknowledging Arnold's genius in "Hellenism versus Hebraism" and "Literature versus Dogma" as "immortal by reason of the exquisite clearness", Shorthouse tried to explain "a new view of Humour...a *synthesis* of Revelation (on the divine principle) with Humour, *not* their *opposition*". Extolling Cervantes' *Don Quixote* and the works of Jean Paul Richter as the nearest approach to his conception of "Humour...in the very highest sense in which the word can be understood--a sense beyond, perhaps, that in which it ever has been understood", Shorthouse honours Arnold with a commission: "It is reserved to *you* to reveal [this conception of Humour] to men." Tracing Arnold's "sweet song" back to the "sweet reasonableness" described by Agathon in Plato's *Symposium*, Shorthouse exhorts, "Do not let it die away till you have made its full diapason sound within the hearts of men." As Shorthouse understood, the "sweet song" unites the "enthusiasm of our sacramental hours", which proves the "divine principle...is at work in every one of us, constantly endeavouring to permeate our daily life", with the "everyday life of ourselves and others". The discrepancy between the sacramental experience and daily life, for most men, "is so appalling, and the distance of ourselves and others [from] the effort of this principle...to enter into human life", that a great question "seems forced upon us": "Is the Christ we have sufficient for these things, or do we look for another?" Shorthouse does not question the "sufficiency of the Christ" but rather the sufficiency of "the Christ we have", the contemporary interpretation of the Christ which "needs...to be seen in a new light, in accordance with the changes wrought by the contemporary spirit."[42] Attempting to give psychological validity to the interpretations of Christianity led Jung to "the question of Christ as a psychological figure", just as trying to synthesize differing Christian points of view led Shorthouse to "the idea of Christ", not to considerations of the "historical Jesus" or to the "person of the Christ".[43] Jung found synthesis by demonstrating the "parallelism between the Christ figure and the central concepts of alchemy", and by relating the psychology of Individuation to the historical legends of Parsifal, Merlin, and Mercurius, he created "an essentially alchemical vision of Christ...as a union of spiritually alive and physically dead matter".[44]

Shorthouse's appeal to Arnold to write "the great book" earned him a brief letter from Arnold within two weeks' time. Arnold acknowledged the "notions and aims" of Shorthouse's argument had "long been present" to him, but he excused himself from such an undertaking because of the work he had already set for himself.[45] Twenty-seven years later Shorthouse still regretted that Arnold had not undertaken the challenge:

> I look back upon his career with regret, for I am firmly
> persuaded that, under more favourable circumstances, he
> might have produced one of the great prose *books of the
> world*...alas! the great book never came. He had every
> qualification for it.[46]

Because Arnold rejected the challenge, Shorthouse himself had to take it up. Thus, he developed the principle of "the subjective influence of the Christian Mythos" into the "religion of *John Inglesant*".[47] Later, he wrote "The Humourous in Literature" to clarify his theory to the public. From this concern, Shorthouse developed the conviction that only a great "musical romance written by one who combined technical knowledge with artistic and emotional insight [could] resolve the mysteries of life". Soon realising that the public had not understood his synthesis of "Revelation and Humour" in *John Inglesant*, he felt the necessity of enspiritualising philosophy itself, and thus began to compose spiritual romances to integrate musical analogies to enhance his themes. Eliot, too, recognized that "whether in Argos or England / There are certain inflexible laws / Unalterable, in the nature of music"[48] and that man could become "Transfigured in the vision of some marvellous creation"[49] through music. The need to modernize and reinterpret the Christian message through "The Music of Poetry"[50] inspired Eliot to compose *Four Quartets* as analogies of Beethoven's late four string quartets[51] and dramatise music as religious vocation in *The Confidential Clerk.*[52]

Shorthouse began examining the possibilities of enspiritualizing romances as he studied the differences between nineteenth-century romances and eighteenth-century novels. In "The Successor of Monsieur Le Sage", also published in volume two of *LLLR*, Shorthouse *contrasts* George Borrow's *Bible in Spain* against Alain Rene Le Sage's *Gil Blas*. He selected the two works because each of them contains more than "mere opinions of a writer upon certain elevated subjects" and because neither of them is a "book full of fine writing and magnificent ideas, which find no echo in our own breasts". In both *Bible in Spain* and *Gil Blas*,

> we are reading the story of one of ourselves, walking
> upon the same earth, and looking at strange or familiar
> things with the same eyes, thinking of them with the same
> ideas, affected by them with the same emotions as we
> ourselves (64).

Although he has never visited Spain, Shorthouse declares, "life in Spain is more in a dream than a reality"; the nation lives "in a perpetual dream over its former greatness...the whole people resting...contentedly centuries behind the world" (69-70). Because *Bible in Spain* possesses "the spirit of simple and trusting faith", it also has "a sustained and united sympathy", qualities lacking in *Gil Blas*. Gil Blas is a "clever, good-natured scoundrel, with no aim in view but a selfish one of his own aggrandisement", whereas passages in Borrow's romance "reminds us of one of the heroes of the old stories of Christian Chivalry, half saint, half knight, riding through wild moors and desolate haunted forests on some holy mission or quest" (66-67). Shorthouse admires a scene in which Borrow depicts his experience at an execution for murder in Madrid. As the culprit dies on the scaffold, a priest shouts "*Pax et misericordia et tranquilitas*" and shouts louder and louder "just as if he would pursue the spirit through its courts to eternity, cheering it on its way". "The effect", Borrow states, "was tremendous", and he himself joins in the shouting. What is crucial, however, follows:

> God was not thought of, Christ was not thought of; only
> the priest was thought of, for he seemed at that moment to
> be the first being in existence, to have the power of
> opening and shutting the gates of heaven or of hell, just as
> he should think proper (68).

The presumption of priestly power, Borrow proclaims, represented a "striking instance of the successful working of the Popish system, whose grand aim has ever been to keep people's minds as far as possible from God, and to centre their hopes and fears in the priesthood." Shorthouse judges against *Gil Blas* because it has a "perfectly worldly spirit and looks at everything in a worldly way"; he accords high praise to *Bible in Spain* because it is a romance with "unsurpassed painting of scenery" (71). The most interesting aspect of "The Successor of Monsieur Le Sage", however, concerns Shorthouse's interest in narrative technique.

Noting that when Borrow began *Lavengro* "he evidently intended to produce a correct three-volume novel, having a plot, a beginning, an end, a hero, and a villain", Shorthouse discerns that Borrow was "as incompetent to perform [such a literary task] as Le Sage would have been himself". Borrow begins the novel "with the utmost propriety" and brings all the characters "on the stage in the most correct way", but he soon begins to struggle "under the trammels of a plot which he will soon cast off to follow his own way...As we go on the incidents and conversations are not those of a novel. There is none of that unnatural chain of events tending towards the final *denouement*" (76). The plot is such that "the hero sees persons and things which have no effect on the story, though they all leave a carefully marked result on his own mind". Shorthouse admired the technique as an advance from the "typical novel": "This [*Lavengro*] certainly is not a novel, but it is something better. We feel it is a real man living, and that the education of his life is on going on all the while" (76). Shorthouse extols how the hero gathers "as much truth and philosophic reasoning" from "*any* class of people" he meets, and he asserts,

> ...the description of [characters] and of scenes and incidents [is] beyond all praise. The language (perfectly simple, plain, and unaffected) has a force and strength rarely surpassed, and not unfrequently reaches a poetic beauty and a lofty sublimity which the finest writers but seldom have had the good fortune to attain to (78).

Noting that wandering and travels gave Borrow "an intense aversion to the conventionalisms and deceits of modern society" and agreeing that there is much to be decried in modern society, Shorthouse suggests, however, that Borrow was one-sided "through ignorance of the highest society" and accuses Borrow of "puppyism", which Borrow associates with "that 'badge of the low scoundrel puppy, the gilt chain at the waistcoat pocket'" (82). "To imagine that there is no courage or manliness but in prize-fighters or the leaders of a Chartist mob", Shorthouse argues, "is no more free from puppyism and conventionalism (though of the opposite kind) than that 'gentility nonsense' against which Borrow is so severe" (82-83).

Another of Borrow's severities, however, Shorthouse approves: "There is far too much reviewing and trusting to reviews in the present day." Any man, Shorthouse contends, who has a "noble library at command", can read up "in half an hour sufficient to talk very learnedly upon a subject, however deep, and any moderately clever man...can find faults anywhere". Far too many people, he agrees with Borrow, "have no time to read the books themselves; they must read the reviews and so keep themselves up with the current literature of the day". Shorthouse condemns such reading as "superficial and useless" and concludes, "Surely one good book well read were worth a million such glimpses of books" (84).

In "The 'Paradise Lost'" he takes the Friends Essay Meeting to task for how they once accepted two essays on Milton's great poem, one of which possessed "a very superficial acquaintance with the poem itself". He has, he tells the Friends, "the best possible reason for knowing this", for he was himself the irresponsible essayist.

"Paradise Lost" raises

> those questions before whose stupendous difficulty the human intellect, even when assisted by revelation, has ever quailed, and towards whose solution it has never been able to advance one step, --the origin of evil, free-will, the divine attributes of infinite power and mercy considered in connection with a creation full of misery (124).

If any of the Friends suspected Shorthouse of being too dreamy or too given to romantic feeling about myth, he challenged their perceptions by arguing that Milton had failed because he did not consider the great questions of human life "solemnly and soberly, in the light of reason and of prayer". Milton considered his themes poetically in the darkness "of dim traditions, and through an antique region of pagan and medieval mythos" (122-123). Milton described "the divine persons themselves in language and by ideas which, being human and sensuous, are naturally revolting and inadequate" (124-125). Milton's suffered

> a stormy and distracted life, a home rendered unhappy by a stern, unyielding temper and an intolerant creed, and a public life stained with violent party passions and degraded by the purchased pen of a political hireling, and by the malignity which pursued its enemies even beyond the grave (125-126).

To appreciate the "Paradise Lost", Shorthouse argues, we must "forget the story" and read the entire poem "in such an allegorical light as will enable us to separate the beauties from the dross in which they are enclosed". The narrative, he judges, is "so gross...and so unworthy...that no amount of allegorical interpretation can render them otherwise than disgusting" (127). The beauty and power of the poetry, however, are not entirely lost if we "allegorise the whole book" and take Adam "as simply the mouthpiece of humanity" and the "wealth of description of scenery [as] imagery of the different aspects in which the visible things of earth and heaven appear to affect us" (128). Judging by the tone and the rhetorical pattern, negative criticism followed by supposedly self-evidently beautiful passages of description, Shorthouse probably wrote "The 'Paradise Lost'" about the same time he composed "The 'Morte D'Arthur' and 'Idylls of the King'" (1864?), though it was bound in Folio VI (1865-1869?). In "Literature" he returns to "the peculiar dangers and causes of decay [of] literary societies like ours". The intellectual element in them is "narrowed to one phase, and that a somewhat peculiar one--pure literature". He recounts how and when he "first saw something of the delightful possibilities of 'literature' properly so-called". Attending a course of lectures in Birmingham delivered by "a gentleman of the name of Lord", Shorthouse discovered "that science which treats of the effect of the contact of human nature with matter", which, he asserts, "to be very nearly an exact definition" of literature. Literature always has "individual human feelings as its centre" (138-139). Distinguishing between "Personalists and Impersonalists", he declares that Personalists are interested "in anything" which relates "in some plain way to individual human life"; Impersonalists "delight in nothing but the consideration of abstract phenomena...which have no connection, or at least a very remote one, with human life" (139-140). As if he wished to provoke his audience, he admonishes:

> And does it not seem more than probable that a society
> whose members are given to pursuits the reverse of all
> this, must be content to go on in future, as it has gone on
> for a considerable part of its existence, drinking tea, and
> eating 'trifle' and bread and butter?

He abruptly drops his direct criticism of the Essay Meeting and asks them to think of the work of the historian, the writer on natural history, the philosopher, the preacher, the writer of novels and tales. Exhorting his listeners to expand what they consider suitable for the Essay Meeting, he continues:

> It is the great fault of modern followers after pure reason
> to pursue but one object, blinding themselves to every
> other. All that makes a man combine in his mind more
> ideas than one, more science than one, more conceptions
> of the appearances of things than one elevates him in the
> scale of existence, carries him nearer to his Creator, and
> disposes him to listen to that system, catholic over nature
> as over the human race (143).

Because "all the sciences blend with and assist each other", the more "we use their aids the more we shall discover the master principle, the *summum bonnum*, of the ancients, in which all wisdom is contained" (143-144). "The more our learning enables us to see all the various points of view, and all the lights and shadows of this picture of Our Lord" the more we shall "appreciate its relative position in the history of our race" and more fully realise the "highest possibilities of that human nature which it is our overwhelming responsibility to share with Him" (144). Had Jung been present at the reading of Shorthouse's "Literature" he would undoubtedly have praised Shorthouse's enthusiasm, his boldness in working to expand the Society's intellectual scope, and the direction his thinking was beginning to take. In three other essays, Shorthouse approaches subjects very near Jung's concerns.

"Ars Vitae" reiterates Shorthouse's conviction that "every influence which serves to graft Christianity more strongly into our intellectual life should be taken advantage of" and accords "humour" the status of "a new art, or faculty of the mind". With the "increased toleration which follows upon enlarged culture" and because humours differ from man to man, "no one has any reason to assume his superiority to another" (225-226). Once associated with "certain phenomena of the body", the humours have come to represent "mind and conduct". Shorthouse does not explore the four humours individually, but he does trace essential differences between Hellenic and Hebraic traditions, differences he absorbed from Arnold's work. "That higher seriousness...which clothes itself in irony and humour", he observes, "was unknown to the Jews, while the simple grandeur of their literature seems unreal and grandiloquent to the European." The Bible, he asserts, affords "no encouragement to the sharply-wrought reasoning faculty of the Caucasian race", which owes its development to the Greeks. Thus, "Hebrew is unknown, except to theologians, while the study of Greek becomes a passion to every man of culture" (228-229). The "perfect self-sacrifice of the Platonic Socrates [failed] altogether to influence the masses of mankind", and the superiority of Christianity asserts itself precisely because the "exquisite word-science, the brilliant dialectic, the dramatic colouring, [and] the alluring life" of the Greeks failed. As he had called Christ the "noblest of gentleman" in one of his earlier essays, he now proclaims that "Christ Himself was, in the highest sense to which we have attached the word, a more perfect 'Humanist' than any who have hitherto spoken in His most Holy Name" (229). "Ars Vitae" touches on the fringes of a profound study, but Shorthouse stops short. He again confronts the "fragile" limitations of the Essay Meeting, and presumably the group takes a break for "tea and trifle".

In "Fragilia" he tries a more philosophic approach, yet one that is more suited to his audience. Recalling the powerful remembrance of a picturesque view over the plain of Worcestershire one summer morning at sunrise, Shorthouse meditates on the brevity of such pleasures. However brief life's pleasures, "It is a necessity of their existence that men should partake of the spirituality of nature", and that, as "they are only perceptible to cultured thought and feeling, they should be clearly marked by the fragility of their existence, as belonging to mind and to eternity and not to matter and to time" (167). "Fragilia" defines a fundamental conviction about time that Shorthouse developed in his early childhood. In the beginning lines of "Burnt Norton", Eliot asserted a hypothesis about the nature of time, stating that "all time is eternally present". In his pre-Einstein cosmos, Shorthouse has a different view: "We cannot be said to have any present":

> ...every moment as it comes to us becomes instantly the past, and as well cannot be said to live in what is no longer ours, and as it is impossible that we can exist, except metaphorically, in the past, we can therefore be said to live nowhere but on the very point which is neither future nor present, but is just on the verge of becoming present (160).

Because "The immediate future is of little value and interest to us, and the present is gone as soon as it is here", we are driven "to the necessity of seeing that the really valuable possession is not the past, but what the past has brought to us and what it has left us...the real existence of the world of ideas", which is independent of matter, therefore of time. Study of this world of ideas, he states, is the only means by which we "can realise what spirit *is*, and what relation it has to our present visible life" (161). To accommodate ourselves to the world of ideas and its idealism, yet to keep our "feet in this world", we reconcile "ideality with personality"; that is, as Jung might have said, we project an anthropomorphic vision of the universe "out of our own bodies".

Like Jung, Shorthouse believed that humanity shares a united instinct that is forever opposed to "pure scientific materialism and to profligate scepticism". "No idea", he asserted, "has been more familiar or more perpetually present to our race in all stages of its existence than that of *another* world...the *spiritual*" (163). "Fragilia", written about 1870, offers no evidence that Shorthouse is directly responding to Darwin or the Victorian "Battle of the Churches", but the essay states his final resolution to the multifarious problems. "In the end", Shorthouse asserts, it will "be found that spirit and matter, science and faith, are not separable, but are both wanted to make a complete man" (163). To Shorthouse, "Spirit can never be apprehended or known or understood or seen or felt by matter." What we realise when in "some wonderful and inconceivable way" we know "spirit" is influencing or moving matter is "the kindred spirit within us which feels and is sensible of the approach of it" (164). It requires little accommodation of words and metaphors to see Shorthouse's argument as fundamental to Jungian thought. Jung resolved the same dilemma for himself by conceiving of his psychology as analogous to alchemy, biology, and physics and of thinking about *spirit* as analogous to libido and psychic energy and as inseparable from the relationships of mind to psyche and body to matter.[53] For Shorthouse, the uniting instincts of spirit and matter may be collectively named *music*, especially "music without words", which makes us:

> conscious of the presence of a sensation we cannot feel,
> of words which we cannot hear, of thoughts which we
> cannot grasp, of a world of intellectual being which like a
> phantom is close to us, but which, from instant to instant
> as we think ourselves on the point of entering, always
> eludes our consciousness and vanishes away (164-165).

Eliot certainly agreed and urged that "the poet is occupied with frontiers of consciousness beyond which words fail, though meanings still exist",[54] yet he insisted that "the music of poetry is not something which exists apart from the meaning."[55] Confronted with the relativity of time and space, Shorthouse asserted that "to spiritual man already there is no more time" (165), or in Eliot's words in "Burnt Norton", "All time is eternally present". Struggling against the fragility of thought in time-space relativity to name that "something... something abstract, which, once created, is independent of circumstance and change" (166), Shorthouse approximates Jung's "archetypes of the collective unconscious".

In "Religio Historici" Shorthouse questions whether the study of history is "useful and improving" and asserts, "The object of any study can only be the knowledge of ourselves, our duties, and our powers", but in an age of scientific enquiry, the study of history cannot readily be validated: "...there is a want of mathematical proof of the exact amount of the benefit" of historical study (168). The same, of course, may be said of any behavioural science. "We may take it for granted...that [the study of history] raises us from the merely animal life of the present moment, and from the petty sympathies of our mediocre natures, to an existence in many distant ages, and to friendship and a sympathy with the highest and noblest of our race" (169). Yet, "the great evil" has befallen the science of history. "Professors have been too fond of particular theories of their own... [and] facts have been taken to support the favourite theories of different historians." In the psychological sense, the historian's mind projects its own unconscious needs, perhaps even its own unconsciousness, onto the "facts" which it seeks, selects, and orders into theory. "It is surely as fair to argue on the passing opinion of the day in *favour*...as against" (170). Here, too, his reasoning provides an echo of Jung's later assertion that to argue against religion and life after death or "particular myths" is no more valid than to argue in favour of such ideas: "Belief proves only the phenomenon of belief, not the content of belief."[56] "Interpretations are only for those who don't understand." Paradoxically, "It is only the things we don't understand that have any meaning."[57]

"One of the acknowledged facts of our earliest history", Shorthouse asserts, "is the similarity in the traditions and theologies of the most widely separated nations" (170). Those who believe in a common origin of all mankind have posited "extraordinary theories", tracing the nations of the earth from Adam and Eve through "the supposed journeys of the ten lost tribes of Israel". The Jews in the north of Scotland and the tribe of Dan, which was settled in Ireland, have both received visits, according to some theories, from Jewish "missionaries of Buddha--who had previously been converted to that religion in India!" Such theorizing is "unphilosophical, and almost childish", Shorthouse asserts, then wonders: What do we think if we "set aside all theories?"

> [If we take] for granted what modern science as well as orthodox antiquity would seem to teach, that men originally came from one parent stock, is it not more rational to take such coincidences as the result of the workings of a common human intellect? (171).

Examining several of the coincidences as though he were tracing "the history of the God-idea", Shorthouse arrived at the same conclusion Jung later reached:

> In psychology the concept of God is a definite entity, which must be reckoned with, just as much as with 'affect', 'instinct', 'mother', etc. [but] the perpetual confusion between object and image [makes it impossible to discern] a difference between 'God' and the 'imago of God'... [We] suppose that we are speaking of God and giving a 'theological' explanation when we are really speaking of the 'idea of God'.

Psychology, Jung concluded, "has only to reckon with the function of an image of God, in accordance with the actual facts".[58] To Shorthouse, it is a fact that we have "well-defined traditions", like that of "some primeval and supreme conflict...between gods and inferior demons, or between gods and men themselves", but such traditions may derive from man's innate, *a priori* need to tell stories, to mythologize. "It would be a very curious study to trace [such traditions] to their origin", Shorthouse surmises, but in the instance of the "war in heaven", for example, we would have "to see how much of the belief of orthodox minds...is formed from the 'Paradise Lost' and how much from other non-scriptural sources (172-173).

Religious and mythological traditions themselves "are not mere coincidences, much less are they the result of direct communication by word of mouth and teaching", Shorthouse argues. They are "one of the strongest proofs of the common origin of our race, not so much because of the resemblances themselves, which might be accidental, or arise from many causes, but because we see in them and through them we can see the same mind working, the same ideas, the same ignorance, the same desire for instruction" (174). We can see, he asserts, "human nature very nearly by itself [though the] structure of theology, poetry, tradition, history, physics, and ethics [presents] human nature, perhaps, under its most picturesque aspect." In Jung's view, such literary traditions and storytelling itself derives from what Shorthouse called "the same mind...the same ideas". To Jung, such representations of the mysteries of life encoded psychically and linguistically into myths are "first and foremost psychic manifestations that represent the nature of the psyche...symbolic expressions for the inner and unconscious psychic drama that becomes accessible to human consciousness by way of projections--that is, by being mirrored in the events of nature."[59] Shorthouse understood psychological projection as the "half-understood promptings in the secret chambers of the human heart itself" which make "much of the history and writings of the classic ages sound more like allegory than history or philosophy" and which help explain man's anthropomorphic realisations of God.

Archaeological and anthropological pursuits of his Victorian contemporaries attracted Shorthouse far more than the "Battle of the Churches", and he found it more profitable to indulge his antiquarian and topological interests through the sciences of his age than to pursue theology. As Jung would later do, Shorthouse began looking for the origins and sources of conflicting opinions, rather than actively engaging himself in advocating and arguing any particular contemporary viewpoint or theory. "If we allow ourselves to realise the childlike and totally unoccupied state of the human mind in its early ages", he felt, "we shall understand many peculiarities both in ancient and modern history", and we shall see "that God left Himself a witness" both in Nature and in the "half-understood promptings in the secret chambers of the human heart itself" (175).

"Religio Historici" was composed while Shorthouse was at work on *John Inglesant*, and it reflects how he sought to find answers to the intellectual questions of his age and to resolve the problems through philosophical romance. By experiencing the childlike state of the human mind, he discovered that "Revelation only touched very slightly upon man's intellect, or upon his knowledge of his dwelling-place", and he recognized "the writings of the seventeenth century show no great dissimilarity to those of Greece and Rome" (175). What he saw most prominently and felt most intensely was the historical tradition of focusing conscious attention on "individual character and action". The historical tradition, however, only continued, he believed, "to very recent times", and then it drastically changed. "Formerly individual human interest was supreme: ascertained facts were very few, and those few of a nature (such as death) that added to, rather than detracted from, individual prominence and influence." "Now", he laments,

> facts are everything--science is crushing individuality out of the world; we live and move scientifically and in masses; we may be said to think by machinery and steam; there is no scope for individual action; the science of law fixes exactly what every man is to do...Nothing separates history from our own era so much as this want of commanding individual interest (176).

Thus, in *John Inglesant* he concentrated on the picturesqueness of individual interest and individual. Having complained earlier in his essays about novels which cannot "endure heroes [like] a king who, at the head of his armies, took the field...for 'the glory of God and the relief of man's estate'", Shorthouse began to advance his argument that what modern man desperately needs is the picturesque. To Shorthouse, "Picturesqueness in fact and individuality are the same things, for picturesqueness always accompanies individual thought and action and their productions" (177).

This picturesqueness is not unlike Jung's understanding of *mana*, "the primitive notion of an all-pervading vital force, a power of growth and magic healing". *Mana*, in Shorthouse's terms, is the "Divine Spirit...some portion of its indwelling".[60] Pondering it led Shorthouse to what Jung called the "archetypal question". As he began "Religio Historici" by questioning whether man profits from the study of history, so he ends the essay pondering "the great question": "...whether any advance, or indeed any alteration, has taken place in the individual mental standard of mankind", and he recognizes that fundamentally "it is to individual minds then and now that we must look for an answer" (175).

Study of individuality leads, however, to an "impassable gulf" which exists, he asserts, "between the pursuit of truth in material sciences and in the immaterial existence of which Revelation treats". Revelation is "fixed", he argues in "Religio Historici" which echoes the final argument of *John Inglesant*; no further discoveries can be made, and the "human mind has not advanced one step in the knowledge of the immaterial world since the earliest Homeric days":

> The mind of the earliest, the most uncultivated

> Greek...saw as clearly the answer to the great riddle of
> Life and Death as (without the Christian faith) *we* see
> it...Standing by our grave-sides, as the earth rattles on the
> coffin-lid, just as dense a veil, just as impalpable a void,
> cuts us sharply off from the life beyond, baffling our
> intensest efforts, our keenest glances, as they baffled his
> (178).

Indeed, "The more grandiose, the more comprehensive the image that has come into being and been handed on, the further is it removed from our experience. Nowadays we can feel our way into it and perceive something of it, but the original experience is lost" (179), or, as Eliot realised, we may have had the experience, but we have lost the meaning: "There is, it seems to us, / At best, only a limited value / In the knowledge derived from experience...And approach to the meaning restores the experience in a different form".[61] Religion, "the vital link with psychic processes independent of and beyond consciousness," Jung explained, leads but to "the dark hinterland of the psyche"[62] but does not enable modern man to understand more than the primitive did, nor does it necessarily empower modern man to experience even the understanding itself. In fact, Jung, asserted, faith itself may be "the arch sin [for it] forestalls experience", and, for Jung, "in religious matters only experience counts".[63] How, then, may highly civilised modern man make any advances at all that will gain him greater insight or more certain knowledge than that which the primitive mind possessed and experienced?

Shorthouse's answer was, first of all, to define the "religion of the historian", a religion which enabled the historian to see

> full evidence of a common humanity, of a mysterious
> similarity of ideas, of a singular property in all history,
> tradition, poetry, and literature, as if all these forms of
> human thought contained in them something more than
> met the eye (178).

He names this "something": "apologues and types, the outward manifestations of a secret power which, through many and dark ages, was silently, but imperceptibly, working towards a certain end...to understand something of the connection between the human and the Divine" (179-180). Shorthouse believed such a religious outlook would enable an historian to see beyond and through his own projected theories. Seeing the mistakes and misdirections of other historians and seeing his own psychological projections, the historian must realise that, as he studies:

> a phantasmagoria of men and events floats before him...in
> a vain show; the more he inquires into men and creeds,

the more he is perplexed--he finds none which he can say is absolutely right, no one fully wrong (181).

"Perhaps gradually", Shorthouse was convinced,
> one fact comes out more clearly in all his study; a fact not dependent on any theory--far above all theory; a fact so infinite...that no theory could have invented it; a fact so absolutely one with humanity...the fact which all history, literature, and human life before a certain period pointed forward to, and to which all history, literature, human life after that period points back (179-180).

Of course, for Shorthouse and his audience, this fact is "a life so intensely human that every human heart at once bears witness to its truth...the life round which all history centres" (181-182). Idealistically, rather unrealistically for a man living through the "Battle of the Churches" and the conflicts between the sciences and the diversity of religious persuasions, the seeming idols of his age, Shorthouse proclaims, "All creeds, doctrines, disputes of different churches, theories of inspiration--all lost themselves in one single command, one single doctrine--belief in Him." In their "disputes about doctrine men have forgotten the Person" and in "discussions on what His servants have taught they have forgotten His own teaching" (182). "It seems", he summarizes, "that the religion of the historian, more than that of any other, should lead him to cling tenaciously to the belief in the Person of Christ" (183). The importance, here, is not to explore the logical fallacies or shortcomings of argument in "Religio Historici". He all too obviously failed "to set aside all theories" and addressed an audience that readily agreed with his conclusions. Yet, reading "Religio Historici" today, one senses that Shorthouse was arguing with an audience much broader than that of the Essay Society Meeting, that he was, in fact, projecting his argument towards the audience he imaginatively addressed as he wrote *John Inglesant*. As if "ideas were truly in the air" or were developing gradually in Victorian consciousness, Shorthouse was responding to influences other than those suitable to the Society of Friends. His "apologues and types" predates Lady Welby's "links and clues" but is contemporary with James Hinton's resolutions to *The Mystery of Pain*, which he must have read during the composition of *John Inglesant*. Welby's and Hinton's works, however, were undoubtedly appropriate for the Essay Meeting's considerations. What was not suitable, of course, was Shorthouse's desire to read and compose his own book as a romance. Thus, the philosophical aspects of *John Inglesant* owe their vitality to Shorthouse's active membership in the Friends Essay Society; the romantic aspects of the novel illustrate the strength of his personal interests and modes of imaginative thought which were unsuitable for the Society and which directed him towards the Church of England. His Early and Middle Essays reveal his preparation for *John Inglesant*, but more importantly, they disclose how we should read the historical and religious aspects of the novel as "philosophical romance". "The author of *John Inglesant*" composed the "philosophical romance" as a study of individual human life because he discerned "the half-promptings in the secret chambers of the human heart itself" and, more importantly, he had to project these promptings of intuitive self-knowledge and their romancing of the Self in order to understand them himself. *John Inglesant* is a text that derives its pretext from the psychic life of J. Henry Shorthouse, just as surely as it derives its historical and cultural picturesqueness from the vitality of the similarities between the seventeenth century and the Victorian era.

As Jung confessed,

My words can be regarded as stations along my life's way. All my writings may be considered tasks imposed from within. I permitted the spirit that moved me to speak out...I have the feeling that I have done all that it was possible for me to do...more was not within my power.[64]

John Inglesant is also a personal confession as well as a romantic formulation of religious quest and intellectual synthesis. In his recreation of the spirit of the Church of England, Shorthouse created a literary symbol, which for him and countless others contains archetypal power.

Shorthouse's psychological Individuation may seem to end in his first novel, because in composing *John Inglesant* he worked out a comprehensive personal philosophy that needed no later refining. Individuation, though, is never merely mechanical, never finished, not even in death.[65] As Eliot knew,

...what the dead had no speech for, when living,

They can tell you, being dead: the communication
Of the dead is tongued with fire

beyond the language of the living.[66]

To regard *John Inglesant* as the one great novel of J. Henry Shorthouse is a presumption that his communication ceased in 1880, a presumption that makes him metaphorically "dead" and prevents our hearing and attending to the "tongues of fire", the spirituality of his later novels.

Notes to Chapter Two

[1]All references from Shorthouse's "Early Essays" are taken from Sarah Shorthouse's *Life, Letters, and Literary Remains of J. H. Shorthouse*, vol. II, (London: Macmillan, 1905).

[2]No reason for the change of titles is given in the Shorthouse/Macmillan correspondence.

[3]Sarah Shorthouse notes that the family reminiscence is by "one of the cousins", but she does not identify the relative by name. Internal evidence suggests Margaret Southall.

[4]J. Henry Shorthouse, Letter to Matthew Arnold (23 October 1871), *LLLR*, vol. I, 83-90.

[5]C. G. Jung, *Psychological Reflections: An Anthology of the Writings of C. G. Jung*, selected and edited by Jolande Jacobi. (New York: Harper and Row, 1953), 67, rep. New York: Pantheon Books, 1953.

[6]William Wordsworth, *The Prelude: 1799, 1805, 1850*. ed., Jonathan Wordsworth, M. H. Abrams, and Stephen Gill. (New York: W. W. Norton Co., 1979), 154-159.

[7]C. G. Jung, *Psychological Reflections* 66, 65, 56.

[8]C. G. Jung, *Psychological Reflections* 46, 58.

[9]C. G. Jung, *Psychological Reflections* 61, 57.

[10]C. G. Jung, *Psychological Reflections* 55, 63.

[11]William Wordsworth, "Lines Composed a Few Miles above Tintern Abbey...", *The Complete Poetical Works of Wordsworth*, ed. A. J. George (Boston: Houghton, Mifflin, 1932), 91-93.

[12]C. G. Jung, *Psychological Reflections* 65.

[13]James A. Hall, *The Jungian Experience: Analysis and Individuation* (Toronto: Inner City Books, 1986), 93. "Characterized by concentration, limitation, and exclusion", consciousness censors dreams so that dramatic structure and the purpose or meaning of dreams may be changed "in the telling". (See also *Psychological Reflections* 49.)

[14]Sarah Shorthouse, *LLLR*, vol. 1, 29.

[15]J. Henry Shorthouse, Letter to Margaret Southall (16 August 1853), *LLLR*, vol. 1, 39-41.

[16]J. Henry Shorthouse, Letter to Margaret Southall (Undated [? 1854]), *LLLR*, vol. 1, 50-52.

[17]James A. Hall, *The Jungian Experience* 97.

[18]Anthony Stevens, *Archetypes: A Natural History of the Self* (New York: Quill, 1982), 215.

[19]Morris Philipson, *Outline of a Jungian Aesthetics* (Chicago: Northwestern University Press, 1963), 9-10.

[20] T. S. Eliot, *The Complete Poems and Plays* (London: Faber and Faber, 1969, rep. 1987), 171. According to E. M. Stephenson, *T. S. Eliot and the Lay Reader* (London: The Fortune Press, 1944, rep. 1948, 80), Eliot took the epigraph from the German "standard text of pre-Socratic philosophers", that of Hermann Diels, *Fragmente der Vorsokratiker*, but, as Stephenson quotes Eliot, "No one translation, however can be considered as anything more than a limited interpretation since the meanings of key words in Greek philosophy can never be completely rendered in a modern language. That is the reason for my putting the Greek text instead of an English translation of it." Professor Lawrence Dunlop, Marymount College, California, provided the translation used here.

[21] F. J. Wagner, *J. Henry Shorthouse* (Boston: Twayne, 1979), 48.

[22] Sarah Shorthouse, *LLLR*, vol. 1, 60.

[23] Jessie Douglas Montgomery, "Some Personal Recollections of Mr. Shorthouse", *LLLR*, vol. 1, 397-407, 405.

[24] J. Henry Shorthouse, "The End of Learning", *LLLR*, vol. 2, 193-194. (Parenthetical page references are cited hereafter.)
25. J. Henry Shorthouse, Letter to Sarah Shorthouse (10 April 1857), *LLLR*, vol. 1, 57-59.

[26] J. Henry Shorthouse, Letter to Margaret Southall (Undated: ? 1854), *LLLR*, vol. 1, 50-51.

[27] "Chronological snobbery" or compensatory experiencing of time and meaning is a term C. S. Lewis used in his "great war" with Owen Barfield. Jung defined the *anima* as that "she" which "goes back into pre-history...embodies the contents of the past...[and] provides the individual with those elements that he ought to know about his prehistory". Symbolizing "all life that has been in the past and is still alive in him", the *anima* creates historical perspective.

[28] T. S. Eliot, "Tradition and the Individual Talent", *Selected Essays*, third enlarged edition, (London: Faber and Faber, 1951), 16.

[29] J. Henry Shorthouse, "Bede", *LLLR*, vol. 2, 106.

[30] C. J. Jung, *Psychological Reflections: Anthology of the Writings of C. G. Jung*, selected and edited by Jolande Jacobi. (New York: Harper and Row, 1953), 133.

[31] C. G. Jung, *Memories, Dreams, Reflections* (New York: Pantheon Books, 1961), 389. (Cited hereafter as *Memories*.)

[32] C. G. Jung, *Memories* 389-390.

[33] F. J. Wagner, *J. Henry Shorthouse* (Boston: Twayne, 1979), 45.

[34] Sarah Shorthouse, *LLLR*, vol. 1, 8, and 180-184.

[35] Paul Elmer More, "J. Henry Shorthouse", *Shelburne Essays*, Third Series, (Boston: Houghton, Mifflin, 1905), 213-215.

[36] Paul Elmer More, "J. Henry Shorthouse" 229.

[37]Sarah Shorthouse, *LLLR*, vol. 1, 64-65.

[38]J. Henry Shorthouse, Letter to "-----, at Weston", (undated), *LLLR*, vol. 1, 65-68.

[39]Raymond Chapman, "For God and King Charles", *The Sense of the Past in Victorian Literature* (New York: St. Martin's Press, 1986), 103-122, 108.

[40]C. G. Jung, *Memories* 209.

[41]Arnold Toynbee and Jane Caplan, "The Relativity of Historical Thought", *A Study of History* (Oxford University Press, 1972), 30-38, 38.

[42]C. G. Jung, *Memories* 210.

[43]C. G. Jung, *Memories* 200-237.

[44]C. G. Jung, *Memories*, 211.

[45]Matthew Arnold, Letter to J. Henry Shorthouse (3 November 1871), *LLLR*, vol. 1, 89-90.

[46]J. Henry Shorthouse, Letter to Arthur Galton (Sunday before Advent, 1898), *LLLR*, vol. I, 350-351.

[47]J. Henry Shorthouse, "Preface" to *John Inglesant* (London: Macmillan, 1882), x.

[48]T. S. Eliot, *The Family Reunion, Complete* 329.

[49]T. S. Eliot, *The Confidential Clerk, Complete* 465.

[50]T. S. Eliot, "The Music of Poetry" (Glasgow University Press, 1942), reprinted in *On Poetry and Poets* (New York: Farrar, Straus and Cudahy, 1957), 17-33.

[51]Thomas R. Rees, *The Technique of T. S. Eliot: A Study of the Orchestration of Meaning* (The Hague: Mouton, 1974), 305. Several critics have followed Helen Gardner's lead in writing about "The Music of 'Four Quartets'", *The Art of T. S. Eliot* (New York: E. P. Dutton, 1950), 36-56. Gardner asserted that "each poem is structurally a poetic equivalent of the classical symphony, or quartet, or sonata, as distinct from the suite" (36-37). Rees cautioned, "Many critics have come dangerously close to subscribing to the tenuous proposition that a nearly exact formal analogy exists between the structure of Eliot's poem and that of Beethoven's late string quartets. In reality the exterior structure of the *Four Quartets* stands merely as a rough approximation of the form of Beethoven's quartets. Nor does Eliot's poem, as a literary adaptation of musical form, have a strict formal correspondence to any other quartets or symphonies" (305). Rees judged it better "to consider the entire work as *one quartet*" than to regard each poem as a separate musical analogy.

[52]The plot of *The Confidential Clerk* develops around Colby Simpkins' discovery of his true parents, and the discovery of his true identity interrelates with his realisation that he understands himself by "translating" self-realisation "Into terms of music" (464).

[53]C. G. Jung, *Memories* 200-201.

[54]T. S. Eliot, "The Music of Poetry", *On Poetry and Poets* 22-23.

[55]T. S. Eliot, "The Music of Poetry", *On Poetry and Poets* 21.

[56]C. G. Jung, *Memories* 319.

[57]C. G. Jung, *The Archetypes and the Collective Unconscious,* vol. 9, part 1, *Collected Works,* Bollingen Series XX, 2nd ed., (Princeton University Press, 1969), 31.

[58]C. G. Jung, *Psychological Reflections* 300.

[59]C. G. Jung, *Psychological Reflections* 15.

[60]C. G. Jung, *The Archetypes and the Collective Unconscious* 33.

[61]T. S. Eliot, *Four Quartets, Complete* 179 and 186.

[62]C. G. Jung, *Psychological Reflections* 314-315.

[63]C. G. Jung, *Memories* 94, 98.

[64]C. G. Jung, *Memories* 222.

[65]C. G. Jung, *Memories* 248.

[66]T. S. Eliot, "Little Gidding", *The Complete Poems and Plays of T. S. Eliot* (London: Faber and Faber, 1969), 192.

Chapter Three: "John Inglesant" in England

When Alexander Macmillan offered to publish *John Inglesant*, Shorthouse insisted his manuscript be published "*as it is*": "I have not adopted the form and manner of the book without consideration...the book as it stands with all its peculiarities is just what I intended it to be!"[1] Precisely what he had intended it to be remains somewhat unclear. As Wagner notes, Shorthouse "wrote himself into the book"; during the ten years the Birmingham manufacturer devoted to composing his romance, it became "an exposition of [his] inner life, the life beneath and behind his domestic, social and business life".[2] After publication of his final novel, *Blanche, Lady Falaise*, Shorthouse realises, "*John Inglesant* is, of course, the work into which I put my life", and he concedes, "I can never write such a book again."[3] *John Inglesant* distills his thoughts on "the actuating force of his life--religion",[4] and formulates his religious intuitions into philosophical romance. In his later works, he continues to explore and illustrate his belief that spirituality creates the essence of personal integrity, that aesthetic religious discipline refines higher sensibilities, and that sin corrupts both personality and individual character. From about 1876 until the end of his life, he maintains the psychological *persona* of "the author of *John Inglesant*". To develop the argument of this thesis, this chapter will explore relationships between Shorthouse's intentions and his historical imagination, and through examination of his psychological *persona*, it will develop analogies between his religious philosophy and the Individuation of "John Inglesant" in England.

Shorthouse explains the form and manner of the book in the "Preface" to the 1881 edition, but he offers no insight into the origins of his desire to become an author. As a youth he had wanted "to write a book; if it was only quite a little book which nobody read".[5] At nineteen, he declares his admiration for Nathaniel Hawthorne and vows, "...if ever I write anything, I intend to make my début as one of his disciples."[6] In her contribution to *Life, Letters, and Literary Remains of J. H. Shorthouse*, Margaret Southall, his cousin, claims that Hawthorne's literary works had a permanent influence on the Birmingham author. Shorthouse, however, never credits Hawthorne in any of his letters or essays as having influenced *John Inglesant* or any of his other novels, though the Roman setting of *The Marble Faun* (1860) and its study of sin and evil suggest possible influence. Southall herself observes that Shorthouse may have outgrown his fascination with Hawthorne's studies of sin and evil as he outgrew most of his other literary enthusiasms. There are two clear exceptions. He was a lifelong devotee of Wordsworth, and when Tennyson became Poet Laureate in 1850, Shorthouse quickly "passed under [his] spell".[7] Tennyson's revival of Arthurian romance directly influenced *Sir Percival*. Combining his youthful admiration of Malory with his more mature respect for Tennyson, Shorthouse derives both the plot and central theme of *Sir Percival* from *Morte d'Arthur* and *Idylls of the King*. Shorthouse, in fact, spent many years reading voraciously and passing through personal interests and private fascinations to new literary and historical enthusiasms. As he collected excerpts and descriptive passages, he developed habits of mind that explain the narrative structure of *John Inglesant*. As noted in chapter one of this thesis, Shorthouse interlards the episodic and loosely joined narrative of *John Inglesant* with numerous borrowings from his antiquarian and topographical reading and from his religious and romantic literary interests. Despite the popular success of the novel, critics and reviewers do not notice the incorporated borrowings for more than two decades after Shorthouse's death.

In 1925, W. K. Fleming, the first critic to attack *John Inglesant* as "a miracle of ingenious dove-tailing...of a quantity of unacknowledged verbatim quotations from 17th-century writers", offers the public "a sufficiently imposing list" of Shorthouse's "plagiarisms":

> --for the account of Little Gidding, we have the Life of Nicholas Ferrar by his brother, John, and the 'Lives' by Peckard and by Jebb; then there are Turbervile's 'Booke of Hunting'; John Aubrey's 'Brief Lives, chiefly of Contemporaries'; Burton's 'Anatomy of Melancholy'; Antony à Wood's 'Athenæ Oxonienses,' and his 'Life'; Thomas Wright's 'Letters relating to the Suppression of the Monasteries,' in the Camden Series; 'England's Black Tribunal'; Ward's 18th-century 'Life of Henry More'; Hobbes' 'Leviathan'; Ranke's 'History of the Popes,' and the Diaries of Evelyn, of Lady Fanshawe, of Reresby, and of Ellwood.[8]

Exposing "Some Truths About *John Inglesant*", Fleming offers direct comparisons of Shorthouse's sources and asserts his discoveries prove the need for a new edition. "Appreciative and critical editing", he urges, will add "greatly to the worth of the book as the representation of the atmosphere of thought and the play of events in the 17th century."[9] Although Fleming demonstrates that Shorthouse modernizes spelling and changes specific words and punctuation to suit his own purposes, he fails to uncover any patterns or techniques that explain the "habit of mind that indulged in their use". He concludes that "their use is simply baffling."[10] The use of the borrowings may baffle some readers' temperaments, but most readers of *John Inglesant*, including scholarly critics, concur with Montague Summers, who, after publishing his own discovery of Shorthouse's technique, concludes:

> I would add that personally, in spite of these excessive
> borrowings, which I recognized many years since, and in
> spite of manifest faults not a few, I shall never cease to
> regard *John Inglesant* as one of the most delightful and
> winning books I know in any literature, a romance whose
> words have a music and a charm, whose pages reveal an
> atmosphere of peace and beauty, which afford the
> sweetest and securest of retreats.[11]

Polak disagrees vehemently, and after examining Sotheby's *Catalogue of the Library of Joseph Henry Shorthouse*, he adds to Fleming's list. "Subjoin[ing] some items of the Catalogue, notably all those which contain one of the 'sources' of *John Inglesant*, and besides several others showing the peculiar range of Shorthouse's interest",[12] he, nonetheless, fails to distinguish which items are sources and which books Shorthouse found simply interesting enough to add to his library. Quibbling over Shorthouse's changing the names of real historical persons to create fictional characters (Lady Fentham for Lady Fanshawe, for instance, and Lady Conway for Lady Cardiff, Cardinal Rinuccini for Cardinal Doughi, and Sir John Harris for Sir John Harrison), Polak ignores the fact that Shorthouse's borrowings, like his inclusion of real characters among fictional ones, is "a common device of the historical novel to give verisimilitude to imagination".[13] Polak notes in his chapter on "Plagiarism" (52-71) that Fleming does not make use of Sotheby's "Catalogue of the Library of Shorthouse" and expresses the hope that Fleming will "welcome [it] as a solid support for the disclosures [he has] made" (66). Brodrick, Fleming, and Polak, however, overlook Berington's *Memoirs of Gregorio Pangani*, "of which", Shorthouse admits, "I made great use in *John Inglesant*".[14] They also ignore Hamilton's *Life of James Bonnell, late Accomptant-General of Ireland*, which was "rarely absent" from Shorthouse's bedside and of which he said, "I have used this book as a constant devotional manual for many years."[15] No publisher has yet recognized the value of Fleming's proposal for an annotated edition, nor has any publisher produced an illustrated edition with Lady Jane Lindsay's watercolours and drawings.[16] An illustrated edition might revive interest in *John Inglesant*, and an annotated study would show how Shorthouse tried to achieve his initial ambition:

> When I began the book, my principal, perhaps sole object
> was to endeavour for my own pleasure to realise, if
> possible, something of that exquisite age-spirit which
> combined all the finest feelings of our nature, and all the
> sympathies of our existence, with a certain
> picturesqueness of tone and result, which seems to me to

mark the seventeenth century.[17]

Indeed, even Polak admits "strong proof that Shorthouse achieved his ambition" and notes that when the "lifted" passages are examined individually they

> obviously have a seventeenth-century ring, but they blend splendidly with the general tone of the narrative, and are so neatly woven into Shorthouse's own exquisite nineteenth-century English as to appear native to their environment.[18]

Shorthouse himself shed some light on his narrative practice. As we know from his letters, he believed it:

> ...a very strange thing that we are able to transmit...ideas at all, and still more the affection or 'rapport', as the clairvoyance people call it, that springs up between the author and those of his readers who appreciate him, or some-times, failing that, the friendship which seems to exist, with me at least, between myself and the book itself; it seems to me as if a favourite book knew me, and knew what part in it I wanted, and opened there...[19]

Sarah Shorthouse testifies that Shorthouse did not search for a narrative form but for a plot: "I am quite ready to begin a book", he assures his wife, "only I want a plot."[20] Over two decades later, he explained to Rawdon Levett, to whom he dedicated *John Inglesant*, how he found the one incident around which he could weave his hero's story. "I am quite justified in saying", he wrote Levett in 1894, "that *John Inglesant* was written to lead up expressly to this one incident, and I do not think it would have been written if I had not chanced upon the beautiful story" of Giovanni Gualberto. From Shorthouse's point of view, the many inclusions find him or find their way from his favourite books into the narrative as though they are participating in *John Inglesant's vraisemblance*. As he writes in "The Humorous in Literature":

> ...the most delightful part of [an author's] experience is the way in which characters do grow and develop, as it seems, independently of their author. They form their own story, and pursue their own course.[21]

Thus, in quest of *vraisemblance*, Shorthouse deliberately includes scenes, paragraphs, and particular sentences, and either from cryptomnesia or "undesigned coincidence",[22] he allows them to fit themselves independently into his narrative.

The clearest exception to this compositional process is, of course, his finding the story of St. Gualberto. Shorthouse looks consciously for a plot episode, a symbolic event around which he could weave Inglesant's story; nonetheless, he does not identify the actual source of this "singular incident". Instead, as he tells Levett, he "took the story from a few lines in a very old book". Only later did he learn the story of the founder of the Order of Vallambrosa, the "Shady Valley", is "a well-known guide-book story" of the crucifix above the altar in the church at San Miniato.[23] Shorthouse may have come upon the story in Alban Butler's *The Lives of the Saints* or in Caxton's edition of *The Golden Legends*, but his statement that the story is contained in "a few lines", suggests Robert Mannynge's "Handlynge Synne", a paraphrase of a thirteenth-century French song by Robert de Brunne, as a possible source. Given Shorthouse's interest in chivalry, another probable source is Kenelm Digby's *Tancredus*, volume two of *The Broad Stone of Honour: or, the True Sense and Practice of Chivalry*. Shorthouse mentions neither of these books in his letters or essays, though he includes mention of Digby in a brief scene when Inglesant is in Paris. Father St. Clare declares Digby "mad" and "dangerous", and Inglesant comments offhandedly that he has heard of him (205). There is, however, no evidence that Shorthouse owned these particular books. The popularity of *The Broad Stone of Honour* and its role in reviving and defining chivalry in accord with Victorian and Christian perspectives of the British Empire suggest that Shorthouse might have been as fascinated by Digby's work as were his contemporaries.[24] Although Shorthouse admires the Pre-Raphaelites,[25] he gives no mention of the work of Sir Edward Coley Burne-Jones or of the 1863 watercolour, "The Merciful Knight". Born in Birmingham one year before Shorthouse, Burne-Jones had "a lifelong absorption with the chivalric world of Chaucer and Sir Thomas Malory's *Morte d'Arthur*",[26] and he painted scenes from "The Legend of St. George" in 1863, the same year he worked on "The Merciful Knight". "The Merciful Knight" poignantly and beautifully illustrates the same incident in the Italian saint's life that Shorthouse appropriates for the climax of his novel. Digby gives the story simply:

> St. John Gualbert, a Florentine noble of the eleventh century, who, in his later years, founded the great monastery of Vallambrosa, near that city, cherished a deadly vengeance against a nobleman who had murdered his only brother Hugo. It happened that riding home to Florence, on Good-Friday, he met his enemy in so narrow a passage, that it was impossible for either of them to avoid the other. John seeing the murderer, drew his sword, and was going to dispatch him; but the other alighted from his horse, fell upon his knees, and with his

arms across, besought him by the passion of Christ, who suffered on that day, to spare his life. The remembrance of Christ who prayed for murderers on the cross so overcame the young nobleman, and meekly raising the supplicant from the ground, he said, 'I can refuse nothing that is asked of me for the sake of Jesus Christ. I not only give you your life, but also my friendship for ever. Pray for me, that God may pardon the sin of my heart.[27]

Believing that "Jesus Christ was the most perfect knight, the noblest born and best-descended gentleman",[28] Shorthouse combines the spiritual and chivalric qualities of Christ with those of St. John Gualbert and St. George, England's patron saint. Chapter thirty-two of *John Inglesant* is virtually a reenactment of "The Merciful Knight". The Christ figure leans forward from the cross to kiss the Cavaliere di San Giorgio, who, dressed in splendid armour, offers his sword as a sacrifice upon the altar.

In *The Mystery of Pain*, which Shorthouse responds to in the "Preface" to *John Inglesant*, James Hinton expresses the belief that "only in the form of that which we call sacrifice can our true good be given us,"[29] and he argues that the "possibility of love is given us in our power to sacrifice".[30] Moreover, Hinton declares sacrifice to be an archetypal human condition: "Whatever else may pass or change, of this we may be sure, that till God cease to love us we shall stand face to face with sacrifice."[31] The sacrifice in *John Inglesant* is not, ultimately, the hero's forgiveness of his enemy nor his surrendering his sword upon the altar in a wayside chapel. Although the scene is central to the plot and serves to consummate the spiritual meaning of the novel, the climactic incident prefigures and prepares for the philosophical climax of the last chapter. The dialectic of the novel permeates the plot and leads to Shorthouse's concluding declaration about truth, human reason, and the necessity "not for a larger intellectual view, but for faith; for that which is the common and inevitable basis of all religion."[32]

Of course, a writer who defines his composition as a romance need not present a step-by-step reasoned analysis of his hero's religious conversion and certainly need not self-analyze his own faith. Yet, as the elderly Inglesant "spoke more to himself" (445) than to Valentine Lee, the curious recorder of Inglesant's last words, so the narrative addresses a general, rather ecumenical audience who want to follow "the laws which our instinct and conscience tell us are Divine" (444). The final message has obvious appeal to readers who share Shorthouse's quest for unity among Christian churches; it has special appeal for readers who share his particular social temperament and/or his psychological typology. Yet, it must be remembered, Shorthouse wrote *John Inglesant* for his personal satisfaction and for his wife's amusement. If anything in the novel suggests that

Shorthouse imagined or hoped for a wider audience, it is his balancing of Inglesant's romantic adventure and philosophical quest as "an allegory of his own spirit" (176). His representation of Quakers in both the English and in the Italian sections of the novel suggests he was writing with his family and religious Friends in mind. Among the Quakers at Oulton, after his brother's death, Inglesant discovers that "the mystical doctrine which he had studied [under the Jesuit's direction] was not unlike much that he would hear from Quaker lips" (183). Likewise, the episodes in Paris, especially those involving the Benedictine, Serenus de Cressy (197-204), and the scenes in Italy involving Miguel de Molinos, the Quietist (269ff.), ground Inglesant's spiritual struggle in "contemplative devotion" (269) and continual remembrance of the "stillness and peace unspeakable" (59) of the Sacrament at Little Gidding. If Shorthouse's Quaker family and friends wondered at his conversion or transition from the Society of Friends to the Anglican Communion, he did not keep them guessing. As the Roman Catholic mass and its "sense of pathetic pleading and of mysterious awe" had failed to convince Geoffrey Monk "that there was more under that gorgeous ceremonial than may be found under the simpler Anglican ritual of the Blessed Sacrament" (4), so the aesthetic glories of Catholic churches that Inglesant enjoys throughout Italy do not alter the simpler form of faith he experiences in the quiet days at Oulton. Convalescing after his release from the Tower among the Quakers at his sister-in-law's estate, Inglesant "began to adapt himself to a course of religious life from which he never altogether departed...to the end of his life" (185). Shorthouse, recovering from a childhood illness at his grandmother's home at Moseley, adapted himself to quiet, interior devotion which his later love of ritual never disturbed. About "the religion of *John Inglesant*", however, much needs to be considered before the novel can be more formally examined from a Jungian perspective.

Shorthouse modelled Father St. Clare on Christopher Davenport (1598-1680), an Englishman who became a Catholic while living on the Continent. Davenport joined the Franciscans in 1617, took the name of Franciscus a Sancta Clara, and returned to England, where

> For more than fifty years, he labored incessantly to promote the papal cause, by gaining many disciples, raising money among the English Catholics to carry on public matters beyond the seas, in travelling from one country to another,...During the civil wars of Cromwell's time, he disappeared from public life, ... [though he was] sometimes in London, at times in the country, and then at Oxford...He became theologist or chief chaplain [to Charles II's Portuguese queen, Catharine]. He was four times chosen provincial Minister of his order for the

province of England, and was accounted its greatest
pillar, and the person most to be consulted in their
affairs.[33]

The author of *God, Nature and Grace* and *A Periphrastic Exposition of the
rest of the Articles of the Anglican Confession* (1634), Fr. Davenport
laboured to reunite Christendom by interpreting the Church of England's
"Thirty-nine Articles" as compatible with doctrines of Rome. Davenport's
Exposition has been described as "more ingenious than convincing",[34] and
certainly the same may be said of *John Inglesant*, especially by Catholic
readers. Much of the confusion and controversy about the religion of John
Inglesant concerns Inglesant's personal loyalties and the credibility of Fr. St.
Clare. Shorthouse conceives Fr. St. Clare as

a man of the world, and not a mere tool of his Order. He
sacrifices Johnny to his purpose, as he would have
sacrificed his own life, but in return he trains his pupil to
a broad perception of life and men, which developed, step
by step, into a perfect toleration of and indifference to all
creeds and opinions, as alike the outcome of a central
light, which, to his own satisfaction at least, was
sufficient to illuminate the dark puzzles of his life.[35]

"Whether such a Jesuit is true to nature or not", Shorthouse continues, "is
another question", a question that did not excite him to further clarification
or to historical investigation. The Jesuit serves Shorthouse's philosophical
and narrative purpose; he trains Inglesant to religious and political
indifference. Inglesant could be "loyal to apparently opposite interests...to
the Jesuitical Order and to the cause of *religious freedom*", because he was
"loyal to an *idea*". Shorthouse explains:

I do not think he can be said to have been loyal even to
the Jesuit--it was the idea of devotion with which the
Jesuit had inspired him. Much less could he be said to be
loyal to the King...He was not loyal even to his lady-love,
for he deserted her at the call of the dominating instinct.[36]

The dominating instinct, Shorthouse confesses, "is not very easy to put into
a few words":

He had been taught to prefer ideas to men, to believe that
all men were actuated more or less by good and noble
ideas; that the noblest of such ideas was self-sacrifice and
obedience; that therefore, whatever came, he supposed
self-devotion and obedience were most becoming...His
instinct reminds us a little of Socrates' demon--'a kind of
voice which from childhood always diverts me from what

117

I am about to do, *but never urges me on*.[37]

To critics who argued that he had given "no clue to John Inglesant's extreme nobleness of character", Shorthouse responds:

> ...the clue to John Inglesant's life was evident on every
> page of the book--his devotion to the "*ideal of Christ*"...
> [which] is entirely independent of all particular dogma".[38]

Inglesant's "dominating instinct" expresses Shorthouse's own spiritual motive and his capacity to maintain inner conviction of Quaker truth while outwardly preferring High Church ceremonial. To Shorthouse, "the *idea* is the *reality*",[39] and the "idea of Christ" symbolizes "the forces that *are* Christ, not *were*".[40] In his reasoning, religious thinkers often confuse factual or material realities, which are "nothing but...outward garb and voice, which may vary according to need and circumstance", with the true life of the Church, sacramentalism. Devotion to the Holy Sacrament is the clearest and most certain of John Inglesant's ideals.

While "Johnny" was a teenager at Westacre, Fr. St. Clare "took pains to prevent his becoming attached to Popery" (33); when "John" became "actively and enthusiastically [interested in becoming] a Papist" (63), the Jesuit took him to Thomas Hobbes. Hobbes argues that Inglesant's "idea of the Catholic system is a dream, and has no real existence among the Papists" (65). While he is imprisoned in the Tower awaiting execution, Inglesant asks for "a Priest, either of the Roman Catholic or the English Church, he [is] indifferent which" (158). Later, when Inglesant is in Paris, Monk interjects:

> It would appear that about this time he must have been
> formally received into the Romish Church, for he
> confessed and received the sacrament at low mass; but no
> mention of the ceremony occurs, and it is possible that the
> priests received instructions respecting him, while there is
> clear proof that he attended the services at the
> Ambassador's [Sir Richard Browne's Anglican] Chapel
> (192).

While Inglesant is still in Paris, the Jesuit arrives, and the confusion continues. Fr. St. Clare concedes his work in England has been a failure and assures his pupil, "I do not wish to influence you any more, nor to involve you any longer in any schemes of mine" (205). After offering this seeming release, the Jesuit quickly urges him to go to Rome as an accredited agent of Queen Henrietta Maria. The Queen wishes Inglesant to become a Catholic, but the Jesuit knows that Inglesant will be "a more useful agent" if he does not formally "take orders, as a priest" (206). Inglesant arrives in Rome "recommended to the Jesuits' College, almost an accredited agent" (261), yet he tells Count Vespiriani, a supporter of Molinos, that, because he believes in "the freedom of the Blessed Sacrament", he has "always been attracted to the Protestant Episcopal Church of England" (273). As Inglesant asserts, "too much freedom" has "utterly ruined and laid waste" England, the narrative voice defines "the greatest of all problems, that of granting religious freedom, and at the same time maintaining religious truth" (276). Had Inglesant become a Roman Catholic? Not "properly speaking", according to Shorthouse himself; John Inglesant "never consciously went over to Rome at all."[41] Did he *unconsciously* "go over to Rome"? The "religion of *John Inglesant*" teaches, in the words of Fr. St. Clare,

> that all creeds and opinions are nothing but the mere
> result of chance and temperament; that no party is on the
> whole better than another; that no creed does more than
> shadow imperfectly forth some one side of truth (74).

Change "chance and temperament" to "psychological typology", and the view accords with Jung's. "What we call culture, national politics and religious and social movements are created", in Jungian perspective, "by the psyche and a particular typology that expresses itself through the members of each particular social, ethnic or religious collective."[42] Shorthouse's rector of the Jesuit College in Rome agrees:

> ...things are true to each of us according as we see them;
> they are, in fact, but shadows and likenesses of the
> absolute truth that reveals itself to men in different ways,
> but always imperfectly and as in a glass (264).

In *John Inglesant* the "shadows and likenesses" provide "opportunities of mental study of absorbing interest" (294), and, although various characters define the imperfect ways to truth, Inglesant often repeats the views of Thomas Hobbes. As Hobbes observes, "One disputant grounds his knowledge upon the infallibility of the Church, and the other on the testimony of the private spirit" (68). With the Jesuit rector, Inglesant urges another view, one he attributes to "our service in England", namely, that all men "are branded with the mark which He puts upon His sheep--the innate knowledge of God in the soul" (264). Later, conversing with Cardinal Rinuccini and his dinner guests, Inglesant notes that Thomas Hobbes has given the world a third authority: "We had first the authority of a Church, then of a book, now Mr. Hobbes asserts the authority of reason..." (292). Confessing that what Hobbes teaches "would require more skill than I possess to explain", Inglesant observes that

> ...it proves the acuteness of the Anglican divines that they
> have detected, under the plausible reasoning of Mr.

Hobbes, the basis of a logical argument which would, if unconfuted, destroy the authority of Holy Scripture (292).

The narrator notes that "the subject did not seem to possess great interest to the company at table", and the argument is dropped for over a hundred pages. Shorthouse, to his credit, avoids dogmatic assertion of "the religion of *John Inglesant*" by keeping its tenets and practices amongst the "shadows and likenesses", which, admittedly, makes his Anglo-Catholicism rather ambiguous.

In defining his technique of narration in the 1881 "Preface" as "an attempt, and an honest one, to blend together these three in one philosophy-- the memory of the dead--the life of thought--the life of each one of us alone", Shorthouse acknowledges his aim to capture "the religious and social tone of the seventeenth century" (7), not to adhere to historical details. Yet, as Mary Drew knew, even Lord Acton, "the greatest historical authority of his day", devoted several pages of a letter to criticizing Shorthouse's historical inaccuracies, because he felt the "veil of mirage" created by the novel's romantic qualities. In her words, "The very name [of John Inglesant] has something of that virility and melody that make his story never less than magical", and because Shorthouse wrote it "for himself, into it he put himself...he fused it with the electric fires of his own spiritual--So thus [sic] at last, it emerged, with all this intensity of personal experience to enrichen and *ensoul it*."[43] Because his "interest in the period was not that of the historian, to show the century as it really was, nor of the realist, to portray the external likenesses beneath changed exteriors",[44] he did not write a historical novel but recreated the seventeenth century through his historical imagination as a setting for his religious philosophy. He did not write, as Landis notes, "to present a picture of the seventeenth century, but to propound a religious philosophy of the nineteenth by means of a seventeenth century story."[45] Because Shorthouse's personality was that of an introverted feeling type with strong secondary intuition, he should have had considerable difficulty had he tried to present a historically accurate picture of the seventeenth century. *John Inglesant*, in Elton's judgment, "stands aloof from the historical and religious novels of its time",[46] because it does not attend to external details, as, for instance, *Lorna Doone* does. In *Lorna Doone* the details are "of a material and external nature; whereas in *John Inglesant* they [are] spiritual and internal".[47] Shorthouse demonstrates ability to handle the problems of historical fiction in various scenes, notably in the Oxford episode in chapter nine and in the Chester episode in chapter twelve. In Landis's judgment, Shorthouse did not "possess the requisite knowledge" of historical details,[48] but, as Jungian critics argue, such extroverted, sensate knowledge has little meaning for introverted, feeling types. The nature of Shorthouse's fiction becomes more distinctive when compared with the work of a few of his contemporaries.

Although Shorthouse never acknowledged a specific debt to Scott, he owned a complete set of first editions of Scott's novels,[49] and *John Inglesant* follows a narrative pattern that posed artistic problems familiar to readers of Scott. Because Scott "present[ed] great crises of historical life in his novels" and depicted "hostile social forces, bent on one another's destruction", he risked the narrative danger of presenting "warring forces... [as] a merely external picture of mutual destruction incapable of arousing the human sympathies and enthusiasms of the reader."[50] As Scott had frequently done, Shorthouse presents his hero's character and fortune so that he belongs to what Lukács has called "a 'middle course' asserting itself through the struggle of extremes".[51] Unlike Scott, Shorthouse chose no "mediocre, prosaic hero",[52] like Waverley or Colonel Everard of Scott's *Woodstock*, who shared Inglesant's Civil War/Restoration time period, nor did he chose an adventurous model like Amyas Leigh of Kingsley's *Westward Ho!* Instead, he modeled John Inglesant on his ideal of Christ, chivalrous gentleman and knight, and attempted to create a fictional "world-historical individual" in contrast to a "maintaining individual". As Lukács explains, the true world-historical figure belongs more properly to drama and becomes, at best, only a minor character in a novel, which is true of Cromwell in *Woodstock* and King Charles I in *John Inglesant*. After reading *John Inglesant*, however, one wishes that the hero had actually been real, because his lifetime excites the reader's imagination with what seem to be "quintessential moments of historically authentic"[53] characters and events. Thoroughly idealized, however, Inglesant is an historically incredible "maintaining individual". Even the most dramatic episodes of his story do little more than intensify the "show and tell" of the before and after of the historical events in the novel, and, at best, Shorthouse depicts the popular life and character in England and Italy through the eyes of a narrator who only catalogues what Inglesant saw and felt. The catalogue descriptions of London and Rome are picturesque and inviting beyond "local colour", and, in combination with the novel's musicality and discussions of music, they leave the sphere of historical fiction and become, as Shorthouse intended, romance in which historical authenticity is not as artistically important as psychological realism and idealism.

What Lukács neglects, however, are precisely the psychological and romantic aspects of the historical process upon and within the hero. Acknowledging the importance of the authenticity of historical details in the novel as "the sensuous mediator of this specific quality, this peculiar process", he accepts the process as "historical necessity [which] asserts itself at a particular time, in a particular place and within certain class relations, etc."[54] His concern is with the historical spirit of "bourgeois literature", and he virtually ignores psychological theory which interprets literary genre and forms as conscious metaphors of human nature and as symbols of unconscious human experience. When Mary Gladstone Drew states, for instance, that "For a book to live, it must possess some quality that is independent of times and seasons, of fashions, of atmosphere", she is responding to a specific form of historical necessity, one of the particular perspectives of literary criticism that emerged during her lifetime. More importantly, her argument expresses the historical vitality of an approach to literary criticism that draws its definitions of necessity from human nature itself. "What is", she asks, "the quality which makes Shakespeare, Scott, Dante, and Cervantes immortal?" Her answer represents the historical understanding of her time, a convention of popular criticism:

> It is reality. It is that which appeals to human nature which is common to us all, that touches our personal experience, that deals with the eternal verities, the things that lie deepest in man.[55]

What she means by "reality" and "the eternal verities" is subject, of course, to the kind of critical and historical interpretations Lukács and Jung offer. Lukács concerns himself with social realism and with the time-bound limitations of literary forms that an author expresses "at a particular time, in a particular place and within certain class relations, etc." Yet, as Sanders concludes, Lukács's social realism "blinds him to the real diversity of Victorian historical fiction, and, moreover, to the advances...breaking away from the well-explored confines of social realism."[56] Jungian critics would relate Mary Drew's belief in the "eternal verities" to psychological typology and projection and to archetypal theory. If the truths she admires could be traced to her personal psychology, the truths would cease to be "eternal" because they would not belong to her personal unconscious, not to the realm of the Collective Unconscious. The rhetoric of Gladstone's daughter does, however, represent a collective, a social-psychological one. She expresses the ethnocentric, limited perspective of Victorian England, which Shorthouse echoes in Constance Lisle, the narrator of *Sir Percival*. Constance believes that the "beneficent march of civilisation" owes its great victories to the "glorious English race" and their innate, "supreme gift--of leadership" (15-16). A Jungian approach to the expressions of Mary Drew or Constance Lisle would necessarily limit itself to study of the psychodynamics under and behind their thinking, and in its own analogous terms, would respect the sense of historical necessity inherent in Lukács's social realism. The social context that Shorthouse creates within *John Inglesant* is nationalistic primarily in terms of its religious views. The novel does not show or argue any "flag waving" or patriotic nationalism, yet it does argue that the Church of England is a product of native English character, and, with few exceptions, the novel depicts Italians as "of the nature of children--children who are naughty one moment and sincerely penitent the next" (264), controlled by "two passions--jealousy and revenge" (227), and children controlled by a distinctive "Italian devil". Indeed, Shorthouse's narrator asserts "no man can doubt" that "the character of the inhabitants of any country has much to do in forming a distinct devil for that country" (327). He quickly informs the reader that neither Malvolti nor the despicably immoral Cavaliere di Guardino is the Italian devil. "Born of the fleshly lusts of the people", the Italian devil has no power to tempt Inglesant or others of "higher natures". Nowhere in his writings, however, does he equate "higher natures" with the English. Quite to the contrary: if the Italians support a system of religious politics and are subjected to the power struggles of the Papal Curia, the English, as Hobbes argues, contrive their civil government to embody "the vicar of Christ" (64), and under Cromwell they behead their king, leaving their country "in the hands of butchers and brewers" (164), an act presumably of the collective "English devil". If Shorthouse himself experienced an English devil, the devil appears in the development of his religious views and expresses what Jung calls a psychological complex in the personal unconscious. Shorthouse's personal views will be outlined briefly here, and an analysis of them as a psychological complex will be presented in the next chapter.

While still a young Quaker, Shorthouse began to find the "idea of an historic and national church peculiarly attractive to him",[57] and after formal baptism into the Church, he accepts and advocates the legal authority of the Church of England. He rejects "primitive Quakerism" as a "dead sect" and tells a Quaker lady who is distressed by his decision to join the Church of England that even the "most important truth" of the Friends, "the indwelling of the Divine Word" is but "a portion of the *whole* [sic] glorious system, the whole of which is to be found in the Church of England."[58] Within the Church he finds the freedom and the "free thinking" he needs. Believing that "Everything may be a sacrament to the pure in heart", he publishes "The Agnostic at Church" in *Nineteenth Century* (1882) and urges that in the Church of England, "an Agnostic should certainly offer himself as a communicant".[59] From the time he wrote the final chapter of *John Inglesant*, however, he projects genuine animosity upon the Church of Rome and champions the "wonderful Church of England" as "the only fruit of Christianity (so far as thought is concerned) of any vitality or standing in practical existence".[60] In private letters he describes the Church of Rome as "hopelessly narrow and sectarian"[61] and as "that fairyland (I will not say fools' paradise) in which modern Catholics live",[62] and he contributes the preface to *The Message and Position of the Church of England* damming the Papal Curia:

The Papal Curia is founded upon falsehood, and falsehood enters, consciously or unconsciously, willingly or unwillingly, into the soul of every human creature that comes under its influence. It has poisoned the wells of religious life. Its story is one of horror, and of crime, and of cruelty. As I have said elsewhere, it always has been, and is now, the enemy of the Human Race.[63]

Shorthouse wrote "the enemy of the human race" (without the capital letters) as least twenty-three years earlier as part of Inglesant's final judgment "between the Churches" (442). Indeed, it is not easy to reconcile or explain the difference between Inglesant's departing comments to the rector of the Jesuit College in Rome ("I shall go away with nothing but sadness and affection in my heart; with nothing but gratitude towards you, Father, with nothing but reverence towards this city—the mother of the World.") and Shorthouse's personal animosity against Rome. In the novel, the final scene serves its philosophical purpose, as in Shorthouse's personal life, his animosity towards "the Romish system", serves his personal psychological needs. Both are examined in greater detail in the next chapter.

Shorthouse intended all his characters to introduce philosophical purposes, not to be "mere representatives of life",[64] though his characters generally embody religious satire as much as they represent philosophical points of view. Because Inglesant is virtually the only questing character in the novel, the epistemological challenge Hobbes offers him also serves the reader as the criterium of religious perspective. "...how do you know that your private spirit, that his divine life within you, is other than a belief grounded on the authority and arguments of your teachers?" (68) troubles Inglesant to the last page, and the question helps Shorthouse balance his satire. Mr. Thorne's puritanical "perpetual struggle ...between his real nature and the system of religion which he had adopted" (80) is opposed by Cardinal Rinuccini. Handsome as a "pagan god", the Cardinal is "content to live from day to day...sweetening life" as he can "with some pleasing toys here and there, to relish it" (254). Content that he "did not make the world" and is "not responsible for its state" (254), his "philosophical paganism" embraces "life as a spectacle, 'in theatro ludus'" (255) and indulges Inglesant's love of art, music, and entertainment. Through his influence, Inglesant sees the world and his own role as political-religious "agent" with necessary detachment, which Shorthouse defines as "the true field of humour" (285). Intellectual concern with the "infinite distance between ...the aspirations and the exhortations of conscience...and the actual circumstances and capacities of the individual" (284) defines Shorthouse's understanding of humour, which is compatible with his psychological typology, and the tone he tries to achieve in *John Inglesant*. He had, as he realised, "to leave out a great deal of detail which, being absolutely *real*" would have diminished both his philosophical intent and "that exquisite age-spirit which combined all the finest feelings of our nature, and all the sympathies of our existence, with a certain picturesqueness of tone".[65] Attempting to recreate "real life and philosophy with sufficient *vraisemblance*", he could, like other successors of Scott, represent the reality of the past "as if it were an act of personal memory". As Sanders observes, to artists after Scott, "history was contemporary, synchronic and enveloping; it was living and vibrating in the present".[66] However, Sanders recognizes that Shorthouse "remained unconscious of, and oblivious to, most contemporary developments in the novel".[67] In the "Preface", Shorthouse expresses minimal concern with the artistic work of his contemporaries, and confines himself to defining the philosophical intent of his work and to defending the power of romance. That he did not change the novel's subtitle in later editions suggests he was content to advertise the novel as "a romance".

As Shorthouse explains in the preface, he realises *John Inglesant: A Romance* is "a somewhat hazardous venture...an attempt at a species of literature which I think has not hitherto had justice done to it" (vii). Although he had never deliberately sought a reading audience, he recognized the popularity of romances and realised that his novel would reach a wider audience if the public thought of it as a romance. Feeling "the responsibility of introducing real historical characters and orders of men" into his work, he offers a "general defence": "I have written nothing which I should not equally have set down in an historical or a controversial work" (x). What the preface fails to confess, however, is that Shorthouse loathed controversy, especially in public, as unbecoming to a gentleman. It is difficult to imagine he did not realise the controversial nature of his work, though none of his correspondence with the Macmillans concerns the title or the controversy the book occasioned. Somewhat ironically, the complete title declares historical intentions yet omits both philosophy and romance, and it seems merely to append Inglesant's "religious doubts and experiences":

Memoirs of the Life
OF
MR. JOHN INGLESANT
SOMETIME SERVANT TO KING CHARLES I
WITH
AN ACCOUNT OF HIS BIRTH, EDUCATION, AND TRAINING BY
THE JESUITS
AND
A PARTICULAR RELATION OF THE SECRET SERVICES
IN WHICH HE WAS ENGAGED

ESPECIALLY IN CONNECTION WITH THE LATE
IRISH REBELLION
WITH
SEVERAL OTHER REMARKABLE PASSAGES AND OCCURRENCES,
ALSO,
A HISTORY OF HIS RELIGIOUS DOUBTS AND EXPERIENCES
AND OF THE MOLINISTS OR QUIETISTS IN ITALY
IN WHICH COUNTRY HE RESIDED FOR MANY YEARS
WITH AN ACCOUNT OF
THE ELECTION OF THE LATE POPE
AND
MANY OTHER EVENTS AND AFFAIRS

(The complete title adequately outlines the plot; for a summary, please send endnote.[69]) To organize memoir, account, particular relation, remarkable passages, and history, Shorthouse relies on a conventional narrative frame. The framework enables him to avoid what Lukács called the "central problem on which minds divided in Scott's time": the "false inheritance" of earlier historical novels that modernize the psychology of characters though they try to keep "genuine historical psychology" intact.[70] Geoffrey Monk, an Oxford student, writing presumably in the mid-Victorian period, offers a personal "Introductory Chapter" to explain his finding "a considerable collection of papers" in the basement library of a Roman Catholic family who live in Shropshire near the Welsh border. Presenting the Inglesant papers as a compilation, of course, enables Shorthouse to incorporate seventeenth-century sources, as it helps readers imagine the narrative is faithful to the psychology and prose rhythms appropriate to his story. The narrative ends with a letter purporting to be from Valentine Lee, a chirurgeon of Reading to Anthony Paschall, a physician in London. The letter is the only document from the "compilation of papers" with a specific attribution. The spelling has been "modernized throughout", evidently to make Victorian readers feel the break in the historical imagination, and, thus, feel more directly the impact of the argument. The narrative break, like the twenty-year lapse in Inglesant's personal history, enables Shorthouse to speak more immediately in his own voice than he is able to through his fictional narrator. Indeed, the inclusion of the letter with its passionate declaration of the hero's philosophical conclusions and religious convictions allows Shorthouse to proclaim "the religion of John Inglesant" as his own.

In Geoffrey Monk's "Introductory Chapter", Shorthouse uses another Victorian convention, portraiture, to excite antiquarian interest and establish Gothic tone. Portraiture frames the plot in imagery, and references to music and musical analogies provide an underlying, sensual harmony of theme. A portrait of the young John Inglesant "with a tonsured head...in a

126

very simple monk's dress" (2)[70] captivates Monk's interest. In the final chapter, the elderly Inglesant performs "a descant upon a ground bass in the Italian manner" that gives Lee "thoughts [he] had long sought and seemed ever and anon on the point of realizing" (439). Together, Inglesant's music and Lee's latent thoughts conjure the reader's imagination, and Shorthouse evokes a powerful mental portrait of elderly Anglican hero outside Worcester Cathedral after the Restoration. As the music gathers up and brings together all the "dying falls and closes", creates joy, transforms joy into sorrow, and transfigures sorrow into peace, so the philosophical themes and psychological energies of the plot converge and merge into the archetypal image of the wise old man ready to summarize his life's experience. Drummond's analysis of the scene neglects Shorthouse's gathering and building dramatic energy into a romantic, symbolic image, yet Drummond offers interpretive insight that encapsulates the religious philosophy in historical perspective. He sees the ending as a carefully prefigured presentation of "the necessity of intuitive religion as a preservative against dead traditionalism, to offer a dynamic 'walking by the spirit' against both the 'propagandist machine' (Romanism) and the narrow, insular formalism so typical of the Oxford Movement."[71] Monk's interest in the portrait of young Inglesant excites his historical curiosity, especially when he sees the contrasting, formal portrait of John's twin, Eustace.

Victorian readers of romances were, of course, accustomed to expect stories to follow when characters in novels look at portraits, and modern readers can only wonder how Shorthouse himself responded to the eighth chapter of *Woodstock*. Scott uses a Vandyke painting of Charles I to provoke Cromwell into an outburst, a "spontaneous unburdening of his own bosom". "As if pleading in his own defence before some tribunal", Scott's Cromwell praises the Vandyke:

> ...what a power he has! Steel may mutilate, warriors may waste and destroy--still the King stands uninjured by time; and our grandchildren, while they read his history, may look on his image, and compare the melancholy features with the woful tale.[72]

Pondering the contrasting portraits, Monk turns inward, and, as he ruminates on the Catholic and Anglican services he has attended at Monk's Lydiard, the mystery of the wild look in the "monkish" John Inglesant's eyes and in the "greater strength and resolve" of his portrait prompts him to tell Inglesant's story. In the final chapter, of course, the reader wonders why Shorthouse has dropped Monk as narrator and replaced him with Valentine Lee. As he frames the novel with youthful and elderly portraits of his hero, Shorthouse also frames the novel with Anglican and Catholic narrators whose interests are romance and philosophy. Monk is an Anglican, cautious of the appeal of the Roman liturgy; Lee, a Catholic, sees the Church of England as a "compromise" and provokes Inglesant with a personal assertion: "...the Church of Rome never falters in its utterance, and I confess seems to me to have a logical position" (443). Monk's fascination with the romance of Inglesant's history and Lee's curiosity about the philosophical conclusions of Inglesant's religious mind complement the novel's theme and form.

Typically, Shorthouse suggests that "very singular" stories are attached to portraits, and he develops plot incidents and thematic implications to excite his reader's interest in the relationship between the past and the present. He draws upon the visible world of art objects to draw forth the invisible world of spirit, to enspiritualise daily life with divine meaning. His technique is more subtle than Eliot's deliberately drawing Becket's assassins into twentieth-century England in *Murder in the Cathedral*, and it is more nebulous than Eliot's defining of time parallels in *The Family Reunion* and *The Cocktail Party*. Eliot makes it clear that the past directly impinges upon the present and that the implications of the past may be intuited as meaning in the present. In Eliot's dramas the past and present cohere, and his characters only understand the meaning of their present experiences when they recognize that the past is "living and vibrating in the present". Such awareness in Eliot's plays can only be "hinted at / In myths and images" and, because the world of the past "does not take the place of this one",[73] Eliot's theatre audience and play readers can experience the present and understand its meaning only in historical perspective, not, however, through imagination. As "Some presage of an act / Which our eyes are compelled to witness, has forced" the chorus of Canterbury women "Towards the cathedral",[74] the Eumenides "spy" on Lord Harry, follow him into the drawing room, and force him, and eventually his family, to realise that the past has "been preparing always" for the meaning and action of the present.[75] Thus, too, Edward realises in *The Cocktail Party* that his life "was determined long ago"[76], and when Celia chooses to live in accord with the determining forces of her life, Alex, Julia, and Dr. Reilly invoke "the Guardians" to "Watch over her" and to "Protect her from the Voices [and] Visions" of "the phantasmal world / Of imagination, shuffling memories and desires."[77] In Inglesant's world, the "thousand fancies and feelings which have no adequate cause among outward things" (41) serve as intuitive intimations "to prove the reality", not of imagination, but "of our obedience to the voice of the Church" (417).

Based on the early essay "My Fever" (1857) and the story "A Midsummer Night's Dream" (1857-60?), it is probable that Shorthouse uses the convention of portraiture to express his own voice through fictional characters. "My Fever" and "A Midsummer Night's Dream" are autobiographical fantasies, and the fact that Charles I figures in the story and in two novels, *John Inglesant* and *Sir Percival*, suggests Gosse and Shorthouse's other "saucy friends" had good reason for calling him "the Marquis" and mildly chiding his "love of beautiful apparel".[78] Afflicted, as King Charles was, with a lifelong stammer, Shorthouse compensates for his inability to articulate his thoughts clearly and elegantly through meticulous attention to personal apparel and through the eloquence of his writings. He labours to perfect elegant, metaphoric descriptions of the natural world, because, as Inglesant's first schoolmaster teaches: "Faded flowers have something, to me, miraculous and supernatural about them" (41). Like Dr. More, the Quaker, Shorthouse thought himself *Incola coeli in terrâ* and found the "effect of nature upon my soul...inexpressibly ravishing, and beyond what I can convey to you" (188).

Shorthouse discovers refined emotions and expresses exquisite moments of psychological and spiritual insight as though he finds the divine essence of human character in artists' portraits, personal letters, the costumes of masques, and especially in the spiritual powers of music. In the most poetic passages of his writings, Shorthouse draws analogies between music and spirituality to urge his readers to under-stand and extend their spirituality. He wrote one of his most musical passages in *John Inglesant* while attending a service in Wells Cathedral:[79]

> Streaks of light, transfigured through the coloured prism
> of the prophets and martyrs that stood in the painted
> glass, lighted up the wreaths of smoke, and coloured the
> marbles and frescoes of the walls and altars. The mystic
> glimmer of the sacred tapers in the shaded chapels, and
> the concluding strains of the chanting before the side
> altars...filled the Church with half light and half shadow,
> half silence and half sound...The low, melancholy
> miserere--half entreating, half desponding--spoke to the
> heart of man a language like its own; and as the theme
> was taken up by one of the organs, the builder's art and
> the musician's melted into one--in tier after tier of carved
> imagery, wave after wave of mystic sound. All conscious
> thought and striving seemed to fade from the heart, and
> before the altar and amid the swell of sound the soul lost
> itself, and lay silent and passive on the Eternal Love.
> (389)

Visual contrasts between worldly and divine knowledge and the paralleling of the past with the historic present begin early in the novel when the priest takes Monk into the drawing room to see a portrait of John Inglesant's twin brother, Eustace:

...a magnificent picture...representing a singularly handsome young man, in a gorgeous satin court dress of the reign of Charles the First, [with] long hair and a profusion of lace and ornament...softened by the peculiar genius of Vandyke...[into] a combination of splendour and pathos. (3)

The artist of John's portrait had also combined the elements of his subject to indicate, not splendour and pathos, but "a slightly wild and abstracted look, indicating either religious enthusiasm, or perhaps unsettlement of the reason within" (4). The priest offers no interpretation of either picture but confirms that John Inglesant had established a "hospital for lunatics", a detail that is otherwise ignored throughout the novel. Through the contrasting portraits and Monk's reflections on music, the Anglo-Catholic tensions begin.

When Monk attends High Mass at the chapel, "exquisite, plaintive music" confirms "the sense of pathetic pleading and of mysterious awe, as if of the *possibility of a Divine Presence*", and, although the Mass produces on him "the same effect it does on most educated Churchmen", it fails to convince him "that there [is] more under that gorgeous ceremonial than may be found under the simpler Anglican ritual of the Blessed Sacrament" (4). Music complements the visual contrast between the portraits of the twin brothers as the "gorgeous ceremonial" of the High Mass competes with the "simpler Anglican ritual" and "the Sunday stillness" that Monk experiences when he visits Inglesant's tomb. Although Shorthouse played no musical instrument, he represents music as the agency of psychological and spiritual unity and extols repeatedly "the power that music has over the passions of men" (240). Having dedicated *John Inglesant* to his friend Rawdon Levett, Shorthouse included a tribute to friendship in chapter twenty-two by introducing "The Vielle-Player's Story" as proof of the power of music to resolve spiritual and intellectual dilemmas. After forty days of confinement in a pest-house during a plague in Italy, Inglesant is confined for another forty days. The details of the plague and Inglesant's confusion during his first confinement echo numerous Old Testament parallels: the forty days and nights Moses spent "in the mount of God" (Exodus 24:13) and the forty days of Noah's flood (Genesis 7:12), as the physical ordeal and mental temptations of his second confinement suggest New Testament analogies: the forty days and nights of Jesus' fast (Matthew 4:2) and the forty days of Jesus' temptation in the wilderness (Mark 1:13). During his second confinement, he befriends another inmate, a musician who plays a vielle and tempts him to understand its secrets. The vielle, "a curiously shaped instrument...somewhat like a child's toy, with four strings, and a kind of small wheel instead of a bow" (239) is described without apparent symbolism, though the vielle and the vielle player's story allegorise

Inglesant's condition and suggest a psychological interpretation, a resolution of his spiritual and intellectual dilemma.

Explaining the vielle as "this poor little friend of mine, who will speak to me though to none else", the musician discourses on the philosophy of sound in terms analogous to Inglesant's need for psychological balance:

> ...the principles of harmony prevail in the dead things of the world, which we think so blockish and stupid; and what is more wonderful still, the passions of men's souls, which are so wild and untamable, are all ruled and kept in a strict measure and mean, for they are all concerned in and wrought upon by music (239-240).

Fascinated, Inglesant listens intently to "The Vielle-Player's Story", which tells how two friends, opposites in musical talent and tastes, eventually attained "perfect sympathy" with each other. While one dies in the Royalist cause at Colchester, the other realises "the consonance is complete" and dies simultaneously in Rome. England and Rome are suggestively united "as in a dream" through the allegorical story of how the "mystic haze" of music appeals to "the secret and intellectual faculties, so that the music [becomes] not only an exponent of life but a divine influence" (241). Life and freedom are gifts, therefore, to those who live in perfect sympathy with the laws of musical harmony. Shorthouse would have understood the proclamation of the chorus in Eliot's *The Family Reunion*: "There is no avoiding these things...whether in Argos or England / There are certain inflexible laws / Unalterable, in the nature of music."[80] Although he lacked musical training, Shorthouse understood music as a symbolical, spiritual force, through which "he was transported out of himself" (243).

Perhaps he unconsciously felt kinship with Kingsley, who also suffered from a stammer. If he did not directly borrow from or imitate Kingsley's *Ravenshoe* (1862), he certainly shared his contemporary's use of music as the most abstract force that complements or controls human emotion. In effect, Shorthouse's descriptions of music provide an echo to passages like the following one taken from the eighteenth chapter of *Ravenshoe*:

> The music began with a movement soft, low, melodious, beyond expression, and yet strong, firm, and regular as of a thousand armed men marching to victory. It grew into volume and power till it was irresistible, yet still harmonious and perfect. Charles understood it. It was the life of a just man growing towards perfection and honour.
>
> It wavered and fluttered, and threw itself into sparkling sprays and eddies. It leapt and laughed with joy

unutterable, yet still through all the solemn measure went on. Love had come to gladden the perfect life, and had adorned without disturbing it.

Then began discords and wild sweeping storms of sound, harsh always, but never unmelodious: fainter and fainter grew the melody, till it was almost lost. Misfortunes had come upon the just man, and he was bending under them.

No. More majestic, more grand, more solemn than ever the melody reasserted itself: and again, as though purified by a furnace, marched solemnly on with a clearness and sweetness greater than at first. The just man had emerged from his sea of troubles ennobled.

Generally, Shorthouse does not provide interpretive program notes as Kingsley does, though he does define the allegorical implications. In Sienna, for instance, when Inglesant studies violin, he recognizes:

The whole of life is recited upon the plaintive strings, and by their mysterious effect upon the brain fibres, men are brought into sympathy with life in all its forms, from the gay promise of its morning sunrise to the silence of its gloomy night (210).

Music, however, does not save the Vielle Player's life; he dies soon after he tells his life's story to Inglesant. The doctor in the pest-house realises that music alone cannot cure Inglesant of his illness, and he prescribes "philosophic treatment" (249). When Inglesant begins to explore the diverse philosophies of Rome, he discourses on music as "that [which] fostered and encouraged in Rome an easy tolerant philosophy" (281). Drawing upon his fanciful story, "A Midsummer Night's Dream", Shorthouse reiterates through Inglesant his belief in "creatures which live in sound":

As the air and fire are said to be peopled by fairy inhabitants, as the spiritual man lives in the element of faith, so I believe that there are creatures which live in sound. Every lovely fancy, every moment of delight, every thought and thrill of pleasure which music calls forth, or which, already existing, is beautified and hallowed by music, does not die. Such as these become fairy existences, spiritual creatures, shadowy but real...which live in melody, and float and throng before the sense whenever the harmony that gave and maintains their life exists again in sound. They are children of the earth...as in an allegory or morality...The pleasures and delights of past ages thus live again in sound... (280-281).

By the end of the novel, Inglesant has become famous as a lutinist and player of the violin, and as he performs in a concert in Worcester Cathedral, the narrator acknowledges:

> It seemed to me as though thoughts, which I had long sought and seemed ever and anon on the point of realizing, were at least given me, as I listened to chords of plaintive sweetness broken now and again by cruel and bitter discords--a theme into which were wrought street and tavern music and people's songs, which lively airs and catches, upon the mere pressure of the string, trembled into pathetic and melancholy cadences. In these dying falls and closes all the several parts were gathered up and brought together, yet so that what before was joy was now translated into sorrow, and the sorrowful transfigured to peace, as indeed the many shifting scenes of life vary upon the stage of men's affairs (439-440).

In Kingsley's description, music is programmatic and mirrors the hero's spiritual condition; in Shorthouse's descriptions, music is allegorical; it mirrors the hero's inner condition as it urges his mind towards self-reflection and philosophical meditation. Shorthouse, in fact, extends his fanciful philosophy of spirituality and music into all of his later novels and tales. In *A Teacher of the Violin* and in *The Countess Eve*, the main characters gain spiritual recognition of their ancestral pasts through music. To most critics, however, *John Inglesant* is Shorthouse's masterpiece, not an apprentice novel. Dalglish is almost alone in her appreciation of the "moments" in Shorthouse's complete work "when the lower and restricted self has to make way for that in the soul which is higher, and is thereby raised far above the highest ascent of the intellect". Believing that "progressive interior simplification...develops with the development of the inner life", Dalglish wonders "if the technique and pageantry of *John Inglesant* is not, after all, on a lower level than the spirituality of those later novels."[81] In *John Inglesant*, Shorthouse's musical analogies complement the hero's psychological and religious condition and serve as preludes to his culminating philosophical judgment. Astonished by Inglesant's musical performance in Worcester Cathedral, Valentine Lee realises that "In these dying falls and closes all the several parts were gathered up and brought together...as indeed the many shifting scenes of life vary upon the stage of men's affairs" (440), which prepares the reader for the gathering together of the elderly Inglesant's personal philosophy.

As musical allegories dramatise the hero's spiritual condition, visual imagery develops his psychology. As the young Shorthouse had looked up at "a sun with rays" on the canopy of his sickbed in "My Fever", so in death John Inglesant looks upward at another sun with rays on the ceiling of the chapel, and the inscription surrounding his effigy posits the heart of his philosophic dilemma. Represented in the gown of a "bachelor of civil law...with tonsured head", his effigy depicts the earthly quest and the spiritual rest of the man who sought to serve civil law in humble obedience to the divine law. After Geoffrey Monk attends service with Father Arnold, an Anglican priest and an accomplished musician, he tries to persuade the priest to write Inglesant's story. When Father Arnold declines, as Matthew Arnold had declined Shorthouse's challenge to make the "full diapason" of "sweet reasonableness...sound within the hearts of men",[82] Monk gives himself up unreservedly to the task of compiling and narrating Inglesant's story and his attention to imagery and detail is, like his creator's, quite conscious. As Shorthouse says:

> ...the *descriptions of scenery*...spring from my own feeling. I do not think that there is a waking moment of my life in which I am unconscious of my *surroundings*. I cannot *think* of my characters apart from the scenery and environment.[83]

Trusting that the antiquarian interests and Gothic tone of his narrative will excite imagination, Monk quickly prods his reader's intellect with curiosities of detail that lend themselves to psychological interpretation. It is in the "drawing-room" that Eustace Inglesant's portrait first attracts Monk's attention, in the "dining room" that John's portrait claims notice; so, too, it is the Catholic Mass that pleases his aesthetic taste, yet it is the Anglican service that supplies him with the spiritual food of the sacrament. Shorthouse plays with image and word. Geoffrey Monk, Monk's Lydiard[84], and Inglesant's portrait dressed in a monk's garb suggest word play that hints at deeper meaning: *lydia*-yard may suggest *Lydia*, home of the mythological, wealthy King Croesus, or it may suggest *lydian*, a mode of Greek music characterized as soft and feminine, like the music Monk hears in the Roman Catholic chapel. Even at the end of the novel, Inglesant plays his violin "in the Italian manner" (439) as though he were still in quest of historical continuity between the churches of Rome and England. Monk quickly extends the contrast between the portraits of John and Eustace to one between the Roman chapel and the Anglican parish church, and after he ponders the graves in the churchyard at Monk's Lydiard, he sits in the library beneath the Fisher manor house and wonders about the documents that contain Inglesant's story. While exploring the manuscripts, Monk sits in "a very curious room below the level of the ground, and in the oldest part of the house", and the library is "crammed with books, the accumulation of four hundred years". To readers of Jung, the ancestral house and its library suggest the cultural accumulation of the collective unconscious.[85] Having suggested he will explore "the possibility of a Divine Presence" in the Mass and having noted the artist's representation of John Inglesant's "unsettlement of the reason within", Monk begins the story of the twin brothers with the "sins of their father" upon them.

Born in 1622[86] the younger twin of his father's namesake, John Inglesant inherits the burden of his father's religious deception and must atone for the crimes committed by both his father and his grandfather. When Richard Inglesant, John's grandfather, was charged with securing the submission of Westacre Priory to Henry VIII in 1537, he was frightened by the commission and threatened "with unknown penalties and terrors which he dare not face" (10-11). Had he known how to interpret his dreams, he might have foreseen that his confrontation with the Prior would have consequences in the lives of his children. A mysterious priest who practised alchemy and was "said to be in possession of the Elixir of Life" (11), the Prior responds to the King in his Sunday sermon. A small, quiet man, the Prior begins his homily with a Latin text, *Omnes qui relinquunt patrem, domos, uxorem*, then stuns Inglesant and his congregation with a defiant response and a personal transfiguration:

> ...suddenly throwing aside all reserve, and with a rapidity of utterance and a torrent of eloquence that carried his hearers with him, he rushed into the question of the day, brought face to face the opposing powers of State and Church, hurled defiance at the former, and while not absolutely naming the King or his Council, denounced his policy in the plainest words...Then...shrank back, to all appearance, into the quiet, timid monk (13).

The abrupt intensity of the scene prefigures Inglesant's dramatic pronouncements at the end of the novel, as Richard's receiving Westacre as a gift from the King prefigures John Inglesant's receiving the Villa-Castle of San Giorgio as a gift from the Duke of Umbria. Richard soon learns that his earthly reward, a dispossessed monastery, is not truly "dispossessed", as his grandson will later learn that San Giorgio, a wedding gift, also means death and the extinction of the Inglesant family.

The first night Richard spends in his new residence he has a nightmare, the first of the many precognitive dream motifs in the novel. In the dream, he senses "a fierce contention of the elements and of some powers more fearful than the elements". Rising from bed, he goes out into the courtyard, where the wind swept fiercely and "strange voices cried to him in an unknown language, and undistinguished forms seemed passing to and fro" (16). The Chapel was "all alight, and low and mournful music came from it, as for the dead". Fascinated with terror, he obeys an "irresistible impulse" and enters the Chapel:

> ...cowled forms filled the stalls, and chanted, with hollow, shadowy voices, a dirge for the departed. A hooded and black form stood before the altar... ghostly forms...thronged about him. Voices called from without, and were answered from within... Rushing sounds filled the air as though the trees were being torn up, and the Chapel and house rocked...wild and ghostly lamentation was made by beings no longer of the earth (15-16).

Feeling "dread and inexpressible sorrow [as though] all whom he had ever loved and known lay before him in death", he awakens only to re-experience the dream. The ghostly form of the Prior draws magic figures upon a stone wall, follows the geometrical figures and his shadow projected on the wall, and removes "an antique glass or vial, of a singular and occult shape" from its hiding place. Startled by Richard, he shatters the vial and with it his own sanity. If he had possessed the Elixir of Life, the Prior destroys it--accidentally--at the sight of Richard Inglesant. Nothing, however, is accidental or acausal in the Victorian conventions of Shorthouse's providential aesthetic. The strange forms and ghostly voices in the nightmare elect Richard's grandson to "strain and struggle...to come to consciousness", which, in Jungian terms, means that John Inglesant must re-discover the Elixir of Life in another magical container, the Self. As Eliot's Lord Harry learns in *The Family Reunion*, "knowledge must precede the expiation" of sin, and, in his case, the knowledge involves his unconscious relationships with three women: Amy, his domineering mother; Agatha, his mystical, childless aunt; and Mary, his childhood sweetheart. John Inglesant, "chosen / To resolve the enchantment" inflicted by his grandfather upon his "unhappy family",[87] must likewise define and resolve three unconscious influences upon his life: the conflict between Culture and Fanaticism, the character of Sin, and the subjective influence of the Christian Mythos. Shorthouse identifies these three in the "Preface" (x) as the "distinct threads" or themes of *John Inglesant*. Amid the "tangled web" of conflicting political, philosophical, and religious ideals of his era, John Inglesant must grapple with intuitions of ancestral "karma". Because Richard's role in the dissolution of Westacre Priory was against his conscience and against the religion of his heart and because his son, "a Catholic at heart" who "conformed outwardly to the religion of the hour" (18), John must atone for "the wages of sin" earned by his grandfather and his father. To integrate his outward life with his inner quest for conviction,

John must choose consciously between the Church of Rome and the Church of England, and, in part, his dreams influence his conscious choices.

No single dream, according to Jung, has significant meaning unless it is seen in context with other dreams.[88] Richard's precognitive nightmare, however, represents the typical pattern of all other dreams Shorthouse incorporates into the narrative. Shorthouse uses the dream motif to prefigure and give metaphoric suggestiveness of deeper meanings, though, typically, too, he understates the significance of details. Of course, in his judgment, the character of "John Inglesant is *understated* all through".[89] Thus, the implications of details, such as Inglesant's being named after his mother's brother, "a priest of Douay who was executed in England for saying mass, and refusing the oath of supremacy" (20), his founding of a "hospital for lunatics in the chapel in which his tomb is still standing" (2), and his son's name, which the text never gives, are left to the reader's imagination and to the reader's interpretation of understatement. Understatement creates an emotional tone and implies a textual background from which the reader infers meaning, as the dream motifs create a rhythm of intuition and imagination that urges the reader's mind to interpret Inglesant's actions in light of his philosophical quest, to seek harmony between Inglesant's knowledge and his experiences, and to balance the contrary tensions between Inglesant's faith and his susceptibility to superstition.

When Inglesant is in Scotland, an elderly Highlander tells him that if he is not already "a seer" he soon will be able "to see apparitions and spirits" (71), which may first strike the reader as superstition, although it prepares the reader to willingly suspend disbelief and to accept the appearance of Strafford's ghost in King's bedchamber (76-79). So, too, Inglesant's surprising ability to read and interpret horoscopes in colourful, cryptic detail (169-171) startles and prepares the reader to accept the wizard's crystal ball scene (173-176), in which the wizard attributes Inglesant's extraordinary perception to the purity of his motives, his loyalty to King Charles. Thus, the mystical vision of the "gracious figure [that] entered into Inglesant's soul" at Little Gidding (59) prefigures narrative counterpoints, meditative, self-reflective scenes of "stillness and peace unspeakable" (59) which alternate with intensely dramatic episodes to prepare the reader to accept the miracle of the crucifix in the climatic scene. As numerous descriptions of nature metaphorically complement human affairs, the dream motifs juxtapose and parallel insights into character and religious faith to create a subtle rhythm that enables the reader to accept the improbable and the historically impossible as a mirror of the truth of imagination. Holding "the mirror up to nature: to show...the very age and body of the time his form and pressure"[90,] Shorthouse constructs a mirror of the Ego/Self axis that reflects the dynamics of the Individuation process. As a character of fiction, Inglesant is, of course, "historically impossible" and "individually improbable", but he is also fully believable because of his "studied neutrality".[91] The objectivity and subjectivity of point of view create a narrative rhythm, a pervasive sense of paradox, that invites the reader's imagination to believe in the myth of John Inglesant's reality just as surely and just as unconsciously as the reader accepts that Geoffrey Monk is not J. Henry Shorthouse but a fictional persona or an *alter ego*. Through the eyes of Monk and the numberless, nameless writers from whose documents Monk has supposedly compiled the story, and from shifts in point of view and shifts in perceptual mode, the reader sees Inglesant represented, as it were, "from the point of view of the ego, then from that of the psyche".[92] The "as in a dream" motif signals narrative transitions from ego-oriented perception to mythic mode, a technique Shorthouse uses as if he were experimenting with the possibilities of stream-of-consciousness narrative. Only rarely, however, does Shorthouse present Inglesant's thoughts directly as though they were taken from personal letters or other documents. Even in Inglesant's trance-like and aberrant states of consciousness, the reader remains aware of the subtle presence of an objective, omniscient narrator. The seeming stream-of-consciousness passages express Shorthouse's understanding of the mythic mode.

Jung defines the mythic mode of perception as "the natural and indispensable intermediate stage between unconscious and conscious cognition",[93] which aptly describes Inglesant's "studied neutrality" in psychological terms. In *John Inglesant* the hero's religious neutrality serves practical political purposes; to be useful as an agent he must maintain in public a studied indifference between religious and political divisions. Within England, of course, he is attached to the Royalist cause as the pupil of Fr. St. Clare and must be loyal to the King, but to be useful to the King he must win acceptance and trust from both the High Church and Roman Catholic parties. Later, in Italy, although he attends Anglican services and never formally becomes a Catholic, he is attached to the Catholic cause as the political agent of the Queen and finds himself caught between conflicting parties within the Catholic Church, parties that represent political loyalties and religious sensibilities. Throughout his known, active political life, Inglesant studies indifference as though to be an agent he must be an actor. Indeed, in England he does act in comedy and masque, perhaps as a compensatory entertainment against the tragedy and seriousness of real life. As Ollard observes, during the English civil wars, "Participants on both sides thought of themselves as involved in a general collapse, as actors in a tragedy. Actors, not authors. The parts assigned them had been written, most of them believed, by God."[94] Inglesant's public roles in political and religious life often position him into psychological neutrality, towards the "hypothetical point between the conscious and the unconscious", which Jung calls the Self.[95] Within *John Inglesant*, Shorthouse creates tension between the reader's active emotional and imaginative involvement in the hero's religious quest. The alternating rhythms of Inglesant's self-reflective, philosophical thinking and his dramatically intense actions affect the "studied neutrality" and balance of historical romance and philosophical discourse, as his religious devotions and discussions at Little Gidding alternate with his secular ponderings and speculations with Hobbes. As Shorthouse excites and parallels his readers' historical imagination with the Victorian sense of contemporaneity, he creates an Anglo-Catholic vision, a psychological myth which asserts that individuals of conflicting religious differences may attain spiritual unity in spite of the earthly, political divisions of Christianity. His religious liberalism seeks an adequate expression of religious freedom in Victorian England. Ironically, the first historical parallel he develops involves the suppression of Catholic freedoms in Tudor England.

Henry VIII's suppression of Roman Catholicism informs the first of Shorthouse's parallels between the Reformation and Victorian England. On 18 July 1870, the Vatican Council issued *Pastor Aeternus*, which proclaims "that the Pope is infallible when he speaks *ex cathedra* on faith and morals even without the formal agreement of the church".[96] The Vatican Council's proclamation of papal primacy and infallibility forced Shorthouse and his contemporaries to make decisions of faith and conscience, and in the early chapters of *John Inglesant*, Shorthouse dramatises the effects of Henry VIII's 1534 "Act of Supremacy" upon his fictional characters. Indeed, as he illustrates, the Elizabethan Settlement of 1559 did not resolve the dilemmas of faith and conscience but forced English Catholics to conform outwardly to "the religion of the hour" (18). As Pickering argues, the forces of political necessity imposed on individual conscience developed into the historical and theological ambiguities of Anglo-Catholicism.[97] As the coffin image in Richard Inglesant's nightmare suggests, not even death can box in the religious turmoils of his era. The coffin image gives Richard a premonition of his entire family's death, and only the childless death of his grandson John fulfills and ends what Jung recognizes as "karmic law" or psychological necessity. Old Testament admonitions warn that the sins of the father may be inherited by his sons, that the Lord "visits" the iniquity "of the fathers upon the children" (Exodus 20:5), and New Testament verses assert that the laws of God are written "not in tables of stone, but in fleshy tables of the heart" (2 Corinthians 3:3). According to St. Paul, when God proclaimed His new covenant, He said, "I will put my laws into their mind, and write them in their hearts" (Hebrews 8:8-10). Jung believes so insistently in the archetypal, "internal origins of religious reality" that he declares "that if the religions were eliminated today, they would be reborn from within tomorrow".[98] To Jung, the "making of religion" is the process of making symbols.[99] Believing "that the future is unconsciously prepared long in advance", he cautions against "rushing impetuously into novelty" in search of new symbols, which one is apt to do when "unconsciously caught up by the spirit of the age":

> The 'newness' of the individual psyche is an endlessly varied recombination of age-old components. Body and soul therefore have an intensely historical character and find no proper place in what is new, in things that have just come into being...The less we understand of what our fathers and forefathers sought, the less we understand ourselves.[100]

Thus, Shorthouse's desire to capture the "spirit of the age", which he identifies as "the religious and social tone of the seventeenth century" in the "Preface" (7), leads him to a "recombination of age-old components", the formulation of the "religion of John Inglesant" as a defence of Anglicanism. Inglesant's Italian physician, Signore Zecca, has "no faith in the new doctrine of chemical medicines", yet argues that one "well grounded in the old way may do strange things" with the new medicines through "philosophic treatment" (251-252). A manufacturer of chemical medicines, Shorthouse expresses his hope in the "Preface" that his philosophical romance will do more good for "sorrowing hearts" than Dr. James Hinton did through his treatise, *The Mystery of Pain*.

Shorthouse offers no new speculations in *John Inglesant* about how "history repeats itself", but he does interweave the "philosophic treatment" of his story into psychological insight about how the past impinges upon the present. He studies "the character of Sin" and its consequences, "the wages of sin" (392), in Inglesant's obsession for revenge, Malvolti's nefarious intrigues, and di Guardino's evil nature, and through images which function as "objective correlatives", he hints at the transforming power of the Christian Mythos. The accidental destruction of the mysterious, the magical liquid, the Prior's "Elixir of Life", suggests analogous metaphors: the saving blood of Christ, the shedding of Eustace's blood in a vengeful murder, the poisoned wine that Inglesant is offered at a masked ball, and the drying up of his family's male potency. Shorthouse, in fact, studies the consequences of sin in each of his novels and relates sin to his hero or heroine's unconscious inheritance, which is one of the thematic similarities between his works and Eliot's dramas. In the creative work of both authors, the resolution of the "sin" within the unconscious serves as the impetus for Individuation. Shorthouse's Victorian sensibility and Eliot's modernist vision echo Hamlet's cry, "My fate cries out!"[101] and both authors require their readers to interpret the "ghosts" which cry out for conscious representation. In Jungian terms, the ghosts are psychological complexes and psychic projections of the intuitive potentialities of Individuation, and their manifestations, in whatever form, express the urgency of the Self to relate to the Ego. The compelling motives of Shorthouse's main characters and Eliot's protagonists urge them to investigate their respective ancestral histories, and, as their heroes and heroines explore the past, they come to new awareness of their identities and gain new meaning in their lives.

Shorthouse grounds Inglesant's exploration of his ancestry in non-rational thinking. Eustace and John look "so exactly alike that it [is] impossible to tell them apart" (19), so their father dresses John simply and keeps him at Westacre, where the young boy learns "strange stories" from superstitious servants. He sends Eustace, the elder twin, to London where he dresses and receives education in accord with the highest standards of court life. John, as Shorthouse himself was, is a delicate child who mixes and mingles "reality and shadows" and is "very susceptible of fascination ...superstition and romance...day-dreaming and ...metaphysical speculation" (22). "Johnny", as Shorthouse inconsistently calls him, spends three formative years with an old curate who instills in him "some faint prejudice, some lingering dislike" of Catholicism, which prevents him "in after years and under great temptation, from formally joining the communion of the Church of Rome" (21). When the old curate dies in 1632, John moves into the household of the vicar at Ashley. Platonist, Rosicrucian, and believer in alchemy and astrology, the vicar teaches John the Rosicrucian theory of "vital congruity" of terrestrial, aerial, and ethereal or celestial spiritual "vehicles". Essentially, the vicar's teaching prepares John to experience the two modes of development Jung identifies as natural individuation and Individuation. Natural maturing and understanding of the body and of physical senses develop ego-consciousness, and the Ego; Individuation, the psychological analogy of the Christian spiritual myth, is, as Jung most succinctly writes, "the self-realisation of God in human form".[102] Jung translates Plato's terminology and Rosicrucian theory into his own psychological typology, and thereby establishes continuity between alchemy and psychology. Rosicrucian theory combines two of Plato's four aspects of soul, *noeis* (intelligence or pure reason) and *doxa* (opinion, belief, or faith for conviction), into the terrestrial vehicle, and teaches that the soul must learn to sensate (think-feel and feel-think) before it can become conscious of the aerial genii of *dianoia* (understanding and demonstration). Mastering terrestrial and aerial vehicles, the soul develops celestial capacities, *ekasia* (imagination, conjecture, and perception of shadows), and through "vital congruity", the soul "melts into Divine Love and loses itself in joy in

141

God".[103] Translated into Jung's theory of personality integration, *noeis* and *doxa* name the Thinking and Feeling functions as *dianoia* and *ekasia* represent Sensation and Intuition. From the vicar's theories, young Inglesant learns to interpret myth as though it represents "a secret recipe for the philosopher's stone" and to trust astrology more than recorded history. As the vicar instructs, the "life of Priam can be read more surely in the stars than in history" (23).

To some of his critics, Jung's interests are as non-rational, but to others his
> bold pursuit of unconscious manifestations--the irrational,
> the illogical, the nonscientific, the fantastic, the esoteric
> and occult, alchemy, astrology, gnosticism, mysticism,
> para-psychology, Eastern religions, and primitive rituals--
> may have earned him the censure of the intellectual
> establishment while it rewarded him with his most crucial
> insights, namely the recognition of the symbolic and
> transpersonal nature of psychic phenomena.[104]

In like manner, Shorthouse's religious aestheticism, his love of nature, and his studies of Plato and "The Platonism of Wordsworth" earned him, he believed, "an entrance into the world of abstract thought", into the "fourth dimension of intellectual space" in which "thought, and that alone, is subjective and objective at once".[105] Shorthouse never records when he seized upon philosophical romance as an intellectual synthesis of subjective and objective thought, of mystical intuition and philosophical argument, but he does record his conviction that literary genius proves itself by "basing... idealism upon recognized facts". In his essay on Wordsworth's Platonism, he recognizes both the *Dialogues* and Wordsworth's poems to be "Philosophical Romance". According to Wordsworth, the intellect derives its "visionary character" by projecting itself upon objects in nature. There is, he writes, "a dark / Inscrutable workmanship that reconciles / Discordant elements, makes them cling together... Within my mind...when I / Am worthy of myself!"[106]

Jung accords high value to the keeping of secrets as a means of defining and establishing self-worth, as does Shorthouse's vicar. Inglesant's philosophical quest begins when the vicar admonishes him to "follow the Divine Light" and insists that Inglesant will be able to discern "the voice of God from the Inner Light" only by being obedient to external authority. "You are not placed here to reason", he insists, "but to obey", and he enjoins spiritual silence:
> Do not talk of these things, but keep them in your heart;
> hear what all men say, but follow no man... What [the
> Divine Light] is no man can tell you...You know very
> well, it is not here or there, as men shall tell you...It will

reveal itself when the time shall come (24).

He seems to echo Polonius's advice to Laertes about proper conduct: "Give thy thoughts no tongue...Give every man thy ear, but few thy voice".[107] Ironically, if Polonius's advice culminates in "To thine own self be true" as an admonition about Laertes's apparel,[108] the allusion foreshadows one of Inglesant's constant concerns, his attire. Inglesant's almost constant concern about being dressed as a fine gentleman expresses his appropriate desire to dress properly as an esquire of the King's bedchamber and as an important political agent. However, his concern also betrays the compensatory activity of the *persona*, which accommodates his need to be secretive about the insecurity his spiritual confusion causes him. It may also represent, of course, Shorthouse's compensation for his speech impediment. Shorthouse, as noted earlier, enjoyed dressing "with a flair", although his manner of dressing may have had as much to do with a fashion of Victorian gentry, who "were fond of dressing up as Roundheads and Cavaliers",[109] as with his own personality. In a metaphoric sense, philosophy itself serves Shorthouse as a "dress" or "disguise" for his real interest, spiritual romance, which he began writing almost as soon as Macmillan published *John Inglesant* and "the author of *John Inglesant*" gained popularity.

From his studies of the secrecy of the Rosicrucian and other occult societies, Jung recognizes secrecy as a form of psychological agency, "an intermediary stage on the way to Individuation". He warns that even though a person may be outwardly protected, as Inglesant is by the Society of Jesus, "he will have no defence against his inner multiplicity" until he is able "to differentiate himself from all others and stand on his own feet". "There is", Jung writes, "no better means of intensifying the treasured feeling of individuality than the possession of a secret which the individual is pledged to guard."[110] Before Inglesant leaves Westacre for London, Fr. St. Clare warns him of the necessity of "keeping secrets which would, if revealed, bring the highest heads in England, not to speak of my own, to the block" (43). Later, during the Irish negotiations and the surrender of Chester, Inglesant protects the King's honour, although he certainly does not experience any "treasured feeling of individuality" during his imprisonment in the Tower of London. The Parliamentary forces rightly suspect him of protecting the King, but they are unable to coerce him into a confession. He maintains his silence and, thereby, his integrity as an obedient servant of the King and of the Jesuit's purposes. His silence, though it may appear honourable, proves merely that "his purpose was not so much a part of him as he was a part of it" (123). His obedience has been disciplined and commanded, first by his father, then by his teachers, by Father St. Clare, and by the King himself. Inglesant does not learn to "stand on his own feet" until he learns to discern the difference between the Inner Light, which derives from and expresses his Ego-centred personality, and the Divine Light, which symbolizes the spiritual agency of the Holy Spirit, or, in Jung's terms, the psychological dynamics of the Self.

Shorthouse's Quaker background and his understanding of the doctrine of the Inner Light are different from those of Eliot, yet the contrast between their views is minimal. Eliot's Unitarian upbringing, his gradual conversion to Anglo-Catholicism, and his reputation as a Christian apologist make him cautious of using terms and labels without clear definitions. The connotations of obedience to the dictates of individual conscience offended his conservative religious sensibility, as the "obscurities of 'humanism'"[111] disturbed his intellect. To Eliot, Secularism has corrupted the religious doctrine of the Inner Light as it has corrupted "the whole of modern literature".[112] Attacking humanism, especially that of Irving Babbitt, as "alarmingly like very liberal Protestant theology of the nineteenth century", Eliot declares that humanism "is, in fact, a product--a by-product of Protestant theology in its last agonies".[113] He accuses those who believe that humanism is "an alternative to religion" of "trying to build a Catholic platform out of Protestant planks" and challenges, "What is the higher will to *will*, if there is nothing either 'anterior, exterior, or superior' to the individual?"[114] Had he responded to the "religion of *John Inglesant*", Eliot might have accused Shorthouse of trying to build a Catholic platform out of Church of England planks. Shorthouse, however, draws distinctions between the Inner Light of Inglesant's youthful, Ego-centred personality and the Divine Light of his more mature years, and Eliot would surely have approved the distinctions, because they assert the primacy of the supernatural and the spiritual over natural life.[115] In Eliot's view, "the humanitarian has suppressed the properly human" and "the humanist has suppressed the divine", leaving modern man "with a human element which may quickly descend again to the animal".[116] "It is doubtful", he states, "whether civilisation can endure without religion, and religion without a church", and, like Shorthouse, he rejects the ultramontane view:

> One may feel a deep respect and even love for the Catholic Church...the hierarchy in communion with the Holy See...but if one studies its history and vicissitudes, its difficulties and problems past and present, one is not the more tempted to place all the hopes of humanity on one institution.[117]

Inglesant's first confusion about the Inner Light is a direct result of his reading a copy of *The Flaming Heart, or the Life of St. Theresa*, a gift he received from a Roman priest. The book asserts the need for spiritual direction, and recommends "obedience and entire submission" (35) to the authority of priests. Yearning for self-confidence to identify "the transcendental voice of the Platonic Reason in the silence of the soul" (36), Inglesant studies "Aristotelian irony or what", Shorthouse adds, "might perhaps be called 'Christian Agnosticism'".[118] Although he never clarifies what he means by "Aristotelian irony", Shorthouse connects the concept with satire of the Early Oxford Movement, whose members sought resolution of contemporary Christian dilemmas in the writings of first century Christian fathers. Inglesant consults the aged vicar of Ashley, who searches the "ancient and later Platonists, Greeks and Arabs, Heathens, and Mohometans" because he can find "nothing in ancient Christianity to answer the conflict" between priestly authority and an individual's Inner Light. This essential question of authority, of course, has divided the Church into churches, into what Shorthouse calls "parties", a term that suggests social and sociological criteria may explain such divisions. In his personal letters, Shorthouse rarely refers to specific parties within the Victorian Church. Writing to relatives and friends, he addresses more general concerns; responding to correspondence from readers of *John Inglesant*, he becomes more specific. Thus, writing to a cousin whose only son has just died, Shorthouse offers consolation through a vague fancy:

> I sometimes fancy (for it does not attain to a thought) that
> this life, with all its fleeting joys and its enduring sorrows,
> has nothing whatever to do with the spiritual life, that
> they run altogether upon different lines, parallel but never
> touching, and that no reasoning can be drawn from one to
> the other.[119]

If anything does connect the parallel lives, he suggests, it is "recollection and sympathy". His vague notion of parallel lives is, however, one of Jung's essential concerns, the duality of the structure of personality and divisions within the duality. Shorthouse's "this life" names what Jung calls "consciousness centred in the Ego", and Shorthouse's conception of "the spiritual life" accords with Jung's "psyche", which contains the Ego within it. In this sense, recollections and sympathy define by analogy the psychodynamics of the Ego/Self axis, and the defining and developing of analytical psychology deny Shorthouse's sense that the parallel lives never touch and that "no reasoning can be drawn from one to the other". Writing to a correspondent, Shorthouse connects, again rather vaguely, on Aristotle's idea "of the receptivity of matter" with the "becomingness" of Hegel's dialectical philosophy, and reflects: "Perhaps the fundamental idea of *John Inglesant* is the intense difficulty of revealing the Infinite in any degree to the finite", of "search[ing] out the Divine scheme".[120] The letter and the parallel dualities of Inglesant's experience in England and Italy demonstrate that Shorthouse conceived of philosophical romance as a dialectical synthesis of romantic imagination and philosophical thought. Ultimately, the "religion of *John Inglesant*" obviates priestly authority, vitiates "the Romish system", and recommends recollection and sympathy as forms of obedience to "the laws which our instinct and conscience tell us are Divine" (444). Inglesant's life story dramatises his struggle to respond to "the law of life we feel within" (445) and is synonymous with Shorthouse's "intense difficulty of revealing the Infinite in any degree to the finite". Again, by analogy, the "law of life we feel within" is Individuation, and the "intense difficulty" of the psychological dialect between the infinite Self and the finite Ego describes the process through which the Divine Light transforms John Inglesant into John "English-saint".

Notes to Chapter Three

[1]J. Henry Shorthouse, Letter to Alexander Macmillan (20 January 1881), British Museum MS. 54933.

[2]F. J. Wagner, *J. Henry Shorthouse* (Boston: Twayne, 1979), 50.

[3]J. Henry Shorthouse, Letter to Francis A. Jones (18 June 1891). The letter is in the Berg Collection, New York City Public Library; Wagner refers to it on page 50 and cites the reference in Note 1, 170.

[4]F. J. Wagner, *J. Henry Shorthouse* 50.

[5]Sarah Shorthouse, *LLLR*, vol. 1, 76.

[6]Sarah Shorthouse, *LLLR*, vol. 1, 39-40.

[7]Margaret Southall discusses Hawthorne's influence on Shorthouse in *LLLR*, vol. 1, 28.

[8]W. K. Fleming, "Some Truths About 'John Inglesant'", *The Quarterly Review*, vol. 245, no. 485, July 1925, 130-148.

[9]W. K. Fleming, "Some Truths About 'John Inglesant'", 147-148.

[10]W. K. Fleming, "Some Truths About 'John Inglesant'", 147.

[11]Montague Summers, quoted by Meijer Polak, *The Historical, Philosophical, and Religious Aspects of John Inglesant* (Purmerend: J. Muusses, 1933), 54-55.

[12]Meijer Polak, *The Historical, Philosophical, and Religious Aspects of John Inglesant* 67-69.

[13]Raymond Chapman, *Faith and Revolt: Studies in the Literary Influence of the Oxford Movement* (London: Weidenfeld and Nicolson, 1970), 110-111.

[14]J. Henry Shorthouse, Letter to Arthur Galton, *LLLR*, vol. 1, 365.

[15]J. Henry Shorthouse, Letter to Arthur Galton, *LLLR*, vol. 1, 358, and Sarah Shorthouse, *LLLR*, vol. 1, 384.

[16]One of Sarah Shorthouse's letters to George Macmillan (21 June 1905) confirms that her brother-in-law, John William Shorthouse, saw Lady Jane Lindsay's twenty-six illustrations before they were published in a limited edition (250) by Dickinsons of Bond Street. (British Library MS. 54934: f. 65, f. 66 (24 June 1905) notes the official London exhibition of the illustrations), and f.72 (15 November 1905) reports that twenty-four of the illustrations have been published), and f.73 (20 November 1905) contains Sarah's appraisal: "[She] has drawn houses--horses--landscapes & figures with such grace and power, & some of the scenes are extremely touching and beautiful."

The Birmingham Reference Library has Copy 2 (Ref. AE 741.64) of the folio size *Drawings by Lady Jane Lindsay Illustrative of "John Inglesant"* (Dickinsons, 1906), which contains wash drawings and photogravure illustrations of scenes from the following chapters:

I.The Prior of Westacre preaching from an outdoor pulpit before Richard Inglesant and the Sheriff.

IV:The Thames at Whitehall: Inglesant being presented to Queen Henrietta Maria by Fr. St. Clare.

IV:Inside the Chapel Royal, Whitehall: King Charles at the altar presents the Epiphany offerings.

V: Inglesant see the apparition of Strafford passing through the anteroom to the King's bedchamber.

VI: The King examines Inglesant about the vision.

VI: Little Gidding: Inglesant kneeling before Mary Collet.

VII: The King on horseback being welcomed as he crosses a bridge at Little Gidding.

IX: Oxford: John and Eustace perform *The Comedy of Errors* before the court.

X: The execution of Archbishop Laud on Tower Hill.

XII: Lord Biron examining Inglesant at Chester.

XIII: Inglesant brought to Parliament House for trial.

XIV: London Bridge: Condemned to death, Inglesant meets the disguised Jesuit.

XIV: Charing Cross: The scaffold for Inglesant's execution.

XVIII: Paris: Inglesant visits Mary Collet on her deathbed.

XXI: Florence: Inglesant gives Holy Water to Lauretta.

XXV: Borghese Gardens, Rome: Inglesant discusses the doctrines of Molinos with a Spanish priest.

XXV: Belvedere Gardens, Rome: Inglesant and a friend hold up a crucifix to compare it with the statue of Apollo.

XXVI: Urbino: Inglesant intervenes in a street tumult to rescue a prisoner.

XXVI: Grand Ducal Palace, Florence: Lauretta meets Inglesant at night as they prepare to flee.

XXXII: The climactic scene: Crossing the mountains to meet his bride,

Inglesant confronts Malvolti.

XXXII: In the armour of St. George, Inglesant offers his sword to the altar in a wayside chapel.

XXXIV: The plague in Naples: Inglesant searches the river quay for di Guardino.

XXXIV: The plague in Naples: Inglesant and Signore Mauro recruit slaves to help bury the dead.

XXXVII: Rome: At a great meeting in Don Agostino's palace, Inglesant defends Molinos.

The above list of drawings is included here because the illustrations are virtually unknown and because of a strange omission. Having chosen to illustrate thirteen scenes in England, one in Paris, and ten in Italy, Lady Jane neglected unaccountably the final, triumphant scene before Worcester Cathedral.

[17]J. Henry Shorthouse, Letter to Edmund Gosse, *LLLR*, vol. 1, 190-191.

[18]Meijer Polak, *The Historical, Philosophical, and Religious Aspects of John Inglesant* 71.

[19]J. Henry Shorthouse, Letter to Margaret Southall, *LLLR*, vol. 1, 40-41.

[20]Sarah Shorthouse, *LLLR*, vol. 1, 76.

[21]J. Henry Shorthouse, "The Humorous in Literature", *LLLR*, vol. II, 252.

[22]J. Henry Shorthouse, Letter to Alexander Macmillan, *LLLR*, vol. 1, 166.

[23]J. Henry Shorthouse, Letter to Rawdon Levett, *LLLR*, vol. 1, 329.

[24]Mark Girouard, *The Return to Camelot: Chivalry and the English Gentleman* (New Haven: Yale University Press, 1981), 56-66. According to Girouard, Burne-Jones kept a copy of Digby's *The Broad Stone of Honour* and his *Mores Catholici* next to his bed (63-64). Only one of Digby's ideals would not have appealed to Shorthouse, namely that of the "natural gentleman" (65). Shorthouse, who believed in the greater sensibilities of the aristocracy, would probably have rejected the idea that a common man could be "as much, if not more, of a gentleman than the greatest aristocrat" (65).

[25]J. Henry Shorthouse, Letter to Margaret Southall, *LLLR*, vol. 1, 38.

[26]Ian Warrell, *Burne-Jones: Watercolours and Drawings* (London: Tate Gallery, 1993), 1.

[27]Kenelm Henry Digby, *The Broad Stone of Honour: or, the True Sense and Practice of Cavalry* (London: R. Gilbert, 1828), 244-245.

[28]J. Henry Shorthouse, "The 'Morte D'Arthur' and the 'Idylls of the King'", *LLLR*, vol. 2, 113.

[29]James Hinton, *The Mystery of Pain: A Book for the Sorrowful* (London: Smith, Elder, and Co.,

1867), 43-44.

[30]James Hinton, *The Mystery of Pain* 36.

[31]James Hinton, *The Mystery of Pain* 44.

[32]James Hinton, *The Mystery of Pain* 24. Hinton was not, of course, writing about *John Inglesant*, but his argument is similar to Shorthouse's final declaration. Truth, according to Hinton, must be "freed from the limitations of our perceptions" (24); Shorthouse argues, "We cannot say how we know it" and urges, "Whether we are free...we can at least... resolve" (444).

[33]A. Benedict Davenport, *History and Genealogy of the Davenport Family in England and America, 1086-1850* (New York: S. W. Benedict, 1851), 78-80.

[34]George Leopold Hurst, *An Outline of the History of Christian Literature* (New York: Macmillan, 1926), 318.

[35]J. Henry Shorthouse, Letter to Dr. Abbott, *LLLR*, vol. 1, 125.

[36]J. Henry Shorthouse, Letter to Dr. Abbott, *LLLR*, vol. 1, 126.

[37]J. Henry Shorthouse, Letter to Dr. Abbott, *LLLR*, vol. 1, 126-127.

[38]J. Henry Shorthouse, Letter to Mrs. Moller, *LLLR*, vol. 1, 288-289.

[39]J. Henry Shorthouse, Letter to Lady Welby, *LLLR*, vol. 1, 157.

[40]J. Henry Shorthouse, Letter to Dr. Talbot, *LLLR*, vol. 1, 174.

[41]J. Henry Shorthouse, Letter to Edmund Gosse, *LLLR*, vol. 1, 192.

[42]Eugene Pascal, *Jung To Live By* (New York: Time Warner Books, 1992), 43. As Pascal interprets, "In the history of Christianity, Eastern Orthodoxy and Roman Catholicism went their separate ways in A.D. 1054, due to theological and cultural (read 'typological') differences; Protestantism and Roman Catholicism diverged four hundred years later, also for typological reasons, among others" 43.

[43]Mary Gladstone Papers, Vol. LII, British Museum MS.46,270, f. 412 and 415.

[44]Paul Nissley Landis, *The Development of Nineteenth Century English Historical Fiction Dealing with British History from 1640-1688.* Diss. University of Illinois, 1923, 236.

[45]Paul Nissley Landis, *The Development of Nineteenth Century English Historical Fiction* 243.

[46]Oliver Elton, quoted by Landis, *The Development of Nineteenth Century Historical Fiction* 232.

[47]Paul Nissley Landis, *The Development of Nineteenth Century English Historical Fiction* 243-244.

[48]Paul Nissley Landis, *The Development of Nineteenth Century English Historical Fiction* 243.

[49]After his death, most of Shorthouse's library was auctioned by Sotheby, Wilkinson, and Hodge, 20 September 1909. The *Catalogue of the Library of Joseph Henry Shorthouse, Esq.* provides most of the information about Shorthouse's literary taste used in this thesis.

[50]Georg Lukács, *The Historical Novel* (London: The Merlin Press, 1962), 36.

[51]Georg Lukács, *The Historical Novel* 37.

[52]Georg Lukács, *The Historical Novel* 34.

[53]Georg Lukács, *The Historical Novel* 151-152.

[54]Georg Lukács, *The Historical Novel* 151.

[55]Mary Gladstone Papers, Vol. LII, British Museum MS.46,270, f. 412.

[56]Andrew Sanders, *The Victorian Historical Novel, 1840-1880* (New York: St. Martin's, 1979), 10.

[57]Sarah Shorthouse, *LLLR*, vol. 1, 64.

[58]J. Henry Shorthouse, Letter to "----, at Weston", *LLLR*, vol. 1, 65-68.

[59]J. Henry Shorthouse, "The Agnostic at Church" was reprinted from *Nineteenth Century* (April 1882) in *LLLR*, vol. 1, 150-155.

[60]J. Henry Shorthouse, Letter to the Reverend Charles Black, *LLLR*, vol. 1, 307-309.

[61]J. Henry Shorthouse, Letter to Dr. Talbot, *LLLR*, vol. 1, 304.

[62]J. Henry Shorthouse, Letter to Dr. Abbott, *LLLR*, vol. 1, 125.

[63]J. Henry Shorthouse, "Preface" to Arthur Galton's *The Message and Position of the Church of England* (London: Kegan Paul, Trench, Trübner and Co., 1899), xiv.

[64]J. Henry Shorthouse, Letter to Dr. Abbott, *LLLR*, vol. 1, 126.

[65]J. Henry Shorthouse, Letter to Edmund Gosse, *LLLR*, vol. 1, 191.

[66]Andrew Sanders, *The Victorian Historical Novel, 1840-1880* 31.

[67]Andrew Sanders, *The Victorian Historical Novel, 1840-1880* 34.

[68]Raymond Chapman presents the following plot summary in *Faith and Revolt: Studies in the Literary Influence of the Oxford Movement*, 110:

> John Inglesant, child of a family which had kept Roman Catholic sympaties during the turmoil of the sixteenth century, is brought up under covert Jesuit influence and finds himself involved on the Royalist side in the Civil War. He undertakes secret missions for the King which

bring him to trial and almost to execution when he is repudiated by his royal master. After a brief reunion, his twin brother is killed by an Italian called Malvolti. Inglesant goes to France where he is tested by the demands of the active and contemplative lives, and then to Italy in the service of the Jesuits. His faithful work is rewarded with an estate and he marries an Italian girl. Ever seeking revenge for his brother's death, he cannot kill Malvolti in cold blood when he meets him, and consequently dedicates his sword to peace in a country church. Later he meets Malvolti again, now blind and the devoted member of a religious order tending victims of the plague in Naples. After the death of his wife he goes to Rome, is involved in the Molinist controversy and imprisoned. Eventually he returns to England for a quiet life in communion with the Anglican Church.

[69]George Lukács, *The Historical Novel* 60.

[70]For convenience, page references to the one-volume edition of *John Inglesant* will be cited parenthetically. Issued in 1883, the one-volume edition reached a circulation of about 110,000 copies by 1929, and is therefore the most readily available. The pagination of the smaller Macmillan Sixpenny Edition is consistent with that of the 1883 edition.

[71]A. L. Drummond, *The Churches in English Fiction* (Leicester: Edgar Backus, 1950), 88-89.

[72]Walter Scott, *Woodstock* (London: Macmillan, 1925), 147-148.

[73]T. S. Eliot, *The Cocktail Party, Complete* 438.

[74]T. S. Eliot, *Murder in the Cathedral, Complete* 239.

[75]T. S. Eliot, *The Family Reunion, Complete* 339.

[76]T. S. Eliot, *The Cocktail Party, Complete* 381.

[77]T. S. Eliot, *The Cocktail Party, Complete* 422, 419.

[78]Sarah Shorthouse, *LLLR*, vol. 1, 57, records that her husband always had a love of "beautiful apparel", and surely his manner of dress explains why John Inglesant was always, even in his most distressful moments, elegantly attired.

[79]J. Henry Shorthouse, Letter to Miss Southall, *LLLR*, vol. 1, 148.

[80]T. S. Eliot, *Complete Poems and Plays* (London: Faber and Faber, 1969), rep. 1987, 329.

[81]Doris Nellie Dalglish, "The Novels of J. H. Shorthouse", *Friends Quarterly Examiner*, LIX (July 1925), 221-235.

[82]J. Henry Shorthouse, Letter to Matthew Arnold, *LLLR*, vol. 1, 88-89.

[83]J. Henry Shorthouse, Letter to Dr. Talbot, *LLLR*, vol. 1, 299.

[84]Shorthouse never explained his use of *Lydiard*, but he did confirm in a letter to his cousin that

he had a particular house in mind when he described Monks Lydiard, the home of the Berrington family, Little Malvern Court: *LLLR*, vol. 1, 132.

[85]Houses, castles, and other dwellings which appear in dreams suggest compensations which help identify personality structure. Jung documents his first conscious realisation of the relationship between alchemy and psychology from dreams involving house imagery in his autobiography, *Memories, Dreams, Reflections* (New York: Pantheon, 1961), 202-204 and 213-215.

[86]Wagner notes that in the private edition of 1880, John Inglesant was born in 1612, but that Shorthouse changed the date to 1622 in the Macmillan edition of 1881, perhaps "to bring Inglesant's life into line with John Aubrey's (1626-1697), or more likely with John Evelyn's (1620-1706)." *J. Henry Shorthouse* 172, note 20.

[87]T. S. Eliot, *Complete Poems and Plays* (London: Faber and Faber, 1969), rep. 1987, 333.

[88]C. G. Jung, "Dream-Analysis in its Practical Application", *Modern Man in Search of a Soul*, trans. W. S. Dell and Cary F. Baynes, (New York: Harcourt, Brace and Co., n.d.), 1-31.

[89]J. Henry Shorthouse, Letter to Lady Welby, *LLLR*, vol. 1, 159.

[90]William Shakespeare, *Hamlet* (III.ii.22-24).

[91]Paul Nissley Landis, *The Development of Nineteenth Century English Historical Fiction* 10.

[92]C. G. Jung, *Memories, Dreams, Reflections* 314.

[93]C. G. Jung, *Memories, Dreams, Reflections* 311.

[94]Richard Ollard, *This War without an Enemy: A History of the English Civil Wars* (New York: Atheneum, 1976), 216.

[95]C. G. Jung, "The Detachment of Consciousness from the Object", *The Secret of the Golden Flower: A Chinese Book of Life* (New York: Harcourt, Brace and World, 1962), 124.

[96]Owen Chadwick, "Great Britain and Europe", *The Oxford Illustrated History of Christianity* (Oxford University Press, 1990), 371.

[97]W. S. F. Pickering, *Anglo-Catholicism: A Study in Religious Ambiguity* (London: Routledge, 1989). Pickering defines the theological ambiguities of Anglo-Catholicism in his "Introduction", 1-12, and outlines their historical development in his second chapter, 41-64.

[98]John P. Dourley, *The Psyche as Sacrament: A Comparative Study of C. G. Jung and Paul Tillich* (Toronto: Inner City Books, 1981), 42.

[99]John P. Dourley, *The Psyche as Sacrament* 45-46.

[100]C. G. Jung, *Memories, Dreams, Reflections* 235-236.

[101]William Shakespeare, *Hamlet* (I.iii.81).

[102]C. G. Jung, *Memories, Dreams, Reflections* 328.

[103]Jung develops the historical continuity between alchemy and psychology and elaborates his theory in *Psychological Types*, revised by R. F. Hull from the translations of H. G. Baynes, *Collected Works*, vol. 6, Bollingen Series XX, (Princeton University Press, 1971). P. W. Martin compares Jung's theory with Plato's in *Experiment in Depth: A Study of the Work of Jung, Eliot, and Toynbee* (London: Routledge and Kegan Paul, 1955), 17-35.

[104]Karin Barnaby and Pellegrino D'Acierno, *C. G. Jung and the Humanities: Toward a Hermeneutics of Culture* (Princeton, University Press, 1990), xxiii.

[105]J. Henry Shorthouse, "The Platonism of Wordsworth", *Wordsworthiana: Papers Read to the Wordsworth Society* (London: Macmillan, 1889), 3-16.

[106]William Wordsworth, "The Prelude", *The Complete Poetical Works of Wordsworth* (Boston: Houghton Mifflin, 1932), 129: 341-350.

[107]William Shakespeare, *Hamlet* (I.iii.59-81).

[108]James Kirsch, *Shakespeare's Royal Self* (New York: G. P. Putnam's Sons, 1966), 28-30. Kirsch notes that the modern psychological interpretation of Polonius's advice ["This above all, to thine own self be true..."] is a misreading and mis-interpretation of Polonius's speech. According to Kirsch, Polonius is concerned about his son's wardrobe and manner of dress, which, Kirsch insists, should not be confused with the Delphic oracle's "Know thyself" (28-30).

[109]Richard Ollard, *This War without an Enemy: A History of the English Civil Wars* 214.

[110]C. G. Jung, *Memories, Dreams, Reflections* 342-343.

[111]T. S. Eliot, "The Humanism of Irving Babbitt", *Selected Essays*, third enlarged edition, (London: Faber and Faber, 1951), 480.

[112]T. S. Eliot, "Religion and Literature", *Selected Essays* 398.

[113]T. S. Eliot, "The Humanism of Irving Babbitt", *Selected Essays* 475.

[114]T. S. Eliot, "The Humanism of Irving Babbitt", *Selected Essays* 478.

[115]T. S. Eliot, "Religion and Literature", *Selected Essays* 398.

[116]T. S. Eliot, "The Humanism of Irving Babbitt", *Selected Essays* 473.

[117]T. S. Eliot, "The Humanism of Irving Babbitt", *Selected Essays* 480.

[118]J. Henry Shorthouse, Letter to W. A. Wickham (5 October 1883), published in the *Guardian* (18 March 1903).

[119]J. Henry Shorthouse, Letter to Mrs. Evans, *LLLR*, vol. 1, 315-316.

[120]J. Henry Shorthouse, Letter to Madame de Steiger, *LLLR*, vol. 1, 392-394.

Chapter Four: "John Inglesant" in Italy

Throughout *John Inglesant* Shorthouse relies on the intuitive and imaginative appeals of romance to create interest in his characters, and, although he does not divide the novel into formal parts, he uses a symbolic, three-part narrative structure. An interlude in Paris separates Inglesant's experiences in England from those in Italy, and the chapters set in Italy, XVIII--XXXIX, parallel the hero's philosophical and religious quest in England with further adventures in Italy. This chapter continues the examination of *John Inglesant* in the light of Jung's theory of Individuation and argues that "John Inglesant in Italy" represents Shorthouse's testing of the spirit of Anglicanism and the expression of his personal dogma. As his letters prove, especially those to Victoria Welby,[1] he was well aware of the necessity to use the suggestive power of romance to confront "the paradoxes of language". Jung denies the possibility of absolute knowledge and of reasoning "not liable to error", and he recognizes that the nature of language and the limits of discursive language force psychologist and creative artist alike to use paradox and symbol, especially when their minds confront "immediate experience" or the mysteries of human life. "Whatever one can say", Jung observes, of transpersonal experiences, such as love, for instance, "no words express the whole."[2]

Moreover, to Jung, religious dogma have greater value "from the standpoint of psychological truth" than scientific theories, which are soon superseded by other theories. Jung states that "the dogma expresses an irrational entity through the image". As he explains,

> ...the dogma owes its existence and form, on the one hand, to the so-called 'revealed' immediate experiences, such as the God-Man, the Cross, the Virgin Birth, the Immaculate Conception, the Trinity, and so on, and, on the other hand, to the ceaseless collaboration of many minds and many centuries.[3]

Dogma confront consciousness with "immediate experience", yet, paradoxically, "a dogma is in itself the very thing which excludes immediate experience".[4] According to Jung, "Before people learned to produce thoughts, the thought came to them"; thus, dogma "originated from visions, dreams, or trances" spontaneously.[5] Shorthouse rejects the "Romish system" because it institutionalized dogma too early in human history, "before thought had taught itself to grapple with religious subjects" (442). In his view, the Roman Church sacrificed "individual conscience or reason", which he dramatises through Inglesant's defence of Molinos. Dogma, whether defined as authoritative statements of religious truth, as tenets of a systematized philosophy, or as "a point of view or alleged authoritative tenet put forth...without adequate grounds",[6] may appear spontaneously, Jung argues, and he recommends that one should take St. John's *probate spiritus*[7] with deep seriousness. "Life is a test of the truth of the spirit", he asserts, and life also tests the "truth within us [which] creates ideas", including the dogmatic idea of truth.[8] Generally, Shorthouse uses the testing of spirits for satirical purposes, but at the end of the novel he denounces the Church of Rome as "the enemy of the human race" and dogmatically proclaims the Church of England is "like the Divine Being Himself" (442).

Early in the story, Inglesant investigates a rumour that a local parson has "brought down an angel from heaven". Shorthouse uses Inglesant's visit to the parson to satirize Tractarian ritualism, as he uses Inglesant's final scene to satirize "the principles and system of the Jesuits".[9] The parson looks "on forms and ceremonies with the greatest reverence" and shows his young visitor books on "taking off the hat at the name of Jesus; another on the cross in baptism, and kneeling at the communion; a third on turning to the east...a fourth on the use of the surplice" (39). Because the parson is so "totally incapable of telling [him] anything of that mystical life he [is] so anxious to realise", Inglesant abruptly leaves the parson and returns to his first schoolmaster. Later, after his brother's murder, Inglesant stays with the Quakers at Oulton, and Dr. More redefines the old schoolmaster's teaching in terms of Christian Platonism and philosophical Deism. Inglesant's first teacher had taught him "the alchemy of the immortal spirit, which...transmutes... all the things of life...into immortality in our own nature!" (41). In the teachings of Dr. More, Shorthouse expresses the "dogma" of his personal convictions and defines his favourite literary theme, the enspiritualising of daily life so as to live *Incola coeli in terrâ*.

As a co-inhabitant of heaven and earth, Inglesant begins to study "the workings of the minds of men" (43), and he begins to study his own conscience and nature in earnest when Fr. St. Clare announces, "The time is ripe for you to play the part your father and I have destined for you, and to play it--to a great extent--alone" (43). Inglesant is not at all ready to think for himself, but he is prepared to become a player, an agent, an actor, and from this point on, the psychology of Inglesant's personality parallels the development of Shorthouse's philosophy and the combination of the two dynamics begins to define the "religion of *John Inglesant*". His shadowy religious doubts and his philosophical quest in Italy comprise "a complex and powerful juxtaposition of time planes, perspectives, and analytical perceptions"[10] and express unconsciously hidden, repressed psychological attitudes which he must "inextricably link together...with good qualities-- normal instincts and creative impulses"[11] before he becomes able to "play his part...alone".

Had Shorthouse composed *John Inglesant* as historical fiction, the novel would function only as "signal art-work" and "reaffirm [the reader's] previously established knowledge and values". Through the imaginative power of romance, however, Shorthouse "effect[s] symbolic values which stimulate [the reader] to new knowledge and new values" and transforms plot, character, image, and philosophical theme into "symbolic art-work". As Jung advises, in the work of an author who attempts to transform signal into symbol,

> We should expect a certain strangeness of form and shape, thoughts that can only be apprehended by intuition, a language pregnant with meanings, expressions that would have the value of genuine symbols, because they are the best possible expressions of something as yet unknown...[12]

In the ancient Greek sense, *symbolon* combined *sym* ("together, common, simultaneous with, or according to") with *bolon* ("that which has been thrown") to represent "thought...independent from what it represents".[13] To the Greeks, the symbol represented a "tally...a half of a bone or coin or other object which two parties broke between them in order to have proof of identity".[14] Individuation psychology regards consciousness itself as symbolic and recognizes the historical and spatial elements of self-reflective thinking: The "I-that-am" wonders and ponders the "I-that-was" to affirm the Ego's sense of continuous identity. "We live in the 'here' as something of our own", as Spengler observed, "and experience the 'there' as something alien and uncanny."[15] The "I-that-am" seeks the other part of the "tally", the "I-that-was". Throwing, as it were, the two senses of "I am this" and "I was that" into a unity, Ego-thought orders relativities of time- and space-bound experiences, and, in the contemporaneity of memory, creates the dynamics of *religion*. The Victorian sense of "history [as] contemporary, synchronic and enveloping... living and vibrating in the present" that Sanders attributes to the achievements of historical fiction,[16] coincides with the popularity of religious novels during the Victorian period. As the *Oxford English Dictionary* states, *religion-em* is of "doubtful etymology", but it was "connected [by Cicero] with *relegere*, 'to read over again', but by later authors with *religare*, 'to bind'". In Jungian thinking, literature which expresses or creates a bridging or connecting of past and present moments of self-realisation is "symbolic-art work", which, by etymological definition, also is religious. Such instants or moments of "rereading and binding" inform the Ego with the sense of historical continuity and create stable identity, a kind of "metaphysical stasis". As literature of "the symbolic quest" lends itself readily to analysis in terms of "basic concepts of analytical psychology",[17] the religious experiences in *John Inglesant* provide both the reader and the novel's hero with "temporary relief from the anxiety of questing". According to the historical reasoning of Moris, because Inglesant's identity rests in some authority outside himself, the novel represents Catholic psychology, which "can be equated with the classical vision, the systematic, rounded, infallible, dogmatic and integrated view of life" as "Being" as opposed to the "world of Becoming".[18] In the stages of his "Being", Inglesant is obedient to his father, whose presence and parenting are negligible in the novel; to his spiritual director, whose triple identity as Mr. Hall/Fr. St Clare/the Jesuit dominates Inglesant as long as they are both in England; and to King Charles, whose authority Inglesant accepts for three reasons: because the Jesuit has trained him to, because Hobbes' philosophy induces him to, and, quite simply, because Charles is the King. In Italy, however, Inglesant experiences the "world of Becoming", and by the time of the final scene in England, he seems to have achieved a final "metaphysical stasis", to have become a stable identity grounded in Anglo-Catholic psychology. Yet, as Valentine Lee describes the "dazzling splendour" of Worcester, "dark rain clouds" threaten the "fairy radiance and light", and he realises the moment "bathed in life and hope" is but a *breve gaudium*. As *breve* once meant an authoritative, royal or papal letter and evolved into *brief*, a term still used to denote a papal letter, and into the concept of a *breviary*, a stable form of liturgy, the connotations of "brief" (quick, short, momentary, short-lived, etc.) threaten the meaning of the word and pose paradoxes, some of which are inherent in the metaphoric nature of language. Literary critics and psychologists alike seek to define meaning and values and to establish the methodology of their practices. Yet, no matter how a critic interprets the idea of a "text" or a psychologist defines the complex materials involved in an analysis, other problems remain, new problems arise or are discovered, and both stability of process and criteria of judgment become relative to their own terms and to the assumptions of their various methodologies. Thus, Paul Kugler, a psychoanalyst, compares the developments in psychological theory to those in literary criticism: Modernism "was guided by the implicit assumption that the true meaning was to be found in authorial intention"; New Criticism "shifted the focus of textual analysis from history and content to form, emphasizing 'imagery' as the constituent of form itself...[and] emphasized the autonomy of the text and the presence of meaning within it"; Structuralism "envisioned a new science called semiology", the linguistic analysis of how signs and representational qualities "mirror nature or the human psyche", reformulated "the Freudian topographical model of the mind", and sought archetypal patterns within and between texts; Deconstructionism "has seriously called into question our Western metaphysical tendency to ground the act of interpretation in 'absolutes' such as Truth, Reality, Self, Center, Unity, Origin, and even Author"; and, finally, Postmodernism, which posits that a text is not "a closed entity with definite, decipherable meanings" but is rather "irreducibly plural, oscillating between literal and figural significance [and] can never be fixed to a single center, essence, or meaning".[19] According to Kugler's analysis of literary and psychological theory, "...language has subtly trapped us inside [its own] logic". Because "Our theories of interpretation have no location outside language", he asserts: ...the idea of a detached observer is being replaced by the an intersubjectivity in which the images in the text interfuse and alter the lens of the viewer reading the text. We not only read texts, but we read the world through texts.[20]

Jungian theorists are familiar with the problems, and Jungian analysts confront them in their patients as they do in themselves, as do authors of literature and literary criticism. The analyst trying to read the "objective psyche" through the "text" of a patient's personality must "remain resolutely postmodernist", Edward Casey argues, because "the objective psyche is at the same time a collective psyche, at once prepersonal and pluripersonal (or more exactly, omnipersonal)."[21] Casey asserts that language "is no more a matter of an individual speech act...than primordial images are affairs of the isolated ego. Each proceeds from a level of the psyche that is profoundly impersonal..."[22] In the hero's quest for truth, Shorthouse mirrors this search for objectivity and impersonality, but he does so in religious terms. As a depth psychologist searches for the location of consciousness,[23] Inglesant looks for authority.

When Eliot begins to define his impersonal theory of poetry, he insists that "*significant* emotion...has its life in the poem and not in the history of the poet. The emotion of art is impersonal."[24] From the Jungian perspective, it follows, therefore, that if the emotion of art proceeds from a level of the psyche that is profoundly impersonal, the emotional qualities of art are inseparable from the archetypal qualities of "immediate experience". Assuming some qualifications of background and intelligence, sensitivity, education, and sensibility, a critical reader may do more that naively induct from "the enumerative bibliography of literature" which depends, in Frye's estimation, on chronology and the "magic word 'tradition'".[25] Certainly, Eliot recognizes the problem in his early essay, "Tradition and the Individual Talent", and rather than cross "the frontier of metaphysics or mysticism", he allows the essay to halt at the proposition,[26] as if the essay were writing itself or as if it were defining and composing some objective stance between tradition and his own poetic talent. As explained in the introduction of this thesis, Frye's assumption of the "total coherence" of literature and Eliot's recognition of "the mythical method", which makes "the modern world possible for art", represent their attempts to formulate critical theories that accommodate the personal and the impersonal in literature. As Eliot says:

> Words, after speech, reach
> Into the silence. Only by the form, the pattern,
> Can words or music reach
> The stillness...[27]

He qualifies the reach into stillness: the poet must surrender "himself wholly to the work to be done",[28] or he warns in "Little Gidding", the cost to the personality is "not less than everything".[29] If it requires "an escape from personality"[30] for a poet to reach the objective psyche, what must a reader do to achieve "direct knowledge of life" from reading?

Reading the world through fiction, of course, compounds the intellectual problems of reading analytical or discursive prose, yet, in as much as the experience of reading fiction excites imagination and elicits or inspires intuition, it engenders moments during which readers may examine how they understand themselves and how they understand life in general. As Eliot explains:

> Direct knowledge of life is knowledge directly in relation
> to ourselves, it is our knowledge of *how* people behave in
> general, of what they are like in general, in so far as that
> part of life in which we ourselves have participated gives
> us material for generalization.[31]

"Knowledge of life obtained through fiction is only possible", Eliot concludes, "by another stage of self-consciousness", awareness that such knowledge cannot be generalised but must be accepted as what it is: "the world as seen by a particular mind".[32] Shorthouse concurs, though he allows the generalisation:

> If success be ever attained by the writer of what we call
> fiction, it must be when men of culture perceive in his
> stories lessons and glimpses of truth such as they have
> discovered in life itself ...I am glad to think of any work
> of real art that opposite lessons may be read *into* it,
> through not, perhaps, *from* it; if it be a true glimpse of
> life, it must bear different interpretations, as life does.[33]

Interpreting *John Inglesant* in terms of Individuation theory is, according to Shorthouse's idea, reading into the text, as would be using any of Shorthouse's suggestions about how to read his own work in accord with his intentions. Shorthouse suggests that he has drawn parallels between religious life in the seventeenth century and the Victorian era, but to illustrate "the subjective influence of the Christian Mythos" upon his hero, he virtually ignores Church history, and whatever parallels he intended, they remain unclear. As he introduces his characters with philosophic purpose, so he chooses a religious spectrum that distinguishes Inglesant's spiritual quest, while he ignores the "Battle of the Churches", as if he were asserting that, if Christianity be a true glimpse of spiritual reality, it must bear with different churches, as human thought bears with different philosophies. Inglesant's direct experiencing of "Christianity without the Bible" (187) delineates "the subjective influence of the Christian Mythos" as the "particular mind" of his author. With spiritual roots in the Society of Friends, Shorthouse accepts one of the fundamental ideas of the Quakers, that true brotherhood exists among all believers in Jesus, regardless of church "denomination or none".[34] He divides the setting and the treatment of the hero's psychology into two dominant halves and organizes the narrative into five parts: Monk's introductory chapter and Valentine Lee's concluding epistolary report frame Inglesant's life. We see his childhood and young adulthood in England, his maturing experiences in Italy, and, between them, a transitional interlude in Paris. As explained in the introduction and chapter one of this thesis, Individuation is a process of psychological integration, of relationship between five archetypes. The Ego and the Self function as the two basic structuring principles of consciousness within the psyche, as the archetypes of *persona*, *shadow*, and *anima/animus* direct and control the Ego/Self axis.

The pattern, however, is not a formula, and the autonomous complexes which express symbolic aspects and activities of the archetypes cannot be reduced to anything more than a general outline of psychological development. Individuation theory defines the uniqueness of each human personality, as, in effect, the application of Individuation theory to a work of literature affords only a single interpretation among many possible interpretations. The "particular mind" of the analyst or critic cannot be generalised so as to assert a "correct" Jungian interpretation. Jung's own writings about literature and literary works comprise no more than "arbitrary", not authoritative or definitive, attempts at understanding meaning. Jung himself denies the "Jungian theory of dream interpretation": "I have no theory about dreams."[35] He explains:

> I am convinced that there is no absolutely reliable method
> of interpretation...Also, when we consider the infinite
> variety of dreams, it is difficult to conceive that there
> could ever be a method or a technical procedure which
> would lead to an infallible result.[36]

As Philipson concludes, "Jung's writings on art present a defense of criticism".[37] Eliot, too, warns against over valuing knowledge derived from personal experience:

> There is, it seems to us,
> At best, only a limited value

In the knowledge derived from experience.
The knowledge imposes a pattern, and falsifies,
For the pattern is new in every moment
And every moment is a new and shocking
Valuation of all we have been.[38]

Knowledge derived from others, Eliot recognized, may be more fully appreciated than knowledge derived from one's own experience, for such knowledge is "Unqualified, unworn by subsequent attrition". Self-knowledge, such as Inglesant seeks, is subject to the effects of aging and maturation and represents the psychological mode, the attempt to mediate between consciousness and the personal unconscious. He discovers, however, that "as one becomes older...the past has another pattern, and ceases to be a mere sequence-- / Or even development".[39] Thus, his final defence of the Church of England is, in effect, a "shocking valuation" of all he has been in the novel, for he is never presented as an Anglican; he is not even always presumed to be one. Although profoundly attached to the Jesuit, Inglesant is adrift in the world, and even in his final scene, he defends the Church of England but does not proclaim his membership in it or his identity as an Anglican. What he maintains throughout the novel is his *persona*, an agent between the King and the High Church party and the Catholic Church. As discussed in chapter three of this thesis, Inglesant's discovery of the *persona* and his constant concern for his manner of dress and the dignity of his behaviour are outward "masques" that serve his political purposes. Only in the sense that his outward *persona* truly reflects his inner quest and that his quest is subject to his tastes and preferences does the *persona* play a significant role in his story. Inglesant's Christianity "was ignorant of doctrine and dogma of almost every kind, and concentrated itself altogether on what may be called the Idea of Christ" (187). The same may be said of his politics. His loyalties portray him as only "a good and faithful servant". As he confesses to Mary Collet, "I am not my own. I am but the agent of a mighty will, of a system which commands unhesitating obedience--obedience which is part of my very being" (85). He is loyal to that system until the abrupt final chapter, and it is only from the last scene that the full effects of the *shadow* and the *anima* may be interpreted.

Perhaps the most interesting way to apply Individuation theory to *John Inglesant* is to regard the characters, who, after all, serve as figures to advance philosophic purposes, not as genuine literary characters, as symbolic aspects, or personifications, of complexes of archetypes. Complexes, as Jung defines them, are

> psychic fragments which have split off...appear and
> disappear according to their own laws...behave like
> independent beings [and may] even take on a personal

ego-character like that of the spirits who manifest themselves...[40]

Stevens defines them as "a collection of associated ideas and images all linked together by a common affect" and summarizes, "Complexes are archetypes actualized in the mind."[41] When personified as a literary character, a complex extends its range of ideas and associations into an archetypal energy field. Even though a particular character may personify an aspect of the archetype, several images or figures may collectively define the field or complex of the archetypal energy. The *shadow* in *John Inglesant* does not express itself through a single character or one personification. Malvolti, for instance, personifies one aspect of the *shadow*, but his negative, underworldly energies connect him with di Guardino, as Inglesant's personal shadow extends into his religious doubts. As part of their structure, complexes represent aspects of both the personal and collective unconscious, as a mother figure or character is rooted in the archetype of "mother". If a complex may be given an image, Hopcke writes,

> ...one could say a complex is like a plant, part of which
> exists and flowers above the ground, in awareness, and
> part of which extends unseen beneath the ground, where
> it is anchored and fed, outside of awareness.[42]

John Inglesant (or Shorthouse writing as Geoffrey Monk) has no problem identifying his personal shadow and containing its energy until he meets the first personification of the *anima*, Queen Henrietta Maria, who appears to him in a barge resting on the Thames "in a gleam of sunlight" (48). Dressed in new apparel which makes him feel "astonished" at his own image in a mirror (47), he receives a simple directive from the Queen: "You wish to be one of my servants...Father Hall will tell you what to do" (49). The Queen's smile transforms him, and he looks "out for the first time on the world" and, under the influence of the *anima*, converts all that he sees "into spiritual visions". To please the Queen, Johnny begins to play in public with his new *persona*; he becomes an actor in court masques. John and Eustace, "more alike than ever and much admired at Court as a pair", perform "parts somewhat similar to the brothers in *Comus*, but requiring greater resemblance, as in Shakespeare's *Comedy of Errors*", and, because he can "keep in character", John earns the praise of King Charles. Until the moment of that meeting, Inglesant, as a younger twin brother, never views himself apart from his father and brother; that is, he never questions, but simply assumes, his identity. At once he finds himself courted by "persons of all ranks and opinions in the Court", and, plays indeed upon his physical likeness to his brother. He and Eustace perform in "the Queen's Masques", and his personal shadow, rather like an *alter ego*, exerts only a positive affect, though he slowly becomes conscious of how different he is from Eustace, and just as gradually, Eustace takes on aspects of the archetypal *shadow*. Worldly and pleasure seeking, Eustace involves John in a social escapade in which his younger brother has to literally "cover up" for him to avoid serious social embarrassment and potential danger. By this time, the relationship between the brothers has developed into a complex one. Socially identified with his twin, he dissociates his listening "for the utterances of the Divine Voice" from his "tastes and training" (103), and cannot distinguish his developing ego from the worldly dictates of the *persona*. Hence, his inner spiritual quest begins to compensate, and he distances himself from his brother. He suspects "his brother of caring very little for him" (93); nonetheless, he loses his "own identity in [the] passion of brotherly regard" (172), and for a time, "the whole world seems to be centred in his brother" (178). His suspicion grows unconsciously, and in the wizard scene (173-176), he envisions the murder of his brother, compensating for his own feelings by projecting the *shadow* as the murderer and rationalising the murder as retribution for his brother's pursuit of worldly pleasures. For a moment, he cannot tell whether the murder victim is his brother or himself. Refusing to look again into the crystal ball, a metaphor for the unconscious, he suffers psychological denial, becomes profoundly confused, and loses contact with the real world. The hallucinating affects of the *shadow* disappear, his nerves steady, and his brain clears only when he sees his brother's murdered corpse (182). Instantly, he projects the *shadow* and transfers its energy onto the nameless Italian assassin.

Not only does the plot thicken, but the psychology of the novel becomes more complex. To find his brother's assassin, Inglesant needs his connection with another Italian, the Jesuit, but to identify the murderer, he needs only the image within his own mind. While Inglesant stays at Oulton, the *shadow* begins to integrate into his ego; he recovers physical health and receives material compensation from the *anima*: Lady Cardiff, his sister-in-law, whom he never meets, bequeaths his brother's wealth to him. Conversations with the Quakers confront Inglesant with the growing awareness that the Inner Light and the Inner Voice he seeks to obey and to keep secret are not the same as the Divine Light and the Divine Voice. As Jung describes the Ego/Self axis, the Inner Light and Inner Voice are "signs" within the Ego, the voices of conscience confronting the Ego with the necessity of making conscious choices and moral judgments; the Divine Light and the Divine Voice are symbolic expressions of the urgings of the archetypal Self. If awakened, however, to the Divine Voice, the dictates of Individuation, the Ego is burdened with its own potentialities and confronts the dilemma of obeying ego-consciousness, which may mean little more than ego-gratification, or the inner laws of psychological necessity which create meaning itself. When the Ego perceives inner necessities, it may well share the agony Eliot expresses in "Gerontion": "After such knowledge, what forgiveness?"[43] Or, in persons of exceptional psychological self-knowing, the Ego may grasp the wisdom of silence and, in awe, share Job's great apology to God: "I have uttered things too wonderful for me, which I knew not...I have heard of thee by the hearing of the ear: but now mine eye seeth thee" (42:3-6). As long as Inglesant remains in the grip of the *shadow*, he cannot escape his need for spiritual direction, thus he must project his ego as if it were "a relatively constant personification of the unconscious itself", a mirror image in which the unconscious may become "aware of its own face".[44] The Ego can withdraw its projections and integrate the *shadow* through the influence of the *anima*. Fortunately, Inglesant's conscious religious questioning leads him to the personification of the *anima*.

After reading Valdesso's *Divine Considerations*, Inglesant determines to visit the translator, Nicholas Ferrar, founder of the religious household at Little Gidding. At Little Gidding, Inglesant examines his religious quest with Ferrar, and he personifies his personal *anima* and projects it onto Mary Collet. Shorthouse borrows freely from Peter Peckard's *Memoirs of the Life of Mr. Nicholas Ferrar* (1790), to create Mary Collet as "a creature of fiction" whose "words and aspirations and life" accord "with those of her real prototype".[45] As Inglesant internalizes the spiritual advice of Ferrar, he becomes enamoured of Mary Collet, one of the seven young ladies of the Little Gidding household who devoted their lives to religious worship and spiritual discipline. The story of Mary Collett and the Ferrars of Little Gidding charmed readers of *John Inglesant* with its idealization of a spiritual or Platonic relationship, and, as argued earlier, may have inspired Eliot. Shorthouse's Mary Collet does not possess the mysterious and transcendental qualities of the Eliot's *anima* representations in "Ash-Wednesday",[46] yet Shorthouse uses the character of Mary Collet to direct his hero towards divine, rather than human, love.

Shorthouse uses the serene and picturesque Church of St. John the Evangelist to focus Inglesant's Anglo-Catholic quest upon religious authority. Inglesant notices that all of the women are dressed in black, except one, Mary Collet, who wears a friar's grey gown. Two of the ladies, he knows, have expressed the desire to become "veiled virgins", report of which has contributed to the controversial reputation of Little Gidding as the Protestant or "Arminian Nunnery".[47] The family's ordered, devotional life has attracted considerable public notice. "Strange and romantic", the whole scene appeals to "his fancy", and he cannot "keep his eyes from this one passive face, with well-cut delicate features, and large and quiet eyes" (55). Next morning, he visits the family's hospital room, where he encounters

Mary Collet, known in the community as "the Patient", alone. He asks "if she [has] lost her own name in her assumed one", a simple, yet serious question for the young actor and political agent and one that prefigures his later transformation into the Cavaliere di San Giorgio. Mary has "not entirely lost her own name in her assumed one", as John Inglesant remains John Inglesant when, for "a patience" of time he becomes a personification of St. George. "Aglow in her presence", as if receiving the benediction of the *anima*, he seeks private conference with Nicholas Ferrar, "chiefly to know his opinion of the Papists and their religion" (54). Ferrar cautions Inglesant against "exalting the inward spiritual life above the foundation of holy Scripture", and the poet Richard Crashaw, who often visited Little Gidding while he was a student at Cambridge, warns Inglesant that "the English Church [has] not sufficient authority to resist the spread of Presbyterianism". Crawshaw states that he sees "no safety except in returning to the communion of Rome" (58). Under the spell of his *anima* projection, of course, Inglesant feels the authority implicit in the community's way of life, and the advice he receives from Ferrar, Crawshaw, and Collet, leaves him in the same dilemma Geoffrey Monk experienced in the introductory chapter. Receiving the sacrament in the Anglican chapel, Monk readily believed it as spiritually efficacious as that supplied by the "gorgeous ceremonial" of the Catholic Church. Monk's experience, however, dulls into "signal art" in comparison with Inglesant's numinous, mystical experience:

> Above the altar, which was profusely bedecked with flowers, the antique glass of the east window... contained a figure of the Saviour...The form was gracious and yet commanding, having a brilliant halo round the head, and being clothed in a long and apparently seamless coat; the two fore-fingers of the right hand were held up to bless. Kneeling upon the half-pace, as he received the sacred bread and tasted the holy wine, this gracious figure entered into Inglesant's soul, and stillness and peace unspeakable, and life, and light, and sweetness, filled his mind. He was lost in a sense of rapture, and earth and all that surrounded him faded away (59).

The "gracious figure" is the first half of Inglesant's mystical experience, the Anglican vision, which is later complemented by miraculous experience in the wayside chapel in Italy. Thus, it is in England that, under the spell of Mary Collet and his *anima* projection upon her, "Heaven itself seemed to have opened to him, and one fairer than the fairest of the angelic hosts to have come down to earth" (59). As a projection of Inglesant's *anima*, Mary Collet's symbolic function is not to replace deity, but to point at the divine and help him to understand his destiny. Because Inglesant's "purpose was not so much a part of him as he was a part of it" (122), his Platonic relationship with Mary accentuates his sense of destiny.

Shorthouse's idealized picture of Little Gidding accords with the most recent scholarship, which finds that "in the context of their time [the Little Gidding community of the Ferrar family] were an 'ecumenical' community...not only a haven, but a parable of peace, a place where king and commoner, Catholic and Protestant, could find welcome." Little Gidding "transcended the party spirit which divided the Church and represented a unity between her two traditions of spirituality".[48] Although Shorthouse never visited Little Gidding, he found in its history the perfect symbol to express his Quaker-Anglican and Anglican-Catholic sensibilities and his hope for Christian unity. Eliot uses a mystical voice, the "murmuring shell of time", to admonish pilgrim travellers in "The Dry Salvages" to "consider the future / And the past with an equal mind".[49] Shorthouse employs Nicholas Ferrar to offer Inglesant a practical appraisal of his quest:

> You are very young and are placed where you can see
> and judge of both parties. You possess sufficient insight
> to try the spirits whether they be of God. Be not hasty to
> decide, and before you decide to join the Romish
> communion, make a tour abroad, and if you can, go to
> Rome itself (61).

Then he confesses, "I am now, and I shall die, as I believe and hope shortly, in the Communion of the English Church" (61). Echoing Geoffrey Monk's earlier testimony, Ferrar concludes, "This day, as I believe, the blessed sacrament has been in the Church before our eyes, and what can you or I desire more?"

What Inglesant needs, in Jungian terms, is an internal marriage, the *mysterium coniunctionis* of Individuation, the symbolical process in which ego-consciousness and archetypal *shadow* psychologically unite through the agency of the *anima*, transform the Ego, and create the Self, "the hypothetical summation of an indescribable totality".[50] Appropriately, once Inglesant has felt the fatherliness of Nicholas Ferrar and the Neoplatonic influence of Little Gidding,[51] "Father" St. Clare begins to represent the *shadow*; he becomes "the Jesuit", and Inglesant begins to become conscious that how he thinks and why he believes is more important than what or whom he believes. Thus, when Inglesant returns to London, the Jesuit restates his earlier declaration that party differences are "unimportant and slight" in terms that echo Shorthouse's "Christian agnosticism":

> When you have lived longer in this world and out-lived
> the enthusiastic and pleasing illusions of youth...your

admiration and attachment to any particular party or opinion will fall away altogether...This is the most important lesson that a man can learn--that all men are really alike; that all creeds and opinions are nothing but the mere result of chance and temperament; that no party is on the whole better than another; that no creed does more than shadow imperfectly forth some one side of truth (74).

Reinforcing the urgency of Ferrar and Hobbes that Inglesant become conscious of the needs and choices of his situation, Father St. Clare insists:

Hereafter it will be of little importance which of these new names, Cavalier or Roundhead, you are called by, whether you turn Papist or Puritan, Jesuit or Jansenist, but it will matter very much whether you acted as became a man, and did not flinch ignobly at the moment of trial. Choose your part from the instinct of your order, from your birth, or from habit or what not; but having chosen it, follow it to the end (74).

The attitude of Shorthouse's Jesuit anticipates that of Jung. Jung stresses the importance of making conscious choices, arguing that, if one does not consciously make choices, one can only unconsciously follow the conventions of moral, social, political, philosophic, and religious ideals.[52] Because "right choice" implies living in accord with one's own nature, Inglesant's loyalties and his denial of external authority makes his life a symbolic quest to be free of external laws and entanglements. Only in such freedom can he actualise "the unique law of Self",[53] which dictates that to individuate one must "concentrate on self-knowledge then live in accordance with the truth about himself...One must be what one is...must aim for that ideal point towards which nature appears to be directing us."[54]

In Shorthouse's religious aesthetic and in Jung's psychology, obedience to one's own nature requires forgiveness of others, or acceptance of one's own projections. Inglesant withdraws his projections when he forgives Malvolti. His forgiveness of his brother's murderer is an archetypal reenactment of the meaning of the central mystery of Christianity, the crucifixion of Christ, and, because Inglesant is dressed in the armour of St. George, the climactic act restates Shorthouse's dictum: "God prefers culture to fanaticism."[55] More importantly, the response of the Christ figure validates the spiritual efficacy of the Anglican sacrament. To Jung, fanaticism, whether for personal or political ends, leads to ego-inflation, such as Inglesant feels when, echoing Macbeth,[56] he declares, "I bear a charmed life; no steel can touch me, nor any bullet hurt me, till my hour comes" (221). Fanaticism as self-will run riot or self-glorification of the Ego distorts perception and leaves an individual in conflict against his own nature, as Inglesant realises when he confronts the puritanical Mr. Thorne. The crucifixion of the Ego, however, transforms personality by replacing the Ego with the Self as the new centre of the personality. Psychological transformation, according to Jung, is analogous to religious conversion, because

> Christ is our nearest analogy of the Self and its meaning...
> [The] great symbol tells us the progressive development
> and differentiation of consciousness leads to...nothing less
> than a crucifixion of the ego, its agonizing suspension
> between irreconcilable opposites.[57]

The seemingly irreconcilable opposites in the novel are both personal and archetypal, in accord with Jung's view that the psyche comprises personal and archetypal realms or dimensions. Inglesant's religious turmoils are imposed upon him by conditions in seventeenth-century England and Italy, but his fate is determined by his capacity to become conscious of the roots of the conflicts within himself. The Ego/Self axis and the respective political and religious claims of the Church of Rome and the Church of England mirror his psychological condition. Because psychological opposites contend in the "reformation" and unity of personality, the historical contentions of Protestant and Catholic churches may ultimately individuate into the unification of Christianity. Jung asserts that, as "Protestants hypostatize the Bible, illegitimately making it the supreme authority, regardless of its contradictions and controversial interpretations", Roman Catholics hypostatize papal authority.[58] According to Jung, "The psychological rule says that when an inner situation is not made conscious, it happens outside, as fate. This is to say, when the individual remains undivided and does not become conscious of his inner contradictions, the world must perforce act out the conflict and be torn into opposite halves."[59] Applying Jung's rule to *John Inglesant*, one might say the Civil War in England expresses the division within "the conscience of the King". Such reconciliation of the opposites often begins in the projection and ends in the *mysterium coniunctionis* of Individuation, as in the historical drama of the King, the story ends in martyrdom, almost in sainthood.

In *John Inglesant*, Shorthouse ends the hero's *mysterium coniunctionis* by fully integrating the *shadow* and the *anima* into a transforming symbol, the Church of England, but the *shadow* dominates the chapters set in Italy. In England, the *shadow* manifests itself in a variety of ways as an aspect of religious and political confusion and strife. Shorthouse was well aware that Inglesant's loyalty to the Jesuit would have been controversial to "all right-thinking Englishmen" in seventeenth-century

England and to many of his contemporary Victorians. He knew that he could not create John Inglesant into a believable character without having his hero pronounce some judgment on the Society of Jesus. The Jesuits, he asserts from his contemporary viewpoint, symbolize "a vague and intangible designation...standing...as a synonym for all that was wicked, base, and dangerous" (142) in the seventeenth-century church. "Lost to all sense of right and truth", the Jesuits intrigued and plotted for "supremacy over the popular mind", as within the Roman Church, the Jesuits secured their power through their manipulation of "the frailty of the human heart" (142). Indeed, the history of the Society of Jesus in England sometimes deeply implicates them in nefarious intrigues, such as that of William Parry and Father Benedict Palmio, who plotted to assassinate Queen Elizabeth I in 1584, and that of Henry Garnet, the Anglo-Jesuit provincial, who was involved in the Gunpowder Plot to assassinate James I. Shorthouse admits making "great use of the agency" of Gregorio Pangani (or Panzani) in characterizing the Jesuits in *John Inglesant*,[60] but his representation of them evokes little invective or rancor today. Panzani worked with Cardinal Barberini, nephew of Pope Urban VIII, and with Father Philip, an English Capuchin and confessor to Queen Henrietta Maria. Believing the "court very accessible of bribes" and knowing the King's enthusiasm for art, Barberini "was quite prepared for his protégé Panzani to rob Rome of her most valuable ornaments, if, in exchange, 'we might be so happy as to have the King of England's name among those princes who submit to the Holy See'".[61] Shorthouse, however, balances the shadowy reputation of the Jesuits in England by criticizing the character of King Charles I, and his treatment of the Jesuits in Italy accords them both criticism and respect.

In England, the King's duplicity and his failure to protect Strafford evoke a personification of the *shadow*, Strafford's ghost; in Italy, the shadowy political intrigues of the conclave that elects Cardinal Chigi elicit the "overpowering apprehension of some approaching existence" (346). Shorthouse expresses his own admiration of Strafford and comments on the King's lack of conscience:

> That such a man, by the simple clamour of popular
> opinion, should have been arrested, tried, and executed in
> a few days, with no effort but the most degrading and
> puny one made on his behalf by his royal master and
> friend, certainly must have produced a terror and
> excitement, one would think, unequalled in history (76).

Malvolti, slinking stealthily along the Cardinal's corridor, serves as a representative of the "Italian devil" and evokes more than an image of "a phantom murderer"; his presence calls forth "the phantom of murder itself" (347). However, unless one reads Inglesant's final words in Rome as satire, one can only conclude that by the end of his experiences in Italy, Inglesant has withdrawn all spectres of the *shadow* from the Jesuits: "I have nothing to say of the Society but what is good. It has ever been most tender and parental to me. I go away with nothing but sadness and affection in my heart... with nothing but gratitude...nothing but reverence" (432-433).

In England, Inglesant observes Mr. Thorne, the only Puritan character of significance in the novel, and is "attracted to him in a strange way"; he sees Thorne as a man

> in...perpetual struggle...between his real nature and the system of religion which he has adopted, but in whom the original nature has been subdued and nearly extinguished, until some event, apparently of recent occurrence, has renewed this conflict and excited the conquered human nature once more to rebellion (80).

Expressing an aspect of the *shadow*, Thorne contorts St. Paul's admonition that "the letter killeth, but the spirit giveth life" (2 Corinthians 3:6) into "There is no need for us to go beyond the letter of the Spirit" (82). Ironically, Thorne calls Inglesant his "shadow", and it is the "shadow" of the Jesuit that takes Inglesant from Mary Collet and Little Gidding. The moment he receives the summons to London to begin the Chester negotiations, Inglesant sees Mary Collett kneeling with "sunlight from the west window shining" upon her, and the messenger of the Jesuit "in the dark shadow under the window" (121). The contrast develops into Inglesant's most important choice in England, which prefigures his choice not to join Cressy's Benedictine monastery in Paris. Inglesant offers himself to Mary, but, true to her nature and her namesake, Mary is aware of the needs and spiritual yearnings behind and beneath her would-be lover's infatuation, as, Jung notes, only a psychologically mature woman can be.[62] Inglesant idealizes Mary as a "holy as a saint of God", and he yields himself to her as a repentant son might to a mother: "Do with me what you will...I am yours--my life belongs to you" (85-86). To accord with Shorthouse's setting, the real Mary Collet would have been forty-two years old, and she was indeed the mother-figure of the Little Gidding community after the death of Nicholas Ferrar's mother in May 1634. Shorthouse changes Mary Collet's age and position within the community, yet depicts her motherly qualities accurately to serve the needs of his psychological realism, just as Eliot uses the legend of Charles's third visit to Little Gidding to give drama and mythic quality to *Four Quartets*.[63] According to the facts of history, the King made his second visit to Little Gidding on 15 March 1642, seven months before the Battle of Edgehill, 23 October. According to legend, he made his third visit alone and arrived "like a fugitive at nightfall".[64]

As a theologian might search for "the historical Jesus" or an archaeologist might excavate a particular land site hoping to uncover artifacts, an historically minded critic might search for the historical John Inglesant in the first part of the novel. Shorthouse boldly places his hero in England in the heart of public life in historical events, and then withdraws him to quietude and momentary obscurity. He continues the pattern of projecting his hero into public life and real historical events in Italy, then withdrawing him for self-reflection into churches, monasteries, or country villas. The pattern of John Inglesant's behaviour in Italy, of extroverted action and introverted thinking, creates narrative continuity, and, most significantly, creates religious feeling and tone. The parallels between the two parts of the novel effect the "gathering together" or "binding together" implied in the etymology of *religion*. The religious, social, and political aspects of Inglesant's life in Italy mirror and complement his life in England. Although they are grounded in the quest theme of Inglesant's philosophical approach to religious experience, the connecting figures serve more as metaphors than as literary characters. That is, they, too, serve Shorthouse's philosophical purpose. Because his purpose throughout the novel is to teach truth "under the form of apologue and romance", not "by set treatises",[65] his characters embody ideas more than they express human personality. The psychological realism of their purpose and function is more important than their realism as characters, because that realism creates what might best be called "religious coherence".

As several of Shorthouse's characters form into complexes that define and identify archetypes, a few of them have complex identities. Other than John Inglesant himself, whose psychological goal is individuation, the characters tend to blend or meld together, to become indistinct. The tripartite identity of Mr. Hall/Fr. St. Clare/the Jesuit dominates Inglesant's life in England, but the character fades out of the story after Inglesant leaves Paris. Reversing the process, The Italian/Malvolti/Fr. Grazia provides a counterpoint: shadowy and mysterious in England, he becomes frightfully present and nightmarish in Italy; for about a third of the novel, he personifies evil, then, in the final third, he personifies the archetypal image of the humble, caring, Christian servant. As Fr. St. Clare and his political purpose disappear in the novel, Fr. Grazia and his spiritually-transformed nature dominate. Likewise, in England, Inglesant is an agent for the Jesuits, the Royalists, and the King; in Italy, he serves as an agent for the Jesuits, the English Catholics, and the Queen. When he returns to England, he serves a single role as defender of the Church of England in the cause of religious freedom. The psychological agency which mediates the coherence of characters into a complex is the *anima*, and the transforming agency which individuates and gives "religious coherence" to "the religion of John Inglesant" is the archetypal *imago Dei*, the Self.

Although *John Inglesant* has a clearly defined central character, the *anima* archetype within the philosophical romance is not easy to define. Jung asserts that the *anima* "forms an extremely dramatic content of the unconscious" which may be described "in rational, scientific language", but that to do so "entirely fails to express its living character." "Therefore", he continues:

> in describing the living processes of the psyche, I deliberately and consciously give preference to a dramatic, mythological way of thinking and speaking, because that is not only more expressive but also more exact than an abstract scientific terminology..."[66]

In dramatic literature and in mythology, the *anima* corresponds to goddesses, spiritual guides, and to the feminine principle within men that enables them to psychological wholeness. In a general sense, the *anima* in *John Inglesant* may be defined as the totality of all female characters in the novel who mediate between Inglesant's conscious and unconscious, between his conscious quest for philosophical understanding of religion and his often unconscious struggle to understand his religious experiences. In varying degrees of significance, such a list includes: his Catholic mother who dies giving him birth, his nurse, Mary Collet, Queen Henrietta Maria, Lauretta, the Contadina who saves him from drinking poisoned wine, and the nameless "lady in the velvet masque" (427) who betrays him to the inquisitors at the trial of Molinos. Of these, however, only Mary Collet, the Queen, and Lauretta have significant impact on him or in his life.

Mary, "holy as a saint", serves him as a spiritual director, and after her death he remembers her with "sentiment that commended itself to his reason and his highest feelings" (229). From the moment he first sees Lauretta, however, he is "conscious of a half-formed fear, of a sense of glamour and peril, and of an alluring force independent of his own free will" (229). Archetypes are simply "not subject to will and conscious control",[67] but their autonomy may be integrated into consciousness:

> The autonomy of the collective unconscious expresses itself in the figures of *anima* and *animus*. They personify those of its contents which, when with-drawn from projection, can be integrated into consciousness.[68]

Jung qualifies his assertion:

> ...though the *contents* of *anima* and *animus* can be integrated they themselves cannot, since they are archetypes. As such they are the foundation stones of the psychic structure, which in its totality exceeds the limits

of consciousness and therefore can never become the object of direct cognition.[69]

Thus, the assertion that Mary and Lauretta personify Inglesant's *anima* implies that the two women represent some "psychic content" that Inglesant can understand only by withdrawing his projections from them, only by integrating their meaning into his consciousness.

When Mary hears Inglesant call Fr. St. Clare "an angel of light", she instinctively realises that the Jesuit may require Inglesant to do "something conscience cannot approve". He asserts that she knows him better than he knows himself and offers himself completely to her: "I am yours--my life belongs to you" (85-86). She argues, but her plea produces "no effect upon his purpose", and she realises, "We have both of us other work to do, work laid out for us, from which we may not shrink; a path to walk in where there is neither marrying nor giving in marriage" (86). By recognizing the proper limits of their relationship, she enables him to withdraw his *anima* projection from her, and, as Shorthouse typically uses nature to complement: "The evening sun that lighted all the place went down suddenly behind the hedges of the garden, and the room grew dark" (86). Inglesant himself describes the content of his *anima* projection in the only words adequate: "...the gates of heaven may still open,...I dare not face the radiance that even now issues through the opening space" (85). As Whitmont says, "The acceptance of the *anima* as an independent other personality to which one is bound transforms her into an ally",[70] and it is as intimate allies that they meet for the last time. Attending her deathbed in Paris, he again pleads with her for spiritual direction: "Tell me how I can serve Him, Mary, and I swear to you I will do whatever you shall say" (196). In her wisdom, she help him realise he is already following the Inner Light, and she leads him towards the Divine Light in his own heart: "...the path you have already chosen...only follow your heart as unflinchingly, when it points you to Him" (196).

Under the spell of a *shadow* personification, the Jesuit, Inglesant becomes directly involved in the King's "unholy alliance" with the Irish Catholics; however, when he and the Jesuit meet in Paris, Fr. St. Clare releases him. At the same time, the Jesuit commends him to the service of the Queen. As he had easily withdrawn the *anima* projection from Mary Collet, he has no difficulty in serving the Queen. Before his meeting with Fr. St. Clare, Inglesant rejects the offer of Serenus de Cressy to join the Benedictine monastery at Douay:

> Life was not yet over with him; perchance he might yet
> find what he sought in some other way. He saw the path
> of perfect self-denial open before him,--renunciation, not

of pleasure, nor even of the world, but of himself, of his
intellect, of his very life,--and distinctly of his free choice
he refused it. (203)

In search of his brother's assassin, Inglesant pursues the world of
pleasure as his brother had done. As an agent of the Queen, he travels
towards Italy in deep internal conflict. Pursuing the delights of art and
music, reflecting on his rejection of de Cressy, he experiences deep spiritual
apprehension and guilt and becomes profoundly troubled in mind. As he
had been unable to "face the radiance" of heavenly service, he stands on a
summit overlooking Sienna, "the most wonderful and beautiful sight he had
ever seen" (214). Abruptly, he throws himself upon the ground; "and
overwhelmed with a sudden passion, he repented that he had been born"
(214). Shorthouse explains:

> So palpably did the consciousness of his choice, worldly
> as he thought it, cause the presence of evil to appear, that
> in that heavenly solitude he looked round for the
> murderer of his brother. (214)

Having seen the ghost of Strafford, a personification of the King's guilty
conscience, he now looks for a personification of his own internal division.
The *shadow* does not appear, although, Inglesant often walks hereafter "as
in a dream". Shorthouse depicts Inglesant in continuous states of trance or
dream in much of the Italian section of the novel; for more than a hundred
pages, Inglesant experiences little conscious reality but moves "as in a
dream":

> ...his mind and imagination...in that state in which, from
> the inward fancy, phantoms are projected upon the real
> stage of life, and playing their fantastic parts, react upon
> the excited sense, producing conduct which in turn is real
> in its result. (219)

Through "the intricate pathways of a dream" (330), "as though he were
moving in a delicious dream" (332), "like a man speaking in a dream" (337),
enjoying "the delusive pleasures of a dream" (338), he is led "in a confused
and troubled dream" (346) to Malvolti. His dream states are most intense
when he gambles, attends theatre and concerts, pursues various pleasures,
and, ironically, after the death of Pope Innocent X and throughout the
Vatican conclave. The "visible links in a chain of unconscious events",[71]
dreams represent "the theatre where the dreamer is at once scene, actor,
prompter, stage manager, author, audience, and critic."[72] Thus, at the theatre
with his violin teacher, Inglesant sees the Italian of his nightmarish dreams
and trances for the first time as the personification of the *shadow*. With his

eyes "fixed as though fascinated...spell-bound and unable to turn away" (233-234), Inglesant listens to the "fantastic music...in which gaiety and sadness were mysteriously mingled" (233). The music in this scene, as in others, expresses the abstraction of the *anima*. Hearing the "bass viols and a shrill plaintive note of the treble violins", Inglesant receives an image, "a clearer perception of those paths of intrigue and of danger in which he seemed to walk" (234).

Music is "specially receptive of symbols" from the unconscious, and "archetypal musical sound-patterns [express] an astonishing unity of basic conceptions".[73] Jung wrote little about music, yet he believed that "Music expresses in sounds what fantasies and visions express in visual images...music represents the movement, development, and transformation of motifs of the Collective Unconscious." He excuses himself from exploring music as he explores literature and the visual arts: "I am not a musician and would not be able to develop these ideas...in detail."[74] Shorthouse, too, was no musician, but throughout his complete works, from his early essay "A Midsummer Night's Dream" to his final novel, *Blanche, Lady Falaise*, he attempts to define an art realm peopled with living presences. In Shorthouse's imagination, people live "in all the pictures that hang upon the walls...in sound...in scent...in colour...and in form". He introduces the idea in "A Midsummer Night's Dream" through a young girl's dream,[75] and in *John Inglesant* he develops the idea into Inglesant's philosophy. Inglesant played "the violin a little in England", but in Italy he discovers that "whole of life" may be "recited upon the plaintive strings" of the violin, and, most significantly, that through "their mysterious effect upon the brain fibres, men are brought into sympathy with life in all its forms" (210).

Shorthouse places a musical allegory, "The Vielle-Player's Story", in the centre of the novel as the bridge between the two great divisions in John Inglesant's life, his experiences in England and the maturing of his philosophy in Italy. As an allegory, "The Vielle-Player's Story" explains Inglesant's psychological division and the potentialities of his individuation. Two musicians discover "a common existence and sphere of life" in music, and later when they are separated by war, one in England and the other in Italy, they feel the "mysterious presence" of the other through musical consonance (243-245). Later, when Inglesant discusses "philosophical paganism" with Cardinal Rinuccini, the Cardinal echoes the vielle-player and subtly suggests an analogy between the Churches of Rome and of England:

> To a solemn bass of mystery and of the unseen, each man
> plays his own descant as his taste or fate suggests, but this
> manner of play is so governed and controlled by what

seems a fatal necessity, that all melts into a species of harmony; and even the very discords and dissonances, the wild passions and deeds of men, are so attempered and adjusted that without them the entire piece would be incomplete. (255)

Walking to the Cardinal's for dinner with a Roman gentleman, Inglesant puzzles over the "wonderful contrasts with which Rome abounds", and the gentleman declares: "We are Catholic and Pagan at the same time" (279). At dinner, Inglesant expounds upon "the power of music upon the mind" and declares his belief in "creatures which live in sound" who "kindle in us a love of our own kind and a tolerance of the petty failings and the shortcomings of men" (281). As such, art, and especially music, is Shorthouse's answer to unity within the Church. As man bears "the innate knowledge of God in the soul" (264), he has the power to transform life into "a fine art" (254) through religion. When Inglesant rescues a Lutheran fanatic from a mob, he discourses with him on art as in England he had discussed art with the Puritan, Mr. Thorne. Inglesant declares that art speaks to him "and in indistinct and yet forcible voice, of that common sympathy-- magical and hidden though it may be--by which the whole creation is linked together" (316). Thus, to Shorthouse, art in all its forms serves as the *anima*, guiding human thought towards common sympathy and unity. Besides his brief mention of King Charles's love of Church music (246), however, Shorthouse says little of art in England, and it is in Rome itself, "the visible symbol and representation of the Christian truth", that he sees life as "a perpetual masque or holy interlude of the life of the Saviour" (263).

It is in Italy, too, that Inglesant begins to discern the *shadow* affects and evils of the Romish system. The "nearer he approached the Papal capital the more wretched and worse governed did the country appear on every side" (260); the greater the contact he had with the Italian aristocracy, the greater his awareness became of "bad government, and the oppression and waste caused by the accumulated wealth and idleness of the innumerable religious orders" (217); and the more he came into contact with the common people, the more he heard "muttered complaints [against] the tyranny and oppression of the society of the Jesuits" (260). When deadly plague ravages the countryside and depopulates Italy's most beautiful cities, Inglesant connects the plague with political and religious in-fighting, and when he intellectually confronts the causes of the plague, he comes to understand that "the Churches...spread the contagion" (383), and he cannot distinguish whether the plague or the Romish system is the "terrible enemy of mankind" (382). Nonetheless, he creates authentic "holy interlude" in the "perpetual masque". Psychologically, his forgiveness of Malvolti and of the Cavaliere di Guardino are expressions of Ego/Self alignment; spiritually, they are epiphanies, transcendent visions of the Christ.

By transforming Malvolti from a personification of evil, a metaphor of Jung's *shadow* archetype, to Father Gratia, a living symbol of spiritual grace, Shorthouse dramatises the archetypal agency of the Self in its purest Christian form. At the moment Inglesant surrenders Malvolti to divine justice before the altar in the Chapel of San Miniato, Inglesant sacrifices more than his ego-centred obsession with revenge. As he accepts the Divine Light and the prompting of the Divine Voice before the altar, he sacrifices, in Shorthouse's terms, his philosophical quest, his human reason, and his human will. In Christian terms, he surrenders his evil nature, his personal will, and his soul to "the adorable Name of Jesus" (367). As Jung understands such experiences, Inglesant surrenders both his personal *shadow* and the collective *Shadow*, and his ego-consciousness and the Ego to the Self. His mind is clear and he speaks distinctly until he hands his sword to the priest. As the priest lays the sword upon the altar, Inglesant becomes confused "by the sudden overmastering impulse upon which he had acted" (368), and when he gives "his embroidered purse, heavy with gold" to the priest to have masses said for his brother's soul, he "totally forgot to name his brother" (368). Acting in accord with the dictates of the Self, Inglesant temporarily displaces ego-consciousness and moves "as in a dream". "One must never forget", Jung cautions, "that one dreams primarily, and, so to speak, exclusively, about oneself and out of oneself."[76] Had Inglesant named his brother, he would have merely personified his personal *shadow* as Eustace. Had Shorthouse adhered to the details of the story of the miraculous crucifix in San Miniato or to Burne-Jones' painting of the scene, as discussed in the last chapter, this dramatic scene should indeed have been the climax of the novel, the dissolution of the *shadow*.

Shorthouse's scene captures for the religious imagination the power of forgiving of an enemy, but it lacks the dramatic power the reader might have expected as the culmination of Inglesant's obsessive quest for revenge. In chapter thirty-two of *Westward Ho!*, for instance, Kingsley's hero, Amyas, madly pursues his brother's murderer, and when he hurls his sword into the sea, nature responds with a crash of lightning that blinds Amyas. Inglesant's action has the reverse effect; it gives rise to a "popular tradition" that the virtue of his "magic sword" protects the village: "...no harm can befall the village, no storm strike it, and, above all, no pillage of armed men or any violence can occur" (368). Inglesant has other important matters to attend to, his marriage to Lauretta, and as if his marriage has not ended the power of the *shadow*, the old Duke dies at the moment Inglesant and his daughter are married.

The personification of the *shadow*, however, transfers from Inglesant's hatred of Malvolti to Malvolti's hatred of di Guardino, Lauretta's brother. Jung gives an apt description of what happens psychologically to Inglesant. Although he sacrifices his ego-consciousness at the altar, he cannot extinguish the Ego itself, and he can, at best, transfer the projection of the *shadow*. "Naturally", Jung writes, "there can be no question of a total extinction of the Ego, for then the focus of consciousness would be destroyed, and the result would be complete unconsciousness." He explains:

> The relative abolition of the Ego affects only those supreme and ultimate decisions which confront us in situations where there are insoluble conflicts of duty. This means, in other words, that in such cases the Ego is a suffering bystander who decides nothing but must submit to a decision and surrender unconditionally.[77]

As Shorthouse dramatises the psychology, Inglesant's "shadow" must itself sacrifice the *shadow*; the psychological complex he has experienced is but a manifestation of the archetype. It remains for Malvolti, Inglesant's personal *shadow*, to deprive the archetype of all energy, which he can only accomplish by withdrawing the collective archetypal *Shadow* into his own consciousness. To do so, Malvolti must experience religious conversion and become an agent of "the supreme effort of Divine mercy...which shapes the faltering and unconscious actions of man into a beneficent and everlasting work" (403). Seeking revenge against his former "ally in evil", di Guardino, who has destroyed his family, Malvolti arrives at the Ara Coeli in Rome on Christmas Eve. Blind and attended by a faithful boy, Malvolti sees "in [his] mind's eye" (397), the total transformation of Rome. In "mystic white light", he sees the Christ descend the steps of the Ara Coeli into the Campidoglio and hears the Christ demand, "Knowest thou not that thou art mine?...thou wast given over to me by one who is a servant and friend of mine" (398-399). Transformed into an archetypal image, Father Grazia is protected by the power of Christ over the plague in "the city of the dead". As he wanders from city to city, nursing and attending to the victims of the dead, he is protected from the plague by his faith that "no poison could hurt me, no sword slays me" (397). Unless poison and sword are metaphors, he suffers from ego-inflation as Inglesant had earlier. Inglesant recognizes Fr. Grazia madness, and he wonders at the "particular form" it has taken. Soon, however, Inglesant stands beside Fr. Grazia and the dying leper, di Guardino. As the friar whispers prayers in di Guardino's ear:

> ...there passed across Inglesant's bewildered brain the vision of Another who stood beside the dying man. The halo round His head lighted all the hovel, so that the seamless coast He wore, and the marks upon His hands and feet, were plainly seen, and the pale alluring face was turned not so much upon the bed and upon the monk as

upon Inglesant himself, and the unspeakable glance of the
Divine eyes met his. (407)

This moment of eye-to-eye seeing represents the fulfillment of Inglesant's spiritual quest. When the "gracious figure [of Christ on the cross] entered into Inglesant's soul" (59) at Little Gidding, it activated an internal recognition of Individuation. Because "the relationship of the Self to the Ego is reflected in the relationship of Christ to man",[78] Inglesant's philosophical quest represents his need and desire to become conscious, to contain the numinous, mystical figure within the Ego, to translate the Divine into human reason.

It is not possible from Shorthouse's text to determine if the image of Christ originated within Inglesant, from his unconscious, and projected itself outward upon the crucifix or whether the image originated outside him and then entered into his psyche. What is clear, however, is that Inglesant would not have had the experience had he not been in the presence of a projection of the *anima*, Mary Collet. As Inglesant watches Fr. Grazia praying into the ear of di Guardino, whose leprous, plague-ravaged body presents a "spectacle of inexpressible loathing and horror" (406) to his sight, "there passed across Inglesant's bewildered brain the vision of Another" (407). Of spiritual visions and numinous psychic experiences, Jung insists, "We are unable to distinguish whether these actions emanate from God or from the unconscious. We cannot tell whether God and the unconscious are two different entities."[79]

In his quest to validate either "the infallibility of the Church" or "the testimony of the private spirit" (68), Inglesant must consciously chose his path, as Mary Collet, Nicholas Ferrar, Fr. St. Clare, Cardinal Rinuccini, and the rector of the Jesuit College in Rome insist, and he must be certain to follow his chosen path to its end. As a result of his encounter with Thomas Hobbes, his philosophical quest becomes a psychological one. "Hobbes's doctrine was new to him...the particular form it took was peculiar to Hobbes, and perished with him", but, inserts Shorthouse, "the underlying materialism which in some form or other has presented itself to the thinkers of every age" (68), and he presents Inglesant with a new challenge.

Thus, he questions himself: "How do I know indeed that this divine life within me is anything but an opinion formed by what I have heard and read? How do I know that there is any such thing as a divine life at all?" (68-69). As he gains sufficient, albeit subjective, experience to be able to address the questions consciously, the questions transform. Hobbes makes him aware that to answer the questions for himself, from within himself, he should have to "pretend to a direct revelation" (67). The *anima* guides him through the Inner Light towards the Divine Light; the *shadow* leads him through philosophical and religious doubts and through physical and intellectual agonies. It also leads him to the collective ravages of the plague and to the "greatest of all problems", that of "granting religious freedom, and at the same time maintaining religious truth" (276).

In his defence of Molinos, Inglesant challenges the possibility of attaining "the highest spiritual walk, and the purest condition of spiritual worship...within the Church of Rome" (418). He seeks the "liberty of reason" (418) for himself and for "those farthest advanced in the spiritual life" (417). "If it were possible for the spirit to be free", he reasons, "while fulfilling the outward observances, and participating in the outward ordinances of the Church, so also it must be possible for the reason to be free too" (418). Thus, he demands "spiritual freedom--the freedom of silence" from the General of the Jesuit Society. The General himself is silent, and when Inglesant leaves Rome, he leaves with the blessing of the Jesuit, and he leaves in silence.

Shorthouse never described his own inner struggles while composing *John Inglesant*, but, as noted earlier, he insisted to Macmillan that "the book as it stands with all its peculiarities is just what I intended it to be!" The imposed structure of the narrative suggests that Shorthouse's final intuition and understanding of his own transition from Quaker to Anglican was a "leap of faith", which he expresses through the metaphor of missing manuscripts that leap over the hero's story. The insertion of "NOTE: The MSS. are here imperfect." at the end of chapter twenty-two and the twenty-year break in the narrative between chapters thirty-eight and thirty-nine, accord with Shorthouse's final declaration that "We cannot say how we know . . ." (444). Inglesant's final answer in Rome, like that of Job, who also sees God eye-to-eye,[80] is silence, but his final answer in England is an impassioned, eloquent defence of the Church of England grounded in Shorthouse's psychological realism.

In the final scene outside Worcester Cathedral, Inglesant sacrifices the authority of reason itself, yet, ironically, he reasons himself into an absolutist position, and he does not speak alone; he speaks with the authority of his author. He acknowledges the "logical position" of the Church of Rome as the "inspired exponent" of the revelation of absolute truth (443), and then, in his own defence, he formulates a personal dogma about authority. Shorthouse uses a reasoning process that is remarkably similar to the response "post-Jungian" analysts make to Postmodernism. Postmodernist critics interpret archetypes through a representational theory of language, thus they assert that archetypes do not express eternal, unquestionable absolutes, but "are rather *temporal and linguistic by-products*".[81] Theoretically deprived of the grounding of their clinical and analytical authority, Jungians today must continue to use the Self as a "god term", as the ultimate explanatory principle of their psychological practice, despite their awareness that their "'ultimate' is no longer so absolute, so ultimate" as Jung conceived it to be.

The "ultimate ground of depth psychology" today is, however, precisely what Jung declared it to be, the unconscious itself, and the only response Jungians can make to their paradoxical dilemma in and through language lies in Jung's definition of the unconscious as the "ultimately unknowable".[82] Shorthouse delivers his response to the dilemma through "the religion of John Inglesant", which completes the philosophical quest that permeates the romance even as it asserts a spiritual grounding for the hero's religious thinking. The final page of the novel declares faith in "the method which Christ followed", of being "in harmony with that law of gradual development which the Divine Wisdom has planned" (445). Shorthouse does not involve himself or his hero in the Victorian debates between the science of evolution and biblical creationism or in the "Battle of the Churches". Rather, he contends "Absolute truth is not revealed" (443), to human reason, only the "physical and psychical laws" of "harmony" have been revealed (444). Christ "won the world by placing Himself" in harmony with the ultimate "law of gradual development" (445), which Jung's analytical psychology defines and describes as the dynamic process through which the inner laws of the human psyche individuate personality.

When Cardinal Rinuccini and Inglesant discuss the failure of Christianity to be of "use" to human needs, they recognize the need and the potential for "a purer Mythos". The Cardinal acknowledges that "the myths of the world are slow to change"; Inglesant responds, "The cross of Christ is composed of many other crosses--is the centre, the type, the essence of all crosses", and all crosses ultimately unite "undefined, unknown, yet sure and irresistible, with the iron necessity of law" (259). Even though "the position on which [the Church of England] stands seems to be illogical", Shorthouse declares, it is "an agency by which the devotional instincts of human nature are enabled to exist side by side with the rational" (442). *John Inglesant* does not define Anglicanism, because, as Neill concludes his study of Anglicanism, "There are no special Anglican theological doctrines [and] there is no particular Anglican theology".[83] Nonetheless, the "religion of John Inglesant" Shorthouse's Anglo-Catholic conviction that the Church of England is the Catholic Church in England. Eliot, who inherited "the religion of John Inglesant" and the literary tradition of Anglo-Catholicism, discovered at Little Gidding that "what the dead had no speech for, when living / They can tell you, being dead: the communication / Of the dead is tongued with fire beyond the language of the living".[84] He honours tradition:

...if the desirability of [Church] unity be admitted, if the
idea of a Christian society be grasped and accepted, then

it can only be realised, in England, through the Church of England...I am only affirming that it is this Church which, by its tradition, its organisation, and its relation in the past to the religious-social life of the people, is the one for our purpose--and that no Christianisation of England can take place without it.[85]

Notes to Chapter Four

[1]Sarah Shorthouse selected nineteen of her husband's letters to Victoria Welby for publication in the first volume of *LLLR*. Shorthouse deeply admired Welby's *Links and Clues* (1883), which she sent him as a gift to express her gratitude for his study of religion in *John Inglesant*. Although sufficient evidence does not exist to define the extent of her influence upon Shorthouse's development from philosophical romance to spiritual romance, his letters to her confirm her influence on his attention to spiritual ideas and distinctions. In his letter of 25 June 1882, he quotes from a paper she had sent him, and his response typifies his general understanding of "significs" and language: "...the answers to some of the things which most baffle us...are contained...not directly in words, but in Himself...the Incarnate Word is the Revelation", *LLLR*, vol. 1, 159.

[2]C. G. Jung, *Memories, Dreams, Reflections* (New York: Pantheon, 1961) 353-354.

[3]C. G. Jung, *Psychological Reflections* (New York: Harper, 1953), 239 and 321.

[4]C. G. Jung, *Psychological Reflections* 321.

[5]C. G. Jung, *Psychological Reflections* 321.

[6]Webster's *Third New International Dictionary* (1961).

[7]St. John admonishes: "Beloved, believe not every spirit, but try the spirits whether they are of God..." (I John 4:1), which Jung discusses in "A Psychological View of Conscience", *Collected Works*, vol. 10, 444 and in "The Phenomenology of the Spirit in Fairytales", *Collected Works*, vol. 9,I, 215.

[8]C. G. Jung, "Spirit and Life", *Contributions to Analytical Psychology* (London: Kegan Paul, Trench, Trubner and Co., 1928), 98.

[9]The Reverend J. Hunter Smith, who wrote the introduction to *LLLR*, comments that *John Inglesant* "is to a large extent a satire, and not altogether a fair one, on the principles and system of the Jesuits."

[10]William R. Siebenshuh's *Fictional Techniques and Factual Works* (Athens: University of Georgia Press, 1983) explains that in writing autobiography the author must "play the role of both participant and observer, actor and critic... [and] must imaginatively extend himself to recreate emotional experience", which may result, as it did in the autobiographical works of Gosse and Newman, in "a complex and powerful juxtaposition of time planes, perspectives, and analytical perceptions".

[11]Joseph L. Henderson, "Ancient Myths and Modern Man", *Man and his Symbols*, C. G. Jung and Marie-Louise von Franz, eds., (Garden City, New York: Doubleday, 1964), 118.

[12]Morris Philipson, *Outline of a Jungian Aesthetics* (Chicago: Northwestern University Press, 1963), 118.

[13]Philipson, *Outline* 27.

[14]Philipson, *Outline* 28.

[15]Oswald Spengler, *The Decline of the West* (London: Allen and Unwin, 1922), 167, quoted by Philipson, *Outline* 29.

[16]Andrew Sanders, *The Victorian Historical Novel, 1840-1880* (New York: St. Martin's, 1979): See page 160 of this thesis for a brief explanation of Sanders' observation.

[17]Edward C. Whitmont's *The Symbolic Quest* (New York: G. P. Putnam's Sons, 1969), for instance, illustrates more of the "Basic Concepts of Analytical Psychology" from examples in literature than it does from the analyst's clinical practice.

[18]Kevin L. Moris, *The Image of the Middle Ages in Romantic and Victorian Literature* (London: Croom Helm, 1984), 18-19.

[19]Paul Kugler, "The Unconscious in a Postmodern Depth Psychology", *C. G. Jung and the Humanities: Toward a Hermeneutics of Culture* (Princeton University Press, 1990), 307-318.

[20]Paul Kugler, "The Unconscious in a Postmodern Depth Psychology", *C. G. Jung and the Humanities* 315.

[21]Edward S. Casey, "Jung and the Postmodern Condition", *C. G. Jung and the Humanities* 322.

[22]Edward S. Casey, "Jung and the Postmodern Condition", *C. G. Jung and the Humanities* 323.

[23]When Jung was a young boy between seven and nine years old, he often sat alone on a stone that jutted out on a slope in front of his family's garden wall. Sitting alone, he played "an imaginary game that went something like this: 'I am sitting on top of this stone and it is underneath.' But the stone also could say 'I' and think: 'I am lying here on this slope and he is sitting on top of me.' The question then arose: 'Am I the one who is sitting on the stone, or am I the stone on which *he* is sitting?'...my uncertainty was accompanied by a feeling of curious and fascinating darkness. But there was no doubt whatsoever that this stone stood in some secret relationship to me." As Jung explains in "First Years", *Memories, Dreams, Reflections* (10-23), he later realised that "the world of my childhood...was *eternal*" and that his fascination with the "superior intelligence" of the eternal and the "soul stone" motivated his later discovery of the collective unconscious.

[24]T. S. Eliot, "Tradition and the Individual Talent", *Selected Essays* (London: Faber and Faber, Third Enlarged Edition, 1951) 22.

[25]Northrop Frye, *Anatomy of Criticism: Four Essays* (Princeton University Press, 1957), 16.

[26]T. S. Eliot, "Tradition and the Individual Talent" *Selected Essays* 21: "This essay proposes to halt at the frontiers of metaphysics and mysticism, and confine itself to..."

[27]T. S. Eliot, "Burnt Norton", *The Complete Poems and Plays* (London: Faber and Faber, 1969, rep. 1987), 175.

[28]T. S. Eliot, "Tradition and the Individual Talent", *Selected Essays* 22.

[29]T. S. Eliot, "Little Gidding", *Complete* 198.

[30]T. S. Eliot, "Tradition and the Individual Talent", *Selected Essays* 21.

[31]T. S. Eliot, "Religion and Literature", *Selected Essays* 395.

[32]T. S. Eliot, "Religion and Literature", *Selected Essays* 395.

[33]J. Henry Shorthouse, Letter to Canon Ainger, *LLLR*, vol. 1, 205-296.

[34]Helen Cadbury Alexander, *Richard Cadbury of Birmingham* (London: Hodder and Stoughton, 1906), 356-357. Cadbury was one of Shorthouse's childhood playmates; his "What is my Faith?", *Friends Quarterly Examiner* (July 1878), defines the Quaker beliefs most familiar to Shorthouse.

[35]C. G. Jung, "Aims of Psychotherapy", *Modern Man in Search of a Soul*, trans. W. S. Dell and Cary F. Baynes, (New York: Harcourt, Brace and Co., n.d.), 71.

[36]C. G. Jung, "The Meaning of Psychology for Modern Man", *Civilization in Transition*, vol. 10, *Collected Works*, 1964, 150.

[37]Morris Philipson, *Outline of a Jungian Aesthetics* 178.

[38]T. S. Eliot, "East Coker", *Complete* 179.

[39]T. S. Eliot, "The Dry Salvages", *Complete* 186.

[40]C. G. Jung, *Memories, Dreams, Reflections* 381-382.

[41]Anthony Stevens, *Archetypes: A Natural History of the Self* (New York: Quill, 1983), 65.

[42]Robert H. Hopcke, *A Guided Tour of the Collected Works of C. G. Jung* (Boston: Shambhala, 1989), 19.

[43]T. S. Eliot, "Gerontion", *Complete* 173.

[44]Edward C. Whitmont, *The Symbolic Quest: Basic Concepts of Analytical Psychology* (New York: Harper and Row, 1973), 232.

[45]J. Henry Shorthouse, Letter to Lady Lyell (1899), in *LLLR*, vol. II, 373-375.

[46]Elizabeth Drew, *T. S. Eliot: The Design of his Poetry* (New York: Charles Scribner's Sons, 1950), 101-102.

[47]"The Arminian Nunnery" (1641, rep. The Little Gidding Community Press, 1987) endangered the Ferrar household by accusing the community of practices that form "a bridge to popery" (8).

[48]Robert Van der Weyer, "Nicholas Ferrar and Little Gidding: A Reappraisal", *For Veronica Wedgwood These: Studies in Seventeenth-Century History*, Richard Ollard and Pamela Tudor-Craig, eds. (London: Collins, 1986), 152-174, 171.

[49]T. S. Eliot, "The Dry Salvages", *Complete* 188.

[50]C. G. Jung, *Mysterium Coniunctionis, Collected Works*, XIV, 107, n. 66.

[51]Pamela Tudor-Craig, "Charles I and Little Gidding", *For Veronica Wedgwood These* 175-187, 176.

[52]C. G. Jung, *Psychological Reflections*: "Personality can never develop itself unless the individual chooses his own way consciously and with conscious, moral decision. If either need or choice is lacking, the individual will follow 'the other ways', the conventions of a moral, social, political, philosophic, or religious nature" (279-280).

[53]James Olney, *Metaphors of Self: The Meaning of Autobiography* (Princeton University Press, 1972), 145.

[54]William McGuire and R. F. C. Hull, eds. "Talks with Miguel Serrano, 1961", *C. G. Jung Speaking: Interviews and Encounters* (Princeton University Press, 1977): "Man should live according to his own nature; he should concentrate on self-knowledge then live in accordance with the truth about himself...One must be what one is; one must discover... individuality, that centre of personality equidistant between the conscious and the unconscious; we must aim for that ideal point towards which nature appears to be directing us" (463).

[55]J. Henry Shorthouse, Letter to Margaret (Southall) Evans, (17 July 1880), *LLLR*, vol. I, 121-122. Writing to his cousin about her reactions to *John Inglesant* and his "own reading", Shorthouse states, "My *own* reading of the book is that God prefers culture to fanaticism." His letter to Canon William Boyd Carpenter (7 March 1884), *LLLR*, vol. I, 220-221, concerns *The Little Schoolmaster Mark*, but his statement applies to his lifelong view that "what we want... [is] to understand how religion may be an art."

[56]William Shakespeare, *Macbeth* V.viii.8-13.

[57]C. G. Jung, *Aion: Researches into the Phenomenology of the Self*, trans. R. F. C. Hull, *Complete Works*, vol. 9, part 2, Bollingen Series XX (Princeton University Press, 1959), 44.

[58]C. G. Jung, *Aion* 178.

[59]C. G. Jung, *Aion* 71.

[60]Shorthouse acknowledged in a letter to his cousin Arthur Galton (17 January 1899) that he "made great use" of Joseph Berington's *Memoirs of Gregorio Pangani, and his Agency in England, 1634-1636*, which was published in 1793. See *LLLR*, vol. I, 364-365.

[61]Christopher Hibbert, *Charles I* (London: Weidenfeld and Nicolson, 1968), 135. See also Thomas Griesinger's *The Jesuits: A Complete History of Their Open and Secret Proceedings from the Foundation of the Order to the Present Time* (London: W. H. Allen, 1866), 519-554, which demonstrates the passion of anti-Jesuit feeling during Shorthouse's lifetime, and the account of "Charles the First and the Popish Plot" in J. M. Stone's *Studies from Court and Cloister* (London: Sands and Co., 1905), 178-203, which supports Shorthouse's generalisation.

[62]C. G. Jung, "The Psychological Aspects of the Kore", *The Archetypes and the Collective Unconscious*, R. F. C. Hull, trans., *Collected Works*, vol. 9, part one, Bollingen Series XX (Princeton University Press, 1969), 199.

[63]T. S. Eliot, "Little Gidding", *Complete* 191-192. Eliot uses the legend of the King's third visit in the second stanza of "Little Gidding". He creates tension between a series of "if's", probabilities and potentialities of pilgrimage to Little Gidding, in the second stanza and a series of absolute statements about spiritual experience in the third stanza. The technique complements the probability versus reality theme ("What might have been and what has been") of "Burnt Norton".

[64]Robert Van der Weyer, "Nicholas Ferrar and Little Gidding: A Reappraisal", *For Veronica Wedgwood These*, 168, n. 40. Alan Maycock summarizes the results of the legend of the King's third visit in *The Chronicles of Little Gidding* (London: SPCK, 1954), 68: "In July or August 1646, Little Gidding was raided by Parliamentary troops...The soldiers ransacked both the church and house, tore down the organ at the west end of the church, lit a huge fire with the wreckage and roasted some sheep which they had killed in the pastures. Then, as legitimate loot, they seized all the plate, furniture, and provisions that they could carry off and made away at their leisure."

[65]J. Henry Shorthouse, Letter to Mrs. Moller, *LLLR*, vol. 1, 288-291.

[66]C. G. Jung, "The Syzygy: Anima and Animus", *Aion* 13.

[67]Edward C. Whitmont, *The Symbolic Quest: Basic Concepts of Analytical Psychology* 199.

[68]C. G. Jung, "The Syzygy: Anima and Animus", *Aion* 20.

[69]C. G. Jung, "The Syzygy: Anima and Animus", *Aion* 20.

[70]Edward C. Whitmont, *The Symbolic Quest: Basic Concepts of Analytical Psychology* 199.

[71]C. G. Jung, *Psychological Reflections* 63.

[72]C. G. Jung, *Psychological Reflections* 58.

[73]Gunter Pulvermacher, "Carl Gustav Jung and Musical Art", *Jung in Modern Perspective* (Bridport, Dorset: Prism Press, 1991), 256-267, 259.

[74]Gunter Pulvermacher quotes Jung's letter to Serge Moreux (20 January 1950). Moreux had invited Jung to write about "The role of music in the collective unconscious", an offer Jung declined. "Carl Gustav Jung and Musical Art", *Jung in Modern Perspective* 257.

[75]J. Henry Shorthouse, "A Midsummer Night's Dream", *LLLR*, vol. 2, 329-345: In a dream, Julia meets a magician who describes people who "are born of the union of art and human thought" (341). Pages 298-299 of this thesis discuss the story in detail.

[76]C. G. Jung, *Psychological Reflections* 57.

[77]C. G. Jung, *Aion* 44-45.

[78]C. G. Jung, *Answer to Job* (New York: World Publishing Company, 1970), 153.

[79]C. G. Jung, *Answer to Job* 199.

[80] Job 42.5: "I have heard of thee by the hearing of the ear: but now mine eye seeth thee."

[81] Paul Kugler, "The Unconscious in a Postmodern Depth Psychology", *C. G. Jung and the Humanities* 316.

[82] Paul Kugler, "The Unconscious in a Postmodern Depth Psychology", *C. G. Jung and the Humanities* 316.

[83] Stephen Neill, *Anglicanism* (Harmondsworth: Penguin, 1958), 417.

[84] T. S. Eliot, "Little Gidding", *Complete* 192.

[85] T. S. Eliot, *The Idea of a Christian Society* (London: Faber, 1934), 46-47.

Chapter Five: Shorthouse and his Public,
from *John Inglesant* to *The Little Schoolmaster Mark*

When Shorthouse finished *John Inglesant* in 1876, the "discreet silence" that Inglesant had demanded but failed to receive from the Society of Jesus was nearly over in the author's own life. The "missing documents" of more than twenty years of Inglesant's life, which form the narrative break between chapters thirty-eight and thirty-nine, correspond autobiographically to the twenty years of marriage during which Shorthouse contemplated and composed *John Inglesant* and to the twenty years between his transition from the Society of Friends to the Church of England. From the time *John Inglesant* became publicly known until Shorthouse's death in 1903, another period of just over twenty years filled the silence with a public voice. From 1881, when the novel was first presented to the public, to 1883, when the novel was "taking London by storm", "the author of *John Inglesant*" happily became a public figure, and the pen of J. Henry Shorthouse became an instrument of outspoken, candid, loyal and liberal Anglicanism. Shorthouse found himself "lionized" and sought after by Church leaders, literary critics, politicians, scientists, lords and ladies, and devoted fans. The Prime Minister, the Queen, the Archbishop of Canterbury, the deans and canons of several cathedrals, the Poet Laureate, and professors at Oxford and Cambridge all honoured his philosophical romance with public and private acclaim and appreciation.[1] Almost overnight the quiet Birmingham manufacturer became a celebrity of high Victorian society, and *John Inglesant* became the focus of controversy. Shorthouse's own nature became caught in conflicts that might have divided him from himself had he not been deeply integrated and healthily individuated. During the next decade of his life, he met all public and private challenges with intensified literary and critical work and with devout churchmanship and began redefining and re-mythologizing the essential foundations he had secured for himself in *John Inglesant*. As Individuation continued in him, his persona rigidified, and he both enjoyed and played the role of "the author of *John Inglesant*". Under the influences of the *anima*, however, his masculine, philosophical voice, the narrative "masque" of Geoffrey Monk disappeared, and a new voice of feminine spirituality emerged, one that united the "principle" of Mary Collet with the aristocratic refinement and sophistication of John Inglesant. "Father Rome and Mother England" integrated to form an Anglo-Catholic sensibility.

When Sir George and Lady Sedley requested the pleasure of their dinner guests, 30 January 1882, at 29 Berkeley Square, they included a *nota bene*: "You are particularly asked please not to discuss *John Inglesant* at the dinner table."[2] Of course, it was generally not polite in Victorian society to discuss religion or politics at dinner among guests, but why a host and hostess should so expressly forbid a particular subject "is surely a very singular, one might without fear of contradiction say a unique, kind of embargo".[3] Clearly, the controversy was activated and carried forth in private society and in public notices though very few reviews of *John Inglesant* were published in 1880-1881, and those that were attracted little attention and promoted little controversy. Commenting on "a literary effort which is far too ambitious to be spoken of without respect", *The Athenaeum*, 30 October 1880, observed, "*John Inglesant* affords a capital instance of the way in which inexperienced authors miss success by trying too much at one time" and complained against the "one reason strong enough to damn it--it is much too long." In a lengthy outline of the plot, *The Athenaeum* gave little attention to the novel's philosophy or its romance, but noted that the elderly Inglesant had accepted "for want of anything better the compromise offered by the Church of England".[4] If anyone had real justification for complaint, it was surely Shorthouse, who found himself identified as "Mr. Courthouse" in the review. Shorthouse responded in a letter to Professor William Knight (1 December 1880) that the reviewer had been "rather oppressed by the work" and sent Knight a copy of *John Inglesant* with apologies: "I doubt whether the book is of sufficient interest to justify your spending time over it."[5] A year later (6 December 1881) after correspondence about an article Shorthouse was writing on Wordsworth, Shorthouse thanked Knight for telling him how favourably Prime Minister Gladstone, Professor T. E. Huxley, and Fred Pollock had received the book.

Also during October 1880, the *British Quarterly Review* praised the novel as "a notable book", though one given to "descriptions rather than [to] incidents" and criticized its "disquisitions and descriptions" for "running into excess". The *BQR* also stated that John Inglesant had "become a Catholic" by the time he encountered Molinos, an assertion Shorthouse denied explicitly in a letter to Edmund Gosse (1 April 1883): John Inglesant, "properly speaking, never consciously went over to Rome at all".[6] After praising the novel as "a careful historical study...full of insight and strength", the *BQR* reviewer commended the book as "worthy of being studied", noting it was "compiled with great care and written with great ability". Surely, though, the most interesting and important early review was published in *The Saturday Review of Politics, Literature, Science, and Art* (9 July 1881), a review Shorthouse called "very flattering and beautifully written".[7] Written by Mrs. Humphry Ward, who had served as mid-wife to its publication, the review examined *John Inglesant* at some length and offered both praise and criticism. Admiring its "academic calmness of tone and purity of style", she compared the romantic elements with those of Hawthorne in *Transformation*, and admitted that romance "appeals to a more subtle and unusual range of feelings than are ordinarily stirred by a novel". She directed her criticisms at the literary aspects. The character of John Inglesant, she claimed, should have been presented "through the medium of Inglesant's personality", which would have avoided the abruptive and surprising ending. There are too many "stray characters" and they "are far too apt to talk in the same key and phraseology". Mary Collet is presented as "a beautiful sketch"; Lauretta is "neither a beautiful nor an effective sketch...and Inglesant's relations with her...are scarcely thought out at all". Compared with Thackeray's *Esmond*, the characters, other than John Inglesant, appear "flat and tame". She praises Shorthouse for having "shown great knowledge of many of the deeper and less commonly analysed forces of human thought and feeling" and for having used "unfailing tact and skilfulness in describing them". Finally, she praises the "peculiar religious tone and temper which belonged to the finer and more poetical minds in the Tractarian movement" and to which Shorthouse "[has given] delicate and beautiful interpretation".

Shorthouse responded privately to Mrs. Ward's review. In a letter to his cousin, Margaret Evans, (11 July 1881), he comments that Mrs. Ward "only partially understands the book, and some of her assertions I venture to dispute", but he does not specify his exact disagreements.[8] The same week he wrote to Alexander Macmillan that the review "is beautifully written, and a man must be hard to please who is not satisfied with it; where she differs from the author, *of course*, she is wrong!"[9] He states only one specific instance of her wrong judgment. Because *John Inglesant* "makes no pretention to comparison with *Esmond*: it should rather be compared with such books as William Smith's *Thorndale*, being avowedly a 'philosophical romance'". Critics ignored her suggestion of comparison with *Esmond* and *Transformation*, and no critic found *Thorndale* worthy of comparison with *John Inglesant*. Thus, by the time of the Sedley's dinner invitation, what controversy surrounded the novel was still not defined in print. It must be noted, however, that by the end of 1881 Macmillan had only published 2,750 copies (750 in June and 2,000 in December. In 1882 the book was reprinted almost monthly: some 10,250 copies were released for sale between January and November; 12,000 copies were printed in 1883; 28,000 were printed in London before Shorthouse's death in 1903. When something like 60,000 copies were on the market, Shorthouse braced himself for "the great Roman Catholic attack", and, as he told his cousin Isabel Southall, "I am quite prepared to meet it. I have been too lenient if I have erred at all."[10]

Shorthouse had, in fact, braced himself; he rigidified his views about Roman Catholicism. In a letter to Dr. Abbott (November 1880), he refers to "interesting correspondence" he has had with a Benedictine monk about the character of Father St. Clare. Shorthouse terms the monk's view as being "out of that fairyland (I will not say fools' paradise) in which modern Catholics live".[11] Early in January 1882, Shorthouse wrote Macmillan, who had sent him a letter from Cardinal Manning:

> It is curious that he should prefer the first volume; most Roman Catholics object exceedingly to the character of the Jesuit in it, which they say is an impossibility. I never reason with Roman Catholics: they live in a fairyland of their own.[12]

Later, in October 1881, he wrote Lady Victoria Welby that he objected to "the tendency so often manifested among the most intelligent advocates of freedom of thought to compliment and to pander to the Church of Rome":

> The very perfection of freedom which these men enjoy makes them forget the struggle by which it was won, and the slough of stupid ignorance to which this Church system would have condemned the whole human race.

"These favoured men", he asserts, would have inherited nothing but "the grotesque pantomime which the Roman Church calls history, and the sterile waste which she calls Catholic literature...but for the Protestant princes of Germany". It is his first reference to the German reformers whom he will exalt in his later novels. As if to echo *John Inglesant*, he states,

> The charge against the Roman Church is not that her doctrines do not contain germs of truth, but that having based her system upon the profoundest truths, she has succeeded in making truth itself a life.[13]

The "author of *John Inglesant*" who had maintained his protagonist's indifference, now preferring the Anglican Church, now the Roman throughout most of the novel, had indeed become as anti-Catholic and as pro-Anglican as his fictional hero in the final chapter. Psychologically, it is possible that as Shorthouse dramatised John Inglesant's quest for religious freedom and certitude, he unconsciously projected his own *shadow* onto the enemy and counter-transferred the "infallibility" claims of the Papacy into ego-rigidity. The frustration of the struggle to convince himself intellectually of his own position may explain why he stopped writing "for a period of almost two years". He complained of being "tired [and] that it was of no use to go on [writing], for he would not be able to afford its publication". In 1876 he and Sarah bought Lansdowne, a gracious home at 60 Wellington Road, Edgbaston, where they lived the rest of their lives. Despite finances, what he found somewhat difficult to afford was his privacy. He could not have stated anything critical in writing about the Quakers without offending family and friends, and in joining the Church of

England he had joined the church his mother disliked. There is no evidence, however, of any bitterness, or that he ever felt any need to justify his religious views to the Society of Friends. He felt restricted by their social mannerisms, but if he felt anything unconsciously, he displaced his anxieties and transferred any "*shadow* affects" onto the Roman Church. Shorthouse's struggles were not concerns of doubt or of the finer points of theology that had attracted the Tractarians but were matters of social taste and decorum. As a gentleman, he never spoke offensively against anyone, though his rejection of the Roman "fairyland" seems compensatory and ironic from the man who admitted believing in "fairies" and other supernatural beings.

The early letters after the publication of *John Inglesant* also disclose his awareness of his own unconsciousness, though only in a self-amusing attitude. In a letter of 25 June 1882, he notes that John Inglesant "had not much to complain of at last...and the frame of mind in which he is last seen is one in which many of us are content to rest while hoping [as Goethe had done with his dying breath] for 'more light'". He declared the problems he faced in developing the character of John Inglesant an "impossible task":

> I doubt whether the most superhuman genius could perform such a feat [to create] a character... despised by the one-sided, fanatic, enthusiastic portion of the world, and at the same time to show these people by the simple working out of the character, without preaching it, that he was right and they were wrong.[14]

He began to recognize some unconscious, rather "happy coincidences" of his labours. He enjoyed the sense of synchronicity, as he wrote Macmillan (29 May 1882), when he received a monograph from John Bigelow in New York, who had composed a monograph on *Molinos the Quietist*, "at the same moment independently" that he had been working on the character and ideas of Molinos for *John Inglesant*. It is "very curious coming out at the same moment", he wrote.[15] A few other "happy accidents" also delighted him. In July he wrote Macmillan about "a delightful bit of *undesigned coincidence* in *John Inglesant*". Nathan Bodington of Wadham College, he explained, "tells me that the Founders of Wadham College debated whether they should found a Jesuit College *abroad*, or a *College at Oxford*, and decided on the latter! He thought I knew the fact, and had sent John Inglesant accordingly".[16] Four years later another incident occurred. Apparently the public assumed that Shorthouse had known and corresponded with Bishop Hannington and had deliberately included the story of his tragic death in Africa at the end of *Sir Percival*. Shorthouse knew nothing beyond having read of "an outbreak of war in Africa", but, as his widow surmised, "this fact no doubt influenced the course of his own fictitious story".[17] The point here is a simple one; such unconscious and synchronous coincidences demonstrate how keenly Shorthouse was aware of the "age spirit" which he tried to capture in his novels and how perceptive he had been in suggesting the parallels between the seventeenth-century and his own. Certainly, the recurrence of patterns in human events, in thought, emotion, and belief testifies to the "mystery" inherent in "myth", the validity of archetypal theory as a "human psychology".

In December 1881, Shorthouse expressed the wish to Dr. Talbot of Keble College, who had shown the Shorthouses "the inside of Oxford" in May, that the historian Samuel R. Gardiner would "go into details" in his study of *John Inglesant*. Shorthouse believed Gardiner "most competent" in seventeenth century history.[18] He did not have to wait long, for in May 1882 Gardiner published a review in *Fraser's Magazine*. Gardiner began his criticism with a general discussion of the advantages of the novelist over the historian. The novelist "in being able to throw aside a mass of facts of secondary importance [is able] to embody in creations of his own the life and spirit of a bygone age." With this advantage, however, comes "a greater burden of responsibility", that of presenting "characters and situations which could possibly have existed... [to] teach something worth knowing about the period". Is *John Inglesant* true to the possibilities of the age? Gardiner begins to qualify. If the novel is taken as historical fiction, it succeeds brilliantly within a "few strokes" of bearing the impress of truth", especially the truth about King Charles I. The criteria of historical fiction, however, do not apply to a work that openly proclaims itself a romance. In a romance the author "should take care to let us know that when [he distorts or rearranges historical facts] he does things...intentionally". The writer of historical romance has "no right to irritate those who happen to know something about the subject, by a small number of purposeless blunders". In Shorthouse's case, such errors "lead to nothing except the suspicion that far from having any deep knowledge of the history...Mr. Shorthouse has not thoroughly mastered the small handbooks which supply so many Englishmen with the outlines of history." He cites four such errors, which, "in themselves [are] unimportant" but for another fact: George Eliot "has accustomed us to a different kind of preparation for writing historical romance." *John Inglesant* betrays Shorthouse's own weariness of strife and contention, thus Shorthouse "fixed upon that border-land which lay between the Churches of Rome and England" and he failed to give "allegiance to the stern sovereignty of facts".[19]

Gardiner was the first of many critics to attack the characterisation of Father St. Clare and the first to observe how Shorthouse re-worked history to fit the needs of romance. Father St. Clare, he asserts, is modelled on Christopher Davenport, a Franciscan, whose book *Deus, Natura, Gratia* was attacked by the Jesuits because it showed that "the Articles of the Church of England were susceptible of an interpretation which would not be inadmissible at Rome". Combining Davenport with his fictitious Jesuit, Shorthouse "produced a monster": It is very hard to believe in the existence of such a man, [and] if any Jesuit had come in the reign of Charles I to leave stray souls to their fate, it would be worthwhile telling us who that Jesuit really was. For his purposes, Shorthouse romanticized Father St. Clare, and in leaving John Inglesant freedom of conscience, Shorthouse demonstrated that he "never seems to understand the causes of the permanent hold of the Church upon the English people". The Church of England's history, Gardiner declares, "is one of the most marvelous upon record", and Shorthouse missed a great chance "in drawing out the causes of its success". In Gardiner's judgment, Shorthouse had "overestimated the depth of the movement for bringing about a union between the Churches of England and Rome" and had let his own proclivities colour his reading of history. *John Inglesant* "passes over exactly that which we wish to learn", which is why John Inglesant so adamantly defends the Church of England in chapter thirty-nine and how the Church grew from the beginning of Elizabeth I's reign when "scarcely a voice was raised in its favour" to being "venerated as the Church of the nation" a hundred years later. As for John Inglesant himself, Gardiner comments, "He never could have existed. Even in Utopia there could hardly have been a union of such firmness of decision with such vacillation of purpose".

Gardiner, Shorthouse responded, missed completely "that there are religious phases both of this age of the seventeenth century, and of any other age" because his "habit of exact research has narrowed his perception and grasp of the realities of a past age". Writing to Edmund Gosse (1 April 1883), Shorthouse decried Gardiner's religious sensibilities and stated that "Mr. Gardiner is an absolutely inadequate exponent [and] seems incapable of forming a conception" about the religious phases of history. Gardiner denigrated Shorthouse's treatment of the Archbishop Laud, and Shorthouse, in his letter to Gosse, "venture[d] entirely to differ from Gardiner in his estimate of Laud" as a man who "never feared the face of man".[20] With the declaration that Shorthouse had created a "monster" of Father St. Clare, that Shorthouse had not understood the real historical situation between the two churches, that no one like John Inglesant could possibly have existed, and that Shorthouse did not understand the real nature of the Church of England's position, Gardiner engulfed *John Inglesant* in controversy, and the philosophical romance quickly gained public attention.

The Church Quarterly Review (April 1882) began its review with an assertion: "Those who have not yet heard of *John Inglesant* may well be suspected of...primeval and abysmal aberration".[21] In reading the novel, the

196

reviewer said, "We feel that it is our own inward life which is being searched, and probed, and judged, and clarified", and he praised Shorthouse's work heavenward. The reviewer's complaint, in what little criticism he offered, concerned the plot structure:

> Permanent and vivid impressions [are formed by the book
> but are] not taken up into the story...The public is puzzled
> by a work so vividly dramatic in its separate moments, so
> intentionally undramatic in its effect as a whole...The
> romance has been a little too much for the philosophy.

As Jung later found the psyche itself a "sacrament",[22] so the *Church Quarterly* reviewer found "the hope of an Eirenicon" in *John Inglesant's* vision of the Eucharist: "Worship is more *central*, even, than the Creed itself; it holds within itself the key of the Creed; it is in the action of worship we are all made one." The review ends with a plea:

> We would fervently beg all those to read this beautiful
> book who desire to foster in themselves a strong and deep
> passion of spiritual devotion, and yet are conscious of a
> precious and holy heritage...

Across the Atlantic, Robert Nourse commended *John Inglesant* to readers of *The Dial* (Chicago) with similar urgency and lauded the book: "We have nothing but praise for this fresh and remarkable book...it *is* the greatest romance of the nineteenth century".[23] Nourse, unfortunately, was swept away with the novel's historical fascination and his own highly charged imagination, and presents his own inaccuracies with enthusiastic admiration.[24] *Blackwood's*, meanwhile, declared *John Inglesant* "unique in recollection and unparalleled in fiction"[25] and urged readers to study the novel:

> Style and spirit, tone and colour, are so harmonious, so
> complete and so mutually conducive to the desired effect,
> that [of] music in its mystical perfection.

Blackwood's found fault only with the climax. Inglesant's forgiveness of Malvolti is "too miraculous and highly strained for the rest of the work", though, nonetheless, the book as a whole casts "that spell of unbroken continuity which carries the reader along whether he will or not".

Despite many high praises in contemporary reviews, Shorthouse found the allusion in *The Spectator* (25 March 1881) "more gratifying" than other public notices.[26] "Moral Purpose in Fiction" was the first effort to place Shorthouse's work within a greater literary context. Declaring Shorthouse "the author of the only novel of the day that may take rank" with those of George Eliot, *The Spectator* attempted to define "how little fiction can depend on history for moral purpose, even when its narrative is a mere loan from history":

> The peculiar charm of *John Inglesant*...is that it mirrors
> the subtle complexity with which, in actual experience,
> the proportions of the moral life are blended with the
> unmoral.[27]

It is not just the blending or alternating of experiences of good and evil that the reviewer admired, but the "spiritual experiences... [because] they come in the story, as they come in life". What the reviewer notes specifically is that although Inglesant rejects Cressy's offer of monastic life, he nonetheless "feels the spiritual life flow on with undiminished volume". Inglesant confronted the spiritual paradox that confronts modern man, or Victorian man, in this case, who is aware of his psychological processes and dynamics. What the Ego and the conscience have been taught and disciplined to accept as moral, immoral, and amoral are "relativized by the dynamics of Individuation". An individual may do what is supposed to be morally unacceptable, yet feel free-flowing psychic energy as a result. Individuation "rewards" individuals for obedience to personal psychological dictates. Inglesant "is sensible of worldliness and cowardice, which seem rewarded; his devotion and self-sacrificing loyalty have brought him nothing but ill". As the reviewer explains,

> Right and wrong do not form the only antithesis in human
> life; at strange, inexplicable moments, when the
> unfathomable part of our nature seems opened to us, we
> would say they do not appear to form its deepest
> antithesis.

Then, warning readers against the injurious effects of the "habit of changing description to judgment", *The Spectator* commends fiction which represents the protagonist "as no more than a fragment [of] the whole sphere of goodness", which amounts to an endorsement of Shorthouse's prefatory assertion that in presenting the life of John Inglesant he is presenting "the life of each of us alone" in relation to the Christian Mythos, or, as Jung might have said, of the individuating Ego in its relation to the Self. Moreover, Jung cautioned that the sense of free-flowing energy within the Ego does not in itself provide proof that what the individual has done or is doing is necessarily healthy or "psychologically right". What is wanted in fiction is also what is wanted in Individuation, "discernment of this complex moral life, under the light of intellectual sympathy". Inglesant's relationship with Malvolti combines such discernment with the intellectual sympathies of his intended audience. Had he taken revenge against Malvolti, Inglesant would have taken on, in Shorthouse's terms, the character and nature of a Roman Catholic Italian, and Inglesant's final apology for the Church of

England would have made no sense. Without the final chapter, the novel would have given little offense; the entire story could have been "psychologised" or "written off" as Shorthouse's justification or compensation for his personal religious commitment, but it is far more likely that the final chapter is satirical "revenge" against Papal Infallibility and its foreign sovereignty over English conscience.

When the "attack" against *John Inglesant* began, however, it came from Ireland, not from Rome. Doctor of Divinity William Barry focused theological and literary discernment against *John Inglesant* in *The Dublin Review* (April 1882), and he led an attack upon Shorthouse's religious views that became typical of Roman Catholic attitudes until Vatican II. Barry attempted to argue theological specifics in his review, but his tone is that of sarcasm and parody, which, ironically, works in Shorthouse's favour. Barry's study is over thirty pages long, most unusual for "a review", and it has the added interest of a philosophical dispute about Platonism. Asserting that Shorthouse's Father St. Clare "preferred to hold with Aristotle", Barry delineates the consequences of Inglesant's Platonism, which, he argues, makes the Jesuit priest into a "Machiavellian in league with Fortune" and turns Cardinal Rinuccini into Shorthouse's version of a Roman Aristophanes.[28] Because "ethereal Platonism clings to no one symbol more than another", Inglesant was never forced by Father St. Clare to make a firm commitment to either the Roman or the English Church. Barry considers the characterisation of the Jesuit "utterly impossible", especially because the Jesuit had urged Inglesant that what matters is not Rome or Canterbury but "belief within the heart". Thus, he asserts, for its "communion" the Church of England "must borrow its grace from the heart of the believer".

That Shorthouse was prepared for the attack appears evident, for his response came immediately the same month (April 1882) in *The Nineteenth Century*. "The Agnostic at Church" extends views espoused in an undated letter which Mrs. Shorthouse wisely published in *LLLR*. "To an Agnostic" asserts the sensitivity towards the "idea of Christ" that Shorthouse infused into *John Inglesant*, Christianity without the Bible. Regarding the New Testament as "simply the text-book and historical record of the life and teachings of Jesus of Nazareth and of the early days of Christianity", Shorthouse argues that it "is liable, like any other history, to error and mistake".[29] He was firm in his conviction: "I do not advocate belief in the Bible, I advocate belief in Christ...No infinite truth can be adequately conceived and expressed by human ideas and words." Truth beyond human ideas and words necessitates "seeing Him who is invisible [and] dwelling in the unapproachable Light." To Shorthouse, "The hereafter and the unseen present the highest motive principle of the rational man." Inklings or intimations of truth inspire rationality as they represent and recreate "a spiritual, opposing, and recuperative agency working for good". As the unseen and invisible interact with body and brain, they enforce modern man's need for "a mediator", and, as Shorthouse wrote, "Modern belief in the unalterableness of law only makes this mediator, this atoner, still more necessary." The atoner or "at-oner" is the agency which makes integration and wholeness possible, and whether we accept Shorthouse's "Divine Principle" or Jung's dynamics of Ego\Self relationship, the spiritual and psychological dynamics defy prescriptive or authoritarian statement.

In "The Agnostic at Church", Shorthouse addresses readers in sympathy with *John Inglesant*.[30] The agnostic knows instinctively, Shorthouse argues, that there "is a power *within ourselves* which makes for righteousness, and which may be cultivated." His concern in the essay is to illustrate how "an outward and invisible sign" may express and connect with "an inward and spiritual grace". Spiritual grace, like the Divine Light, is, however, subject to what "may perhaps be...at moments... [the] greatest share [of] consciousness of intellect". Human reason, he asserts, as expressed and believed in by scientists through their methodology, will encounter "more superstition from the pulpit than [it] will ever meet in the ritual of the sacrament". Man cannot avoid superstition "unless he severs himself entirely from his fellow-men". It is this severance that is felt and sensed by the individuating ego when it first begins to heed the promptings of the "higher self", which in the paradoxes of language, is also the "deepest self". Though Shorthouse might have objected to Jung's usage of the word *Self*, he would not have disagreed with Jung's intuitions and attempts to define the agency of the Self. As if imitating the futuristic visions of Tennyson's "Locksley Hall",[31] Shorthouse ponders:

> Looking into the future I sometimes see a glorious Church, which, without faltering in the announcement of what she conceives to be truth, gives her blessing with a kingly munificence, asking nothing in return, and leaving the final result to the decision of the final assize, bestows her sacraments and benediction, like the Divine gift of sunshine, upon all mankind alike.

"The Agnostic at Church" ends with one of Shorthouse's few criticisms of the Church of England's legal position, a position he defends in *John Inglesant*. Stating that the "Romish Church has never risen to the 'height of this great argument' [that God's grace is freely given without earthly qualifications]", he fears that the Church of England, though it has "approached nearer to it", has done so "often [as] the result of the accident of its legal position".[32] Two months later, again only in private correspondence, Shorthouse addresses William Barry's chief argument against *John Inglesant*. Barry attacked "the champions of the mysticism that overspread

Europe in the seventeenth century" as having "carried to perilous excess the doctrine of the Inward Light" and asserted that the doctrine "under the modern name of Free Thought is disintegrating society, as Free Humanism is abolishing morality".[33] Shorthouse wrote Lady Welby (10 May 1882) about his belief that free thought is "the source of faith" and asserted that the "purest Platonism [leads] us to expect...a philosophic system of mathematical certainty which will afford a basis upon which Christian faith may rest secure".[34] Further, he declares, "*It is impossible to start a false myth*", a statement he underscored in his letter before asserting:

> A man cannot sit down in a back parlour and make a myth. No mythos ever yet grew up except from the needs and aspirations of the people among whom it flourished, and to whom it brought spiritual nourishment and help.

Meeting the needs of people from within their daily life is also the grounding of his argument in "The Humorous in Literature", which he published in *Macmillan's Magazine* in March 1883.

Shorthouse hoped to introduce a new understanding about humour, but his essay, though it pleased him, did not define or redefine humour clearly enough to make humour a new criterium of literary value. Beginning with a series of questions--fourteen of them--Shorthouse rather confuses the issue, and fails to resolve the confusion by the end of the essay. "Is all consciousness and intention fatal to the highest literature?" suggests the seriousness and depth of his approach, but he quickly began to see his own difficulties:

> Have you any more questions? the startled reader may reasonably ask; and seeing that we may never be able to answer those already propounded, it may be as well, at least for the present, not to ask any more.[35]

Surveying humour from Aristophanes to Terence through Goethe and his own modern times, Shorthouse tried to ground his argument in historical perspective. He examines Cervantes, for instance, whom he compares with Sterne, then Shakespeare, Ben Jonson, Addison and Steele, Herrick, Pope, Swift, Fielding, Dickens, Arnold, Lamb, Lytton, and, yes, other English authors, then with Irving, La Sage, Richter, and, finally, the Bible. As if to answer Samuel Gardiner's basic objection about intention, exposition, and demonstration in *John Inglesant*, Shorthouse asserts, "It is the function of the true artist [the humourist] to point the moral [and] by the manner in which he does so" to show his skill. Yet, "in Shakespeare we find neither consciousness nor intention". Shakespeare, he argues, presents "nothing but life in infinite variety, fed from the well-springs of human feeling, and ruled by the inevitable forces that keep the issues of life and death". He praises characters that "grow and develop, as it seems, independently of the author", as his own *John Inglesant* had done, and he notes that even Cervantes "may have been unaware of the perfect ending of the whole matter which his genius led him to adopt".

Observing that life in the Middle Ages "was too serious for the individual to grow", he argues that "human life became individual at the Renaissance". With "this new force--this principle of humanism" awakened in the Renaissance, "The antithesis was complete, the incongruities of life flashed upon the human consciousness, and humour became a conscious faculty of the brain." When "this great brain-wave passed over into England", it found "strings of perfect accord". The "sadness and melancholy of the English humour [was] vivified and warmed by this brilliant sunbreak from the lands of colour and of pleasure". The satire of *John Inglesant* reverses the situation; the English scenes of optimism and colourful adventure are followed by the gloomy intrigues and brooding plagues in Italy. Victorian England, he contends, has returned the individual to the condition of the Middle Ages. "Modern centralisation" has boxed in the "little scope" it still leaves the individual, and nineteenth century man must look to the seventeenth and eighteenth centuries to understand true humour. What, though, does he mean by humour?

The answer is clearer in Richard Holt Hutton's "*John Inglesant* on Humour" than in Shorthouse's own essay. Hutton, critic for *The Spectator*, correctly understood that Shorthouse's "The Humourous in Literature" is an exercise in self-definition and self-justification.[36] Hutton commends Shorthouse's essay as "a fine piece of English", then promptly objects to the confusion Shorthouse promoted by limiting "true humour" to a very special kind of literature and by asserting that it is "coextensive with human nature". Hutton defines humour as "coextensive only with the unexpected and baffling caprices of human feeling". Shorthouse argued that humour must "blend with surpassing skill into one life-piece the noble and the frivolous, the simple-hearted and the sarcastic, the pure and the foul" and that such blending results in alternating "laughter with tears" through mental association [into] one source", which is "association of idea". "The incongruities of life, when first they strike the mental retina", Hutton argued, "have the effect of surprise and cause laughter, but, when familiar, are associated with ideas of tenderness which have lain long in deep remembrance." The "two perceptions of the ludicrous and pathetic, this sympathy with the passing joy of a people to whom sorrow is a familiar guest, is what we mean by perfect humour", according to Shorthouse's definition. In practice, however, his final argument fails when he applies his theory to the biblical story of the Prodigal Son. "It is not in the mere blending of joy and sorrow--joy on one account, and sorrow on another",

Holt rejoins,

> that I should ever find an illustration of humour. When the humourist plays upon the blending chords of joy and sorrow, he does so in a manner to bewilder us, to confuse us as to whether we are glad or sorry at the same time, to make us uncertain as to our real feeling, and disposing to confound the pathetic with the absurd...The magic of the humourist consists in producing a certain bewilderment of feeling...so that you do not recognise clearly the true significance of your own emotions.[37]

Perhaps, in an ironic sense, this is what Shorthouse intended in the final two chapters of *John Inglesant*. It must be remembered, though, that Shorthouse appealed to Matthew Arnold in 1871 for help in making his "new view of humour... understood".[38] That Shorthouse did not fully understand the "humourous effect" of the ending of *John Inglesant* is evident from a letter he wrote to his cousin Isabel Southall, in which he thanks her for "pointing out the contrast between the last chapters in Rome and the final one in England". He admitted to his cousin that he "was unconscious of intending it". "This is not wonderful", he hastily added; "I described both, as I believe, absolutely from life, and the result could not fail to be lifelike." To be lifelike, a writer must see more than "part of life", and any one-sided presentation gives little "clear insight into the real facts of the unconscious theory with respect to genius".[39] Because Fielding and other "such writers" only see part of life, they can "only describe part of life".[40] Having deliberately given lengthy description to the weakening dreariness and pessimism of Inglesant's life in Italy, Shorthouse felt the need to show "both sides represented in something like equal proportion". Thus, the abruptive ending of *John Inglesant* serves as "humourous" balancing: the mental condition of Inglesant is drawn out; the emotion is left deliberately brief to intensify the impact of surprise.

Father St. Clare is a remarkable character developed out of Shorthouse's sense of humour; he blends worldly and spiritual qualities convincingly in alternating scenes. In his obedience to the Jesuit, Inglesant must discern the worldly from the religious, an act of judgment he is not able to perform until his is back in England, and not until Father St. Clare is dead. With the death of his spiritual director, Inglesant transfers his loyalties and projects the centre of his own archetypal nature upon "the great symbol of home", the Church of England, which thus makes the Church metaphorically synonymous with the Self. As John Inglesant feared the Church allowed too much freedom of conscience and duty, so Shorthouse believed that the Free Thought of his age needed to be as ordered and disciplined as Nicholas Ferrar's Little Gidding community.

In 1883 Shorthouse made another excursion into publication with a "Preface" to the *Golden Thoughts from the Spiritual Guide of Miguel Molinos, the Quietist*. Seeking to represent "sense in its ideal entirety...form hallowed and mystical, without choice or alternative", he sought to define "the Church Catholic". In noting that "this little book...is not without a singular appropriateness at the present time, when the inquiring intellect is so much in the ascendant", Shorthouse hoped to represent "an eternal principle [of] benign and intelligent energy" which would contain within it the recognizable reality of "a Personal God". He believed that "When we enter with Molinos into the mystical state of 'internal recollection and silence', we leave behind us all the perplexing questions by which religious life in the present day is disturbed."[41] In simplicity, he wonders:

> Is it so strange that we should sometimes think it possible that we might all of us, with our differences and estrangements, in this one thing united as children of a common Father, 'evermore give thanks unto Him in His Holy church'?

Shorthouse believed Molinos had succeeded in "uniting spiritual experience and mystical training with the system and worship of the Church Catholic". Sacramentalism, he declares, "has nothing to do with priestcraft" but is rather "the basis of that idea of the Church which all its abuses in all ages, so far from creating, have only impeded and obscured." He ends his preface with the rhetorical glow that readers of *John Inglesant* surely expected from him.

When Shorthouse read "The Platonism of Wordsworth" to the Wordsworth Society in July 1881, he was responding to a challenge from Professor Knight, who had suggested the undertaking in the autumn of 1880. Shorthouse felt himself unequal to such a task, but he made the attempt nonetheless, and he did so in the same manner of *John Inglesant*.[42] After he had completed the essay and had read it to the Wordsworth Society, he sent a copy to Knight with an apologetic note: "I *sincerely* think little of my paper, which, in fact, consists mostly of quotations"[43] just as *John Inglesant*, though he never acknowledged the fact, consists of many "inclusions". Nonetheless, he wrote Macmillan to see if his publisher had any interest in the essay. Macmillan did not, and when the essay was published it was "privately printed" by Cornish Brothers of Birmingham at Shorthouse's own expense. Another aspect of the essay is evident, too, in its being mistitled. When *The Spectator* reviewed the essay in conjunction with Knight's *Bibliography of the Poems of Wordsworth*, it strongly reacted against the suggestion of the title. Shorthouse was clear; he wanted to work out "the similarity of Wordsworth's teaching to that of Plato" and he qualified his purpose: "I have said the *similarity* of Wordsworth to Plato, because it is not asserted that Wordsworth consciously Platonised; on the contrary, it is not likely that he ever read the *Dialogues*."[44] Beginning with a subtle suggestion that Shorthouse's view of Platonism was "somewhat peculiar", *The Spectator* reviewer promptly asserted,

> Shorthouse misunderstands Wordsworth...we think he perverts him...We do not believe that Wordsworth would have understood Mr. Shorthouse...It seems a serious misinterpretation of Wordsworth.

The complaints hinge on a single idea. Shorthouse ascribed "a philosophy" to Wordsworth; the reviewer insisted the poet "had not a philosophy but a faith". What the reviewer might also have noted but did not was Shorthouse's reading himself into Wordsworth's poetry. Shorthouse calls Plato's *Dialogues* and Wordsworth's poetry, taken as a whole, "a volume of Philosophical Romance". The essay is no better than, and perhaps not as valuable as, some of Shorthouse's earlier essays, but it does show, as a letter to the editor of *The Spectator* makes clear: "...those who would read *John Inglesant* aright must continue to read him in the later writings of the author".[45]

When Shorthouse's "Preface" to a new facsimile edition of George Herbert's *The Temple* appeared in 1882, the truth of the above statement was made evident. With graceful style, "nearly perfect in its kind", Shorthouse extolled the "exquisite refinement which is the peculiar gift and office of the Church" and presented Herbert almost as a model of John Inglesant, forced to chose between "the religious fopperies of Romanism [and] the slovenly attire of Dissent". In choosing the Anglican *via media*, Inglesant dramatised "the peculiar mission of Herbert and his fellows [who had shown] the English people what a fine gentleman, who was also a Christian and a Churchman, might be." *The Spectator* attacked; so did *The Modern Review*.[46] Shorthouse seemed to be celebrating the British Empire, not practicing literary criticism; he proclaimed that the Church of England "had produced a culture unequalled in the world". His newly-won public fame and his personal taste were leading him towards artistic endeavours that stretched his mind towards Europe, especially towards Germany, Italy, and France, and that stretched his literary capacities towards successful publication of short stories, tales, and a series of spiritual novels. During the decade after *John Inglesant*, Shorthouse composed and published as if the reading public were in need of, or were demanding, further explication and clarification of the religion of John Inglesant and the "Church Catholic".

Shorthouse's publications from 1882 through 1891 form something very like the structure of a religious drama. The early creative works, "An Apologue" (July 1882), "The Marquis Jeanne Hyacinthe de St. Palaye" (July 1882), and "The Baroness Helena von Saarfeld" (August 1882), form a prologue and introduction to *The Little Schoolmaster Mark* (Part I, October 1883, and Part II, December 1884). In 1885 the two parts of *The Little Schoolmaster Mark* appeared in one volume as a complete tale. *Sir Percival* in 1886 climaxed the decade of publication and was followed by a sense of resolution in *A Teacher of the Violin and Other Tales* (1887-1888). In the autumn of 1888, *The Countess Eve* appeared, and it was followed three years later by *Blanche, Lady Falaise* in September 1891. The prefaces and essays of 1881-1882 were also followed by other critical works which seem to punctuate and define Shorthouse's creative productivity. After *Blanche*, the voice of "the author of *John Inglesant*" nearly became silent, then erupted in 1899 with a "Preface" to Arthur Galton's *The Message and Position of the Church of England* that serves as epilogue to his career and that resoundingly echoes the final chapter of *John Inglesant*.

One can only speculate about whether the stories, tales, and novels that followed *John Inglesant* would have enjoyed any public reception had they not come from the pen of "the author of *John Inglesant*". What remains a mystery, too, concerns a fundamental change in "the author's" narrative voice. *The Little Schoolmaster Mark* signals a change in Shorthouse's art that is, perhaps, best explained psychologically. Having achieved public success, Shorthouse not only adopted the role of "the author of *John Inglesant*" but he also learned to listen most attentively to a new inner voice. His personal searching for a "Church Catholic" philosophy and his Broad Church sacramentalism centred his self-knowledge and, thereby, his narrative voice, in an androgynous personality. Outwardly in manners and dress, as Edmund Gosse and others noted, he became very much an embodiment of John Inglesant, while inwardly he listened to the archetypal image he had depicted as Mary Collet. Such attention to the *anima* transformed the grounding and centre of his narrative persona from masculine philosophy to feminine spirituality. This is not to suggest that Shorthouse possessed a feminist point of view, though indeed his Quaker background freely accorded equal rights to the spiritually of women. There is no evidence, for example, that he ever sought to redefine the role of women in the Anglican Church. By seeking the best means to express spiritual insight, he changed from masculine personae and philosophical investigations to spiritual self-reflections and self-explorations from the point of view of women. As he allowed his literary characters freedom in his imagination to develop and become themselves, he attended to the *anima*. When he published "The Marquis Jeanne Hyacinthe de St. Palaye" and "The Baroness Helena von Saarfeld", Shorthouse presented the public with experiments in aesthetic religious sensibilities and feminine points of view. Although he maintained and rigidified his own authorial voice in his critical work, he adopted feminine voices to accommodate his audience.

Writing to Lady Welby, whom he regarded as a literary, linguistic, philosophical, and spiritual companion in letters, Shorthouse expressed gratitude for her attentive appreciation of *John Inglesant* and declared,

> It is an unspeakable gratification to me that good women of the highest culture have been so pleased with *John Inglesant*. No higher honour can be obtained by any writer, and no so certain test can be applied to any book.[47]

Remembering that his Early Essays and the "Moseley Pieces" were written in the company of women and were written largely for women, his comment is not too surprising, but a male reader may be pardoned if he reacts, rather startled, to the narrator of *Sir Percival* when she declares, "I am only a woman, and my opinion is of little worth."[48] Perhaps Shorthouse understood Mrs. Ward's criticism that *John Inglesant's* narrative stance distanced readers from the protagonist's experience and sought to address the artistic problem in *Sir Percival*. His feminine narrator quickly confesses, "It jars upon the sense to write down words that reveal the most sacred feelings of the heart".[49] *Sir Percival* intimately studies the hero from a woman's point of view, as if the story of a potential John Inglesant were being written by Mary Collet. Shorthouse was well aware of the problems of narrative persona and voice. He declared to Lady Welby only two months after the publication of *Sir Percival* that "a perfect book would be one which *had no author at all*".[50] Straining towards intimate and sacred feelings of the heart, he stretched his authorial voice not just towards that of an omniscient author, a technique that unites readers' sympathies and tastes into a common view, but towards that of "the absent author", making him a precursor of twentieth-century artistic sensibility.[51] Indeed, his authorial voice strained to become that of "an unknown stranger...in the dark shadows"[52] even as he sought to personify the virtue of spiritual constancy in Constance Lisle, the narrator of *Sir Percival's* history. As Eliot would later do, Shorthouse sought a spiritual vision that would express the mysterious and ineffable qualities that give a unifying agency to the Christian Mythos. By using music and silence to control the tone and attitude of Constance Lisle towards underlying, background themes, he sought to represent the Divine Principle, Individuation, at work.

Over a period of years Shorthouse rewrote the main themes of his philosophical romance into two tales, "The Marquis Jeanne Hyacinthe de St. Palaye" and "The Baroness Helena von Saarfeld". In a letter to Lady Welby (23 July 1882), he defined the themes as a complex of "rank, culture, religion, and art" and described the tales as illustrations of "the culture which comes from *rank* [and] that which comes from *intellect*".[53] Each of the stories explores love, and each studies the effects of "being noble" upon love relationships. The day before the Marquis Jeanne Hyacinthe de St. Palaye signs a marriage contract with Madeleine de Frontenac, he chances upon his intended and her childhood lover, the Chevalier de Grissoles, unchaperoned in a forest on his estate. A gentleman of high breeding and keen sensibilities, the Marquis politely excuses his intrusion and seems oblivious to the social indiscretion. The Count de Frontenac, however, suspects his daughter and the Chevalier, and when he hears a rumour of another intended rendezvous, he attempts to intercept them in the forest. The Marquis follows the Count, then takes a shortcut, and rather leisurely confronts the couple in the forest to warn them of the Count's pursuit. The Marquis betrays his "weariness of life", the weariness of social convention ruling personal and private behaviour, but when the Count takes his daughter to Paris, the Marquis accompanies them. In Paris, the Chevalier discretely manages to see Madeleine, and his valet suggests how the Chevalier may honourably do away with the Marquis. He suggests "a hunting accident". Wearied with the "games of life" and sensing that his own life may soon be over, the Marquis summons his attorney and changes his will, leaving fifty thousand louis d'or to the Chevalier. The irony is soon enacted when, during a boar hunt, the Marquis, just at the moment when he is alone and about to face the boar, is "accidentally" killed by an arrow discharged by the Chevalier. Realizing what has happened, the Marquis tells his assassin, "Ah, Chevalier, that was scarcely fair! Make my regrets to the Marquise. Monsieur Cacotte [the attorney]--will speak to you--about--my--will".[54]

The romantic irony creates a self-reflective echo effect upon the reader, who, at first, supposes the goodness of the Marquis has not opposed "true love", then pauses to realise the Marquis's bequest condemns Madeleine to marry a murderer. Pondering the Marquis's "weariness of life", the reader begins to suspect the nobleman of having helped arrange his own murder and of having transferred the burdens of aristocratic wealth onto the Chevalier. Although the Marquis is "bored" with life, his one-on-one combat with "the magnificent boar" suggests ironic pathos. A metaphor of the Chevalier's rakish character and Madeleine's defiance of her father and disregard of social conventions, the boar is also a metaphor of "culture which comes from rank". Shorthouse demonstrates that, despite the elegance and nobility of manners, the "culture which comes from rank" is as self-destructive as the "romantic love" of the Chevalier and Madeleine and that such culture, however refined, creates only "a haunting legacy" for society.

"The Baroness Helena von Saarfeld" presents the story of a noble woman who stoops below her social level and offers herself to two men who love her but are not socially worthy of her. Both lovers realise their unworthiness and reject her. As in "The Marquis", the story of the Baroness invites a reflective pause to contemplate the Baroness's decision to devote herself to the "mystical religion of the Count von Zinzendorff". As Wagner notes, it is "well-nigh impossible to summarize" the story, though the reader feels that he grasps the significance of the plot. The emancipated Baroness, reared by her father to be quite independent, has no real worldly options. She, too, evokes the memory of Mary Collet, and in giving her life to "mystical religion", she offers her worldly life as a sacrifice to the higher calling. As *anima*, she provokes attention to the mysteries of the unconscious and, like the Marquis, she demonstrates the unworthiness of life lived for the Ego. Her story affords a contrast to Madeleine's and confirms that life lived in accord with the "rank that comes from intellect" preserves social conventions and conserves healthy psychological and spiritual life.

Both stories seem to be literary exercises that might have become chapters of *John Inglesant* had Shorthouse found a way of incorporating them. Madeleine suggests Lauretta as the Baroness evokes Mary Collet. The Marquis' apparent lack of personal interest in Madeleine reminds one of John Inglesant's lack of real interest in Lauretta, even as the two would-be lovers of the Baroness suggest the rivalry between Inglesant and Mr. Thorne for Mary Collet. The story of the Marquis is told by an objective narrator who favours the Marquis at the expense of the Chevalier, while the Baroness's story is told by an anonymous Englishman travelling in Germany. The Englishman incorporates a second point of view into his narrative, that of Herr Richter, an actor. Richter suggests both Inglesant and Jean Paul Richter, whom Shorthouse greatly admired and whose writings Shorthouse emulated in *The Little Schoolmaster Mark*.

During the time he was composing the tale of the little schoolmaster, Shorthouse was also busy trying to pay tribute to the divine who had most influenced his own religious convictions, Frederick Denison Maurice. When Maurice's son published his father's biography, he asked Shorthouse to write a review. *The Life of Frederick Denison Maurice* appeared early in 1884, and Shorthouse's tribute appeared in the May issue of *The Nineteenth Century*. The review is probably Shorthouse's most successful critical prose. Appraising Maurice's "absolute uniqueness" and defining his "almost perfect freedom and toleration of thought with the most entire certitude of conviction and teaching", Shorthouse also defined much of the spirit behind *John Inglesant*. Denigrating "etymological niceties and ethnological refinements", Shorthouse insisted that "all our [theological] difficulties vanish before the simple story of a life like our own" (298). In accord with Maurice's belief in the commonality of human nature "alike in all times", Shorthouse also shared Maurice's conviction that "all little children are Platonists", and he identified the underlying principle that gave equilibrium to Maurice and to human nature in general. Maurice had written "*of* Quakers...*to* Church people", and his theology defined the "God of the natural human race", not the god of human invention. In praising Maurice's appeal to ordinary people, Shorthouse paraphrased the spirit of the "Preface" to *John Inglesant*:

> ...when all our difficulties vanish before the simple story of a life like our own, when the record is revealed to us as being nothing but the history of struggles and failures, sins and repentances, of men and women and people like ourselves, and of the clear and still clearer shining of a light into their hearts and lives by which the mysteries of time and of the future appear, if not altogether vanquished and brought to naught, yet, at least, as ranging themselves on the side of righteousness and development...when instead of the elaborate exegesis we expected, we hear only the charmed rhythm of this divine message through page of story, and prophet's cry, and psalmist's song...our trouble has been in such sort laid to rest.[55]

Then, connecting Maurice with Wordsworth, Shorthouse proclaimed both men were "poets in the highest sense, for they [were] both of them seers" who advanced

> a revolution...in the realm of English thought--the change from pseudo-civilisation, from artificial emotion, from false taste to the true life of simple manhood (314).

Both men worked "to make it possible for the gospel of humanity to be heard again", and both merited the title Shorthouse so approved, that of "Christian Platonist" who "made it possible for the gospel of humanity to be heard again" (314).

Maurice believed himself "sent into the world...to persuade men to recognise Christ as the centre of their fellowship with each other", not factions, parties, or other worldly divisions. Shorthouse shared Maurice's belief that "every human being is the son of God" and lauded Maurice's "combination of tolerance with earnestness" (305). Yet, such tolerance did not extend into either political or religious democracy, which both men detested in their conviction that only men who "are raised above the slime of earth, into the life of the ideal" can respond to such responsibility. Nonetheless, God "enters into human consciousness by virtue of His gracious will, and may be known in consciousness by whosoever seek Him". Shorthouse and Maurice believed, "There is no dogma of Christianity, however grotesque it may appear in its popular form, but what has its germ in the profoundest scientific truth"[56] and that "Christian revelation supplies its own highest evidence, since it and it alone correspond with all the facts of intuition and experience, and thus both correlates and integrates them."[57] He ends his essay with an interpretation of the resurrection of Lazarus. In part, as he notes, he is quoting from a sermon Maurice gave in the chapel at Lincoln's Inn (15 June 1856), a sermon in which Maurice "entered into the Holy of Holies, the 'Cyte of Sarras in the Spyrituel Place'". Thus inspired, Maurice spoke of the resurrection of Lazarus as the "expression of His sympathy in the groan of His creatures". Shorthouse sees the Lazarus story as a command from Christ:

> Come forth out of the lower life: out of the life, lovely in
> its kind--the life of self, of fleshly beauty, the lust of the
> eyes and the pride of life--[Come forth from] the grave-
> clothes of superstition, of formalism, of systems, and of
> burdens laid by human imposition upon the righteous
> (317).

Although Shorthouse himself read and interpreted the Bible as literature, decoding myth into metaphor and symbol, he would not allow that he intended any allegory in *The Little Schoolmaster Mark*, which rivals *John Inglesant* in literary qualities, according to some critics. *Mark* captured and excited intense interest among a select audience, and, as Shorthouse borrowed many passages of *John Inglesant* directly or adaptively from numerous literary and historical sources, he incorporated many suggestions from his correspondents and readers of *The Little Schoolmaster Mark, Part I* into a second part. The first was published by Macmillan in October 1883. Ten thousand copies were printed and the "philosophical tale" also appeared in the November issue of Macmillan's *English Illustrated Magazine*. *Mark* was an instant success, and another five thousand copies were published in December. The first part of *Mark* was clearly Shorthouse's own thinking out of the problems of the relationship between art and life which John Inglesant discussed with Cardinal Rinuccini in chapter twenty-three. Shorthouse wrote to George Macmillan (10 February 1883) that he was contemplating "a German story" that would require "great genius" and that he feared himself "not equal to it".[58]

Why a German story? Shorthouse was convinced that the German Protestant princes had saved the Christian world from the mental imprisonment of Rome, and when the Baron Tauchnitz offered to print an illustrated edition of *John Inglesant*, Macmillan offered Shorthouse a new contract and encouraged his German dream-tale.[59] Dreams and realities, he believed, drawing support from Leigh Hunt, are "but representations of impressions", and when such impressions are represented in books, the books "open for us a world more bright...and create in us a new world".[60] Commending the autobiography of the eighteenth-century German pietist Heinrich Jung-Stilling (1740-1817) in the "Preface" to *Mark*, Shorthouse realised that Jung-Stilling was a healer, a cataract surgeon, who had dedicated his life and work to restoring and giving "new sight" to his patients, as Shorthouse hoped Mark's tale would to his readers. Mark, a tailor's son, is a mixture of Christ-figure and *puer aeternus*, and his story is told in brilliant simplicity in contrast with much worldly sophistication. Shorthouse delighted in foreign phrases and terms, and though he used them sparingly, they give an other-worldly cultural perspective to his story, which helps prepare the reader "to see behind the masques" at Prince Ferdinand and Princess Adelaide's Italianate-German court in 1750.

The plot of Part I is quite simple: a fifteen-year-old village lad locally famed for his piety and storytelling ability is summoned to a princely estate to serve as tutor to the royal children, where he is so assaulted by the frivolous life of the court that, when he is surreptitiously entrapped on the stage of an elaborate and festive masque, he falls from the stage and dies a sacrificial death. Victorian audiences were as used to pitying suffering children as modern readers are accustomed to finding "the Christ figure in unlikely places".[61] Mark, though, is not a Christ figure; he is rather the embodiment of an archetype, and it is the archetypal power of his story that so excited Shorthouse's readers and brought him new correspondents and new friendships. By October, Shorthouse had changed his "philosophical tale" to "a spiritual romance", as the subtitle indicates, thus giving readers reason to expect greater and more subtle spiritual insight that they had received from the philosophical ponderings of *John Inglesant*. That the change from philosophical to spiritual was successful is evident from readers' reactions and the variety of their interpretations.

"I am constantly receiving letters and suggestions upon *Little Mark* (Part I)", Shorthouse wrote Lady Welby, "from every conceivable point of view", and he confided to her that he was "already groping" his way towards a second part.[62] Mrs. Russell Gurney sent him a paper in which she interpreted the characters in *Mark* as allegorical, representing "the conscience or divinely-born spirit...the reason faculty...the earth-born Psyche allied to the outward...the art-winged one...the ethereal clown...the human, sensuous Perception", and she aptly termed the story "a poem".[63] Canon Alfred Ainger preached a sermon on *Mark* at The Temple Church in London and wrote to Shorthouse to confirm his allegorical interpretation of the little schoolmaster as "no other than Religion or the Spirit of Holiness". Interested in the religious aspect of wit and humour, Ainger found "confirmation [in *Mark*] of his own teaching" that "if we try to treat religion as if it was one of the fine Arts, we shall inevitably kill it in the process."[64] Shorthouse appreciated Ainger's interpretation, but he insisted,

> So far as I know, I never wrote an allegory, and never shall; indeed, I scarcely know what such a thing is. With the exception of *Pilgrim's Progress* and of Adam's

Allegories, which I have forgotten, I really do not know what an allegory is.[65]

Earlier, he had written Ainger,

I am glad to think of any work of real art, that opposite lessons may be read *into* it, though not perhaps *from* it: if it be a true glimpse of life it must bear different interpretations as life does.[66]

Shorthouse believed that "all true human life...is symbolical because it is *life*; it is not life because it is allegorical", and he advised Ainger, "Any one who wants to make an allegory out of either *Little Mark* or *Sir Percival* will find all kinds of jarring notes." Ainger, "a sober English Protestant", had, however, no difficulty attempting "perfect agreement with Shorthouse", despite the latter's mystical Platonism, because they were both seeking the "same goal--the spiritualising of life". As Ainger's biographer notes, "Shorthouse want[ed] to turn religion into an art, while Ainger desire[d] to turn all art into religion."[67] Ainger's relationship with Shorthouse took on the flavour of friend, fan, and spiritual partner, and his admiration for *The Little Schoolmaster Mark* and later for *Sir Percival* commended the works to his influential Temple congregation, as the admiration of Bishop William Boyd Carpenter also helped Shorthouse gain a sophisticated audience.

Carpenter, Canon of Westminster, Bishop of Ripon, and confessor to Queen Victoria at Windsor, became intrigued with Shorthouse's work through one of the smallest and least appreciated of his writings, "An Apologue", which first appeared in the July 1882 issue of *The Nineteenth Century*. "An Apologue" refers the reader again to the twenty-third chapter of *John Inglesant* and the discussion about life being like a game of cards. As the Cardinal told Inglesant,

We did not make the world, and are not responsible for its state, but we can make life a fine art, and taking things as we find them, like wise men, mould them as may best serve our own ends.

"An Apologue" develops around the game of bezique and is "a metaphorical form of the Cardinal's argument".[68] Carpenter described the "parable":

The cards were dealt, and as they fell without any sign of order or sequence on the table, and suits were mixed up without one another, the cards, noting the haphazard fashion of their experience said, 'We are the sport of chance'. The cards were gathered up and the game began, and the suits were kept to themselves; spades followed spades, hearts followed hearts, and so, with such regularity that the cards now declared that they were under the rule of inevitable and inexorable law; they said, 'We are the victims of fate'. Then somebody played a trump, and the cards saw that thought and will entered into their destiny, and they said, 'Our lot is ordered by intelligence'.[69]

Carpenter's first letter to Shorthouse also confided that Queen Victoria appreciated the Birmingham manufacturer's work and had taken personal interest in *John Inglesant*. Shorthouse responded with gratitude and sent Carpenter "The Untravelled Traveller", an "obvious adaptation" of a poem by Dean Stanley, which Carpenter included in his autobiography.[70] *The Little Schoolmaster Mark* challenged his ingenuity and he offered Shorthouse his interpretation.

According to Carpenter, Shorthouse,

had a strong feeling that, as the stories which he wrote had been given him, he was but the instrument of transmitting them to the world, and though they were his work, their full or truest significance might be as much a mystery to him as to the reader...The products of his pen were not the results of previous imagination on his part, but were visions with messages which it was for him as well as others to seek to understand.[71]

While Shorthouse was "groping for", as he said, the second part of *Mark*, Carpenter wrote him "An Afterthought", an interpretive ending to the tale.

The plot of Part I is simple, but its working out requires serious religious understanding of psychological effects. Mark may be taken as either an extraordinarily pious, sensitive boy or, to more rigorous minds, as an immature, sickly crybaby. Shorthouse, of course, intended the former, but only a religious-minded reader could avoid being made nervous by the "jarring notes". Because Shorthouse believed his stories were "given to him", Mark speaks when God gives him words, and he is often confused and silent. Before he leaves his father, the village tailor, Mark is simple and naive, though he is also "almost psychic". When the village priest, Father Stalher, asks Mark if he can read, the boy replies, "That is a foolish question, for I am a human being." Amazed, Father Stalher ejaculates, "The devil fetch me...!" and Mark jumps up and looks around the room for the devil.[72] Being interviewed by the court chaplain, Mark asks how he is to address the Prince's children, and rather ironically, the chaplain replies, "Thou must trust in God; He will show thee when to say 'Highness' and when not" (15). Later, at the court, Mark meets Faustina Banti, a beautiful young singer who offers "to take care" of him: "...'come and sit on my lap'; and, sitting down, she spread out her lap for him with an inviting gesture" (33). Her words mean more than even she realises, but her manners and gestures are certainly not a proper way for a young lady to introduce herself to a fifteen-year-old peasant lad. Shortly after Mark meets the Prince's children, a boy and a girl "of about eight or nine years of age", the little girl mocks Mark and tells him to call her "my most gracious and serene Highness". He refuses:

> May God forgive me if I do anything so foolish. I am
> here to teach thee and thy brother, and I will do it in my
> own way, or not at all (36).

Soon Mark meets the four principal members of the court, Prince Ferdinand, a German dilettante and religious aesthete with Italianate tastes; his sister Isoline, an ascetic devoted to good works in an exclusive and pious community; the Prince's wife, Adelaide, who is anti-religious, worldly, and sarcastic; and the Count, Adelaide's urbane and rationalistic *cavaliere servente*. Shorthouse did not intend his four court characters to represent Plato's four aspects of the soul, yet they do correspond to Jung's adaptation of Plato's scheme into representations of the four psychological functions: Thinking (the Count), Feeling (the Prince), Sensation (Adelaide), and Intuition (Isoline). Mark and his childlike innocence has the effect among them of the *puer aeternus*, which "represents not only something that existed in the distant past but also something that exists *now*".[73] "An archetypal content expresses itself, first and foremost, in metaphors"[74]; thus Mark is represented from his first appearance at the court until he falls to his death as "a dying canary". When he first hears Faustina sing, her pet canary falls dead to the bottom of its cage and her singing changes from festive gaiety to "some hidden grief, known before time of all, but forgotten or suppressed" (24-25). The metaphor extends; Mark's life at court is a captivity from which he yearns to escape, and his "wonderful historical stories" become his canary--or "swan song". Most importantly, the functioning and purpose of the child archetype work to effect compensation or correction "in a meaningful manner [of] the inevitable one-sidedness and extravagances of the conscious mind". When "man cuts himself off from roots", as we learn each of the four aristocrats has already done, he confronts two opposing ideals: the "retarding ideal [which is] more primitive, more natural, and more 'moral' in that it keeps faith with law and tradition" and the "progressive ideal [which is] more abstract, more unnatural and less 'moral' in that it demands disloyalty to tradition".[75] Throughout Part I, these two principles work towards Mark's entrapment and death.

Faustina leagues herself with the rational Count and the earthy Adelaide, and they plot an entertainment, a masque, in which Mark is to "be himself" on stage and "to play himself out". The intuitive Isoline forewarns Mark:

> Do not be afraid to die. Instead of your form and voice
> there will be remembrance and remorse...Do not be afraid
> to die. The charm is working now; it will increase when
> sight is changed for memory, and the changeful irritation
> of time for changeless recollection and regret. The body
> of the sown grain is transfigured into the flower of a
> spiritual life, and from the dust is raised a mystic presence
> which can never fade. Do not be afraid to die (80).

Mark does not understand her, but he knows he is going to die, and the reader knows it too. When the festive masque is in progress, "a fairy-like figure" leads Mark deep into the gardens until the woods themselves form "a dark cave or hollow in the wood". When he emerges from the cave, he is centre on stage. Thrust into "a blaze of dazzling sunlight" and thinking himself surrounded "by mystic and awful forms", Mark utters "a sharp cry like that of a snared and harmless creature of the woods". He covers his face with his hands, steps backwards, and falls "some eight feet to the ground". (Eight feet is one of the "jarring notes" of the tale; it does not seem enough of a fall to kill a fifteen-year-old country lad.) At the moment Mark steps onto stage, the director calls for someone to offer himself as a sacrifice and tells Faustina, "You will sing your death-song and the priest will offer himself in your stead." When Mark falls, the Prince and those around him remove their masques "and the play was stopped".

Shorthouse had, perhaps, projected his own one-sidedness onto John Inglesant. As if to compensate and correct the changes effected within his personality by public attention, he composed *The Little Schoolmaster Mark*, and the story combines young John Inglesant at Westacre with young Henry Shorthouse among the more worldly members of the Society of Friends. With the story of the little schoolmaster before the public, Shorthouse felt the tale's incompleteness, but he did not know how to finish it. He welcomed letters of advice, but, like little Mark, he would complete the story in his own way, or not at all. In accord with Jung's analysis of the child archetype, Part II of Mark's story represents psychological compensation. Shorthouse had to compose Part II to balance and effectively correct Mark's one-sidedness. Had Faustina become an *anima* figure, she might have helped Mark, but her alliance with the Count makes her a negative aspect of *anima* and aligns her with the *shadow*. Only the Prince, who expresses fatherly sympathy towards Mark, represents a reasonably balanced personality. Adelaide is too extroverted and worldly to represent the "spiritual affects" of the *anima*, and the Count is little more than a representative of worldly thought. "It has been proved", he tells Mark, "that there is no God" (91), and, as the omniscient, unidentified narrator states, "As the brain consists of two parts, so the mind seems dual also" (93).

Shorthouse played upon the dualities of faith and doubt, art and religion, but Part I leaves Mark either dead or dying, and the court unmasked. To a devout reader, Mark is an appealing character, a "sacrificial lamb", but his effect upon other less pious readers is dubious, though all characters at the court change through their interactions with Mark. The Prince discusses "noble living" and "necessary suffering" with Mark; the Princess Isoline confesses that even in her secluded religious life she has not found happiness; the singer Faustina softens her sarcastic "masque". Mark's sacrifice is well prepared, but a modern reader is left only with the "signal act of unmasking" and looks for allegorical significance. Isoline and Adelaide form extreme opposites, esoteric religion versus worldliness. Faustina seems positioned between them, though at the end she is sympathetic with Isoline's sensibilities. The Count and Mark express opposite extremes with the Prince in the middle. Mark is dead or dying. What is the reader to think? Clearly, the ending of Part I is a "jarring note".

Bishop Carpenter flatly rejected Mark's death and began his "An Afterthought" with an abrupt "But Little Schoolmaster Mark was not dead. He only lay in a trance, motionless and still as death; so that all around him thought he was dead".[76] He continued the tale. The two princesses, Isoline and Adelaide, stand over Mark's body and weep; Adelaide feels "half shame and half pity"; then the Prince stands with them and proclaims Mark "beautiful and good". As the Prince speaks to himself, proclaiming Mark the only one "of all the men I ever knew [who united] both good and beautiful", the ladies speak in chorus, "I wonder why". Mark, meanwhile, experiences an "exquisite repose" and dreams of two birds, a "bird of Paradise, the other...a dull and dowdy-featured bird". A servant, as if from heaven, feeds "pearly white food" to the two birds, and Mark says, "It is manna". Instantly, the dull-featured bird sang and "her plumage brew bright and fair". The other bird also grew beautiful, and "his croak grew into a song, loud and sweet. And the two birds lifted up their voices together and sang till the voices seemed but one, and they shook out their fair wings and made their nest together." The vision faded; Mark awoke, and he responded to "I wonder why" with, "All because of the angels' food". He explains to the questioning Prince, "The only food of angels is love, for they feast their hearts on God, and God is love." The three adults chorus:

I see it now. God is not good that springs not from love,
nor can fair be the fair that grows not from love: love
only is the seed from which alike the fruits of life and the
flowers of life can grow.

They speak no more. The two princesses kiss each other; the Count is banished from court; "sweet songs of praise" are offered "in the little neglected temple", and "Little Mark is at last happy".[77] So, at least, runs

Carpenter's version, one suited, presumably, to amuse the Queen or, to update the situation and please a twentieth-century audience, so ends the "Walt Disney" version.

Shorthouse responded to Carpenter: "Only I think Mark *is* dead, and I fear the Princess (wife) must go through a longer purgation."[78] "We all understand", he admonished Carpenter, "that Art should be religious, but it is more difficult to understand how Religion may be an Art"; then he added, "I am not without hopes that it may gradually work itself out." What worked itself out is Part II; "What was suggestive, in Part I, becomes confusing, even murky, in Part II. If Shorthouse in Part II was 'groping', he apparently did not notice that he was falling over his pen."[79] Part II abruptly changes tone, plot, and point of view. Part I lyrically evokes an introverted, childlike world; Part II debates and confuses, especially the characterization. The two parts, however, form a whole, and the whole provides a provocative view of Shorthouse's progress, or lack thereof, as an artist.

Part I of *The Little Schoolmaster Mark* is divided into seven chapters; Part II into nine. In Part I, each of the chapters advances the tale with little contextual self-reflection; the reader is pulled through the story almost as if charmed. In Part II, the story repeats, and then alters the action; the tale ceases to be spiritual and retreats into philosophical ponderings. Part I reads smoothly, but II jars with presumably deliberate intention. Prince Ferdinand and Princess Isoline momentarily understand each other and their respective relations with Mark. Mark is indeed dead, and both the Prince and Princess blame themselves for his death. Out of their self-accusations comes insight. The Prince admits that he "fancied life was an art" and that he "dreamed that it might be perfected--as a religious art" (127). The Princess argues that art is "simply not enough", even when it is combined with morality, virtue, and love. "Nothing profits", she insists, "save the Divine Humanity, which, through the mystery of sacrifice, has entered the unseen." As they look into each other's eyes, for a brief instant "art and religion [are] at one" (128).

In the second chapter of Part II, the old Carricchio, the court master of entertainments and the Maestro debate whether art ever contemplates "the disagreeable" and whether it is, in its essence, "selfish". "Art has an end, an aim, an intention --if it deserts this aim it ceases to be art. It must be selfish", argues the Maestro, who in Part II becomes an important character. Isoline abandons her reclusive religious life, the Prince takes sudden interest in affairs of state, Adelaide begins to realise she is a mother and that her children need her attention, the little Faustina improves her singing daily, and the Maestro composes his great life-work, an opera based on the story of the little schoolmaster Mark. The relations between Faustina and the Maestro begin to echo the life of the actor and his protégé in "The Baroness

Helena von Saarfeld". All principal characters travel their diverse ways to Vienna, where the Maestro's art and Faustina's singing brilliantly engage all members of their audience except one, the Empress-Queen, who is bored with the show and orders it closed after only two performances. The effects of Mark's death become meaningful: Isoline becomes more worldly, and paradoxically, more Christian; the Prince gives in to his appetites and fancies himself in love with Faustina; and Faustina becomes the living embodiment of Mark's sacrificial mission. She alone makes her life into religious art. The plot reaches climax when the Prince, thinking he has maneuvered the Maestro out of Vienna and Faustina into his arms, declares his passion, or, perhaps it is more accurate to say, he declares his ownership of her. She is shocked, and

> with the entire power of her trained voice, which,
> magnificent as it was, could still but imperfectly render
> the reality of remonstrance and pathetic regret, she uttered
> but one word--'Prince!' (212).

The word, needless to say, has its power, and the Prince leaves her, leaves his wife and children and his courtly life; he travels to Hernhuth as a reformed man to join the religious community of the Count Zinzendorf.[80] At Hernhuth he learns a mystical dream has simultaneously "visited" his two children. In the dream the children are playing in a beautiful garden, "very happy chasing the butterflies", when they encounter an angel, "the Herr Tutor". Mark's spiritual form talks to them "of God, and of angels, and of heaven" and leads them "into a burial-ground [with] open graves...and tall dark trees that bore no flower". In the midst of the cemetery is "a Calvary, and at the foot of the Calvary there was a bier" on which the Prince and Adelaide lay as though dead. Mark vanishes, and the children pray. Christ "came down from the cross, and came to the bier, and touched it", and the seemingly dead parents "stood up beautiful and smiling".

After the children tell Princess Adelaide of their "mystical dream", Adelaide, Isoline, and Faustina attend Mass in a nearby chapel, where the "music of the Mass [speaks] a mysterious language, recognisable to the hearts of every creed" as the three ladies stand beneath a stained glass window of "the three Marys". Having learned from the visionary experience of the children, from the Mass, and from the Prince's visit to Zinzendorf, they all live happily ever after, though also sadder and wiser.

Shorthouse wrote Lady Welby that Parts I and II "should be read together to be understood"[81] and a year later he wrote Edmund Gosse:

> I don't think that *Little Mark* is sufficiently appreciated
> and am inclined to wait till people wake up to estimate
> that work. Ainger is enthusiastic about it, and several
> more whose opinion is most worth having. It is only

meant as a suggestion, but I want it followed up.[82]

To use his terms, no one has "wakened up" or followed up on his suggestion, though exactly what his suggestion is remains unclear. Carpenter was probably close to understanding, and had he considered his appreciation for "An Apologue" as a possible key to *Mark*, he might have perceived a development from chance and to fate "ordered by intelligence". The intelligence of Part II, however, is difficult to appreciate as art. Perhaps critics have been kind in leaving *The Little Schoolmaster Mark* alone. Perhaps, too, Shorthouse failed in Part II because he wrote for an audience rather than for himself. Part I suggests fictional autobiography and displays Shorthouse's imagination almost at its best; II addresses a critical public, and its failures suggest that once Shorthouse had undertaken "spiritual romance" he could not successfully revert to "philosophical romance". Although he believed his stories "came to him", he could no longer find unity and synthesis between art and religion without creating symbols. It is difficult to determine whether the narrator of *Mark* is masculine or feminine, which further suggests that *The Little Schoolmaster Mark* represents a pivotal point in his transition from male personae to female narrators. The most interesting link that *Mark* suggests is to "The Baroness Helena von Saarfeld", and that link is the Count Zinzendorf.

Nikolaus Ludwig, Graf von Zinzendorf (1700-1760) represents Shorthouse's gratitude "for the German Protestant princes who saved Christianity". Zinzendorf's ecumenism and his *Tropen*, methods of religious training, probably suggested to Shorthouse a kind of German Nicholas Ferrar and commitment to communitarian ideals, which Shorthouse mingled with his admiration for Jung-Stilling and Richter. Jung-Stilling's autobiography, suggestive as it is, is not as provocative to a student of Shorthouse as is the *Life of Jean Paul F. Richter*, which appeared in England in 1845, "Compiled from Various Sources, together with his Autobiography".[83] In his autobiography Richter often speaks of himself in third person, an interesting technique for achieving psychological objectivity. Like Shorthouse, Richter had become a writer at a young age, primarily of satirical sketches, and worked for some years as a manufacturer before publishing *The Life of the Little Schoolmaster Wuz* in 1790, which he called "an Idyl, the lowest species of poetic creation" and "a Pedagogical Romance" based on his own teaching experiences. Richter sought to interweave "the romance and reality of one life". Critics of Shorthouse's *The Little Schoolmaster Mark* would probably all share Samuel Taylor Coleridge's exclamation about Richter's *Museum*, though they might substitute Shorthouse's name for Richter's: "O Jean Paul! Jean Paul! This (*die Kraft der Untersuchung*) is not *thy* Forte: a more confused Tangle of common place thoughts I have seldom read!"[84] In presenting his religious and emotional life in third person, Richter prefigured Shorthouse's struggle with Parts I and II. Part I of *Mark* is narrated as if it were "given" to Shorthouse; the narrative persona seems to share in the listening of words as they echo in the readers' minds. Part II confuses the narrative voice. If Part I is thought more musical than II, the analogy works. Twice in Part II the "I" appears, as if referring to a specific person, but no narrator is ever identified, and the other judgments and observations of the "I" which comments on the story from time to time sound very much like "jarring notes",[85] though their effect is more to remind readers of an "ideal musical world" than to advance the narrative through philosophical discussions. Part I is a creative tale that readers of *John Inglesant* could readily admire, but Part II demonstrates Shorthouse's "groping for" another ideal: "Some day a great musical and art novel will be written which will be a revelation to mankind".[86]

After the public acclaim for *John Inglesant*, Shorthouse found himself in a complex situation. As a working man engaged in the commercial life of Birmingham, he had taken time and leisure to inculcate his own interests into a philosophical romance for his own amusement and his wife's entertainment. After 1882 he struggled to become a public voice as if he were himself, not just "the author of *John Inglesant*", but the personification of John Inglesant in Victorian England. His social and religious tastes were those of an aesthete. He courted lords and ladies, deans and bishops, as if he were a spokesman for the religious and social order. Victorian readers who wanted something of the "real life" of the lower-middle class or of the "working classes" could not so much as find the name of a servant or a working-class character in his writings as he changed from silent, listening Quaker to Anglican apologist. In *The Little Schoolmaster Mark*, he found that his own masculine persona failed to reveal or disclose the spiritual insights he wanted to express. To express the psychological and the spiritual, he had to allow himself to be guided by the *anima* and to transform his narrative voice into that of a woman. Part I of *Mark* suggests that Shorthouse was again expressing his own youthful personality and nature, that he successfully compensated for his stammer and inability to fit into "normal schooling" by creating the lyrical rhythms of young John Inglesant and little Mark. Part II reveals his frustration to concretely dramatise and portray his themes of art, religion, culture, and rank. To overcome the difficulties, he tapped deeply into his youthful enthusiasm for chivalric romances and romantic poetry. The effort had succeeded brilliantly in *John Inglesant* and resulted in a synthesis of creative and critical voices. To resolve the "jarring notes" of *The Little Schoolmaster Mark*, he had to dig again into English history and into some of its Germanic roots. As *John Inglesant* creates an imaginative, believable "English-saint", *Sir Percival: A*

Story of the Past and of the Present attempts to revive Arthurian romance into a Victorian setting and to resolve the failures that Shorthouse identified in Tennyson's *Idylls of the King*. *Sir Percival* presents an archetypal or spiritual form of the John Inglesant story from the point of view of a Mary Collet. The voice of the *anima*, once experienced as "that inward consciousness *I am a Me*...like a flash of lightning from heaven...in the holy sanctuary of man"[87] begins to sing and to mythologize, to recreate itself, to "dream the dream onwards and give it modern dress". The "three Marys" of *The Little Schoolmaster Mark* provoked Shorthouse to give them artistic life, and once he finished their separate stories, he ended his literary career.

Notes to Chapter Five

[1]Sarah Shorthouse, *Life, Letters, and Literary Remains of J. H. Shorthouse* (London: Macmillan, 1905), vol. I, 101-175. Mrs. Shorthouse documents, though not always chronologically, "*John Inglesant* and New Friendships", 101-175.

[2]Montague Summers, "Man of One Book", *Times Literary Supplement* (1 July 1926), 448.

[3]Montague Summers, "Man of One Book", 448.

[4]*The Athenaeum* (30 October 1880), 565-566.

[5]J. Henry Shorthouse, Letter to William Knight, *LLLR*, vol. I, 127-129.

[6]*LLLR*, vol. I, 190-193.

[7]Mrs. Humphry Ward's review appeared in *The Saturday Review*, vol. 52 (9 July 1881), 50-51. For Shorthouse's reactions see *LLLR*, vol. II, 132 and 134.

[8]*LLLR*, vol. I, 133.

[9]J. Henry Shorthouse, Letter to Alexander Macmillan (15 July 1881), *LLLR*, vol. I, 134.

[10]J. Henry Shorthouse, Letter to Isabel Southall (7 April 1882), *LLLR*, vol. I, 147-148.

[11]J. Henry Shorthouse, Letter to Dr. Abbott (November 1880), *LLLR*, vol. I, 123-127.

[12]J. Henry Shorthouse, Letter to Alexander Macmillan (6 January 1882), *LLLR*, vol. I, 141-142.

[13]J. Henry Shorthouse, Letter to Lady Welby (22 October 1881), *LLLR*, vol. I, 169-171.

[14]J. Henry Shorthouse, Letter to Lady Welby (25 June 1882), *LLLR*, vol. I, 159-160.

[15]*LLLR*, vol. I, 163.

[16]J. Henry Shorthouse, Letter to Alexander Macmillan (6 July 1882), *LLLR*, vol. I, 166.

[17]*LLLR*, vol. I, 178.

[18]J. Henry Shorthouse, Letter to Dr. Talbot (3 January 1882), *LLLR*, vol. I. 137-138.

[19]Samuel R. Gardiner, "*John Inglesant*", *Fraser's Magazine*, vol. 145, n.s. XXV (May 1882), 599-605.

[20]J. Henry Shorthouse, Letter to Edmund Gosse (1 April 1883), *LLLR*, vol. I, 190-193.

[21]*Church Quarterly Review*, vol. XIV, no. XXVII (April 1882), 134-144.

[22]John P. Dourley, *The Psyche as Sacrament: A Comparative Study of C. G. Jung and Paul Tillich* (Toronto: Inner City Books, 1981).

[23]Robert Nourse, "A Rare Romance", *The Dial* (Chicago), vol. 13, no. 25, (May 1882), 7-9.

[24]Nourse's review defeats its own praise of *John Inglesant* by stating four inaccuracies: 1) the novel had not "run through twenty or more editions in England", 2) Father St. Clare did not have "many *aliases*", 3) Mary Collet was not "a Puritan maiden", and 4) the hero did not "spend his time in sunny Italy".

[25]*Blackwood's Magazine*, vol. 131 (March 1882), 365-374.

[26]J. Henry Shorthouse, Letter to Alexander Macmillan (3 April 1882), *LLLR*, vol. I, 146-147.

[27]"Moral Purpose in Fiction", *The Spectator*, vol. 55, no. 2804 (25 March 1882), 388-390.

[28]William Barry, *The Dublin Review*, 3rd series, vol. 7 (April 1882), 395-426.

[29]J. Henry Shorthouse, Undated Letter "To an Agnostic", *LLLR*, vol. I, 90-96.

[30]J. Henry Shorthouse, "The Agnostic at Church", *LLLR*, vol. I, 150-155.

[31]Alfred Lord Tennyson, "Locksley Hall", *The Poetical Works of Alfred Tennyson*, Vol. II (London: Henry S. King and Co., 1875), 41-60: "For I dipt into the future, far as human eye could see, / Saw the Vision of the world, and all the wonder that would be..."

[32]J. Henry Shorthouse, "The Agnostic at Church", *LLLR*, vol. I, 155.

[33]William Barry, *The Dublin Review*, 3rd series, vol. 7 (April 1882), 419.

[34]J. Henry Shorthouse, Letter to Lady Victoria Welby (10 May 1882), *LLLR*, vol. I, 156-157.

[35]J. Henry Shorthouse, "The Humorous in Literature", *Macmillan's Magazine* (March 1883), rep. in *LLLR*, vol. II., 248-280.

[36]Richard Holt Hutton, "'John Inglesant' on Humour", *Brief Literary Criticisms* (London: Macmillan, 1906), 69-80.

[37]Richard Holt Hutton, "'John Inglesant' on Humour", *Brief Literary Criticisms* 74.

[38]*LLLR*, vol. I, 85.

[39]J. Henry Shorthouse, Letter to Miss Southall (7 April 1882), *LLLR*, vol. I, 147-148.

[40]J. Henry Shorthouse, "On the Humourous in Literature", *LLLR*, vol. II, 262. [Note: *Macmillan's Magazine* printed "humourous"; *LLLR* uses "humorous"; spelling problems plagued Shorthouse in *John Inglesant*, and his letters to Alexander Macmillan often ask advice about spellings, especially of Italian words.]

[41]J. Henry Shorthouse, "Golden Thoughts on the Spiritual Guide", *LLLR*, vol. II. 281-284.

[42]See Shorthouse's letter to Professor Knight, *LLLR*, vol. I: "But I flatter myself that I have not unduly intruded the moral, as few readers [of *John Inglesant*] have perceived it without my

pointing it out" (129-130).

[43] *LLLR*, vol. I, 134-135.

[44] J. Henry Shorthouse, "On the Platonism of Wordsworth", *LLLR*, vol. II, 233-247.

[45] "B.P.L.", Letter to the Editor, *The Spectator*, vol. 55, no. 2826 (26 August 1882), 1109-1110.

[46] "The Author of *John Inglesant* and George Herbert", *The Spectator*, vol. 55, no. 2823 (5 April 1882), 1026-1028. See also *The Modern Review*, vol. 3 (October 1882), 865-866.

[47] J. Henry Shorthouse, Letter to Lady Victoria Welby (10 May 1882), *LLLR*, vol. I, 156.

[48] J. Henry Shorthouse, *Sir Percival* (London: Macmillan, 1886), 15.

[49] J. Henry Shorthouse, *Sir Percival* 64.

[50] J. Henry Shorthouse, Letter to Lady Welby (27 December 1886), *LLLR*, vol. I, 241.

[51] Thomas Docherty, *Reading (Absent) Character* (Oxford: Clarendon, 1983).

[52] J. Henry Shorthouse, *A Teacher of the Violin and Other Tales* (London: Macmillan, 1888), 115.

[53] *LLLR* 161 and F. J. Wagner, *J. H. Shorthouse* (Boston: Twayne, 1979), 110.

[54] J. Henry Shorthouse, "The Marquis Jeanne Hyacinthe de St. Palaye", *A Teacher of the Violin and Other Tales* (London: Macmillan, 1888), 119-184, 183.

[55] J. Henry Shorthouse, "Frederick Denison Maurice", *LLLR*, vol. II, 285-317, 298.

[56] *LLLR*, vol. II, 289.

[57] William Edward Collins, "Frederick Denison Maurice", *Typical English Churchmen* (London: SPCK, 1902), 340.

[58] J. Henry Shorthouse, Letter to George Macmillan, British Library: Macmillan Archive, MS. 54934, f. 43.

[59] J. Henry Shorthouse and George Macmillan, Memorandum of Agreement (26 March 1883), British Library: Macmillan Archive, MS. 54934, f. 46, and (18 May 1883) f. 46.

[60] J. Henry Shorthouse, "Books Versus Books", *LLLR*, vol. II, 16-17.

[61] F. J. Wagner, *J. H. Shorthouse* 94.

[62] J. Henry Shorthouse, Letter to Lady Welby (18 December 1883), *LLLR*, vol. I, 212-213.

[63] J. Henry Shorthouse, Letter to Canon Alfred Ainger (27 April 1883), *LLLR*, vol. I, 223-224.

[64] Edith Sichel, *The Life and Letters of Alfred Ainger* (London: Archibald Constable and Co., 1906), 200-205.

[65]J. Henry Shorthouse, Letter to Canon Alfred Ainger (28 November 1886), *LLLR*, vol. I, 242-244.

[66]Edith Sichel, *The Life and Letters of Alfred Ainger* 202.

[67]Edith Sichel, *The Life and Letters of Alfred Ainger* 202.

[68]F. J. Wagner, *J. H. Shorthouse* 114.

[69]William Boyd Carpenter, *Further Pages of My Life* (London: Williams and Norgate, 1916), 205.

[70]William Boyd Carpenter, *Further Pages of My Life* 207. "The Untravelled Traveller" appears in *LLLR*, vol. I, 222-223.

[71]William Boyd Carpenter, *Further Pages of My Life* 207.

[72]J. Henry Shorthouse, *The Little Schoolmaster Mark* (London: Macmillan, 1883), 10.

[73]C. G. Jung, "The Psychology of the Child Archetype", *The Archetypes and the Collective Unconscious*, vol. 9, part I, *Collected Works*, Bollingen Series XX (Princeton University Press, 1959), 2nd ed., 1968, 151-181, 164.

[74]C. G. Jung, "The Psychology of the Child Archetype" 157.

[75]C. G. Jung, "The Psychology of the Child Archetype" 162-163.

[76]William Boyd Carpenter, *Further Pages from My Life* 209.

[77]William Boyd Carpenter, *Further Pages from My Life* 209-212.

[78]J. Henry Shorthouse, Letter to William Boyd Carpenter (2 March 1884), *LLLR*, vol. I, 220-221; the letter was reprinted in Carpenter's *Further Pages from My Life* 212.

[79]F. J. Wagner, *J. H. Shorthouse* 97.

[80]In "The Baroness Helena von Saarfeld" (280), Zinzendorff is spelled with a double *f*, an error that was corrected in *LSM*.

[81]J. Henry Shorthouse, Letter to Lady Welby (23 November 1884), *LLLR*, vol. I, 227-228.

[82]J. Henry Shorthouse, Letter to Edmund Gosse (20 October 1885), *LLLR*, vol. I, 233-234.

[83]Richter's *Life* was translated by Elizabeth Lee and published in London by John Chapman.

[84]Samuel Taylor Coleridge's marginal note is on page 163 of the 1814 edition (Stuttgart and Tubingen) of *Museum*, now in Doctor Williams' Library at Gordon Square.

[85]*LSM* 142 and 207. "It seems a strange duet, yet I do not know that we should think it strange" (142), and "We shall not care, I think, to see him again" (207), suggest an "I" talking to another

character, to the reader, or to Shorthouse.

[86]J. Henry Shorthouse, Letter to Edmund Gosse (20 October 1885), *LLLR*, vol. I, 234.

[87]Jean Paul Richter, *Museum* (Stuttgart and Tubingen, 1814). Richter records his first experience of self-consciousness: "I stood one afternoon, a very young child, at the house door, and looked at the logs of wood piled on the left, when, at once, that inward consciousness *I am a Me* came like a flash of lightning from heaven, and has remained ever since. Then was my existence conscious of itself, and forever" (32).

Chapter Six: What We Shall Be: Constance, Eve, and Blanche

"Beloved, now we are the Sons of God, but it doth not yet appear what we shall be", proclaims the epigraph of *John Inglesant*, as Shorthouse quotes the first letter of St. John 3:2, alludes to the sacred mysteries of identity, and honours F. D. Maurice.[1] Throughout the philosophical romance, the affairs of the world "act only as a catalyst for the internal events that remain mysterious" and the affairs of the interior life, disciplined by the search for the Divine Light, strive towards "ultimate freedom from family, circumstances, education, and the course of events...freedom from history".[2] To be free from history is not, however, to be lacking knowledge and experience of history. *John Inglesant* illustrates how the experiencing of historical events may lead to deep awareness of a different ordering of time, time lived in the presence of God, God intuited and perceived as the "intimations of immortality" through "active imagination" that bridges and connects the temporal world and the very sense of being alive. For Shorthouse, God-Time and human-time meet in the Holy Eucharist, yet the instant one thinks about the sacramental experience, one is caught in the dualism of thought. Wondering about "the extinction and nothingness of the individual", Shorthouse realised that "you have only to reverse the shield and it seems as though the individual was everything".[3] Because "Everything may be a sacrament to the pure in heart"[4] the purity of the individual becomes the dominant theme of *Sir Percival: A Story of the Past and of the Present*. As the little schoolmaster unconsciously sacrificed his life to raise the lives of others towards higher and nobler spiritual ideals, Sir Percival Massareen sacrifices his life consciously and deliberately in service to the ideals of the Christian Mythos and chivalric romance.

Sir Percival is a daring book, and one that is very difficult to judge. One wonders how the book would have been received by the public had it appeared before *John Inglesant* and searches the text for some logical development or extension of Shorthouse's art, his literary themes, and the religion of "the author of *John Inglesant*". *Sir Percival* illustrates what might have happened to John Inglesant had he followed Mary Collet's spiritual guidance instead of obeying Father St. Clare and serving King Charles I. Sir Percival is motivated by the spiritual idealism of Constance Lisle, who narrates his story as the external fulfillment of her own internal quest. Constance derives directly from "the damoysel...alle in whyte" of Malory's *Le Morte D'Arthur*, and through her persona, Shorthouse attempts to correct the "falseness" of Tennyson's *Idylls of the King*, which he had condemned twenty-five years earlier for "excluding rigorously everything that belongs to the spiritual part and sacred meaning" of Malory's Arthurian romance, "the most wonderful reproduction of the tone of thought and feeling of a past age that has ever been achieved".[5]

When *Sir Percival* was published in September 1886, some thirty-five thousand copies were put on the market; eight thousand more were printed and released before the year was over. The Macmillans and the Shorthouses expected success and were ready to fulfill the expectations of *John Inglesant's* reading public. Critics, however, were more demanding and less kind. *The Academy* "fearlessly damned *Sir Percival* as 'decidedly silly and decidedly dull'".[6] *Blackwood's* denounced it as "a kind of insult to the public...a mystic piece of false sentiment and monkish religiousness"[7], and even the *Church Quarterly Review*, though admitting that "inevitably we measure anything from the pen of Mr. Shorthouse by the lofty standard which he has himself applied in *John Inglesant*", was "aggrieved" that *Sir Percival* was "not better".[8] The *Church Quarterly Review* wanted "more nerve and bone and sinew" and complained that Shorthouse used Sir Percival Massareen as "little more than a by-product of the inner life and quest for meaning of Constance Lisle", whose narrative is "soapy", self-fulfilling, and sentimental.

As if to integrate the German Princess Isoline from *The Little Schoolmaster Mark* into Victorian England, Shorthouse adopted a persona that in itself "makes or breaks" the novel, and the problems of *Sir Percival* are distinctly the problems of Constance Lisle. If John Inglesant were an "impossible character", Constance Lisle is a stereotype that all too easily lends itself to parody. Either the reader accepts her view of reality and thoroughly enjoys her inner explorations and idealistic love for Sir Percival, or the reader jolts at her handicapped personality and hopes she finds a good therapist. In the transition from Geoffrey Monk through the anonymous omniscient persona in Part I of *The Little Schoolmaster Mark* and the anonymous and very nebulous "I" in Part II, to Constance Lisle, Shorthouse crossed the transsexual boundary between fictional personae. Modern feminist critics might have "a real field day" reading *Sir Percival*, but modern readers accustomed to "androgynous vision" will find much to appreciate in considering *Sir Percival* as a companion and a complement to *John Inglesant*. Shorthouse knew what he was about; he did not psychologically project or unconsciously transfer his personality into Constance Lisle. In fact, he created distance between himself and his work. "I always wish them [my books] to stand entirely apart from their author", he wrote Lady Welby, then added, "indeed, a perfect book would be one which *had no author at all*".[9] Shorthouse understood *Sir Percival* as "perhaps a bold a venture as a writer ever wished", and he precisely defined the nature of his venture: "The effort to describe a conscious existence within the grace of God..." Though the effort might be an impossible one, he knew that "To those who are ignorant of such existence it must seem *unreal* [but] to those who happily are familiar with such existence it must seem inadequate." *Sir Percival*, he declared, "is written against a certain very definite school of thought in London", one that "cannot endure the combination of reason and faith".[10] The novel's unavailability today (it was last reprinted in 1910) may be the only cause of its lack of an appreciative audience today. Although it does jar against modern materialistic mentality, *Sir Percival* is a highly imaginative "spiritual romance" and a beautifully written novel that distinguishes love as attraction and sexual passion from love as adoration of the potentialities of "an-Other in the spirit". Suggestive of a *John Inglesant* as told by a Mary Collet, *Sir Percival* defines the archetypal dilemmas of spiritual versus instinctual love, presents some brilliant and "refined portraiture of the high-bred" of Victorian England, and is psychologically compelling.

Constance Lisle, "presumably an old lady writing in 1920",[11] charmingly tells of her life at Kingswood, ancestral home of the Duke and Duchess of Cressy and de la Pole. Her descriptions invite imaginative exploration of curiosities, portraits, armour, and treasures of aristocratic heritage. She vividly shares the "constancy" of the old country estate and the history of "Merrie Olde England". Hints of *John Inglesant* abound, as the charms and mystical atmosphere of Westacre are instilled into Kingswood. References to Charles I and quotations from George Herbert prepare the reader for antiquarian interest in a "quaint little chapel" about a mile from Kingswood where an old painted glass window represents a knight, bareheaded and kneeling in a forest, surrounded by bright light, with a scroll above his head, and one word on the scroll, "Parcyvale". One of the Duke's most valued treasures is a Caxton edition of Malory, and throughout the novel lines from *Le Morte D'Arthur* extend the ideals of Medieval chivalry into the present.

Disclaiming the value of her opinions ("I am only a woman, and my opinion is of little worth")[12], Constance nevertheless praises the glories of England and the greatness of the English race, whose "victories have triumphed over death and hell" and led "the beneficent march" of civilisation around the world. She recalls the spirit of Port Royal des Champs and, recalling the "religion of *John Inglesant*", she tells the story of the Reverend Charles de Foi, the local parish priest, in order to describe Charles Simeon (1759-1836) and "the Cambridge Revival", which enthused new life into the Church of England by starting the "Broad Church Movement". The "muscular Christianity" and the "intellectual renaissance of Simeon's Evangelical Cambridge" would have offended Charles de Foi, but in Shorthouse's Broad Church sympathies, "where a sympathy of nature exists differences of detail are of little importance" (50). Simeon had had considerable influence on de Foi, especially in the notion of extremes. "I am for all extremes", he declared; "The truth does not lie in the middle, or in one extreme, but in both extremes...only remember it is not *one* extreme that we are to go to, but *both*" (51-52). Though given to the ideal of the Golden Mean, Charles de Foi chose to serve the Church after an intimate conversation with Simeon. Simeon told him how he had found his own vocation through a kind of "Bible magic". Praying earnestly for guidance, Simeon had opened the Bible upside down "without intending it" and the first text that caught his eye read, "They found a man of Cyrene, Simeon by name: him they compelled to bear His cross." Rejoicing in his own name, Simeon dedicated himself to "carrying the cross". De Foi received "a sudden flash of light across [his] spirit" and dedicated himself to the Church. Thus, the reader is prepared to accept belief in the magic or *mana* of names, and, recalling the power of one word, "Prince!", which saved Prince Ferdinand from his illicit desire to possess Faustina Banti in *The Little Schoolmaster Mark*, the reader expects "Parcyvale" to have compelling power over the life of Sir Percival, and indeed it does.

Shortly after young Constance, twenty-two, meets Sir Percival when he first visits Kingswood, she tells him the story of Percival as she remembers it from Malory's:

> 'Parcyvale [had] kneled doune and made his prayer
> devoutely unto almighty Jhesu, for he was one of the best
> knyghtes of the world that at that tyme was, in whome the
> verry feythe stode mooste in' (83).

The words of Malory instill Percival with Christian idealism, and everything in the Duke's garden, including "brilliant sunshine and deep shadow" is "enspiritualised". In a thematic sense, the rest of the novel is but the telling of how Percival learns to follow the ideals of his namesake. In the dramatising of it, however, Sir Percival must learn two important spiritual lessons: "See! only see! (92)" and "Be true! only be true! (259)"

Seeing beneath the surfaces of the modern world into its spiritual heritage is an "experiment in depth" into the personal unconscious, then an exploration of the collective unconscious, where the psychological and spiritual heritage of mankind lives and has its being around the archetype of "the centre", the Self. Ironically, *Sir Percival* contains an "odd bit" of art history that enhances the "Only see!" theme. Shorthouse could not have intended the irony, but his Constance Lisle seems to perceive with X-ray vision. Close by the main entrance door of Kingswood hangs a portrait by Gainsborough of "a boy dressed in what the last century chose to call a Vandyke costume--a costume familiar to all from the celebrated picture of the Blue Boy". The portrait was to Constance "the most speaking and life-like portrait" she had ever seen, and, as she tells us in her elderly narrative voice, "I have had good cause to remember it since" (8). Later, we learn that the Gainsborough painting hangs between two doorways, one that leads into the hallway, and one that leads to "one of the numberless staircases of Kingswood". When she first sees Percival, he stands in the doorway that leads to the staircase by the side of the Gainsborough boy (78-79). Later, at a poignant moment in the story, when Constance is singing an air from Handel's *Messiah* and pondering Percival's destiny, she sees "dimly in the background...the Gainsborough Blue Boy" (211). Gainsborough, in fact, painted three portraits of men in the Vandyke blue silk costume, but the most famous one, "The Blue Boy", does contain an ironic "Only see!" message. Gainsborough was "balanced between two extreme positions" at the time he painted "Blue Boy", and beneath the painting of the youthful Blue Boy is another portrait, or at least the beginning of another painting, of an older man discernible only through X-ray photography.[13] Constance believes she sees what Percival is and what he may become, and the portrait serves as an "objective correlative...full of some stuff that the writer could not drag to light, contemplate, or manipulate into art".[14] As Eliot believed, "The only way of expressing emotion in the form of art" is by creating "artistic inevitability" by the "skillful accumulation of imagined sensory impressions" which exactly correspond, or correlate, with external facts. Shorthouse's friend Lady Welby noted, "We cannot attempt to communicate with another 'mind' without first assuming an analogy between that and our own".[15] Welby hoped not merely "to harmonise science and religion", but through the study of "significs" to "show that every form of truth is potential in every other".[16] Eliot's criticism was directed at what can be shown or performed on stage; Welby's study of how language signifies and means was directed at a reading audience. The emotional realities that can be conveyed through a novel far exceed those that can be objectified and presented on stage. A novel writer's

> dreams and buried memories go into his novel along with
> the recognizably objective subject matter; the reader,
> finishing the novel, turns to his own dreams whose
> imagery may be coloured by the events of the novel.[17]

In effect, "the unconscious imagery of one mind enters into the unconsciousness of another", and, as "a writer does not always know what he has written", so "a reader does not always know what he has read". J. Alfred Prufrock exclaims, "It is impossible to say just what I mean!" and finds himself depending on a "magic lantern...to throw the nerves in patterns on a screen".[18] So, too, "The soul must contain in itself the faculty of relation to God, i.e., a correspondence, otherwise a connection [between God and man] could never come about".[19] It is this "faculty of relation to God" that Shorthouse represents in *Sir Percival*. The "Blue Boy", the Duke's manor, even trees in the garden and clouds in the sky correlate Constance Lisle's experience and awareness of God with her transforming influence upon Percival Massareen.

In the process of Individuation, to attain a new level of psychological development one must first detach oneself from one's own emotions and differentiate external facts from one's projections upon those facts, a process Eliot suggested in his separation of "the mind that creates" from the "man that suffers". Once an individual is consciously aware of the distinction between what is empirically real and what is psychologically real, one can "withdraw the projections". Reversing the relationship between John Inglesant and Mary Collet, Shorthouse shows that Constance must detach from being "in love" with Percival to see him as he really is and to help him see himself and intuit his destiny. Though initially "infatuated" with Percival, Constance gains freedom from the projection of her *animus* through meticulous self-scrutiny and self-conscious analysis, and she chooses to sacrifice earthly love in the service of a higher calling.

Under the spell of the British Empire, most readers of *Sir Percival* certainly would not have interpreted their religious values as external representations "of unadorned paganism", as Shorthouse did. To Shorthouse only "the spirit of Christianity" connects the external facts of daily life with the "innate psychic aptitude for God". In Jung's analysis of Western civilisation, psychic conditions

> have remained archaic and [have] not been even remotely touched by Christianity...Christian civilisation has proved hollow to a terrifying degree: it is all veneer, but the inner man has remained untouched and therefore unchanged... Everything is to be found outside--an image...in word, in Church and Bible--but never inside.[20]

To a reader who unconsciously sees the outside as "objective correlative" of his own inner life, the "Aristotelian facts of reality suffice", but to a reader who consciously sees a contrast between the exterior world and his inner being, Platonic ideas and forms are indispensable guides. When Constance praises the English race and extols the leadership of civilisation as "inherent in the English character", Shorthouse satirizes his readers' attitudes. As he wrote Canon Ainger, he was prepared for misunderstanding critics:

> Constance has been sneered at by some of the reviewers *for giving up at once*. She saw, with the insight of *all* clever girls, that Percival could never be hers, and she saw this with a certainty that made all effort, all struggle, useless,--nay, unbecoming and unimaginable; but she was something more than 'a clever girl', she was a *woman*.

In the same letter, he defended his work:

> Except in those parts where *art* is impossible in a novel
> with a purpose, as all my books are, I take it that *Sir*
> *Percival* is *too* good art. It would have been understood
> better in some quarters if the art had been more openly
> shown.[21]

The "art" refers to the external influences upon Percival which counterbalance Constance's "enspiritualised" vision. Percival asks Constance, "Do you really mean that you hear...that you see Him; that you see Christ, as you see me?" "Yes, I do", escapes through her lips, then, she confesses,

> It hardly seemed as though it were myself that spoke the
> words, so suddenly, so confidently, had they leapt forth.
> The boldness of the assertion struck me with a kind of
> awe, and I buried my face in my hands (127).

Under her influence, Percival begins to feel "some new, strange way of looking at things":

> ...things I never thought of were coming into my mind--as
> though I should be able to sometime see and do things
> which I have never seen, never thought that I should do
> (92).

Reality, he says, "simply never looked like this to me before" (153). Then, to test his new mode of perceiving, Virginia Clare enters the story.

Just prior to Virginia Clare's arrival at Kingswood, Constance, meditating on the beauty of the landscape, senses "something in the placid landscape [that seems] to foreshadow and to harmonise with an instinct glimmering [in her] future fate". She returns to the house where the "silent landscapes upon the walls" greet her with "the long fellowship which the entire house and all that it contained seemed to have contracted", a fellowship in which "no jarring note, no inharmonious shade or sound seemed possible". Yet, the moment Constance enters the drawing room, she sees Virginia Clare with Sir Percival and the future of her life is revealed to her. Virginia is outspoken and lacks social decorum; a socialist, she plays the role of "a Petroleuse" (159). Virginia abruptly tells Constance how she detests "everything that is old", which obviously includes Kingswood, and she unceremoniously challenges Percival: "You are rich, are you not?...You must give it all to use. It [the millions he is going to inherit] must all go to the socialist propaganda." Her abrasiveness, however, does not offend at Kingswood, for the Duke, whose attitudes monitor the manners of others, thinks "her socialistic notions sit with a very pretty quaintness upon her" (154). Virginia announces, too, that she is an agnostic and has long given up public worship of any kind, though with a sense of apology, she adds,

I think if I could join any form of faith, I would join the
Quakers. They seem to me to be the most open to all
influences of light. But I have long ago renounced all
forms of faith (160).

Representing an aspect of a negative *anima* projection, she fails to see the
irony of her closed-mindedness in her attraction to the open-mindedness of
the Quakers.

Watching Percival's responses to Virginia, Constance realises her
moment of vision has been correct: "Percival could never be mine...I knew
this with a certainty" (200-201). In the following days the young people
occupy themselves with tennis, horseback riding, exploring nearly monastic
ruins, and pondering their views of a story told by Reverend de Foi. De
Foi's story, like the quotations from Malory, prefigures the plot and enables
the main characters to examine and understand themselves through the story
of Mademoiselle Desessart and Charles de Foi's grandfather, the Vicomte de
Foi. "A Divine Voice" had led the Vicomte to speak about God to a young
lady at a ball. Obeying an inner voice, the Vicomte told Mademoiselle du
Valois-Desessart of "the love of God, of her Saviour, of the unimaginable
joys of the spiritual life". She was startled, for "she had never heard such
words before". Four days after the ball, the Vicomte was summoned to the
Mademoiselle's deathbed by her mother. The mother refused to let the
Vicomte see her daughter, who was dying of virulent smallpox, but she told
him her daughter was dying "happily in the grace of God" and that her
daughter wished her to tell Vicomte to "go on as you have begun" (142).
Readers of *John Inglesant* hear an echo of the dying Mary Collet's voice.

Shorthouse excels in his "humourous" treatment of the relations
between Constance and Virginia. Juxtaposing and balancing their
personalities into "mystical rhythms", he delineates subtle insights, not
"psychological waste-products masquerading as literature".[22] Because
Shorthouse experienced his characters as "given to him" and allowed them
to form themselves outside of his conscious control, Constance Lisle
represents the voice of his *anima*, and his allowing Constance to narrate *Sir
Percival* suggests the novel may have more psychological value than *John
Inglesant*. Indeed, "Sir Percival" has archetypal significance as Constance
Lisle's *animus*. Critics who denigrated *Sir Percival* focused their attention
on the credibility of Constance Lisle as the narrator and on the overdramatic
ending. In a blaze of religious emotion, Constance validates her spiritual
intuition and successfully integrates the *animus* qualities of Percival into her
Ego. When Virginia Clare dies, she dies with one word upon her lips:
"Percival!" (221). Constance realises that Percival's love for Virginia "had
called up an ideal within him", and she determines to help him realise the
potentials of the ideal. Two years pass. Percival moves back and forth

between London and Kingswood, and his relations with Constance become brotherly. Finally, the time arrives for his proposal. Sensing his motives for the visit, Constance invites him to hear Reverend de Foi preach at Rivershead. The novel contains a fifteen-page sermon. De Foi seems to preach directly to Sir Percival:

> [As] every single act, however trivial and small, is not isolated and alone, but is part of a higher life, of a more perfect existence, of a loftier intellect, and a diviner Love, [so] every single act of sacrifice is part of the great sacrifice ...[and] is only possible because it is part of the divine love; nothing can exist save as the result of the existence of its perfect ideal, and the ideal of perfect existence is God (245-246).

Embedded within de Foi's Platonism is also the ideal of "natural laws, forces in harmony with which you work if you make of your daily life an art" (248). De Foi describes "the unconscious world" of which Percival is unaware. Percival returns to Kingswood in silence, and, once there, he centres himself in the gardens by "a sacred well" to listen to his inner voice.

Divided into eleven chapters, the novel's centre is chapter six, "The Garden Door". A simple garden door opens from Kingswood into a world of mystical experience like the door in the rose garden in "Burnt Norton". Opening the door is analogous to entering the unconscious. Midway through the novel, Constance faces "the mysterious door" and reflects:

> I knew nothing of what lay beyond, but it seemed to my childish imagination a vast and gloomy world, full, doubtless, of strange terrors and dangers, and from whence, over the protecting wall, black clouds and storms came drifting...I did not know in those childish days that through this door...I should pass at the most solemn moment of my life (122).

By the garden door, Constance reads "the Keble for the day" to Percival, and their thoughts drift from personal romance towards God and "mystic realities". It is before the garden door that Constance involuntarily declares she "sees God" just as she "sees Percival", and it is at the garden door that Percival proposes marriage to her. Constance confronts the proposal as a woman, as a believer, then as a realist:

> Every word he spoke was honest...but did he know what truth was? Did he know his own mind for a week together? 'I was not worthy of Virginia', he had said. He belonged to her. She did not believe in a God. Should I, who profess to believe in a God... should I take him, who

belonged to her, him whom she had claimed by her dying look and words--take him, who belonged to her, and the Guion money...? Surely, no! (259)

To Constance, Virginia Clare is not dead and Percival still belongs to her: "She is gone to that God whom she died serving, though she fancied that she did not know Him. Percival, she is not dead." Ironically, Constance urges Percival, "Only be true", which, he recalls, were the very words Virginia had spoken to him when he first confessed his love for her. Constance realises quite simply that she is not "in love" with Percival, rather she has "love of him". In Jung's terms, she has withdrawn her projection; in biblical terms, she has removed "the mote" from her own eye, thus is able "to see clearly to cast out the mote from [her] brother's eye".[23] When they approach the garden wall, "The western sun had cast a deep shade from the lofty wall and from the clumps of elms outside it in the chase", but when they open the garden door, "a blaze of light and golden heat over the level lawns" strikes Constance with "a sense of life and hope". She takes many lessons from her readings of nature, and the sunlight tells her she has been right in rejecting Percival and in perceiving his "mote" as "the weakness of undecided action". He is afflicted, as Hamlet was, with no decisive will of his own. Now, symbolically rejected by Virginia's death and by Constance's clear refusal, Percival has no decision to make; he has only "choiceless awareness" of what he must do. Adapting Malory and "enspiritualising" Tennyson, Shorthouse ends *Sir Percival* with "The Finding of the Grail". Percival returns to London and offers his services to Sir Charles Sinclair, who is preparing an expedition to the West Coast of Africa. Shorthouse intended *Sir Percival* to be a "devotional book"[24], but the final scene upset Victorian readers as the ending of Eliot's *The Cocktail Party* upsets modern audiences.[25] Eliot's Celia suffers a horrible crucifixion by the natives she serves as a medical missionary. Modern readers may accept sacrifices for reasonably necessary causes, but crucifixions are another matter; unless carefully presented, they replace "actual suffering...with romantic crucifixion".[26] The holy ideals of *Sir Percival* become too much for Constance Lisle to convey in her narrative, and she repeats, "I am only a woman." The death of Sir Percival disrupts any sense of worldly romance with the shock of "spiritual romance". On a daring mission to rescue an Anglican bishop, with the foolhardy notion that "the presence of an English officer might overawe the natives and their king", Lieutenant Sir Percival Massareen dies of fever in the darkest depths of the jungle surrounded by bloodthirsty savages. His last act is to share in the eucharist with the bishop just before the bishop is killed. With no bread or wine, the Bishop and Percival "eat three blades of grass with intention", a tradition of the Middle Ages, as the bishop verifies, through which a man may receive "the sacrament though

237

other priest were none" (294). Even Shorthouse's friend, the Reverend J. Hunter Smith, found the ending "repulsive".[28]

When Constance receives Percival's last letter, composed as he is dying, she reenacts a scene from Book XI of *Le Morte D'Arthur*: "I sawe a damoysel as me thoughte, alle in whyte with a vessel in both her handes, and forth withal I was hole." With a "thrill of supreme excitement", Constance carries Percival's letter to the chapel like "a sacred thing...a letter to be read nowhere but before the altar of the Lord" (283). In his last thoughts, Percival turned homeward:

> I see the chase and the dark tower, and the flashing waters of the channel gleaming in light, and before me on her horse, beneath the oak-trees, an English girl. Who is this, seated in her saddle beneath the rustling branches of the oak? She turns her head towards me...It is Constance-- Constance with the pleading eyes...in the dazzling light...bright, clear...a long procession of noble forms-- Constance! Constance! Who is this? And the armies that are in heaven follow Him upon white horses, clothed in fine linen...white...clean (298).

Shorthouse achieved in *Sir Percival* precisely what he intended, a story that provokes, rebukes, chastises, and struggles to clean the "mote of unadorned paganism" out of Christianity. Teasingly, he told Lady Welby that he sometimes thought of her "soul (or spirit) [as] a metempsychosis of that of Plato, enlarged and instructed by his experience and growth since he passed into the unseen".[29] He was deeply impressed with the spiritual insight of her writings, especially her attempts to discern "links and clues" of higher, nobler life and to listen to "echoes" of "spiritual reality in daily life". Constance Lisle's character is a composite of Victoria Welby, Mary Collet, an English country girl, and an elderly, aristocratic lady. At least one critic had complained that Shorthouse was "too much identified with his hero's quest [in *John Inglesant*] to adopt the aesthetic distance" needed to attain "the finest evocation of personal experience in the past".[30] His adopting Constance Lisle as his *persona* indicates he was aware of the limiting effect of his third person narration and his autobiographical projection in *John Inglesant*. Through Constance, Shorthouse discovered another role of the *anima*, which is to connect the past with the present, to create historical perspective. Victorian readers who felt the need of a living Mary Collet to inspire ordinary, young Englishmen towards gentlemanly or knightly ideals and behaviour had no cause to complain against Constance Lisle; she inspires her would-be knight towards his spiritual destiny, and she fills her narrative with Malory, Herbert, Keble, Tennyson, and a profound sense of the history of the Church of England. Taken together, *John Inglesant* and

Sir Percival combine masculine philosophical inquiry and feminine spirituality from Medieval through modern Victorian times into religious sensibility. As Shorthouse realised the two parts of *The Little Schoolmaster Mark* need to be "read together" to be understood, *Sir Percival* takes "the sting and the barb" out of *John Inglesant's* defence of the Church of England. The young Sir Percival "Massareen" (a play on "Mass" and "Nazarene") does not argue systems or organizations of religious life, but gives energetic vitality to the spiritual mission of the Church of England. As *John Inglesant* makes the Church and its sacraments worthy of the greatest defence, *Sir Percival* makes the spiritual life worth dying for.

Judging by critical reactions from his contemporaries, Shorthouse's experiment with a feminine persona succeeded. "No appreciation of his writings pleased [him] more than that of good women"[31], and his correspondence and social life included many Victorian ladies of literary reputation: Mary Howitt, Mary St. Leger Harrison (Lucas Malet), Mrs. Sidney Lear (Henrietta Louisa Farrer), Charlotte Maye Yonge, Frances Ware Cornish, Margaret Wilson Oliphant, Lady Victoria Welby, and Mrs. Humphry Ward. His last three novels seem aimed at pleasing his female audience, though in his shorter works he continued to work through male personae. *A Teacher of the Violin*, which first appeared in *Macmillan's Magazine* (November 1887), was published rather cautiously in March 1888. Only three thousand copies were released in book form, even though *A Teacher of the Violin* appeared with *Other Tales*, the stories of the Marquis Jeanne Hyacinthe and the Baroness Helena von Saarfeld, and two smaller pieces, "Ellie: A Story of a Boy and a Girl" and "An Apologue". The collection appeared only once more, in August 1891, when only two thousand copies were printed. Neither of the latter works earned Shorthouse public praise, though "An Apologue" did excite some interpretive curiosity. The psychological and spiritual love stories of the Marquis and the Baroness, artistic as they are, do not compare in interest or quality, however, with *A Teacher of the Violin*, which, despite a weak plot, charms and enchants readers with Shorthouse's near adoration of "musical ideas".

A Teacher of the Violin is a heroic tale that seems to suffocate its central ideal "by wrapping it up into a love story".[32] Its heroism has nothing to do with epic stature in the traditional sense, but with aesthetic nobility and aristocratic sensibility towards life, love, and music in the story of a young boy who grows into manhood with intimate knowledge of

> the harmonies of life, that absorb and hush the discord of the world [and] are heard only in the private walks and daily seclusion in which love and Christian purity delight.[33]

Compensating Shorthouse for his lifelong, convulsive stammer, *A Teacher of the Violin* harmonizes Platonism and philosophical speculation to ineffable limits of expressibility. Through "extraordinary forms of music", Shorthouse hoped to express spirituality in "a great musical novel". In "A Midsummer Night's Dream", one of the Early Essays, he attempted to define an art realm in which "the night side of life" is peopled with living presences, with people who live "in all the pictures that hang upon the walls", the people "who live in sound...in scent...in colour...and in form". "A Midsummer Night's Dream" was not written for the Friends Essay Society, and though Mrs. Shorthouse wanted it published in *A Teacher of the Violin and Other Tales*, Macmillan rejected it without offering any explanation.[34] Although Macmillan did publish the essay in volume II of *The Life, Letters, and Literary Remains of J. Henry Shorthouse*, it is one of Shorthouse's weaker essays. A fanciful tale for children, it is not childlike, but childish. Nevertheless, the essay contains Shorthouse's earliest expression of his belief that art in all its forms has "some effect" upon life and personal character.[35] "Thought", the essay asserts, "when it is once conceived, has an existence of its own, and never dies."[36] What is interesting in "A Midsummer Night's Dream" is not the providential aesthetic, "the awful sphere of consequence in which the smallest leaf never falls impotently to the ground", but the distinction one of "the people who live in sound" draws:

> 'We are the people who live in sound, but we are not born
> of sound...The offspring of thought...We are born of the
> union of art and sound, or rather, we are born of the union
> of art and human thought, wedded in the aisles of the
> glorious cathedral-church of sound' (341).

A Teacher of the Violin declares:

> True music is not heard by the spirit-born but is born of
> the spirit itself...They who are born of the spirit, in the
> turmoil of the world's passion and desire, alone can hear
> (17, 106).

The distinction becomes the central argument of *A Teacher of the Violin*, that "through music [born of the spirit wedded with thought through art]...human thought will be carried beyond the point it has hitherto reached". As the old master teacher declares, "To every note struck anywhere there is an accordant note in some human brain, toiling, dying, suffering, here below" (42). As "Gods and Demons [of the past]...are understood in our 'scientific' age as psychical manifestations of the instincts [so] habitual and universally occurring attitudes and thought forms" yield empirical evidence of "archetypal, basic forms". The psychological "stuff of the Gods" has not died, and "modern consciousness only imagines the god-realities 'lost' [until] a certain general condition brings them back in full force".[1] Shorthouse's story failed, however, to strike the accordant note and *A Teacher of the Violin* did not even capture the attention of his regular readers. Such is the "fortune of mysticism" in literature:

> [It is] generally misinterpreted and misunderstood. Appealing in reality to the highest and most rational in man, its false presentment makes appeal to that which is near to the lowest--those superstitions and curiosities that snatch a fearful joy from the shadows in which wizards peep and mutter.[37]

The failure of *A Teacher of the Violin* is not easy to explain, for, like *John Inglesant*, it appeals to "the highest and most select natures" without "false presentment". Rather than compose *A Teacher of the Violin* as a seamless, fictional autobiography, Shorthouse divided the narrative into three parts. From a psychological point of view, *A Teacher of the Violin* fascinates the relationship between musical sounds of nature (the instinctive, the spontaneous, and the individual) and music composed to express the ideal of individual harmony within social and cultural collectivity. Indeed, the story develops from the realm of the personal unconscious into the collective unconscious, then returns to the personal level and uses music as the agency of psychological transformation. The three parts of the story also correspond to three stages of psychological development: part one is autobiographical and depicts growth from "the unconscious perfection of childhood"; part two, a narrative, focuses on the "conscious imperfection of middle life"; part three returns to the fictional autobiography as "the conscious perfection of old age":

> One moves from an innocent wholeness, in which the inner world and the outer world are united, to a separation and differentiation between the inner and outer worlds with an accompanying sense of life's duality, and then, at last, to enlightenment--a conscious reconciliation of the inner and outer in harmonious wholeness.[38]

Such a pattern is discernible in *John Inglesant* and *A Teacher of the Violin*, although the third stage of growth is more implied in the point of view than it is represented. In the Early Essays, Shorthouse began to experiment with poetic devices and prose rhythms, and his play with assonance, consonance, rhyme, alliteration, and sentence patterns sometimes becomes obtrusive. To accentuate the interior of a church, for instance, from the life outside on the streets, Shorthouse waxes poetic:

> One Sunday evening, the day before he was to meet Cressy, walking along the Rue St. Martin from the Boulevard where he had lodgings, he turned into the

Jesuits' Church just as the sermon had begun. The dim light found its way into the vast Church from the stained windows; a lamp burning before the shrine shone partially on the preacher, as he stood in the stone pulpit by the great pillar, in his white surplice and rich embroidered stole.

Here the embedded stained/stood/stole, shrine/shone/stone, and preacher/pulpit/ pillar are not overly obtrusive but alerts the reader to deliberate sound play. The expectation is soon met:

Over the door and window and pilaster throng and cling the arabesque carvings of foliage and fruit, of graceful figures in fantastic forms and positions --all of infinite variety; all full of originality, of life, of motion, and of character; all of exquisite beauty both of design and workmanship (296).

Often, too, the more lyrical passages and deliberate sound and rhythm play are used to describe dream-like qualities:

In the excitement and nervousness of the hour I was dimly conscious of a solemn blue sky overhead, of the dark foliage of the dying summer rising on the steep hillsides on every hand, of a still afternoon full of sombre tints and sleeping sunlight, of late-flowering china-roses and the tall asters, of massive wreaths of clematis, of a sense of finished effort and growth, and of a hush and pause before decay set in and brought the end of life and of the year: the little stone palace with its carved pilasters and wreaths of fruit and flowers, the weather-stained, moss-tinted statues and urns,--of all this I was dimly conscious as in a dream (61-62).

Even critics who did not admire his themes, plots, or characterizations were unanimous in their praise of his descriptive style, which adds charm and artistic sensitivity more than it detracts with poetic artifice.

The "whispering music" and the "wayward music" assert and argue the "mystic" theme of *A Teacher of the Violin*, and the prose rhythms are often hypnotic in their suggestiveness of "mystic unreality". Two distinct harmonies unite, those of the "wayward music...full, pure, true notes" and those that "whisper in tune with the melodies of heaven". When the true notes of "love and Christian purity" blend in perfect harmony with the melodies of heaven, the result is "supreme music", and the ending of the Ego's personal history: "He that is happy has no history", ends the short novel. Within the story the two different harmonies are metaphors for Otto von

Salle's two loves, Fraulein Adelheid, lady-in-waiting to the Princess, and the Princess Cynthia.

Otto von Salle, the eldest son of the pastor of Waldreich, has great natural musical talent, but in his native environment, he plays only "wild woodland music" and he plays by instinct and alone. He experiences great expectations when his talent is discovered by Herr Veitch, the court music master, who invites Otto to court to learn how to play in concert with other musicians. The music master arranges for Otto to audition before the King and his daughter. As he plays his "wild woodland music", his eyes meet those of the Princess, and he is seized by the power of the *anima*:

> He turned to salute the Princess; but, as he looked up, his
> eyes met her marvellous eyes and were fixed by a magic
> spell, so intense, searching, personal and yet abstracted
> was the look they met. His entire being was caught up
> and rapt into hers in an ecstasy of ravishment (87).

Ego-inflation is immediate; he believes himself "altogether separate from [his] fellows, and to be reserved for some supreme exceptional fate" (91). When invited to meet the Princess in her private garden, he more than fantasizes, he hallucinates. Wandering down the valley by the river, he senses "gibbering passing forms which with intolerable intrusion" seem to force themselves between himself "and the only conceivable event towards which all human history had been tending since the world began" (99). Ravished by an inability to distinguish between the Princess Cynthia and the projection of his *anima*, he nearly destroys himself through "dangerous originality". Fortunately, Otto has been warned by Herr Veitch against "a certain originality" in his performing which expresses "a great snare, indeed fatal in its results" (89), and he quickly masters his "infatuation" by recognizing it as "an exaggeration of delirium" which he suffers "to the highest pitch" (97). Once he realises his error, the "mystic veil [of] fear and embarrassment" quickly dissolves, and "in a clear, true vision", he and Adelheid "see each other for the first time". The two musical harmonies reduce symbolic meaning to metaphoric understanding, and the story becomes a human romance. Otto realises his debt to Adelheid and expresses hope: "You have taught me the violin, but there is another instrument, the strings of which vibrate to even higher tones: will you teach these strings also to vibrate in unison to your touch?" In obedience to the Princess and in love with Otto, Adelheid accepts his offer. Now, properly within his social place, in love in accord with class and rank, he is happy and his personal history comes quickly to an end. "And the Princess?" cajoles the narrator. During the 1806 French invasion, with the Prussian army in full retreat, the Princess rides in noble splendour to the enemy's camp and intercedes. Princess Cynthia's courage is likened to that of "the heavenly Queen", and her intervention saves her Thuringian kingdom from pillage and conflagration. Despite its lack of popularity, *A Teacher of the Violin* is more provocative than *The Little Schoolmaster Mark*. Using music as metaphor and as symbol, Shorthouse represents both the realm of the Ego and its personal unconscious and the greater, more mysterious "psychic vibes" of the collective unconscious. When Otto von Saale plays spontaneously, the Princess intuits "the primeval god-sprung race of the golden hours" (67):

> In its echoing repeats I seemed to hear voices that I had
> never heard before, and yet which seemed as though they
> were the voices of my kin, that told me which I came, and
> who I was, and what I might become (72).

His music evokes the German collective unconscious, and later she thanks and praises him: "You have taught me what I am, and you have shown me what I may become" (105). She is, of course, repeating the import of the biblical epigraph to *John Inglesant*, but, for some reason, Shorthouse used only part of the First Epistle General of John. In it complete context, the scripture states that "The world knoweth us not, because it knew him not", then adds the idea, "We know what we are, the sons of God, but not what we may become." What Shorthouse omits, ironically, is the ending promise: "...but we know that, when he shall appear, we shall be like him; for we shall see him as he is". The "Only see!" admonition underlies all of Shorthouse's creative work and challenges his readers to purify their materialistic perceptions and their religious convictions of "unadorned paganism". To paraphrase St. John's message in Jungian terms, ego-consciousness, the bodily senses, cannot comprehend the Ego's Individuation until it integrates intuitive awareness of the Self. Ego-consciousness is bound by what Blake called "the doors of perception" and, as such, can only abstract and metaphorize self-knowledge. To see "what we may become" is to see the archetypes of the collective unconscious as potentialities of future development. The *anima* in men and the *animus* in women provide internal guiding imagery, but as the Ego watches and attends to the archetypes, the Ego must allow its "personal history" to dissolve, to surrender its individualism and thereby discover its indivisibility, its wholeness. Thus, the Princess feels "born again" as she listens to Otto's violin music.

Unlike the *Other Tales*, the story of Otto is more psychological than spiritual. The Princess becomes a heroic queen, not a reclusive, spiritual seeker after mystical religious experience. The plot, in fact, resembles a case history of what Jung called the *mysterium coniunctionis*, as he titled his "inquiry into the separation and synthesis of the psychic opposites in alchemy". In *Mysterium Coniunctionis*, Jung studies the personification of the opposites in alchemical history in terms of "Rex and Regina" and "Adam and Eve", and he demonstrates that:

physico-chemical procedures [were] external projections onto matter of inward psychic processes whose actual aim...and whose real purpose was the spiritual transformation of the alchemist from within.[39]

Otto von Saale is not an alchemist in the usual sense, but his relationships with Adelheid and the Princess may easily be read as Shorthouse's studies of himself and of his art work, and *A Teacher of the Violin* expresses his most mature awareness of his own psychological Individuation. Composing the story of Otto, Adelheid, and the Princess Cynthia, Shorthouse prepared himself for the final tasks of his artistic career, which led him to the Adam and Eve myth.

The story of *The Countess Eve* serves as an illustration of its epigraph, which Shorthouse took directly from the Litany in *The Book of Common Prayer*:

'That it may please Thee to strengthen such as do stand,
and to comfort and help the weak-hearted, and to raise up
them that fall, and finally to beat down Satan under our
feet.'[40]

The novel dramatises, perhaps too melodramatically, how deeply dependent modern material life is upon "the mysteries of inheritance". The story of five major characters unfolds in terms of their personal philosophies, psychological temperaments or personality types, and "the unfathomable mysteries of the dim aeons of existence when the world lay void and misty and slimy in the pangs of creation".[41] Indeed, the world of *The Countess Eve* proved almost too insanely mysterious for Shorthouse's literary powers, but he carefully delineates the mysteries as far as his capacity allows, as profoundly as his understanding of "the science of sound" and "the science of life" enabled him. As if to explain why John Inglesant and his other characters studied the violin, he declares:

There are partial tones, which are unheard, but which
blend with the tones that are heard, and make all the
difference between the paltry note of the poorest
instrument and the supreme note of a violin.

Then, he asserts that the capacity of such discernment also applies to "the science of life", which he defines as the study to realise:

the unseen presences...unseen forms--Principalities and
Powers and Possibilities [that] happen to all people and in
all places, and during every day and through every night,
as long as human life shall endure (1-3).

The Countess Eve challenges readers "to probe to the uttermost the possibilities not only of the seen but of the unseen existence" and to explore the possibilities of "intense individuality" against the communal life afforded by Christianity (20).

Shorthouse defines the "mysteries of inheritance" and the world of *The Countess Eve* as "part of the great mystery of sound and of the mystery which sound conveys":

> the mystery that transmutes, with a wondrous alchemy, the long, weary hours of pain into the happiest life; the mystery of sacrifice and of pain; the mystery which is in itself a personal, plastic Force; the mystery expressed in sound by concerted discord (76).

The collective "mysteries of inheritance" represents the "hidden, transcendental realm of being... [the] unknowable reality [of] workings and...powers" which are autonomous, which man can neither control "nor can he free himself or escape them".[41] Shorthouse, however, comfortable with the language and rhetoric of "the Church Catholic", transforms the religious aspects of *The Countess Eve* into a study of psychological repression, suppression, and spiritual sin; he unites the two modes of reference into a story of redemption. By the end of the novel, the story of "Sin and redemption", even when studied as "guilt and its consequences", simply cannot be expressed in either religious or psychological discourse and must be cast into symbolic, though traditional imagery, "the greater mystery of Calvary".

The plot of *The Countess Eve* is simple, and the characterization may be easily generalised, though it has its subtleties. About 1785 in a city in Burgundy, Monsieur le Comte du Pic-Adam discovers that his youthful indiscretion with his mother's maid did not cause the woman to commit suicide, and that rather than kill herself, the maid became the Abbess of the Convent of Our Lady of Pity. His brooding guilt over his past temptation and sin has alienated him from his beautiful wife, the Countess Eve. After an evening at the theatre, the Count and Countess invite the principal actor, Felix la Valliere, and his friend, Claude de Brie, to supper at their chateau. In the course of the evening, the four discuss music, acting, and what in modern idiom is called "lifestyles". De Brie, very much a self-representation of Shorthouse, has a deeply sensitive and religious nature and lives his life in orderly accord with moral duty. La Valliere, the most opposite in temperament and manner of living, lives as if he were playing different roles from moment to moment; he believes that "no settled conduct or regular law of action [is] to be expected of society" because "moral law is unknown and physical law also uncertain and insecure" (10). "I seem to live a different life each night", he tells his host and hostess; "I am born again every night" (19). He advocates, "Art must never be crippled or confined. Indeed, all life must be free and untrammelled, or it is not life", and he exalts:

> Give me the man who acts on the impulse of his nature--
> not upon a balanced *bourgeois* consideration of what is
> due to his class, or his character, or his principles (20).

The Count's brooding nature, De Brie's moral sensibility, and La Valliere's enthusiasm for impulsive action awaken the interest of the Countess, whose life is burdened by the mystery of her husband's gloominess. De Brie, a violinist, entertains, and "a plaintive, continuous note, searching back into a past eternity, stretching forward into all time" (27) transforms the "auditory imagination" within La Valliere into a moment of "sudden terror indescribable in words" when he sees "a faint, shadowy figure" emerge out of "weird darkness behind the Countess", to whisper in her ear. Although only La Valliere sees the figure, the Countess's attitude and manner change "inexplicably". The expression on the apparition's face fascinates La Valliere with its bizarre peculiarity, as though "any expression it might wear was only for a moment" (32). La Valliere imagines the "malefic" aspect of his *shadow* is speaking to him:

> 'Be bold! Carry out your own theory of life. Enjoy, prove
> all things. Test the powers that have been given you,
> doubtless for use, by a beneficent Providence. Above all
> things be bold! (34)'

With this fantastical enticement, the action of the plot begins. La Valliere has been tempted, and he will tempt the Countess to commit unknowingly the same sin that her husband had committed some twenty years earlier with his mother's maid. She, however, will be saved, her husband will be redeemed from his past error, and La Valliere will be frustrated and thwarted in his attempt to seduce the Countess by the intervention of De Brie, the discovery of the Abbess and her confession, and the agency of divine grace.

What may seem a story of sin, of misplaced or misused love, does not, however, become such a conventional narrative, because, despite the "one moment of wild delirium" in which the household maid "gave up all" (112) to the Count, the temptation of sin that La Valliere proposes to the Countess is quite different; it is not the sin of passion or lust or illicit love. La Valliere tempts the Countess with a potential change in how she sees reality; he offers her the opportunity "to see and to know something of good and evil...this free life...this tattered, soiled striving with fate--this life which is not shackled by the bonds of wealth and custom, but which knows something of the joys of poverty and of reckless existence day by day" (195). The temptation is complex: to break away from class, rank, and cultured sophistication; to commit a "horrid social indiscretion" by leaving her husband and the court to experience freedom with La Valliere, or, as she understands her situation, "to experience life as men experience it":

> Why should not women also know something of good
> and evil?...If he may leave his home and wander over the
> face of the earth in search of adventures, surely so may I
> (199).

Yet, rather than investigate the possibilities of his unusual plot, Shorthouse reverts to conventional, religious melodrama. The Count and Countess are reunited in their garden, aptly named "Paradise", and as the malefic Abbe, the evil spirit of La Valliere's *shadow*, pursues La Valliere into the garden, he is stopped at the gates of Paradise by the Abbess, who stands "like the archangel of God, the crucifix, that turned its flashing light every way, in her uplifted hand" (240). At the end, all main characters are within the garden of Paradise celebrating their dramatic escape from evil beneath "the tapering spire of the Tree of Life". Only the malefic Abbe, "a clerical Mephistopheles", is denied entrance, presumably by the power of the uplifted crucifix.

Victorian critics responded unfavourably. "A new work by the author of *John Inglesant* always awakens in us eager expectancy", especially when "the story [explores the] mysterious interpenetration of the unseen into the affairs of this garish world...a theme well calculated to call forth Mr. Shorthouse's singular powers".[42] Having read *John Inglesant* as "the biography of a soul", they could do little more than regard *The Countess Eve* as "a rather childish attempt to play a game which was hardly worth playing" and complain that "his stories have a kinship to those which in penny numbers are the reading of shop-assistants and maid-servants".[43] Shorthouse must have been stung by such a judgment, but we do not know his response. The reading public's reactions were predicted by Macmillan's, who released only three thousand copies in October 1888, then released another three thousand in December. Later, in July 1892, Macmillan issued another two thousand copies, but a total of only eight thousand copies proves Shorthouse lost most of his reading audience as quickly as he had gained it. Shorthouse himself regarded *The Countess Eve* as "a kind of sketch of the sort of book which *might* be written",[44] "a great musical novel", a book of "true art--a thing of beauty which never has been seen before, and the exact like of which never will be seen again".[45] We know little of the origins *The Countess Eve*; indeed, the novel is rather "obscured in the mist and silence".[46] That the story "bears signs of hasty production" is justified as one of the reviewer's complained; the two hundred forty pages of the Macmillan edition would fill only seventeen pages of *The Church Quarterly Review*,[47] but neither the rapidity of composition nor the brevity of the story should inhibit a closer look at a novel that Shorthouse considered "powerful". As already established, Shorthouse sincerely believed in the world of spirits and, as his letters testify, he came increasingly to regard modern "realism" in literature as utterly detestable. He wrote to Edmund Gosse,

> I do not know if...you wish to sanction or approve the modern school of fiction, which 'reports' instead of 'creates'. I loathe it beyond the power of expression; more than that, I believe it is *easy* and in fact the only possible school for vulgar and stupid men, who have not the smallest particle of genius.[48]

Shorthouse believed the reading public would respond only "to the call of genius, to something above themselves": "A work of art is nothing if it is not perfect" and a perfect story must have, first of all, "a *root idea* [which] must depend...on *personal development*".[49] Gosse agreed with Shorthouse about the "root idea or spirit". *Spirit*, as Jung well knew, ultimately refers to "an immaterial substance or form of existence which on the highest and most universal level is called 'God... [but which to a psychologist] concerns a functional complex...a psychic phenomenon". The linguistic history of *spirit* proved to Jung that, among the word's "score or so of meanings and shades of meaning", the basic historical tendency has shifted from "unmistakable leanings towards personification" in primitive mentality towards materialistic and rationalistic denial of God and "the universal spirit". To modern realists, then, *spirit* means "merely the sum total of intellectual and cultural possessions which make up our human institutions and the content of our libraries".[50] Shorthouse's Broad Church perspective and his devotion to "Church Catholic" attitudes and his search for "root ideas" suggest he sought what Jung called "theriomorphic spirit symbolism". *The Countess Eve* is not merely an updated allegory or analogy of the Adam and Eve stories in Genesis, nor does it depend on the more esoteric mythology of Adam, Lilith, and Eve. It is rather a psychological investigation and dramatisation of the living power of the root idea, the mythic, psychic phenomenon embodied in "the spirit archetype" which each generation has to "re-invent for themselves".

According to Sarah Shorthouse's evidence, *The Countess Eve* contains more self-projection and self-description than any of her husband's other works.[51] *The Countess Eve*, however, is not especially autobiographical, but it suggests that understanding the novel from the point of view of De Brie better enables us to understand Shorthouse's "spirit" or his *Weltanschauung* and how he understood the operations of the spirit world as they impinge upon, influence, and interfere with the physical, rational world. Eve's "sin" is more than her attempt to break away from her social position and all of its confines. Her story is rooted in the biblical myth only as it involves her desire for knowledge, but the knowledge she needs and seeks is not "of good and evil", nor is it of Life itself. She seeks, as Shorthouse tells us, to understand life as if she were a man. Unable to fathom the mystery of her husband's gloom and personal neglect, she "comes under the domination of the unconscious [and] the darker side of her feminine nature emerges all the more strongly, coupled with markedly masculine traits".[52] Such traits form the root idea of the term *animus*. Seeing character relationships from the point of view of De Brie, who represents the ideal, the "point of purity" in the novel, the reader discerns the psychic link between the Count and the Countess. The malefic Abbe is not just the Count's repressed *shadow*, the personification of his sin, but is also the Countess Eve's *animus* and La Valliere's *shadow*. The Abbe is deeply intertwined as "the third", the psychic phenomenon of unconscious relationship.

Jung's reasoning often derived from sources that to a rationalist or materialist are suspect, sources like alchemy, astrology, numerology, mythology, folklore and fairytales, but the application of his metaphors makes his ideas provocative, if not convincing, to "modern minds". Throughout his *Collected Works*, Jung is often at pains to explain to materialistic thinkers that, though they may "reduce matter" to an idea that makes "spirit entirely dependent on nutrition and environment", they must be mindful that the human intellect does not create spirit; "rather the spirit makes *him* creative, always spurring him on, giving him lucky ideas, staying power, 'enthusiasm' and 'inspiration'." Jung feared modern man "is in the gravest danger of thinking he actually created the spirit and that he *has* it", and he insisted: "In reality, however, the primordial phenomenon of the spirit takes possession of *him*, and, while appearing to be the willing object of human intentions, it binds his freedom, just as the physical world does, with a thousand chains and becomes an obsessive *idee-force*".[53] Thus, a hundred years after the publication of *The Countess Eve*, the imaginative world of spirit that operates in the novel and the historical tradition the novel represents still struggles against "the gravest danger".

One of Jung's numerological examples explains the dynamics of relationship in *The Countess Eve*:

> If one imagines the quaternity as a square divided into two halves by a diagonal, one gets two triangles whose apices point in opposite directions. One could therefore say metaphorically that if the wholeness symbolized by the quaternity is divided into equal halves, it produces two opposing triads.[54]

For example, the Count and Countess and De Brie and La Valliere are couples of distinctly opposites temperaments. Divide the four characters into different relationships, relationships grounded in their personality types, and two triads emerge. De Brie represents the purity and spiritual integrity the Count has lost, and, as opposites, they are attracted to each other, however unconsciously. La Valliere possesses and expresses what the Countess unconsciously desires, a masculine *persona* in touch with the "real world". Eve's *persona*, we are told, so restricts her that she seldom sees objects outside her own Ego. The Count, however much he appears an extroverted man of the world, is haunted by the shadowy aspect of his *anima*: "She must always be near me... always near me, and yet I never see her--never see her." The "she" he mysteriously refers to is mentioned only after La Valliere has seen the ghostly figure of the malefic Abbe whispering in the Countess's ear. The "she" materializes in the novel as the apex of a triad, the Count--the Abbess--Eve, and the ghostly Abbe becomes the apex of an opposite triad, De Brie--the Abbe--La Valliere. The triads are linked together by the "root idea" of opposition, the underlying and unconscious forces of the Abbe's malefic intentions and the Abbess's redemptive power. As Jung says,

> When unconscious wholeness becomes manifest, i.e.,
> leaves the unconscious and crosses over into the sphere of
> consciousness, one of the four remains behind, held back
> by the *horror vacui* of the unconscious.[55]

In the final scene, the malefic Abbe is without the gate of Paradise, and De Brie, though within, has transformed into a symbol of the Self; his purity places him in the centre of the other four: La Valliere enters the garden as would-be tempter, but his seductive power is counterbalanced by the redemptive power of the Abbess, even as the Count's real indiscretion with the Abbess is balanced by the Countess's indiscretion of heart.

However unconscious of psychological design, Shorthouse constructed his story around the triadic relationships that Jung identified as "constellations evident in the history of symbolism". Triads inform the novel: three people fall to their knees at different times (De Brie in prayer when he first learns the chateau is haunted and again when he hears the Abbess's confession; the Count when he sees the Abbess for the first time after presuming her dead for twenty years; the Countess when she escapes from "the Prince of Evil"); three lakes metaphorize and "objectively correlate" with spiritual powers (two beautiful ones--De Brie and the Abbess--and one horridly black and evil, which comprises the collective evil of the Abbe, the Count, and La Valliere). The strongest and most powerful of the triads is formed by the malefic Abbe, De Brie's purity, and the Abbess's devotion and dependence upon the Christ. The story testifies to the power of faith and the redemptive power of man's dependence upon God "in this life"; redemption comes within the story, not in the hereafter. Sin equates negatively with the "failure to resist temptation, and positively [as] the result of evil 'unseen, but not unfelt' which is the cause of temptation".[56]

Sin is presumptuous self-will, ego-centred self-reliance, impulsive and unconsidered action. Given "the uncertainty of all moral valuation, the bewildering interplay of good and evil, and remorseless concatenation of guilt, suffering, and redemption", Jung advises,

> We can never know what evil may not be necessary in order to produce good by *enantiodromia*, and what good may very possibly lead to evil. Sometimes the *probate spiritus* recommended by John cannot, with the best will in the world, be anything other than a cautious and patient waiting to see how things will finally turn out.[57]

Shorthouse makes it clear that mankind, despite the expulsion from Paradise, may reenter through the idea of the Christ, yet he ends *The Countess Eve* with a subtlety overpowered by melodrama that suggests Jung's discernment of "the deep doctrine in the legend of the fall...the expression of a dim presentiment that the emancipation of ego-consciousness was a Luciferian deed".[58] Years after the Count's dramatic reentry into Paradise, he is still plagued by the mystery of Eve:

> Often in the dead of night...he would wake up with Eve's lovely face shining out upon him from the darkness...but through the meshes of her chestnut hair, and across the gleam of her violet eyes, an appalling mystic light--the singe and glow of the flame of the pit (239)!

Behind the allure and providential guidance of the *anima* and the "blessed assurance" of the spirit archetype lurk the forces of the *shadow* and the deception of human perceptions, which are coloured, censored, and selected by the Ego through the *persona*. When the Ego identifies with the *persona*, psychological inflation and spiritual pride may result, as they do in *Blanche, Lady Falaise*. Constance in *Sir Percival* expresses a clarity of perception, a truthfulness to her vision that Shorthouse achieved when he allowed himself to assume a feminine narrative persona. When, however, he stopped listening to the voice of the *anima* and letting "her" write the story, he muddled his artistic persona. *The Countess Eve* is told by an ambiguous persona. Early in the novel a narrator addresses the reader directly: "...or at the time we write of, to the few people we are trying to know something about". Abruptly that "we" asserts, "...but it does seem to me important" (3). Yet, the reader is unaware of a narrative presence until chapter nine in which the anonymous persona very abruptly interrupts the story with almost two pages of direct questioning: "Do you wish me to tell you what they said? Do you ask me what...?...and, if not, why should you demand it of [my characters]?" (180-182). A similar slipping in and out of narrative voice occurs within the story. When the Abbess confesses her part in the Count's history, she begins by speaking in third person. She tells of "the girl" quite objectively until she digresses into De Brie's own history. De Brie's mother had once been a nun; after refusing to obey a visiting superior, she left the convent. Had De Brie's mother not made the opposite choice of the Abbess, De Brie, of course, would never have been born. After establishing this common link between herself and De Brie, the Abbess reverts from talking about herself in third person and confesses, "I have dreaded the pain of revealing myself...I have taken my own course and made my own fate."[59] Her revelation gives De Brie the power of conscious choice, and by intervening to prevent La Valliere and the Countess's intended sin, De Brie reverses and ends the sin of his disobedient mother. Curiously, there is a very brief transition scene between the Abbess's talking of herself in third person and her first-person confession. She receives a message about a young girl's distress in a neighbouring village, an echo of her own distress twenty years earlier. Rather than attend to the girl, the Abbess declares, "I cannot think of her now. I must go to him", and she rushes to the Count. The novel ends with no clear identity of its narrative voice, just as years earlier, the manuscript of *John Inglesant* lay unpublished in a drawer, and J. Henry Shorthouse had no public identity as an author. Whether the Abbess and the Countess Eve are in any unconscious way related to Shorthouse's mother and his wife cannot be determined without more revealing evidence, which is not available. The answer depends upon the extent that De Brie symbolizes Shorthouse as he remembered the "him" who had, perhaps, disobeyed his mother and grandmother by leaving the Society of Friends and was waiting for recognition as "the author of *John Inglesant*". Through his self-projections and self-representations, Shorthouse does invite biographical speculation, and the relationship between De Brie and La Valliere certainly makes one want to know more about Shorthouse's relationship with Rawdon Levett, to whom he dedicated *John Inglesant*.[60] Certainly, in creating Miss Claire Wand to narrate *Blanche, Lady Falaise*, Shorthouse would seem to have withdrawn his masculine self-projection as narrator, yet we know more about the composition of *Blanche* than any of his other works, except *John Inglesant*.

The Countess Eve's day-dreamy, preconscious absorption in her personal unconscious may be attributed to her *animus* and to the *persona* under which she masques herself. Blanche, Lady Falaise, on the other hand, misunderstands the archetypal influences of the Self and identifies herself consciously and deliberately with what she believes to be her natural spiritual superiority. In religious terms, she is guilty of spiritual pride, which connects her unconsciously with the reality of sin. She suffers ego-inflation and the resultant confusion of *shadow* and *animus*, and her story dramatises "the most remarkable mental gymnastics of any character in fiction".[61] Yet, in the simplicity of its sketchy plot, her life story also gives Shorthouse's answer to the extreme difficulties aimed, he believed, at destroying the Church of England. Shorthouse not only "detested religious debate", but he also considered it "in many cases absolutely useless". "However carefully expressed", he wrote, "the sense of *definition* to different minds is so variform as to leave no common form of expression."[62] The Roman Curia's absolute rejection and denial of the validity of Anglican ordination outraged "the author of *John Inglesant*", though for the most part, he continued to avoid public controversy and penned his private thoughts only to family and friends. "I distinguish absolutely between Sacra-mentalism and Sacerdotalism", he wrote his cousin Margaret Evans and went on to explain,

> they seem to be mutually destructive. So long as the clergy confine themselves to their Sacramental office I look upon them as THE channel of grace. When they depart from this, and act and talk out of their own heads, I pay no more attention to them than I do to laymen.[63]

This distinction between priests as agents and performers of baptism, confirmation, the eucharist, penance, extreme unction, orders, and matrimony, and of priests as having supernatural powers that are to be "doted upon" by obedient believers and followers is fundamental to Shorthouse's Broad Church sensibilities and to his characterization of "variform definitions" of Christians in his novels. As "to dote" implies to be "silly, deranged, infatuated, or feeble-minded", Shorthouse despised both the authoritarianism of Roman Catholicism and the self-importance, amounting to self-ordination in Puritanism and to self-righteousness among the more Protestant, fundamentalistic and evangelical members of the Church of England. Those critics who have regarded Shorthouse as "the author of one book" have also collectively confined Shorthouse's religious sensibilities and preferences to questions of class, rank, and taste. Although such a critical habit is not altogether inaccurate, such a stance restricts and overlooks Shorthouse's larger artistic concerns and neglects the brilliance of his religious psychology. His fictional characters are not mere types, for they are studied most carefully and intimately from the inside.

To probe Blanche Boteraux-Falaise and the significant persons in her life's story, Shorthouse invented Claire Wand, but modern readers can only wonder what reaction he hoped to provoke with the novel's beginning: "I am only a woman, and I am going to write this book in my own way..." Likewise, anyone who has read the complete works of Shorthouse must wonder why he called *Blanche, Lady Falaise* "my favourite of my books".[64] Such wonder, however, provokes more critical inquiry than his contemporaries awarded his final novel. *Blanche, Lady Falaise* reads like a companion, a completion of *The Countess Eve*, as *Sir Percival* complements

John Inglesant, but it is, as Shorthouse noted, "more spontaneous" than *Eve*, and was composed more unconsciously. Shorthouse wrote one correspondent, "I do not know if I ever wrote a book in which the characters were so real to me, and seemed to act altogether for themselves, and apart from me".[65] Ironically, of course, his last novel is much more a part of him than it is apart from him, and to his reading public, Blanche is very familiar. Believing "that truth is better taught under the form of apologue and romance than by set treatises",[67] Shorthouse dramatised a familiar theme, one that epitomizes the distinction between natural individuation and the more conscious and "mystical" Individuation process. The two central characters of the novel, Blanche Falaise and Paul Damerle, are true to their ego-selves, the consciousness contained within their respective Ego and *persona* structures, and they both fail to respond to the collective unconscious until the end of the novel. In this sense, Shorthouse's final novel is a moralizing dramatisation of his lifelong purpose: To prove that "that Image after which we were created--the Divine Intellect--must surely be able to respond to the Divine call." "It has taken thousands of years", he wrote only weeks before his death, "to attain the point we have reached, and, judging by the very slow progress made, it will take thousands more."[68] What he had called "the Great Work" when he was a young man, he still recognized as the "greatest advance...ever made...the receptivity of matter", the conscious capacity to listen to "the Divine call".[69] In the same letter, he related the idea of receptivity to "the fundamental idea of *John Inglesant*", namely, "the intense difficulty of revealing the Infinite in any degree to the finite". The narrative of *Blanche, Lady Falaise* struggles to reveal the intensity of "the Divine call" to resolve the Infinite and the finite in "the mystery of the Calvary".

Blanche, Lady Falaise was written and rewritten rather quickly during the winter and spring of 1890-1891, and was published in September 1891. As with *The Countess Eve*, Macmillan issued only eight thousand copies.[70] "All thoughtful readers of English fiction", one review noted, "look with intense interest upon a new work by the author of *John Inglesant*"[71] and, indeed, Shorthouse was well aware of the difficulties of the public's intense interest. "Yes, sir... very good, very good", comments Churchwarden Wike after one of the Reverend Doctor Botereaux's new sermons, "but you won't easily beat the old 'uns, sir". The Rector, with "a twinkle in his eye", responds, "I am very handicapped. I have to compete with myself."[72] Shorthouse sensed his need to compete with "the author of *John Inglesant*", but *Blanche, Lady Falaise* shows more self-repetition than competition. The setting, characterization, descriptions of landscape, the mystic moods, the passages of lofty prose, the narrative appeal to private letters and journals, frequent quotations and references to poets and religious writers, even the

255

theme --all are predictable, designed it would seem, to please the eager and customary audience, even though that audience had considerably dwindled in numbers. Only one element of the novel jars the reader's usual delight in a Shorthouse novel; the punishment at the end is in great excess of the crime:

> In any work of creative imagination...the one thing needful is truth, and this essentially depends upon due sense of proportion...The pursuing vengeance of an avenging fury is concentrated in [Blanche] to a degree that amounts to veritable madness, and so exceptional an instance of a diseased mind does not afford a valid illustration of the providentially designed working of sin.[73]

Had Shorthouse deliberately set himself against the sense of proportion? He knew full well that "Blanche Falaise was insane from the first", that she suffered "a very incipient madness", but he also knew that he had not intended to teach or moralize about anything in the novel. Quite to the contrary, he intended to learn from the novel:

> What Blanche Falaise teaches me, and she teaches me very much, [is that she] acted for herself...The author cannot alter events, even if he wished to do so; he has only to record.[74]

Based on a true story, the characters took on their own identities and acted and narrated for themselves.[75]

Shorthouse knew, too, that

> except where a divine genius walks the earth, and the prompting of a divine spirit is felt, the same old tale is written and rewritten with the same...unwearying pen (30).

He did not think of himself as some new divinely inspired, creative genius, but he must have felt "the prompting of a divine spirit", though *Blanche, Lady Falaise* is morbidly obsessed with sin and with suffering for sin. Although *Blanche* does not end with any echo of the impassioned defence of the Church of England one might expect from "the author of *John Inglesant*", the story of Lady Falaise addresses and reiterates *John Inglesant*'s basic argument, that the spiritual efficacy of the eucharist is as divinely sanctified within the Church of England as it is under the more worldly "system" of authority and dogma of the Church of Rome. Blanche dies "as pure as in her girlhood days", because

> her *intentions being holy and pure*...the Divine Sanctity and Purity (as is natural, both being really but part of the

same principle) co-operated with her, in spite of insanity and mistake, so working out the will of God *by her*.[76]

Blanche is saved "By the purification of the motive / In the ground of our beseeching".[77]

As a young lady living with her father, a former Oxford don, now the rector of Clyston St. Fay in Devonshire, Blanche Botereaux's motives are those of Christian Socialism and personal mysticism. Returning from her French school Neufchatel, Blanche appears "disdainful and discontented" with the charms and beauties of Devonshire village life and yearns for some great work in the slums of East London. With a "lofty, searching look in her brown eyes", she "perpetually waits for the injunction of the Prophet to do some great thing" (40-41). She reads the *Journal Intime* of the Swiss mystic Henry-Frederic Amiel, who, we are repeatedly told, "was more a woman than a man" (63-65). The narrator, Clair Wand, whose name is not without significance, repeatedly disdains men herself: "Men are so strange...They occupy willingly and of their own choice such a low standpoint" (64). Miss Wand quotes retrospectively and freely from Blanche's diary to capture the essence of Blanche's inner life. Though Blanche claims she "doesn't care for words", she revels in the "magic wand of poets, and of romanticists, and of preachers" and quotes from Tennyson's *The Princess* (58). Mixed with Amiel and various readings from Count Zinzendorf, Walker of Truro, and Wesley, the lines formulate Blanche's personality:

> Woman is not undeveloped man,
> But diverse: could we make her as the man,
> Sweet love were slain,...
> Yet in the long years liker must they grow;...
> Till at the last she set herself to man,
> Like perfect music unto noble words;...
> Yoked in all excellence of noble end,
> And so through those dark gates across the wild,
> That no man knows.

Filled with lofty and noble ideals, Blanche yearns for "what she thought was self-denial", but which Miss Wand assures us was truly "profound self-ishness" (62). Into her world comes young George Falaise, the perfectly refined aristocrat, who

> never thought of improving anybody, always of raising himself; selfish in this sense...but with a selfishness that reacted upon those around him to their infinite gain (62-63).

Young George has come to read the Greeks with Dr. Botereaux before he goes up to Oxford. Of course, he falls in love with the beautiful Blanche, and in due time, he proposes, but she, with "a contemptuous irony" refuses him and all his wealth. He will become Premier Viscount of England upon his father's death. Yet, she senses that "her fate was irrevocably bound up with his,...an impending fate that linked her to him" (71, 80). The quiet and charming scenes of their playful romance are disrupted when the Reverend Paul Damerle, the famous evangelist, visits the neighbourhood to preach at Clyston St. Fay. In the zeal of his sermon and of his appeal on behalf of the poor, Blanche discovers her "suppressed and buried life". Echoing Virginia Clare in *Sir Percival*, she insists that George must join the Eton or the Oxford Mission in the East End and must use his wealth and power for the benefit of the poor. Quietly asserting that "no permanent good would arise by [the aristocracy's] giving up their present style of living and slumming it (82)", George nearly destroys what interest Blanche does have in him, and she thereafter directs her attentions towards Paul Damerle and "the Master's service". After subtle courtship, Damerle proposes to Blanche, and she accepts. When, however, Doctor Botereaux explains to Damerle that Blanche and he are "virtually penniless", Damerle goes to London in pursuit of the means to help the poor. There, after not receiving an expected offer of a position in one of the wealthier West End churches, he begins another courtship with the naive but wealthy Lady Elizabeth Poer.

Months pass and his visits to Devon become infrequent. Finally, "the letter" arrives. We are not privy to the exact contents of the letter, but its import is clear. Blanche is shocked and stunned into serious depression by her interpretation of events. Rather than accuse Damerle of breach of promise and faith, Blanche perversely believes she has ruined Damerle. Damerle marries Lady Elizabeth, squanders her fortune on high living, gambling, drinking, and, yes, he ends up in debtors' prison. Meanwhile, Lord Falaise renews his quest of Blanche, and she rather drearily accepts him. Years pass. Lord and Lady Falaise have two sons, but neither husband nor sons give Blanche any cheer. Growing desperate about Blanche's sanity, Lord Falaise persuades her to travel, and eventually on an expiatory pilgrimage to a Calvary in the Austrian Alps, Lady Falaise is killed by lightning at precisely the same moment that Paul Damerle is released from prison. Obsessed with spiritual pride, Lady Falaise believes she has ruined Damerle and bequeathes him fifty thousand pounds in her will. Thus, with a skimpy and somewhat trite plot, the novel's interest lies in the inner workings of Blanche's mind, and even if her interior life seems like extraordinary "mental gymnastics", the intimate and close depiction of sin and pride is fascinating as a balance of Lord Falaise's unbelievable, extraordinary patience.

Most important in the psychological study of sin, guilt, and redemption is Shorthouse's reliance upon the Calvary as the archetypal symbol of redemption. Blanche conscientiously struggles with her ego-inflation, and her belief in her unique specialness to God's work. Near the end of the novel, the extremity of her sin becomes quite clear. As Miss Wand tells her,

> 'You are committing a terrible, almost a nameless sin. You are trying to take this man's sin, this man's punishment upon yourself. There is only One who can do that' (225).

Indeed, Lady Elizabeth Poer-Damerle receives a transcendental vision and sees Blanche in "unspeakable light" standing before an altar, and hears words that tell her what she must communicate to Lady Falaise:

> Thou hast tried to offer a sacrifice which it was not for thee to offer, and to bear a punishment which was not thine to suffer or to bear... [Damerle's] sins, which are many, are forgiven him. He is turned, and shall be saved (287).

Shorthouse clarified his purpose in one of his letters. Damerle assumed self-importance and self-inspiration as, Shorthouse believed, evangelicals and fundamentalists do. He explains,

> The old Rector, in spite of his old-world notions, and (as some would say) imperfections...depended upon the *Church ordinances and services*, while Damerle depended chiefly *on himself...*[78]

Blanche, Lady Falaise addresses the very controversies that Shorthouse preferred to avoid. Through both Paul Damerle and Blanche Falaise, Shorthouse responds to the evangelical and more Protestant elements within the Church of England; in Doctor Botereaux he characterizes churchmanship; in the final scene at the Calvary, he dramatises the sacramental grace available to any and all who seek it diligently; and in Blanche's salvation, he illustrates the efficacy of pure religious intention.

What is sad, however, for anyone who admires Shorthouse, is the inevitable conclusion that, despite the purity and constancy of Constance Lisle, the temptation and salvation of Eve, and the destruction of personality in spite of redemption in Blanche, Shorthouse's feminine trilogy failed to capture readers. The Victorian audience that had responded so enthusiastically to the philosophical romance of *John Inglesant* did not respond to the spiritual romances by "the author of *John Inglesant*". Yet, if it is impossible for man to distinguish the archetypal Self, which he creates or invents in the process of Individuation, from the *imago dei*, the *a priori*, in-born image of the God-head, then Shorthouse's popular failure may be attributed to the psychology of his narrative technique. From *John Inglesant's* "Christianity without the Bible" through *Blanche, Lady Falaise's* salvation through the Calvary, Shorthouse explored and developed "the idea of the Christ", and that he ended his literary career with the necessity of man's acceptance of the Calvary as the only means of embracing "the sacred mysteries" of Christianity is profoundly to his credit. His "sacramental vision" and providential aesthetic may have overtaxed his literary powers, yet his novels develop from masculine philosophical ponderings and religious discussions, the products of Ego and *persona*, to the expression and representation of the voices of the *anima*. It is unfortunate that in order to give expression to such insight he reverted to conventional, melodramatic technique, that he did not possess the originality and literary powers of "major authors". Throughout his life he suffered numerous bouts of illness, and in the course of his physical deterioration, he lost the sight of his right eye, but he never lost the Inner Light of his own integrity or the Divine Light. In the extremities of his physical condition, he experienced "the sense of God's presence" and confessed that, without it, "I should have gone mad".[79] When he knew his "days were numbered" and that his service to God through literature was ended, he confessed:

> God always! God everywhere! If I have done anything, if I have said anything that has been a help to others-- God, God alone! All that He does is right. If He leaves us here, we have work to do still; if He takes us away, 'that which began in him, when he began, is finished. He hath wrought the purpose through of that which made him man'.[80]

Notes to Chapter Six

[1]In *The Life of Frederick Denison Maurice* (Macmillan, 1884), 339-340, Frederick Maurice cites St. John 3:2 in reference to his father's search for "the principle of Catholicity as contrasted with that of separateness or puritanism" in *The Kingdom of Christ*.

[2]Avrom Fleishman, *The English Historical Novel: Walter Scott to Virginia Woolf* (Baltimore: The John Hopkins University Press, 1971), 165.

[3]J. Henry Shorthouse, Letter to Lady Victoria Welby (10 June 1883), *LLLR*, vol. I, 198.

[4]J. Henry Shorthouse, "The Agnostic at Church", *LLLR*, vol. I, 198.

[5]J. Henry Shorthouse, "The 'Morte D'Arthur' and the 'Idylls of the King'", *LLLR*, vol. II, 107-122, 108.

[6]*The Academy* (13 November 1886), 99.

[7]*Blackwood's Magazine*, CXV (December 1886), 793-797.

[8]*Church Quarterly Review*, vol. XXIII, no. XLVI (January 1887), 507-509.

[9]J. Henry Shorthouse, Letter to Lady Victoria Welby (27 December 1887), *LLLR*, vol. I, 241.

[10]J. Henry Shorthouse, Letter to Lady Victoria Welby (5 November 1886), *LLLR*, vol. I, 239, and Letter to Edmund Gosse (30 December 1883), 215-216.

[11]F. J. Wagner, *J. Henry Shorthouse* (Boston: Twayne, 1979), 101.

[12]J. Henry Shorthouse, *Sir Percival: A Story of the Past and of the Present* (London: Macmillan, 1886), 33.

[13]Gainsborough painted Jonathan Buttall, the famous "Blue Boy", Edward Bouverie (1773), and Paul Cobb Methuen (1776?) in the blue silk costume. The exact date of the "Blue Boy" is uncertain. There is no evidence that Shorthouse ever saw the painting; it is more likely he knew it from one of its many reproductions. See Robert R. Wark, "Gainsborough's 'Blue Boy'", *Ten British Pictures, 1740-1840* (San Marino, California: The Huntington Library, 1971), 29-41. Wark's study presents the X-ray details beneath the surface painting.

[14]T. S. Eliot, "Hamlet", *Selected Essays*, third enlarged edition, (London: Faber and Faber, 1951), 141-146.

[15]Victoria Welby, *What is Meaning? Studies in the Development of Significance* (London: Macmillan, 1903), 35.

[16]Victoria Welby, *What is Meaning?* 249.

[17]Zulfikar Ghose, *The Fiction of Reality* (London: Macmillan, 1983), 72.

[18]T. S. Eliot, "The Love Song of J. Alfred Prufrock", *The Complete Poems and Plays of T. S. Eliot* (London: Faber and Faber, 1965), 16.

[19]C. G. Jung, *Psychology and Alchemy*, vol. 12, *Collected Works*, Bollingen Series XX (Princeton University Press, 1968), 10-11.

[20]C. G. Jung, *Psychology and Alchemy* 12.

[21]J. Henry Shorthouse, Letter to Canon Alfred Ainger (28 November 1886), *LLLR*, vol. I, 242-244.

[22]Kathleen Raine, "The Inner Journey of the Poet", *In the Wake of Jung: Selections from "Harvest"* (London: Conventure, Ltd., 1983), rep. 1986, 192-297.

[23]St. Matthew's Gospel 7:3-5, King James Version: "And why beholdest thou the mote that is in thy brother's eye, but considerest not the beam that is in thine own eye? Thou hypocrite, first cast the beam out of thine own eye; and then shalt thou see clearly to cast the mote out of thy brother's eye".

[24]J. Henry Shorthouse, Letter to Mr. Craik (25 June 1886), *LLLR*, vol. I. Craik, one of Macmillan's editors, had proposed publishing *Sir Percival* in *Macmillan's Magazine*; Shorthouse objected: "...such publication is prejudicial to the influence of books meant to last; people read them in a magazine, and forget all about them; if they read them first in a book, they are much more likely to return to them again" (236-237).

[25]E. Martin Browne, *The Making of T. S. Eliot's Plays* (Cambridge University Press, 1969), 218-248.

[26]E Martin Browne, *The Making of T. S. Eliot's Plays* 226-227.

[27]J. Hunter Smith contributed an "Introduction" to Sarah Shorthouse's *The Life, Letters, and Literary Remains of J. H. Shorthouse*, vol. I, IX-XXI; his discussion of *Sir Percival* is on XVIII-XIX.

[28]J. Henry Shorthouse, Letter to Lady Victoria Welby (15 February 1885), *LLLR*, vol. I, 230-231.

[29]Avrom Fleishman, *The English Historical Novel* 169.

[30]Sarah Shorthouse, *LLLR*, vol. I, 247.

[31]F. J. Wagner, *J. Henry Shorthouse* 108.

[32]J. Henry Shorthouse, *A Teacher of the Violin and Other Tales* (London: Macmillan, 1888), 110-111.

[33]Sarah Shorthouse, Letter to George Macmillan (10 August 1904), British Library: Macmillan Archive, MS. 54934, A.21.

[34]J. Henry Shorthouse, "A Midsummer Night's Dream", *LLLR*, vol. II: "The Vandycks...Titians...and the lovely faded Claudes...had some effect upon the children's lives, and made their natures somewhat different to what they would otherwise have been" (332).

[35] J. Henry Shorthouse, "A Midsummer Night's Dream", *LLLR*, vol. II, 342.

[36] C. G. Jung, Letter to Miguel Serrano (14 September 1960). See Miguel Serrano's *C. G. Jung and Hermann Hesse: A Record of Two Friendships* (London: Routledge and Kegan Paul, 1966), 83-88, for a fuller discussion of the argument that the "gods have not died; we have only changed their names".

[37] Edward Mortimer Chapman, *English Literature and Religion, 1800-1900* (London: Constable, 1910), 514.

[38] Robert A. Johnson, *HE: Understanding Masculine Psychology* (New York: Harper and Row, 1989), 6.

[39] Robert H. Hopcke, *A Guided Tour of the Collected Works of C. G. Jung* (Boston and Shaftsbury: Shambala, 1989), 124.

[40] "The Litany", *The Book of Common Prayer* (Oxford: The Society for Promoting Christian Knowledge). Again, Shorthouse takes his epigraph out of context. Practicing Anglicans may find the General Supplication which appears just before the one used for the epigraph even more telling of *The Countess Eve*'s moral: "We beseech thee to hear us, good Lord: That it may please thee to bring into the way of truth all such as have erred, and are deceived".

[41] J. Henry Shorthouse, *The Countess Eve* (London: Macmillan, 1888), 95.

[42] Aniela Jaffe, *The Myth of Meaning in the Work of C. G. Jung* (London: Hodder and Stoughton, 1970, rep. and adapted, Zurich: Daimon Verlag, 1970), 38-39.

[43] *Church Quarterly Review*, vol. XXVII, no. LIV (January 1889), 502-504.

[44] Charles F. Keary, *The Edinburgh Review*, vol. CCII (July--October, 1905), 101-131, 120-121.

[45] J. Henry Shorthouse, Letter to Edmund Gosse (3 June 1893), *LLLR*, vol. I, 327-328.

[46] J. Henry Shorthouse, Letter to George Macmillan (9 July 1890), *LLLR*, vol. I, 281-282.

[47] F. J. Wagner, *J. H. Shorthouse* 115.

[48] *Church Quarterly Review*, vol. XXVII, no. LIV (January 1889), 504.

[49] J. Henry Shorthouse, Letter to Edmund Gosse (9 July 1890), *LLLR*, vol. I, 282-283.

[50] J. Henry Shorthouse, Letter to Edmund Gosse (23 July 1890), *LLLR*, vol. I, 284-286.

[51] C. G. Jung, "The Phenomenology of the Spirit in Fairytales", *The Archetypes and the Collective Unconscious*, vol. 9, part I, *Collected Works*, 207-254.

[52] Sarah Shorthouse, *LLLR*, vol. I, 252-254.

[53] C. G. Jung, "The Phenomenology of the Spirit in Fairytales" 247.

[54] C. G. Jung, "The Phenomenology of the Spirit in Fairytales" 213.

[55] C. G. Jung, "The Phenomenology of the Spirit in Fairytales" 235.

[56] C. G. Jung, "The Phenomenology of the Spirit in Fairytales" 235.

[57] F. J. Wagner, *J. H. Shorthouse* 117.

[58] C. G. Jung, "The Phenomenology of the Spirit in Fairytales" 215.

[59] C. G. Jung, "The Phenomenology of the Spirit in Fairytales" 230-231.

[60] J. Henry Shorthouse, *The Countess Eve*: "She" is used repeatedly (111-118); the change is made to "I" (149-153).

[61] De Brie's "unique and inexplicable attraction" towards La Valliere which "exists only between man and man, and very often between men of singularly opposite nature and opinion" suggests that Shorthouse may have found his *shadow* in Levett. "You always remind me", De Brie tells his friend, "of those old Greek natures, half human, half fay, to whom belonged the secrets of Nature and of the sky, of the elements and of the spirit-world--pure animals" (42-43).

[62] F. J. Wagner, *J. H. Shorthouse* 122.

[63] J. Henry Shorthouse, Letter to Margaret Evans (2 August 1899), *LLLR*, vol. I, 371-372.

[64] J. Henry Shorthouse, Letter to Margaret Evans (8 August 1899), *LLLR*, vol. I, 372.

[65] J. Henry Shorthouse, Letter to George Macmillan (15 July 1894), British Library: Macmillan Archive, MS. 54933.

[66] J. Henry Shorthouse, Letter to Wilfred Jones-Bateman (27 January 1892), *LLLR*, vol. I. 300-301.

[67] J. Henry Shorthouse, Letter to Mrs. Moller (1890), *LLLR*, vol. I, 288-291.

[68] J. Henry Shorthouse, Letter to Madame De Steiger (18 January 1903), *LLLR*, vol. I, 392-394.

[69] J. Henry Shorthouse, Letter Madame De Steiger (18 January 1903), *LLLR*, vol. I, 393.

[70] Three thousand copies were released in September 1891, another two thousand in November, and a final three thousand in March 1892.

[71] *Church Quarterly Review*, vol. XXXIII, no. LXVI (June 1892), 528.

[72] J. Henry Shorthouse, *Blanche, Lady Falaise* (London: Macmillan, 1891), 37.

[73] *Church Quarterly Review*, vol. XXXIII, no. LXVI (June 1892), 528.

[74] J. Henry Shorthouse, Letter to Rawdon Levett (16 November 1891), *LLLR*, vol. I, 296.

[75] Sarah Shorthouse, *LLLR*, vol. I, 250.

[76]J. Henry Shorthouse, Letter to Rawdon Levett (16 November 1891), *LLLR*, vol. I, 296.

[77]T. S. Eliot, "Little Gidding", *The Complete Poems and Plays* (London: Faber and Faber, 1969), 196.

[78]J. Henry Shorthouse, Letter to Wilfred Jones-Bateman (27 January 1892), *LLLR*, vol. I, 300.

[79]J. Henry Shorthouse, Letter to Dr. Gott, Bishop of Truro (1901), *LLLR*, vol. I, 377-378.

[80]J. Henry Shorthouse, Letter to Dr. Talbot (5 November 1901), *LLLR*, vol. I, 378-379.

Chapter Seven: Where Three Dreams Cross

"No connected chain of argument, no worked out theory or system of thought is arrived at or will be found in these pages", wrote Victoria Welby-Gregory in the "Preface" to the second edition of *Links and Clues*. What Lady Welby offered the public were "links between divided souls [and] clues for bewildered hearts".[1] Her approach, like that of James Hinton in *The Mystery of Pain: A Book for the Sorrowful*,[2] defines the form of the complete works of J. Henry Shorthouse, a form in which coherence and unity derive not from any superimposed design or organizational pattern, but from an informing, philosophical attitude[3] of "sacramental receptivity"[4] grounded in religious faith. Faith, "the common and inevitable basis of all religion"[5], has been defined once and for all time for Christians as "the substance of things hoped for, the evidence of things not seen" (Hebrews 11:1) with the dictum that through faith "the invisible things...from the creation of the world are clearly seen" and can be "understood by the things that are made" (Romans 1:20). As man outwardly builds chapels, churches, and cathedrals, so inwardly he constructs his intellect and orders his emotional and psychological nature. As Shorthouse discovered and defined his own nature, he recreated and fictionalized, transferred and projected his inner life into the service of religious aesthetics. During his lifetime he received much praise and deprecation, but no praise pleased him more than that of Dr. Talbot, the Bishop of Rochester, who wrote:

> I feel I owe you great contribution and help towards feeling the beautiful mystery and power and meaning of the Holy Sacrament, as well as an added sense of the beauty of visible things in tones suited to many a modern ear.[6]

Believing, as Hinton did, that human thought, when confronted with faith, "ceases to be a question of argument and balanced evidence"[7] and, as Lady Welby believed, that "the felt necessity and the inherent power" of faith "overcomes the widest differences of standpoint and view",[8] Shorthouse wrote "to indicate the mysticism of the Prayer-Book and the Caroline Divines [as] safe and infinite".[9] He never objected to Catholicism or to "the Church Catholic", but he vehemently opposed the Roman Catholic "system" which denied Anglicans freedom of religious form, usurped national and private conscience in the First Vatican Council's 1870 decree of papal infallibility, constricted and restricted the Blessed Sacrament, and condemned Anglican ministerial orders in the 1896 papal bull *Apostolicae Curae*. Curiously, he did not find the challenges of Charles Darwin and

Darwinianism threatening, for to him such "material sciences" were no threat to the invisible and unseen facts of faith, but, had he lived longer, he would have found the intention of "Freudian faith"—"to free ourselves through psychoanalysis from religious intellectually repulsive and spiritually repugnant.[10] Had he lived long enough to study C. G. Jung, however, Shorthouse would have found a guide to "the personification of the unconscious and the totality of nonphysical life",[11] and he would have found Jung in sympathy with his "sacramental vision".[12] Though one can only speculate how Shorthouse would have responded to the early poetry of T. S. Eliot, there can be no doubt that Shorthouse would have enjoyed and studied "Ash-Wednesday" and *Four Quartets* and that he would have applauded Eliot's dramas, especially *Murder in the Cathedral*, *The Family Reunion*, and *The Cocktail Party*.

Sir Percival is Shorthouse's most successful attempt to find historical continuity in the spiritual meaning of Arthurian romance, just as *John Inglesant* is his most original attempt to create an "English-saint". The "root idea" of both works is the sacramental power of sacrifice, which Shorthouse derived from James Hinton's *The Mystery of Pain* and from the story of St. John Gualberto and the crucifix in the church of San Miniato.[13] Shorthouse was particularly attracted to Hinton's assertion that "The possibility of love is given us in our power to sacrifice; and loving brings the power into immediate action."[14] "The enchanter's wand...the power of Romance", which he declared in the "Preface" to *John Inglesant*, ultimately becomes the pen of Miss Claire Wand in *Blanche, Lady Falaise*, which bears clear traces of Hinton's influence. Hinton recognized the profound, radical "need of a change in human nature" as having "been affirmed by the best members of the human race, as long as history records the thoughts of men". Further, he noted,

> With us, it has become mixed up with theological doctrines, and so has been made the subject of verbal disputes; but it is itself an old and native feeling of the human heart. And the belief that there is an unseen fact beneath all that we are conscious of--that there is something unperceived by us which gives rise to all our experience--also is not new; though it has lately taken a more distinct form and place in the human mind.[15]

Hinton "left untouched the question of sin", but Shorthouse explored "Sin" in all of his novels[16] and tried to define the "terrible consequence of all sin" especially as it is "visited upon innocent victims".[17] Sin and evil are psychological and spiritual "transpersonal" realities to Shorthouse, Jung, and Eliot, which they express respectively as the morbid, oppressive gloom of the plague in *John Inglesant*'s Italy, "the discordant duality and mass

267

unconsciousness of our fallen personality"[18], and "The Waste Land" of dispirited modern human consciousness. Sin and evil, however, express and present the deepest and most impenetrable of mysteries to the human mind through the obscurities, obfuscations, and "obstructions of language". Not the least of such mysteries for Shorthouse, Jung, and Eliot are the relationships of consciousness, meaning, language, and time.

Conscious awareness of time, "thought-time" or "ego-time", grounds itself in experiential paradoxes of self-encounter, memories and self-evaluation of motives, and in experiences of "non-ego" actualities: emptiness, silence, nothingness, and timelessness. "Time past and time future / Allow but a little consciousness", Eliot laments in "Burnt Norton". "To be conscious is not to be in time", he asserts, then instantly qualifies:

> But only in time can the moment
> in the rose garden,
> The moment in the arbour where the rain beat,
> The moment in the draughty church
> at smokefall
> Be remembered; involved with past and future.

As if to set an archetypal seal on the nature of human mind and its apprehension of time, he concludes: "Only through time time is conquered."[19] If there is no time in consciousness, then logically human mind can have no memory of consciousness itself, because memory is in time and can only be experienced through time; paradoxically, however, "timeless moments" are knowable through "projection of consciousness" which is "not the equivalent of reasoning" but is rather

> the projection of the inner light which emanates from the mysterious 'centre' of the person, allowing him to direct himself towards the kingdom of the shadows in a constantly dynamic fashion.[20]

Through such projection, Jung theorized, one can "establish a dialogue between the individual and the universal, without destroying the idea of personality or the Ego".[21] Jung's explanation aligns Shorthouse's "new view of humour" and his "sympathetic perception" with a primitive mode of thought[22] and with the duality of "fallen and risen" man as envisioned by Christianity. Jung sensed the similarities of Eastern and Western thought as an intuition of "a second language" unconsciously parallelling and possibly explaining "the divisiveness found in the Western mind". While Western man was "still barbarously polytheistic", his "natural evolution" was interrupted and "broken by the introduction of a psychology and of a spirituality which had developed from a civilization higher than our own." To Jung, this "culture clash" explained the origin and cause of the "dissociation between the conscious and the unconscious part of mentality". To Shorthouse and Eliot the cause of mental dissociation, was, of course, the "fall of man" in the Genesis myth, and man's potential regeneration at the birth of the Christ became the structure and order of historical time. Does "fallen man" experience time differently than "risen man"? The question focuses on the Ego/Self axis in psychological terms, as it does on the "old self" and the "new self" in New Testament reasoning. In New Testament terms, the First Coming of Christ represents the incarnation, life, and death on the cross; the Second Coming refers to the time at the end of the world when Christ will return to judge the living and the dead. In baptism, which symbolizes death and rebirth, the Christian dissociates his "past life" from "the potential new life in Christ".[23] The old Ego must "die" before one may experience Shorthouse's "sympathetic perception of the divine principle of God in daily living". Clearly, though, in the example of St. Paul's famous "thorn in the flesh" and his teachings to the Romans, sin and the "old will" reassert themselves even after spiritual rebirth and, "It is easier to go to Mars or to the moon than it is to penetrate one's own being",[24] as Jung said. "What lies behind words...is the only thing that is truly there",[25] and "only a poet could begin to understand".[26] Of his own achievement, Jung confessed: "What I have done in my work, is simply to give new names to those ideas, to those realities",[27] and in the final statement of his autobiography he urged a return to traditional religious language

...name the unknown by the more unknown, *ignotum per ignotius*--that is, by the name of God as a final confession of human subjection, imperfection, and dependence and at the same time a testimony to his freedom to choose between truth and error.[28]

To Eliot, history is "a pattern of timeless moments" which may be apprehended and remembered through the mental attitude of "indifference", to observing with both the conscious and the unconscious mind in holistic vision or poetic perception that is at once "the most ancient and the most modern", the most critical and the most creative. Indifference, "being between two lives", is a condition of mind and experience attainable through "love expanded beyond desire". In an Anglo-Catholic sense, "indifference" between Roman Catholicism and Anglicanism is conscious awareness of "still points" or stable "finite centres", moments of faith in which Christian spirituality expands beyond differences of nationality, personality, and thought itself.[29] "In any analysis of knowledge, knowing is assumed...Knowing is inextricably intertwined with processes which are not knowing; knowing...is only an aspect of a continuous reality." The very virtue and necessity of "metaphysical analysis", Eliot contends, derives from its "showing the destructibility of everything", because analysis "gives us something equally real, and for some purposes more real, than that which is analysed".[30] Both his metaphysical philosophy and the assumption of "knowing" are repeatedly asserted and defined in *Four Quartets* around the "finite centres" of the immediacy and the simultaneity of "time and place" as they were earlier in "Ash-Wednesday":

> Because I know that time is always time
> And place is always and only place
> And what is actual is actual only for one time
> And only for one place...

To Eliot's pre-Christian mentality, such knowing yielded only "fragments" which could be "shored against my ruins",[31] but to his Christian intelligence, such knowing declares itself as "a predetermined moment, a moment in and of time...in what we call history: transecting, bisecting the world of time", a moment which literally makes time: "for without the meaning there is no time, and that moment of time [gives] the meaning".[32] The paradoxes of Eliot's Christian understanding of time urge and force meaning into every moment of time as "the actual", which may be lived once and once only and which cannot be explored without great danger to consciousness itself unless "guided by sound theology".[33]

In "Burnt Norton" the intense pressure of seeing experience consciously and unconsciously at the same moment concentrates itself into mystical awareness of "what might have been and what has been", of actuality and of "perpetual possibility" which exists "only in a world of speculation", a world of "looking for". The "door" into what might have been, "the door we never opened", leads Harry in *The Family Reunion* to declare: "So one never passes through the same door / Or returns to open that one overlooked".[34] Realisation of choice is essential to nurturing the process of Individuation and the relocating of the centre of personality from the Ego to the Self, a process that begins in Eliot's poetic vision and in Shorthouse's romantic "enspiritualising" when one moves through the "garden door". Even so, the Four Tempters *Murder in the Cathedral* led Becket through what might have been and what might yet be to an eternal "Now". The "nowness" of "a lifetime burning in every moment"[35] underscores the urgency of self-evaluation, of reflective self-knowing, and forces the mind "Caught in the form of limitation / Between unbeing and being"[36] to see its own worldly pettiness, the "shocking valuations of all that we have been", might have been, and might yet become, and confronts the Christian mind with actual choices in historical perspective:

> To *kneel where prayer has been valid*[37]
> To pray: *Teach us to care and not to care,*
> *Teach us to sit still...*
> *Our peace in His will.*[38]

To know: *The only hope, or else despair*
          Lies in the choice of pyre or pyre--
          To be redeemed from fire by fire. [39]

To be: *...still and still moving*
        Into another intensity
        For a further union, a deeper communion... [40]

To trust: *All shall be well*
           And all manner of thing shall we well. [41]

The choices, of course, may be rephrased and redefined, but within *Four Quartets*, all perspectives are defined by the controlling truth of the epigraph from the *Die Fragmente der Vorsakratiker* Herakleitos: "Although the Word [Logos] is common to all, most men behave as if they had knowledge peculiar to themselves." The *epi*graph or "final word" comes ironically "before the beginning", even as the Christ-to-be in the Second Coming "was before the world was made". Ultimately, the individual "tongues of flame" will become "in-folded" into "the crowned knot of fire" and the seemingly unique self-knowledge of individuals will be seen as "common to all" in a united Christian faith and sacramental vision. The "we" of "The Dry Salvages" who are "content at the last / If our temporal reversion nourish / (Not too far from the yew-tree) / The life of significant soil" may attain "the impossible union of spheres of existence"[42] only "When the tongues of flame are infolded into the crowned knot of fire", and the promised result is mystical Individuation, "the fire and the rose are one":

> From a psychological point of view [the fire and the rose]
> are symbolic of aspects of the process of Individuation,
> particularly the self-realization in man of the Self, indis-
> tinguishable finally from an experience of God, and man's
> realization of himself as a self, as a complex totality
> which is finally a unity of all the opposites in the world.[43]

In *The Cocktail Party*, Eliot describes and explains the essential difference between choice and decision. Because choice derives from intuitive perception of one's nature, it is actually "choiceless awareness", whereas decision, which involves the Ego in time-related thought processes, implies alternatives. In doing so, he dramatises the shift of the centre of personality from the Ego to the Self. Celia Coplestone, suffering the same distress that afflicts Mary in *The Family Reunion*, seeks counsel from Sir Henry Harcourt-Reilly. Reilly, if not a characterization of Jung himself, is remarkably Jungian, a "doctor of the soul". Convinced that the world she

271

lives in "seems all a delusion", Celia suffers an intense awareness of solitude and thinks "that one is always alone". She confesses disillusionment:

> It's not the feeling of anything I've ever *done*,
> Which I might get away from, or of anything in me
> I could get rid of--but of emptiness, of failure
> Towards someone, or something, outside of myself;
> And I feel I must...*atone*--is that the word? [44]

She has come to the solipsistic conclusion that "we can only love something created by our own imagination". Reilly's superior Individuation enables him to understand that her condition is curable, but that treatment must be her "own choice", and he leads her to see alternatives. First, he describes "the good life" centred within the Ego:

> I can reconcile you to the human condition
> [in which] some who have gone as far as you
> Have succeeded in returning. They may remember
> The vision they have had, / but they cease to regret it,
> Maintain themselves by the common routine,
> Learn to avoid excessive expectation,
> Become tolerant of themselves and others...
> Are contented [even though] they do not
>   understand each other,
> Breeding children whom they do not understand
> And who will never understand them.

Then, he describes "another way" for those who have the courage to Individuate:

> The second is unknown, and so requires faith--
> The kind of faith that issues from despair.
> The destination cannot be described...
> You will journey blind.
> But the way leads towards possession
> Of what you have sought for in the wrong place.

Each way, he tells her, "prescribes its own duty" and "Both ways are necessary. It is also necessary to make a choice between them." Raising alternatives to consciousness gives the Ego power to make decisions, but if one alternative presents itself as an intuition of destiny, of potential Individuation, the other will automatically be repressed. When the Ego confronts alternatives and de-*cides* between or among them, it selects one of the alternatives, allows it to remain in consciousness, and "kills" or suppresses the other(s) into the unconscious. Choosing from faith or intuition, however, directs the Ego and ego-consciousness with specific intention but does not "kill off" alternatives. Choosing holds alternative possibilities as potentialities within the Ego. In Celia's case, although she cannot know the destination of her chosen way, she will consciously know what her life "might have been" had she chosen the other way. She will "avoid the final desolation / Of solitude in the phantasmal world / Of imagination, shuffling memories and desires". By holding both "what might have been" and what actually is in consciousness, Celia will live what Jung called "the symbolic life", a sharp contrast to the Canterbury women of *Murder in the Cathedral* who go on "living and partly living" until they realise the meaning of Becket's martyrdom. Living with dynamic symbols of transformative energy, Celia's new life of faith will enable her to unfold the Self, to invent a new centre of personality, even as the Canterbury women begin to experience the new saint within themselves.

Although Shorthouse placed emphasis on "the idea of Christ" more than he did on the *imago Dei*, his "sacramental vision" envisions the lives of his protagonists as they come into contact with the "transcendent function of symbols". As Celia is guided into her new life by Reilly, a personification of the healing power of the *animus*, so Inglesant and Percival are guided by healing *anima* representations, Mary Collet and Constance Lisle. Shorthouse grounds his characters' actions in discernment and active opposition to the world of ego-time. The world of common sense, society, politics, and philosophy interact through the agency of the Self's potentiality, which Shorthouse expresses as Inner Light (conscience, self-knowing, and self-knowledge) and the Divine Voice, the transcendent power of sacramental vision.

A brief examination of three particular life choices helps us understand how Shorthouse, Jung, and Eliot responded to the symbolical processes of Individuation which they consciously experienced. Although it is not possible to isolate a single event within the life of each of these three authors as *the* moment of ego-transcendence or the moment when their respective egos broke through the personal unconscious into the collective unconscious, a series of inner choices and outer actions in each of their lives may be taken as symbols of how they chose to live symbolic, psychologically rich and spiritually abundant lives. Events in the world are rather meaningless to introverts who aspire towards intuitive thinking, and when introverts are naturally gifted with literary imagination, they instinctively self-project and express the dynamics of their inner lives through unconscious transferences to create "symbols of transformation".

In Shorthouse's case, the essential, symbolical life choices were two, which were synchronistically related. The first is his transition from the Society of Friends into the Church of England, and the second is his composing and publishing *John Inglesant*. Publication of the philosophical romance richly compensated Shorthouse for his lifelong stammer; it removed him from the "sweet silence together" of the Society of Friends and persuaded him to dedicate his articulate and imaginative voice to Anglican churchmanship. Believing that "communion with God is given to those who seek it diligently, not to those who despise it or pass it lightly by" and that communion with God is "entirely independent of all particular dogma", Shorthouse chose "the most efficacious means of proving this intimate communion with God", composing and publishing *John Inglesant* as dynamic testimony to the "scientific truth of God" and to the communal ideals of Little Gidding.[45] Because he consciously intentionalised his literary work to validate and give material form to the unseen and invisible world of spirit, his novels, tales, and essays represent rational attempts to capture and contain the irrational aspects of spirituality and "to enspiritualise" daily life into a myth of spiritual romance.

In "Ash-Wednesday" Eliot describes the condition of the persona's Ego in ego-time as

> Wavering between the profit and the loss
> In this brief transit where the dreams cross
> The dreamcrossed twilight between birth and dying.

Experiencing the autonomy of the unconscious as a kind of "grace", the persona confesses, "though I do not wish to wish these things", then witnesses itself being transformed within its sensual, ego-consciousness:

> From the wide window towards the granite shore
> The white sails still fly seaward, seaward flying
> Unbroken wings
>
> And the lost heart stiffens and rejoices
> In the lost lilac and the lost sea voices
> And the weak spirit quickens to rebel
> For the bent golden-rod and the lost sea smell
> Quickens to recover
> The cry of quail and the whirling plover
> And the blind eye creates
> The empty forms between the ivory gates
> And smell renews the salt savour
>   of the sandy earth.

In the "never and always...time of tension between dying and birth" and at "The place of solitude where three dreams cross...", Eliot experienced conversion and consciously chose a new religious orientation that he adhered to the rest of his life. Later, his visit to Little Gidding and his regular worship at St. Stephen's, Gloucester Road, sealed the fundamental ideal of Christian communal living ordered by devotion and worship into an apt symbol of transformation, and posits the Church of England as a psychic and spiritual home where individual personalities share "the common Logos of meaning".

By the time Eliot received formal baptism into the Church of England, he was recognized as an important and leading poet and literary critic. He was baptized 29 June 1927 rather secretly and privately by William Force Stead in Finstock Church, Oxfordshire, and was confirmed the next day in the Church of England by Thomas Banks Strong, Bishop of Oxford. Having lapsed "from Unitarianism into agnosticism, and out of agnosticism, after inclining towards Buddhism around 1922, to the Catholic idea which he preferred in its Anglican form",[46] Eliot gradually, rationally found "a satisfactory explanation both for the disordered world without and the moral world within". In Anglo-Catholicism, he discovered respect for individual conscience and judgment and abundant opportunity for the growth of love.[47] He quickly made his new Christian voice public in prose and poetry, in criticism and broadcast talks, and addressed his attention to reordering and reclaiming one of his greatest loves, English history. As if the "different voices" of "The Waste Land" had indeed found synthesis in a new "finite centre", and, as if the gasping, halting urges towards prayer in "The Hollow Men" had found divine acceptance, Eliot received new vitality and poetic inspiration. With new vision and new purpose, he accepted an offer from the London Forty-five Churches Fund and gave his poetic talents to writing "a book of words", the choruses of *The Rock*. The fund-raising pageant play was heralded by *The Times* (29 May 1934) as "a new thing in the theatre...a notable reunion between the theatre and its 'long-lost child... the English Church'". Success was immediate. *The New Statesman* (2 June 1934) acclaimed, "Mr. Eliot shows himself a greater master of theatrical technique than all our professional dramatists put together."[48] Having found the place for his individual talent within the greater tradition, Eliot accepted a daunting challenge, a new play about Thomas Becket to be performed in the Chapter House of Canterbury Cathedral.

It is, indeed, difficult to conceive of a greater and more daring undertaking for any poet-critic. Believing that "the whole of modern literature" had been "corrupted by Secularism", Eliot entered the realm of intellectual debate as the champion of the English Church. "It is not enough to understand", he explained, "what we ought to be, unless we know what we are; and we do not understand what we are, unless we know what we ought to be". He approached the paradox with a simple assertion of the need for synthesis: "The two forms of self-consciousness, knowing what we are and what we ought to be, must go together."[49] Shorthouse believed he had found the probability of such a synthesis in "Revelation (on the divine principle) with Humour, *not* their *opposition*" and had appealed to the greater intellect of Matthew Arnold to undertake making the synthesis, believing only "a *poet* [who is] a disciple of Christ" is capable of making "*the* Saviour" available to all ranks and classes of men.[50] As readily as Arnold rejected Shorthouse's challenge, Eliot rejected "Arnold's religious campaign" as a virtual "divorce" of "Religion from thought", an attempt "to affirm that the emotions of Christianity can and must be preserved without the belief".[51] Through his silence on Shorthouse's work, Eliot, in effect, rejected Shorthouse with the same criterion he used to explain "Arnold's failure". Arnold, and in this respect Shorthouse too, holds his place in English literature "by the power of his rhetoric and by representing a point of view which is particular though it cannot be wholly defined".[52] With his greater intellect and greater critical and creative powers, Eliot could not hope, as Shorthouse had done, that another author would share his mission and work it out for him. Eliot accepted the commission to write *Murder in the Cathedral* out of profound Christian dedication and genuine self-knowledge.

When *The Times* (2 November 1935) proclaimed *Murder in the Cathedral* as "the one great play by a contemporary dramatist", the reviewer noted that Eliot's own declaration through his protagonist could not have been more clear, more decisive, or more personal: "Now is my way clear, now is the meaning plain..."[53] However any critic analyzes Eliot's personal psychology or reads autobiography out of the creative works, the testimony of Eliot through Becket and its repeated definition and validation in all his later critical, poetic, and dramatic works is quite clear in Jungian terms: the Self replaced the Ego as the centre of Eliot's personality and gave him "new life". No longer a poet-critic whose personal psychology and intimate life depended upon the "whims of ego-consciousness", Eliot positioned himself with an urgency as resolute and absolute as Shorthouse did in the final chapter of *John Inglesant*. When the youthful Eliot argued that "the progress of an artist is a continual self-sacrifice, a continual extinction of personality" and that "the more perfect the artist, the more completely separate in him will be the man who suffers and the mind which creates",[54] he aligned himself, however unknowingly, with one of the fundamental tenets of analytical psychology.

"Great poetry [and by extension, great literature] draws its strength from the life of mankind, and we completely miss its meaning if we try to derive it from personal factors." In the struggle to become impersonal, Eliot stressed that the poet has "a particular medium" to express, not a personality, and, when the medium itself derives its psychic energy from the archetypal dynamics of the collective unconscious, new, great art redefines and reorders tradition:

Whenever the collective unconscious becomes a living

experience and is brought to bear upon the conscious outlook of an age, this event is a creative act which is of importance for the whole epoch. A work of art is produced that may truthfully be called a message to generations of men.[55]

Working from their respective historical perspectives, Shorthouse and Eliot both directed their intellectual and creative energies outwardly at what Jung calls "the psychic malaise": "An epoch is like an individual; it has its own limitations of conscious outlook, and therefore requires a compensatory adjustment."[56] As it was not Goethe who created *Faust*, but *Faust* that created Goethe",[57] so it was *John Inglesant* that created J. Henry Shorthouse and the other novels and tales that defined him, as it was the complete critical and creative works that synthesized the intellectual and emotional integrity of T. S. Eliot. Likewise, the *Collected Works of C. G. Jung* comprise the personal history of the Swiss psychologist and document the discovery of the archetypal nature of the collective unconscious. Unlike the life-creating moments of Shorthouse's and Eliot's choices, Jung's experience has the exactness of methodical self-study recorded through scientific empiricism.

Having resolved to begin a "voluntary confrontation with the unconscious as a scientific experiment", Jung recorded his experience with graphic objectivity.[58] Within days Jung had other visions which he was able to interpret through the same technique Wordsworth used in Book V of *The Prelude*. He regarded the series of dreams as though they were "empirical evidence" from another source, as though they were not his own subjective experiences. Objectifying the visions as messages from the unconscious, Jung realised the "I" of the visions, like "Parcyvale" in *Sir Percival*, was grounding his identity and attempting to give him a message in an historical perspective. At one point in the dream series, Jung heard a voice commanding him: "You *must* understand the dream, and must do so at once! If you do not understand the dream, you must shoot yourself!"[59] Because he knew a loaded revolver lay in the drawer of his night table, he became frightened and pondered again: "...and suddenly the meaning of the dream dawned upon me". As interaction with the Arab-Quixote dream figure caused Wordsworth to "wake in terror" only to discover his vocation to become a poet, so Jung awakened in fright to the realisation that the Self was struggling against his personal ego-will, that he must "sacrifice his ideal and his conscious attitudes":

> ...my secret identity...and my heroic idealism had to be abandoned, for there are higher things than the ego's will, and to these one must bow.[60]

277

Sacrifice is the key to understanding Shorthouse's sacramental vision as it is in Eliot's Christian apologetics. Because sacrifice requires a surrendering or giving up of ego-will, ego-thought, and ego-time, sacrifice requires consciousness greater than ego-consciousness, self-consciousness, and that of the Ego itself. Thus, interactive perception between audience and protagonist enables the audience to perceive dramatic irony in literature, and, thus the interplay of paradoxes of identity create "ironic consciousness". As an audience witnesses Becket, for instance, confronting the Fourth Tempter in *Murder in the Cathedral*, the audience already knows Becket's destiny and literally watches Becket gain knowledge of his inner nature. Thus, too, readers know the end of John Inglesant's religious quest from the beginning of the novel and confront, if they read with sensitivity, a satire cloaked in dramatic irony. Readers must locate "authority" within the text itself, accept the epistemological challenge Hobbes offered young Inglesant, or redefine their own artistic sensibilities. Although a reader may indeed "trace the outlines of his own personality", as Bodkin suggested, a reader must also recognize that "A work of art is not a human being, but is something supra-personal" and must therefore accept the value of impersonality.

> [A work of art] is a thing and not a personality; hence it cannot be judged by personal criteria. Indeed, the special significance of a true work of art resides in the fact that it has escaped from the limitations of the personal and has soared beyond the personal concerns of its creator.[61]

John Inglesant escapes the "limitations of the personal" by exciting readers' intuitive, imaginative powers to find parallels or comparable groundings, in other times and other places--the mysticism of the sixteenth and seventeenth-century Anglican divines and *The Book of Common Prayer*. Through its imaginative qualities, its evocative prose rhythms and poetic descriptions, and its philosophical and historical parallels, *John Inglesant* does "soar beyond the personal concerns of the creator". Nothing in the novel itself excites interest in the personality of Shorthouse or invites curiosity to explore his personal life. However, through the narrative persona of Geoffrey Monk, and during Shorthouse's ten-year process of composition, *John Inglesant* does create "the author of *John Inglesant*". As "the one great religious novel of the English language"[62] that "speaks immediately to human intuition... without regard to the reader's own faith or philosophy"[63] *John Inglesant* affords insight into the essential differences between Jungian literary criticism and archetypal criticism.

Jungian criticism took root in England during the 1920s' through the work of John Thorburn and Herbert Read, then took a decided turn towards archetypal criticism in the 1930s' and late 1940s' through the influence of Maud Bodkin and Elizabeth Drew.[64] Studying "archetypal patterns" in poetry, Bodkin tried to explain how literary works activate emotional responses in readers, how artistic techniques excite unconscious forces. As Jungian criticism directs attention at an author's growth and development in relation to the theory of Individuation, so archetypal criticism aims at analysis of formal structures that excite readers' responses. Looking for underlying unity within or between works of art, archetypal critics help elucidate and define what literature is and how it attains its ends; thus archetypal criticism seeks to discover the "Grand Unification Theory" and to establish literary criticism as a science. Archetypal criticism may well suspect "that literary value-judgments are projections of social ones...that Rhetorical value-judgments usually turn on questions of decorum...the difference between high, middle, and low styles." However, because "any criticism motivated by the desire to establish or prove" its value ultimately becomes "merely one more document in the history of taste", archetypal criticism risks self-confounding its artistic value in its determination to prove itself scientific.[65] Jungian literary criticism accepts "the presence of incommunicable experience in the centre of criticism" and the irrational and the ineffable within literary texts, and insists that criticism is at best an interpretive art which can never become scientific. Jungian and archetypal critics both tread the nebulous and indistinct borderland between science and art, a distinction as difficult to make as that between "the man who suffers and the mind which creates". The "Jungian facts" of any "anatomy of criticism" argue that the deconstruction any literary text merely reduces symbols to metaphors, translates and describes but does not explain. Jung's theory of Individuation aptly describes the dynamics of how *John Inglesant* created "the author of *John Inglesant*" and why "the author" continued to explore his spiritual insights in other creative works, and it insists that, at best, such analysis can only transform the complete works of Shorthouse into a "metaphor of Self", an illustration of how an artist transformed his personal myth into meaning for his readers.

Henderson's "case study" of Eliot and some observations about Shorthouse afford insight. Asserting "a certain advantage" in knowing little of an artist's personal experience, Henderson affirms it is "impossible to separate the poet's personality from his poetry" unless the "personality ceases to be only personal [and] becomes a kind of personal myth which gives meaning to the typical experiences of numerous people living at the same time".[66] Thus, the "myth of T. S. Eliot" does not lead to reductive interpretation: J. Alfred Prufrock does not represent Eliot's *persona*, Sweeney does not express Eliot's "personal *shadow*", and the women and images of women in Eliot's poetry and plays do not correspond to his "unfulfilled feeling function". To the contrary, they represent modern man in relation to the *persona*, the *shadow*, the *anima*, and, most importantly, to the Ego/Self axis. Thus, Marie-Louise von Franz's biographical study of Jung became an analysis of "his myth in our time", Aniela Jaffe's study of Jung developed into "the myth of meaning" and "the myth of consciousness", and Laurens van der Post's biography of Jung became "the story of our time".[67] Analogously, Shorthouse's becoming "the author of *John Inglesant*" transforms or individuates his personal psychology into a new transpersonal myth, a myth that is at once traditional, in that it represents unconscious ways of feeling and acting, and orthodox, in that it recognizes "a tradition without intelligence is not worth having" and insists upon intelligence that is consciously Christian.[68] Myth relates present consciousness to ultimate, ineffable mysteries, and because *mythos* is the linguistic "dressing of the *Logos*", mythology apprehends and contains the *Logos* as metaphor:

> Metaphor emits energy in both directions; it is at once a projection of psyche onto the face of the universe, and a satisfaction of psychic experience, a macrocosm contained in the full image of itself.[69]

The parallels Shorthouse drew between the spirit of *John Inglesant*'s historical era and Victorian England are in themselves metaphors that lead to the novel's central symbol, its *Logos* in action, the uniting of two sacramental visions: As "the figure of the Saviour" first entered Inglesant's soul and filled his mind with "stillness and peace unspeakable, and life, and light, and sweetness" when he knelt in adoration before the east window at Little Gidding, so "the figure of the Saviour" miraculously leaned from the crucifix towards "The Merciful Knight",[70] the Cavaliere di San Giorgio, and embraced "the blessed St. George himself" with a holy kiss before the altar in San Miniato.

According to Henderson, Eliot's personality was that of an introvert with a primary thinking function; thus Eliot's personality also displayed weak extroversion and feeling. Henderson interprets W. H. Auden's description of Eliot as "composed of three distinct personalities: a precise academician, a player of practical jokes, and an old woman who has known all the sorrows of the world and cannot be comforted". The "old woman" in Eliot he takes as "an incapacity for adequate expression of the feeling function", which represents itself, ironically, as the "little old man". "Gerontion" represents the "ultimate exhaustion of the spiritual life in its attempt to reduce everything to a rational or intellectual denominator". The imagery, conditions, and situations expressed by poetic personae, especially Prufrock, Sweeney, and Gerontion, prepare the unconscious tensions of "a tragical-comical-historical urban drama...the prison of a divided self in the tortures of neurotic conflict". Gerontion's "outward infantilism which has retreated into a passive facsimile of maturity" expresses its own futility and need for "contractual repression". "The sickness of the older person who has exhausted his physical birthright and has not yet achieved a philosophy of life" prefigures the psychological vacuity of "The Hollow Men" and spiritual drought of "The Waste Land". "Waiting for rain", the poems' collective personae yearn for "the healing water of the spirit" as the Sibyl yearns for death in the epigraph.

The potential for healing and "the high expectation of some miracle of healing" signals the first stage of psychological development, when an individual becomes aware of the need to attend to personal problems because archetypal problems have become too difficult or overwhelming. At the onset of the first stage, unused psychic potentialities activate "a rather primitive analogy of the conscious situation in the unconscious"; thus J. Alfred Prufrock pathetically imagines: "I should have been a pair of ragged claws / Scuttling across the floors of silent seas." So, too, earlier modes of persona and ego-adaptation appear through the dominating imagery of water, and the "waiting for rain" generalises unconsciousness and the fragmented consciousness of the many "personages" in "The Waste Land". When rain falls in Part V of the poem, the masculine "personages" (the Fisher King, the One-Eyed Merchant, the Phoenician Sailor, Prince Ferdinand, etc.) melt into the feminine ones (Cleopatra, Juliet, Elizabeth I, the typist home at teatime, etc.) into the transsexual, bisexual Tiresias, whose blind but prophetic "seeing" makes him a "bridging figure", a John the Baptist who prepares the way for the "third who walks always beside you" in Part V. Thus, too, in the weird figures of the Prior of Westacre and the Wizard in London, Shorthouse prepares John Inglesant for interior growth. As Eliot resolves the "personages" of "The Waste Land" into Tiresias, he "melted" all human distinctions in "Little Gidding" into "the familiar compound ghost, both intimate and unidentifiable". Shorthouse does not blend or melt his characters into one, but he does contrive the religious and philosophical ideas of his characters so that they all converge in John Inglesant.

During the second stage of psychological growth, the meaningful figure fades, leaving "the suffering ego at the mercy of the ghosts". In effect, the archetypal *shadow* blocks the "effective action of the ego"; thus, the persona of "The Hollow Men" confronts only "paralyzed force" and can only "whimper" rather than "bang" about the world's end. Such psychic drama also explains the dreaminess, the trances and the near madness of Inglesant even as it prepares him for "the plagues" throughout Italy. Jung described the condition of the second stage as evidence of the need for a "psychological non-ego" to replace "the narrow dichotomy of the ego-shadow combination", as proof that the Ego needs to be displaced by the

Self as the centre of personality. The disidentification of the *persona* with the Ego and its resultant awareness of the *shadow* involve the Ego directly with the unconscious in new and unfamiliar roles. Thus, John Inglesant dons new clothes and new roles as courtier, agent, and actor and begins to realise that the religious and political divisions of the world mirror his own inner conflicts. Thus, too, in Eliot's early poetry Sweeney attempts to dramatise himself as "Sweeney Agonistes". Henderson, generally, expects the third stage

> to be ushered in by an important dream in which the *anima* or *animus*, as images of the soul, appear in their own right and are accompanied by appropriate symbols representing deliverance from the *shadow* paralysis.[72]

The persona of "Ash-Wednesday" sees the "white-gowned Lady" after "three white leopards" have fed to satiety "On my legs my heart my liver and that which had been contained / In the hollow round of my skull". Though "dissembled", "that which had been contained / In the bones" sings ("chirps"), and, as "the silent sister" makes the sign of the Cross, the bones and their contents are "restored", and a voice commands: "Redeem the time. Redeem the unread vision in the higher dream..." Thus, too, Inglesant receives his sacramental vision of the Christ through the agency of an *anima* projection, Mary Collet, and becomes conscious that he must "redeem the time" by visiting Rome before committing himself to either the Anglican or the Roman Churches.

The formulation of "the family myth" and "the recognition of the distortion of the child's natural mind by the arbitrary imposition of the parent's unresolved, perhaps totally unconscious problems" delineates the imagery of the fourth stage. "Freedom from the parent-child situation is required" in this stage, and "it can come only when the individual sees the difference between the real parent and the archetype and is strong enough to continue his journey alone."[73] *The Family Reunion* dramatises the powerful, archetypal story of Harry, Lord Monchensey who is part-Orestes, part-Christ, part-Hamlet, part-Eliot, and part creative imagination. After he acquires new understanding of his family's history by recognizing the superficial *persona*-levels of his aunts and uncles, his unconscious relationship with Mary, with his mother Amy, and with his dead wife, Harry is ready for in-depth confrontation with his *anima*, Agatha, and the personified agents of the collective unconscious, the Eumenides. Harry ends "the family curse" of repressed sins and leaves Wishwood to follow his "bright angels", his new intuitive guides, into new life and spiritual vitality. Once such psychological matter has been resolved or at least sufficiently brought into consciousness, the individual is ready for the second half of life when Individuation may occur:

> Individuation forces recognition of a reality that the human ego could never bear alone and must shrink from until the symbol of Self is strong enough to protect and mediate its acceptance.[74]

In *John Inglesant*, the family myth involves three generations of the Inglesant family, but because the protagonist's father is so inadequate, a succession of father figures help Inglesant gain internal strength: Father St. Clare, Nicholas Ferrar, Cardinal Rinuccini, and the elderly Duke of Umbria. Dying childless, the last of his family, John Inglesant ends the curse of his grandfather's confused loyalties and dedicates himself to a new symbol of Self, the Church of England.

A maturing personality can either stabilize consciousness in the Ego to maintain healthy, normal relations with the personal and collective unconscious (making, perhaps, "the best of a bad job") or it may live, act, and experience its uniqueness in a dynamic relationship with the archetypal Self. One may indeed become an "English-saint". As Eliot intuited and intellectually realised, one may "apprehend / The point of intersection of the timeless / With time", which is indeed "an occupation for a saint", and through "historical perspective" one may also consciously choose to integrate the uniqueness of one's "individual talent" into "tradition". To protect his readers from the dangers of going beyond "the frontiers of consciousness", from the seductions of subconscious imagery and emotions, Eliot integrated rational, philosophical prose passages into *Four Quartets*. In *Murder in the Cathedral* Becket warns the audience, as does the narrative consciousness of "Burnt Norton", "Human kind cannot bear very much reality".[75] So, too, Harry warns the *Family Reunion*'s audience that "life would be unendurable / If you were wide awake".[76] Agonizing over the limitations of his audience, Sweeney states his dilemma: "I gotta use words when I talk to you".[77] The mature poetry of *Four Quartets* fluctuates between poetry and philosophical prose, leading, seducing, cajoling his readers towards poetic vision, then protecting them from the "heaven and damnation" of "now" by weaving his vision back into "the enchainment of past and future".[78] Because "Flesh cannot endure" the intensity of the poetry's mystical vision, "a lifetime burning in every moment", the master poet restores the rational tonality of philosophical speculation and religious metaphor, releases the laughter of children, treasures the family photograph album, and heeds ancestral voices. The "echoes of indifference" in *Four Quartets* evoke semiconscious moments of awareness and juxtapose the "primitive terror" against moments of ecstasy. Eliot's poetical power conjures and shares the sacramental vision of Shorthouse's "enspiritualised" scenes, and behind, below, above, and around both literary talents is the urgency of comprehensiveness, the archetypal validity of spiritual universality, and the "Church Catholic" reverence of the sacraments.

If we accept Jung's contention that consciousness itself is "a myth of meaning", a demanding, intellectual endeavour which takes form in a variety of linguistic discourses, we may apprehend the point of intersection that Eliot and Shorthouse obtained in their Anglo-Catholic sensibilities and that Jung discovered in the Ego/Self axis. The point is not as "ambiguous", as Pickering supposes, nor is it such a "muddle" as might appear to rational minds that flounder in attempts to comprehend the more mystical aspects of Individuation. Rationality and ego-consciousness presume and presuppose Ego-centred personality, which may readily find security and comfort in any number of rational systems of thought and belief which self-proclaim their own authority, but according to the literary and critical testimonies of Shorthouse, Jung, and Eliot, only the suprarationality of the Self can apprehend, comprehend, and integrate the irrationalities of human nature and the archetypes of the collective unconscious into the profound beauty and order of sacramental vision.

Because Shorthouse was an introverted, intuitive feeler, he was not a strong, intellectual or analytical thinker, but everything about him defies the argument advanced by W. J. Conybeare, who defined the Broad Church in the *Edinburgh Review* (October 1883). According to Conybeare's "Church Parties", "The natural indolence of men causes them to pass from the toleration of unimportant differences to the belief that all differences are unimportant." Ironically, when Arthur Stanley first introduced the term "Broad Church" in 1850, he did not intend "at all to mark off the lines of a new party, but to protest against party spirit."[78] Shorthouse stressed the unimportance of parties or divisions within the church in *John Inglesant* through both Anglican and Roman exponents, and he carefully delineated his protagonist's intellectual quest, but he did so through the "links and clues" of his intuitive vision, not through discursive logic or the theological "hairsplitting" of the Tractarians. He did not oppose the Christian truths of the Roman Catholic Church; he opposed all *-isms*, particularly the Roman "system", because he believed that "faith is free thought" and that systems of thought constrict the receptivity of sacramental grace. He hoped to protect the intellectual and spiritual freedom of "The Agnostic at Church" as much as he intended and sought to defend the spiritual grace of the Church of England's sacraments. Even the more conservative and conscientiously orthodox Eliot believed that "atheism is often a form of Christianity".[79]

When the First Vatican Council issued *Pastor Aeternus* (18 July 1870) and proclaimed the "irreformable" authority of the Roman Pontiff "when he speaks *ex cathedra*...in defining doctrine concerning faith or morals", the Council stated that such authority was grounded in faithful adherence "to the tradition received from the beginning of the Christian faith". *Pastor Aeternus* acknowledged a triple intent: Authority is necessary for "the glory of our Divine Saviour, the exaltation of the Catholic religion, and the safety of Christian people".[80] Jung grounded the psychology of Individuation in empirical methodology to ensure the safety of personality during "the experiment in depth", the confrontation with the unconscious. Because he understood dogma as "crystallized forms of someone else's religious experience", Jung rejected "dogmatic" as suggesting "the rigidity of a prejudice" and asserted that "in our continued movement toward ever higher levels of consciousness, personal experience becomes the only possible authority" in spiritual matters. The spiritual vitality of a religious tradition can be maintained, he argued, "only if each age translates the myth into its own language and makes it an essential content of its view of the world".[81] The dogma of Papal infallibility offended Protestants and Anglicans in 1870 just as seriously and profoundly as the Roman Church's rejection of Anglican ordination and sacraments did in 1896, a rejection which continues to this day. Despite the Ecumenical Movement and despite Pope John Paul II's sharing worship (but not the eucharist) with the Archbishop of Canterbury in 1982, modern Anglo-Catholics still share the anger and offence of "the author of *John Inglesant*". Modern readers offended by Nicholas Ferrar's protestation "that he did as verily believe the Pope to be Anti-Christ as any article of his faith"[82] are equally offended by Shorthouse's declaration in the last work he wrote for publication.

Contributing the "Preface" to Arthur Galton's *The Message and Position of the Church of England* in 1899, Shorthouse reiterated the vehemence and antipathy towards the Church of Rome that had made, and still makes, *John Inglesant* so controversial:

> Springing from the worst traditions of decadent Pagan Rome, the Papal system never was a Church. It never was anything but a propagandist machine for extracting forced obedience and alms from an ignorant, a deceived, and a terrified world.

As if this were not denunciation enough, he proceeds:

> The Papal Curia is founded upon falsehood, and falsehood enters, consciously or unconsciously, willingly or unwillingly, into the soul of every human creature that comes under its influence. It has poisoned the wells of religious life. Its story is one of horror, and of crime, and of cruelty. As I have said elsewhere, it always has been, and is now, the enemy of the Human Race.[83]

Galton, whom Shorthouse acknowledged as "my friend and distant cousin", had been ordained a Roman priest in 1880, the year *John Inglesant* appeared in private edition. Disillusioned with the Roman Church, Galton renounced his Roman priesthood, took orders in the Church of England, and defended both his personal *Message and Position* and that of other Anglican priests against *Apostolicae Curae*. When Pope Leo XIII condemned Anglican orders as "null and void" in *Apostolicae Curae*, Galton countered that "he ceased to minister in the Church of Rome because he believed that Roman Orders are invalid".[84] Galton's apology, however, did not excite reaction and might have gone publicly unnoticed but for Shorthouse's preface. "No rejection of Roman theology, or recognition of Rome's moral failure in many places", reprimanded the *Church Quarterly Review*, "can justify the language" of Shorthouse's anti-Roman denunciation.[85] Shorthouse was not able to reply or defend the strength of his denunciation. Soon after the publication of Galton's book, Shorthouse was permanently invalided with muscular rheumatism that left him bedridden and suffering. Such a denunciation of the Papal system and the Papal Curia expresses a rigidity and prejudice that may seem unworthy of the liberal-minded Broad Church Sacramentalist, but it expresses the fundamental opposition of Anglo-Catholics to Roman authority and against the Roman "system", and in its passion it restates the final vision of his most successful creation, "the religion of *John Inglesant*". Combining the appeal and transforming power of Romance with "That art of reasoning by which the prudent are discriminated from fools, which methodizes and facilitates our discourse, which informs us of the validity of consequences and the probability of arguments—that art which gives life to solid eloquence, and which renders statesmen, divines, physicians, and lawyers accomplished",[86] *John Inglesant* proclaims, "There is no Art but the Art of Life", and "the author of *John Inglesant*" urges that, as "The whole of modern life has been transformed by the worship of God in *our* Art, so all criticism should serve "this sacrificed and sacrificing God". "Had Victorian artists been chastened by an unselfish, modest submission to the lessons of the past", he believed, "some supreme work of genius would have graced the Victorian reign."[87] *John Inglesant* did, indeed, grace the reign of Queen Victoria with a new synthesis of historical imagination and reason: philosophical romance.

Notes to Chapter Seven

[1]Lady Victoria Welby-Gregory, *Links and Clues* (London: Macmillan, 1883), viii.

[2]James Hinton, *The Mystery of Pain: A Book for the Sorrowful* (London: Smith, Elder, and Co., 1867).

[3]The "philosophical attitude" is that "of the man who starts from a clean slate, the observer who gets rid of his preconceived ideas lest they distort his view of the landscape...[The] landscape is the human being--always original, always unique". George Lauzun, *Sigmund Freud: The Man and his Theories*, trans. Patrick Evans, (Greenwich, Connecticut: Fawcett, 1962), 141.

[4]Lady Victoria Welby-Gregory, *Links and Clues*: "In sacramental reception, it is primarily He who receiveth us, rather than we who receive Him. He is not contracted into our smallness, but we become part of His greatness...our need of knowing God as 'Thou' rather than as 'He' (327)".

[5]James Hinton, *The Mystery of Pain* 23-24.

[6]Shorthouse shared the brief quotation from Dr. Talbot with Dr. Gott, Bishop of Truro; see *LLLR*, vol. I, 377.

[7]James Hinton, *The Mystery of Pain* 76.

[8]Lady Victoria Welby-Gregory, "Preface" to the 2nd ed., *Links and Clues* viii.

[9]J. Henry Shorthouse, Letter to Dr. Gott, Bishop of Truro (1901), *LLLR*, vol. I, 377-378.

[10]Freud "teaches us...to free ourselves through psycho-analysis from religious belief, which calls infantile or neurotic elements into play: 'Cravings for parental protection, narcissistic flight from reality, guilt feelings inspired by a religion based on terror and the castration complex, anxiety wearing the mask—the ridiculously sacred mask—of eternal punishment...'" Gerard Lauzun quotes A. Hesnard, *Sigmund Freud: The Man and his Theories* 144-145.

[11]Robert H. Hopcke's *A Guided Tour of the Collected Works of C. G. Jung* (Boston and Shaftsbury: Shambala, 1989) gives a reliable overview of the problems of Jung's usage of *psyche* and *soul* and clarifies the distinctions, 36-40.

[12]Fr. John P. Dourley, *The Psyche as Sacrament: A Comparative Study of C. G. Jung and Paul Tillich* (Toronto: Inner City Books, 1981), 31-47.

[13]J. Henry Shorthouse, Letter to Rawdon Levett (28 May 1894), *LLLR*, vol. I, 329.

[14]James Hinton, *The Mystery of Pain* 36.

[15]James Hinton, *The Mystery of Pain* 15.

[16]J. Henry Shorthouse, "Preface" to *John Inglesant*.

[17]J. Henry Shorthouse, Letter to Wilfred Jones-Bateman (27 January 1892), *LLLR*, vol. I, 300-301.

[18]Lady Victoria Welby-Gregory, "Duality Within Identity", *Links and Clues* 287-290.

[19]T. S. Eliot, "Burnt Norton", *The Complete Poems and Plays of T. S. Eliot* (London: Faber and Faber, 1969), 173. [Cited as *Complete* hereafter.]

[20]Miguel Serrano, "My First Interview with Jung", *C. G. Jung and Hermann Hesse: A Record of Two Friendships* (London: Routledge and Kegan Paul, 1966), 109. Jung explains: "I was [in India] some time ago, trying to convince the Hindus that it is impossible to get rid of the idea of the Ego or of consciousness, even in the deepest state of *samadhi*...Since the Unconscious really means not-conscious, nobody can gain that state while he is alive and be able to remember it afterwards...In order to remember, one must have a conscious spectator, who is the Self or the conscious being" (48-49).

[21]Miguel Serrano, *C. G. Jung and Hermann Hesse* 46-47.

22. *LLLR*, vol. I, 83-89.

[23]St. Paul's Letter to the Romans, chapter six, explains the paradoxes of perception involved in Christians' baptism and burial "into His death" but "alive unto God", the death of sin and the life of grace which cannot be seen except by "spiritual perception".

[24]C. G. Jung, quoted by Miguel Serrano, *C. G. Jung and Hermann Hesse* 102.

[25]Miguel Serrano, *C. G. Jung and Hermann Hesse* 100.

[26]Miguel Serrano, *C. G. Jung and Hermann Hesse* 60.

[27]Miguel Serrano, *C. G. Jung and Hermann Hesse* 100.

[28]C. G. Jung, *Memories, Dreams, Reflections*, recorded and edited by Aniela Jaffe, (New York: Random House, 1961), 354.

[29]T. S. Eliot, *Knowledge and Experience in the Philosophy of F. H. Bradley* (New York: Farrar, Straus, and Co., 1964), 204-205: "The finite centre, so far as I can to pretend to understand it, *is* immediate experience. It is not in time, though we are more or less forced to think of it under temporal conditions. It comes to itself as all the world and not as one world among others...It is very difficult to keep the meanings of 'soul', 'finite centre', and 'self' quite distinct."

[30]T. S. Eliot, *Knowledge and Experience* 156-157.

[31]T. S. Eliot, "The Waste Land", *Complete* 75.

[32]T. S. Eliot, "Choruses", *The Rock*, *Complete* 75.

[33]T. S. Eliot, "Conclusion", *The Use of Poetry and the Use of Criticism* (London: Faber and Faber, 1933), 150.

[34]E. Martin Browne, *The Making of T. S. Eliot's Plays* (Cambridge University Press, 1970), 98.

[35]T. S. Eliot, "East Coker", *Complete* 182.

[36]T. S. Eliot, "Burnt Norton", *Complete* 175.

[37]T. S. Eliot, "Little Gidding", *Complete* 192.

[38]T. S. Eliot, "Ash-Wednesday", *Complete* 198.

[39]T. S. Eliot, "Little Gidding", *Complete* 196.

[40]T. S. Eliot, "East Coker", *Complete* 183.

[41]T. S. Eliot, "Little Gidding", *Complete* 198.

[42]T. S. Eliot, "The Dry Salvages", *Complete* 190.

[43]Mark Stephen Shearer, *The Poetics of the Self: A Study of the Process of Individuation in T. S. Eliot's 'Four Quartets'*. Diss., University of South Carolina, 1985, 402.

[44]T. S. Eliot, *The Cocktail Party*, *Complete* 412-416.

[45]J. Henry Shorthouse, Letter to Mrs. Moller (1890), *LLLR*, vol. I, 288-291.

[46]*The Christian Register* (19 October 1927) printed "The Modern Dilemma", which was originally an address Eliot gave to Unitarian clergy in Boston. Eliot's self-description of his religious journey to the Church of England is summarized by Caroline Behr, *T. S. Eliot: A Chronology of his Life and Works* (London: Macmillan, 1983), 44.

[47]Eliot's religious conversion has been the study of much scholarly, critical, and appreciative attention. The best analysis and presentation of his inner life is that by Lyndall Gordon: *Eliot's Early Years* (Oxford University Press, 1977) and *Eliot's New Life* (Oxford University Press, 1985). Her chapter "Conversion" also appears in *Modern Critical Views: T. S. Eliot*, ed. Harold Bloom, (New York: Chelsea House, 1985), 77-94.

[48]E. Martin Browne, *The Making of T. S. Eliot's Plays* 32-33.

[49]T. S. Eliot, "Religion and Literature", *Selected Essays*, third enlarged edition, (London: Faber and Faber, 1951), 398.

[50]J. Henry Shorthouse, Letter to Matthew Arnold (23 October 1871), *LLLR*, vol. I, 83-89.

[51]T. S. Eliot, "Arnold and Pater", *Selected Essays* 431-443.

[52]T. S. Eliot, "Arnold and Pater", *Selected Essays* 432.

[53]T. S. Eliot, *Murder in the Cathedral*, *Complete* 258.

[54]T. S. Eliot, "Tradition and the Individual Talent", *Selected Essays* 17-18.

[55]C. G. Jung, "Psychology and Literature", *The Spirit in Man, Art, and Literature*, vol. 15, *Collected Works*, Bollingen Series XX (Princeton University Press, 1966), 98.

[56]C. G. Jung, "Psychology and Literature", 98.

[57]C. G. Jung, "Psychology and Literature", 103.

[58]C. G. Jung, "Confrontation with the Unconscious", *Memories, Dreams, Reflections*: "It was during the Advent of the year 1913--December 12, to be exact--that I resolved upon the decisive step. I was sitting at my desk once more, thinking over my fears. Then I let myself drop. Suddenly it was as though the ground literally gave way beneath my feet, and I plunged into dark depths" (179).

[59]C. G. Jung, "Confrontation with the Unconscious", *Memories, Dreams, Reflections* 180.

[60]C. G. Jung, "Confrontation with the Unconscious", *Memories, Dreams, Reflections* 180-181.

[61]C. G. Jung, "On the Relation of Analytical Psychology to Poetry", *The Spirit in Man, Art, and Literature* 71.

[62]Paul Elmer More, "J. Henry Shorthouse", *Shelburne Essays*, third series, (Boston: Houghton Mifflin, 1905), 227.

[63]Joseph Ellis Baker, *The Novel and the Oxford Movement* (Princeton University Press, 1932), 199.

[64]Jos van Meurs, "A Survey of Jungian Literary Criticism in English", *C. G. Jung and the Humanities*, ed. Barnaby and D'Acierno, (Princeton University Press, 1950), 238.

[65]Northrop Frye, "Polemical Introduction", *Anatomy of Criticism* (Princeton University Press, 1957), 22-25.

[66]Joseph L. Henderson, "Stages of Psychological Development Exemplified in the Poetical Works of T. S. Eliot", *Journal of Analytical Psychology*, vol. I (May 1956), 133-144, and vol. II (January 1957), 32-49.

[67]Marie-Louse von Franz's work, *C. G. Jung: His Myth in Our Time* was published in English in 1975 (New York: G. P. Putnam's Sons); Aniela Jaffe's *The Myth of Meaning: C. G. Jung and the Expansion of Consciousness* in 1970 (London: Hodder and Stoughton); and Laurens van der Post's *Jung and the Story of our Time* in 1975 (New York: Random House).

[68]T. S. Eliot, *After Strange Gods* (London: Faber and Faber, 1934), 29.

[69]James Olney, "Jung", *Metaphors of Self: The Meaning of Autobiography* (Princeton University Press, 1972), 105.

[70]Edward Burne-Jones drew at least three compositional sketches for "The Merciful Knight", a gouache and watercolour that belong to "The Legend of St. George" series. The British Museum houses seven finished paintings (which were painted by Burne-Jones' studio assistant, Charles Fairfax Murray); the Birmingham Museum and Art Gallery has "roughly a hundred studies for the series" and owns "The Merciful Knight" which illustrates the legend of St. John Gualbert (Giovanni Gualberto), founder of the Order of Vallambrosa, "the Shady Valley".

[71]Joseph L. Henderson, "Stages of Psychological Development" 33.

[72]Joseph L. Henderson, "Stages of Psychological Development" 35-36.

[73] Joseph L. Henderson, "Stages of Psychological Development" 44.

[74] W. J. Conybeare, "Church Parties", *Edinburgh Review* (October 1883), 273-342. See also Frederick Maurice's *The Life of Frederick Denison Maurice* 607-608.

[75] T. S. Eliot, "Burnt Norton" and *Murder in the Cathedral, Complete*, 172 and 271.

[76] T. S. Eliot, *The Family Reunion, Complete* 293.

[77] T. S. Eliot, *Sweeney Agonistes: Fragment of an Agon, Complete* 124-125.

[78] T. S. Eliot, "Burnt Norton", *Complete* 173.

[79] In a review of Bertrand Russell's *Why I am not a Christian*, Eliot "maintains that atheism is often a form of Christianity, and that it will be found in its High Church form in Matthew Arnold, its Tin Chapel form in Lawrence, and its Low Church form in Russell". F. B. Pinion, *A T. S. Eliot Companion* (Macmillan, 1986), 37.

[80] H. D. Bettenson, *Documents of the Christian Church* 273.

[81] Wallace B. Clift, "The Language of Religion" and "The Problem of Dogma", *Jung and Christianity: The Challenge of Reconciliation* (New York: Crossroad Publishing Company, 1985), 81-103, 91.

[82] H. P. K. Skipton, *The Life and Times of Nicholas Ferrar* (London: A. R. Mowbray, 1907), 122-123.

[83] J. Henry Shorthouse, "Preface" to Arthur Galton's *The Message and Position of the Church of England* (London: Kegan Paul, Trench, Trubner, and Co., 1899).

[84] *Church Quarterly Review*, vol. LXIX, no. XCVII (October 1899), 201-210.

[85] *Church Quarterly Review*, vol. LXIX, no. XCVII (October 1899), 201.

[86] J. Henry Shorthouse, *John Inglesant* 434-435.

[87] J. Henry Shorthouse, "Of Restraining Self-Denial in Art", *Century Guild Hobby Horse*, III (1888), 3-7. Reprinted in *LLLR*, vol. II, 319-325.

Bibliography

Ackroyd, Peter. *T. S. Eliot: A Life*. New York, 1984.

Acton, Lord John. *The Letters of Lord Acton to Mary, Daughter of the Rt. Hon. W. E. Gladstone* (1904), 135-148.

Adey, Lionel. *C. S. Lewis's "Great War" with Owen Barfield*. Victoria (British Columbia), 1978.

Ainger, Alfred. Letter to Michael Field, 1887. British Library MS. 45851, f. 112.

Albion, George. *Charles I and the Court of Rome: A Study in 19th Century Diplomacy* (1935).

Alexander, Helen Cadbury. *Richard Cadbury of Birmingham* (1906).

Allan, Mowbray. *T. S. Eliot's Impersonal Theory of Poetry*. Lewisburg: Bucknell University Press, 1974.

Alldritt, Keith. *T. S. Eliot's "Four Quartets": Poetry as Chamber Music*. (1978).

Alter, Robert. *Motives for Fiction*. Harvard, 1984.

———. *Partial Magic: The Novel as a Self-Conscious Genre*. Berkeley, 1975.

Altick, Richard David. *The English Common Reader: A Social History of the Mass Reading Public, 1800-1900*. Chicago, 1957.

Alvarez, A. *The Savage God: A Study of Suicide* (1971).

Anglican Essays: The Anglican Communion as Catholic and Reformed (1923).

Anglo-Catholic Principles Vindicated. Oxford, 1978.

Antrim, Harry. *T. S. Eliot's Concept of Language: A Study of its Development*. Florida, 1971.

Aronson, Alex. *Music and the Novel*. Totowa, New Jersey, 1980.

"The Author of *John Inglesant*". Rev. of *The Life, Letters, and Literary Remains of J. H. Shorthouse*. vol. 68, no. 1702 (22 April 1905), 437-438.

Bainston, George. *The Art of Authorship* (1890).

Baker, Earnest A. *The History of the English Novel: The Day Before Yesterday* (1938).

Baker, Joseph Ellis. *The Novel and the Oxford Movement*. Princeton, 1932.

Bantock, G. H. *T. S. Eliot and Education* (1970).

Barfield, Owen. *Poetic Diction: A Study in Meaning* (1928).

———. *Romanticism Comes of Age* (1944).

Barnaby, Karin and Pellegrino D'Acierno. *C. G. Jung and the Humanities: Toward a Hermeneutics of Culture*. Princeton, 1990.

Barnes, Arthur Stapylton. *Bishop Barlow and Anglican Orders* (1932).

Baring-Gould, S. *The Lives of the Saints*. Vol.7, 290-301. Edinburgh, 1914.

Barry, William. "Joseph Henry Shorthouse". *Bookman*. Vol. 28, no. 165 (June 1905), 94-95.

Bartleet, Hubert H.M. "*John Inglesant*, Its Author, and Little Malvern". *Transactions of the Worcestershire Archaeological Society*. Vol. I (May 1923--May 1924), 41-49.

Bates, F. A. *Colonel Graves' Memoirs of the Civil War*. Edinburgh, 1927.

Batho, Edith and Bonamy Dobree. *The Victorians and After* (1938).

Bede, Cuthbert [Rev. E. Bradley]. *Notes and Queries*. Series VII, vol. 7,

341; VIII, vol. 7, 321.

Behr, Caroline. *T. S. Eliot: A Chronology of his Life and Works* (1983).

Bennett, S. Rowe. "John Inglesant's Ideal Church". *The Church Reformer*. Vol. II, no. 3 (15 March 1883), 1-2.

Benson, Arthur Christopher. *The Life of Edward White Benson, Sometime Archbishop of Canterbury.* (1899).

Benson, Monsignor Hugh. "Masterpiece for the Week: Shorthouse's *John Inglesant*". *Everyman.* (13 October 1913).

Berger, Morroe. *Real and Imagined Worlds: The Novel and Social Science.* Harvard, 1977.

Bergsten, Staffan. *Time and Eternity: A Study in the Structure and Symbolism of T. S. Eliot's "Four Quartets".* Stockholm, 1960.

Bigelow, John. *Molinos the Quietist.* New York, 1882.

Birmingham Daily Gazette. Birmingham Biography: newspaper cuttings, vol. 4 (1902-03), 44-45.

Birmingham Daily Mail. Birmingham Biography: newspaper cuttings, vol. 4, 1902-03 (5 March 1903), 43, and vol. 6 (1906-09), 18-19.

Birmingham Gazette and Express. Birmingham Biography: newspaper cuttings, 1906-09, Letter (4 May 1907), 87-88.

Bishop, Morchard. "*John Inglesant* and its Author". *Essays by Diverse Hands.* Oxford: Transactions of the Royal Society of Literature. Oxford, 1958, 73-86.

Blackstone, Bernard. Review of A. L. Maycock's *Nicholas Ferrar of Little Gidding. The Criterion.* Vol. XVIII, no. LXX (October 1938), 154-157.

Blakeney, Edward Henry. "Joseph Henry Shorthouse". *Churchman.* (August 1905), 577-581.

Blamires, Harry. *Word Unheard: A Guide Through T. S. Eliot's "Four*

Quartets" (1969).

Bloom, Harold. *Poetry and Repression: Revisionism from Blake to Stevens.* Yale, 1976.

———, ed. *T. S. Eliot: Modern Critical Views.* New York, 1985.

Bloomfield, Morton W., ed. *In Search of Literary Theory.* Ithaca, New York, 1972.

Bodkin, Maud. *Archetypal Patterns in Poetry: Psychological Studies of Imagination* (1934).

Bowlby, Henry. "Joseph Henry Shorthouse and *John Inglesant*". *National Review.* Vol. 48 (Sept. 1906), 132-145.

Britton, Norman. "A Tract for the Times: *John Inglesant*". *Progress.* (January 1883), 8-15.

Brodrick, James. "A Prince of Plagiarists: John Henry Shorthouse". *The Month.* Vol. CXLVI, no. 736 (October 1925), 338-343.

Brook, Z. N. *The English Church and the Papacy from the Conquest to the Reign of John.* Cambridge, 1931.

Brooker, Jewel Spears. *Approaches to Teaching T. S. Eliot's Poetry and Plays.* New York, 1988.

Brooks, Harold F. *T. S. Eliot as Literary Critic* (1987).

Brown, Ford K. *Fathers of the Victorians.* Cambridge, 1961.

Browne, E. Martin. *The Making of T. S. Eliot's Plays.* Cambridge, 1970.

Burne-Jones, Edward Coley. "The Merciful Knight", 1863. Birmingham Museums and Art Gallery.

Campbell, Joseph. *The Hero with a Thousand Faces.* Princeton, 1949.

———. "Mythological Themes in Creative Literature and Art", *Myth, Dreams, and Religion.* New York, 1970, 138-175.

Campbell, Roy. "Foreword", *On the Four Quartets of T. S. Eliot* (1953).

Carpenter, William Boyd. Letters. Wm. Boyd Carpenter Papers. Vol. VII. British Library MS. 46723.

——. Letters to William Ewart Gladstone: 1872-1893. British Library MSS. 44435-44517.

——. *Further Pages of My Life* (1916).

——. *The Permanent Elements of Religion: Bampton Lectures, 1887* (1889).

——. *A Popular History of the Church of England* (1900).

Carter, C. Sydney. *The English Church in the Seventeenth Century* (1909).

Carter, T. T. *Nicholas Ferrar: His Household and his Friends* (1892).

Casey, John. "T. S. Eliot: Language, Sincerity, and the Self". *Proceedings of the British Academy* (1977), 63.

"Catalogue of the Library of Joseph Henry Shorthouse, Esq. Sold by Sotheby, Wilkinson, and Hodge. Monday, 20 December 1909".

The Central Literary Magazine (Birmingham). Vol. XXII (1915-1916), 107-109.

Chadwick, Owen. *An Ecclesiastical History of England: The Victorian Church* (1966.

——. *The Mind of the Oxford Movement* (1960).

Chapman, Edward Mortimer. *English Literature and Religion, 1800-1900* (1910).

Chapman, Raymond. *Faith and Revolt: Studies in the Literary Influence of the Oxford Movement.* (1970), 252-279.

Charteris, Evan. *The Life and Letters of Edmund Gosse* (1931).

Chasson, Nora. "Sonnet to Mr. Shorthouse". *Westminster Gazette.*
Birmingham Biography: newspaper cuttings, vol. 4 (1902-03), 48.

Clark, G. Kitson. *Churchmen and the Condition of England, 1832-1885*
(1973).

Clarke, Herbert E. "The Author of *John Inglesant*". *British Friend.*
New Series, vol. 14, no. 6 (June 1905), 151-153.

Clift, Wallace B. *Jung and Christianity: The Challenge of Reconciliation.*
New York, 1985.

Coats, Robert Hay. *Types of English Piety.* Edinburgh, 1912, 27-29.

———. "Birmingham Mystics of the Mid-Victorian Era". *Hibbert Journal.*
XVI (April 1928), 485-494.

Conybeare, W. J. "Church Parties", *Edinburgh Review* (October 1883),
273-342.

Cope, W. "J. Henry Shorthouse". *Central Literary Magazine.* XVII
(October 1905), 117-126.

"The Countess Eve". Rev. *The Academy.* vol. 34, no. 866
(8 December 1888), 367.

Craig, Cairns. *Yeats, Eliot, Pound and the Politics of Poetry:*
Richest to the Richest. Pittsburgh, 1982.

Craig, C. Leslie. *Nicholas Ferrar Junior: A Linguist of Little Gidding*
(1950).

Cressy, Dom Serenus [Fr. S. C. Monk, O.B.S.] "Why Are You a
Catholic?" (1686).

Crumb, Lawrence N. *The Oxford Movement and its Leaders: A Biblio-*
graphy of Secondary and Lesser Primary Sources. New York,
1988.

Cruse, Amy. *The Victorians and Their Books* (1935).

Cunningham, Valentine. *Everywhere Spoken Against: Dissent in the*

Victorian Novel. Oxford, 1975.

Daily Graphic. Review of *LLLR.* (19 April 1905).

Dalglish, Doris Nellie. "The Novels of J. H. Shorthouse". *Friends Quarterly Examiner.* LIX (July 1925), 221-235.

———. *We Have Been Glad* (1938).

Damrusch, Leopold, Jr. *God's Plot and Man's Stories.* Chicago, 1985.

Daniell, John J. *The Life of George Herbert of Bemerton* (1902).

Darrall, C. Norman. "The Mystery of *John Inglesant*". *Parish Magazine.* St. John's Church, Ladywood, Birmingham. (August--November 1947; January 1948).

Davis, Walter A. *The Art of Interpretations: A Critique of Literary Reason.* Chicago, 1978.

Dawson, William James. "Religion in Fiction". *The Makers of English Fiction* (1905), 268-289.

"Death of Mr. Shorthouse, the Author of *John Inglesant*, Birmingham's Most Famous Author". *Birmingham Daily Gazette.* Birmingham Biography: newspaper cuttings, vol. 4 (1902-03), 45-46.

"The Death of Mr. Shorthouse". *Birmingham Daily Post.* Birmingham Biography: newspaper cuttings, vol. 4, 1902-03 (5 March), 47-48.

DeLaura, David J. *Victorian Prose: A Guide to Research.* The Modern Language Association of America, 1973.

Denham, Richard D. *Northrop Frye and Critical Method.* Pennsylvania State University Press, 1978.

Digby, Kenelm Henry. "Tancredus", *The Broad Stone of Honour: or, the True Sense and Practice of Chivalry* (1828).

Dorsey, John M . *Psychology of Language: A Local Habitation and a Name.* Detroit, 1971.

Dourley, John P. *The Psyche as Sacrament: A Comparative Study of C. G. Jung and Paul Tillich.* Toronto, 1981.

Drew, Elizabeth. *T. S. Eliot: The Design of his Poetry* (1950).

Drummond, Andrew Landale. *The Churches in English Fiction.* Leicester, 1950.

Durham, James A. *Marius the Epicurean and John Inglesant* (1905).

Eagleton, Terry. *Literary Theory: An Introduction.* Oxford, 1983.

Edinburgh Review. "J. Henry Shorthouse". Vol. 207, no. 40 (January 1908), 178-202.

Edinger, Edward F. *Ego and Archetype: Individuation and the Religious Function of the Psyche.* New York, 1972.

Edwards, E. *Personal Recollections.* Birmingham, 1877.

Eliade, Mercia. *Myths, Dreams, and Mysteries.* Trans. Philip Mairet. New York, 1967.

Eliot, Thomas Stearns. *The Complete Poems and Plays.* (1969), rep. 1987.

Other works in order of publication:

——. "Syllabus for a Tutorial Class in Modern English Literature". University of London, 1916-1918.

——. *Essays Ancient and Modern.* New York, 1932.

——. *The Use of Poetry and the Use of Criticism* (1933).

——. *After Strange Gods: A Primer of Modern Heresy* (1934).

——. *The Idea of a Christian Society* (1939).

——. "Preface" to *The Testament of Immortality* (1940).

——. *Points of View* (1941).

——. "A Sermon Preached in Magdalene College Chapel (7 March 1948)". Cambridge, 1948.

——. *Notes Towards the Definition of Culture*. New York, 1949.

——. *Gedenkschrift zur Verleihung des Hansischen-Goethes-Preises, 1954*. Hamburg, 1954.

——. "Fr. Cheetham Retires from Gloucester Road". *Church Times*. No. 4,856, Vol. CXXXIX (9 March 1956), 12.

——. *George Herbert* (1962).

——. *To Criticize the Critic and Other Writings* (1965).

——. *Selected Essays* (1969), rep. 1987.

Eliot, Valerie. *"The Waste Land": A Facsimile and Transcript of the Original Drafts* (1971).

——. *The Letters of T. S. Eliot, 1882-1921* (1988).

Elliott-Binns, L. C. *Religion in the Victorian Era.* (1936).

Evelyn, John. *Memoirs and Secret Chronicles of the Courts of Europe*. New York, 1901.

Ewer, Ferdinand C. *Sermons on the Failure of Protestantism and on Catholicity*. New York, 1869.

Faber, Geoffrey. *Oxford Apostles: A Character Study of the Oxford Movement* (1936).

Fabricus, Johannes. *The Unconscious and Mr. Eliot: A Study in Expressionism*. Copenhagen, 1967.

Fanshawe, Lady Ann. *Memoirs of Lady Ann Fanshawe, 1600-1672* (1907).

Field, Michael [Katherine Harris Bradley and Edith Emma Cooper].
Letter from J. Henry Shorthouse. (25 May 1886), British
Museum Add. MS. 45,851.

Fleishman, Avrom. *The English Historical Novel: Walter Scott to Virginia Woolf.* Baltimore, 1971.

Fleming, William Kaye. "Some Truths About *John Inglesant*".
The Quarterly Review. Vol. 245, no. 485 (July 1925), 130-145.

——. *Mysticism in Christianity* (1903).

——. "John Aubrey and *John Inglesant*". *Times Literary Supplement.*
(25 March 1926), 236.

Forbes, Mansfield D., ed. "Nicholas Ferrar: America and Little Gidding".
Clare College: 1326-1926. Vol. II. Cambridge, 1930.

Forse, Edward J. G. *Church Times.* Vol. 49, no. 2906 (27 March 1903),
404.

Foster, Genevieve. "The Archetypal Imagery of T. S. Eliot". *PMLA.*
Vol. LX (June 1945).

Frauchiger, Hanna. *Das "innere Licht" in John Inglesant.* Diss.
Zurich, 1928.

Freemantle, Anne. "The Victorian Vision: An Anglican Pilgrim Novel".
Renascence. VII (1925), 129-134.

Frye, Northrop. *The Anatomy of Criticism: Four Essays.* Princeton
1957.

——. *Fearful Symmetry: A Study of William Blake* (1947).

——. *The Great Code: The Bible and Literature* (1982).

Fuller, Thomas. *The History of the Worthies of England* (1662).

Furnivall, Frederick J. *Robert of Brunne's "Handlyng Synne"* (1901).

Gallup, Donald. *T. S. Eliot: A Bibliography.* New York, 1969.

Galton, Arthur Howard. Letters to William Ewart Gladstone, 1887-1897. British Museum MS. 44500.

———. *The Message and Position of the Church of England...with a Preface by J. Henry Shorthouse* (1899).

Gardiner, A. G. *Life of George Cadbury* (1923).

Gardiner, Samuel Rawson. *The Constitutional Documents of the Puritan Revolution, 1628-1660*. Oxford, 1889.

———. "John Inglesant". *Fraser's Magazine*. N.S. XXV (May 1882), 599-605.

Gardner, Helen. *The Art of T. S. Eliot*. New York, 1950.

———. *The Composition of "Four Quartets"* (1978).

———. *"The Waste Land" 1972*. Manchester University Press, 1972.

Garnett, Richard. *Life of John Milton* (1890).

Gatta, John. "Spheric and Silent Music in Eliot's *Four Quartets*". *Renascence*. 32 (1980).

Ghose, Zulfikar. *The Fiction of Reality* (1983).

Gibson, Karen, Donald Lathrop, and E. Mark Stern. *Carl Jung and Soul Psychology* (1986).

Gladstone, Mary. Letter concerning *John Inglesant*. Mary Gladstone Papers, Vol LII., British Museum MS. 46,270.

Goldbrunner, Josef. *Individuation: A Study of the Depth Psychology of Carl Gustav Jung*. Notre Dame, 1964.

Gordon, Lyndall. *Eliot's Early Years*. Oxford, 1977.

———. *Eliot's New Life*. Oxford, 1988.

Gosse, Edmund. "The Author of *John Inglesant*". *Portraits and Sketches*

(1912), 151-162.

Graves, Charles L. *Letters of Alexander Macmillan* (1910).

Hall, Donald. *Their Ancient Glittering Eyes: Remembering Poets and More Poets.* New York, 1992.

Hall, James A. *The Jungian Experience: Analysis and Individuation.* Toronto, 1986.

Hanna, Charles B. *The Face of the Deep: The Religious Ideas of C. G. Jung.* Philadelphia, 1958.

Harding, Esther M. *Psychic Energy: Its Source and its Transformation.* Princeton, 1973.

——. *Women's Mysteries: Ancient and Modern* (1935).

Harris, John F. "J. H. Shorthouse, 1834-1903". *New Witness.* (8 May 1913).

Hart, A. Tindale. *The Eighteenth Century Country Parson: 1689-1839.* Shrewsbury, 1955.

Harvey, Gideon. "Discourse on the Plague" (1673).

Harvey, T. Edmund. "Quaker Language". *The Journal of the Friends Historical Society.* Supp. 15, 1928.

Hays, Alfred. "Men Who Have Influenced Birmingham". *Central Literary Magazine.* XXII (July 1915), 107-109.

Held, Herbert. *John Inglesant und der romische Katholizimus in England.* Diss. Graz, 1940.

Henderson, Joseph L. "Stages of Psychological Development Exemplified in the Poetical Works of T. S. Eliot". *Journal of Analytical Psychology.* Vol. I (May 1956) and Vol. II (Jan. 1957).

Henkin, Leo J. *Darwinism in the English Novel: 1860- 1910.*

New York, 1940.

Henson, H. Hensley. *Studies in English Religion in the Seventeenth Century* (1903).

Hertz, Alan. "The Broad Church Militant and Newman's Humiliation of Charles Kingsley". *Victorian Periodicals Review.* Vol. XIX, no. 4 (1986).

Higham, Florence. *Frederick Denison Maurice* (1947).

Hillman, James. *The Myth of Analysis: Three Essays in Archetypal Psychology.* Chicago: Northwestern University Press, 1972.

Hinton, James. *The Mystery of Pain* (1866).

Hoare, Mary. *Nicholas Ferrar: With Special Reference to the Story Books of Little Gidding.* M.A. Thesis. University of London, 1924.

Holland, Henry Scott. *A Bundle of Memories* (1914), 137-138.

Homans, Peter. *Jung in Context: Modernity and the Making of a Psychology.* Chicago, 1979.

Hough, Graham. "Books in General: J. H. Shorthouse". *The New Statesman and Nation.* Vol. 32, no. 806 (3 August 1946), 83-84.

Howitt, Margaret, ed. *Mary Howitt: An Autobiography* (1889).

Hutchison, William G. *The Oxford Movement: Being a Selection from the Tracts for the Times* (n.d.).

Hutton, Edward. "J. Henry Shorthouse". *Blackwoods's.* Vol. 173 (April 1903), 543-549.

Hutton, Richard H. "John Inglesant on Humour". *Brief Literary Criticisms* (1906).

Inge, Dean W. Ralph. *Christian Mysticism* (1899).

Ishak, Fayek M. *The Mystical Philosophy of T. S. Eliot.* New Haven, Conn., 1970.

Isichei, Elizabeth. *Victorian Quakers*. Oxford, 1970.

Jaffe, Aniela. *The Myth of Meaning in the Work of C. G. Jung*.
    Trans., R.F.C. Hull. Zurich, 1984.

———. *Was C. G. Jung a Mystic? and Other Essays*. Trans., Diana Dachler
    and Fiona Cairns. Einsiedeln, 1989.

James, Louis. *Fiction for the Working Man: 1830-1850* (1963).

Jarratt, F. "J. Henry Shorthouse on *John Inglesant*". *Notes and Queries*.
    Vol. 10, 10th Series (26 Sept. 1908), 246.

Jay, Elizabeth. *The Religion of the Heart: Anglican Evangelicanism*.
    Oxford, 1979.

Jewel, John. *An Apology for the Church of England*.
    Cornell University Press, 1963.

"John Inglesant". Rev. *The Academy and Literature*. vol. 64, no. 1610
    (14 March 1903), 548.

Jones, David E. *The Plays of T. S. Eliot* (1960).

Jones, Joyce M. Meeks. *Jungian Concepts in the Poetry of T. S. Eliot*.
    Diss. East Texas State University, 1975.

Josipovici, Gabriel. *Writing and the Body*. Princeton, 1982.

Jung, Carl Gustav. *The Collected Works of C. G. Jung*. 20 vols., trans.
    R.F.C. Hull; eds., Herbert Read, Michael Fordman, Gerhard
    Adler, and William McGuire. Princeton University Press,
    1953-1979.

———. *Memories, Dreams, and Reflections* (1972).

———. *Psychological Reflections* (1953).

Keary, Charles F. "The Work of J. Henry Shorthouse". *The Edinburgh
    Review or Critical Journal*. Vol. LCCII (July—October 1905),
    110-131.

Keble, John. *The Christian Year* (1827).

Kermode, Frank. "Dissociation of Sensibility". *The Kenyon Review.* Vol.
 XIX, no. 2, (Spring 1957).

Kincaid, James R. and Albert J. Kuhn, eds. *Victorian Literature and
 Society: Essays Presented to Richard D. Altick.*
 Columbus, Ohio, 1984.

King, Rachel A. Albright. "Joseph Henry Shorthouse". *Friends Quarterly
 Examiner.* Vol. 39, no. 155 (July 1905), 391-403.

Kirsch, James. *Shakespeare's Royal Self.* New York, 1966.

Knapp, Bettina. *A Jungian Approach to Literature.* Southern Illinois
 University Press, 1984.

———. *Archetype, Architecture, and the Writer.* Indiana University Press,
 1986.

———. *Machine, Metaphor, and the Writer: A Jungian View.*
 Pennsylvania State University Press, 1989.

Knight, William Angus. *Retrospects.* First Series. New York, 1904.

Knox, R. A. *Enthusiasm: A Chapter in the History of Religion with
 Special   Reference to the XVIIth and XVIIIth Centuries.* Oxford,
 1950.

Kojecky, Roger. *T. S. Eliot's Social Criticism.* New York, 1971.

Kort, Wesley A. *Narrative Elements and Religious Meanings.*
 Philadelphia, 1975.

Kreitler, Hans and Shulamith Kreitler. *Psychology of the Arts.*
 Durham, 1972.

Kugler, Paul. "The Unconscious in a Postmodern Depth Psychology",
 *C. G. Jung and the Humanities: Toward a Hermeneutics of
 Culture* (Princeton University Press, 1990), 307-318.

Landis, Paul Nissley. *The Psychological Treatment of the Historical Novel.* Abstract of a Thesis. University of Illinois, 1923.

——. *The Development of Nineteenth Century Historical Fiction Dealing with British History from 1640--1688.* Diss. University of Illinois, 1923.

Langbaum, Robert. *The Mysteries of Identity: A Theme in Modern Literature.* New York, 1970.

Langdon-Brown, Sir Walter. "The Psychology of Authorship". *Thus We Are Men* (1938), 192-195.

Lathbury, D.C., ed. *Correspondence on Church and Religion of William Ewart Gladstone.* New York, 1910.

Leavis, F. R. *The Living Principle: "English" as a Discipline of Thought.* New York, 1975.

Lee, Elizabeth, trans. *Life of Jean Paul F. Richter: Compiled from Various Sources, Together with his Autobiography* (1845).

Lee, Vernon [Violet Paget]. Rev. of *The Little Schoolmaster Mark The Academy.* Vol. 24, no. 608 (29 December 1883), 426-427.

——. Rev. of *Sir Percival. The Academy.* Vol. 30, no. 758 (13 November 1886), 320-321.

Levy, William Turner and Victor Scherle. *Affectionately Yours, T. S. Eliot.* New York, 1968.

Lindauer, Martin S. *The Psychological Study of Literature: Limitations, Possibilities, and Accomplishment.* Chicago, 1974.

Lindsay, Lady Jane. *Drawings by Lady Jane Lindsay Illustrative of John Inglesant* (1906).

Linnell, Charles. "The True Story of *John Inglesant*". *Athenaeum.* (27 July 1901), 127, and (17 August 1901), 222.

"*The Little Schoolmaster Mark*". Rev. *The Academy.* vol. 27, no. 617 (14 March 1885), 185.

Lloyd, Thomas. "The Literary Life". *Sunday Sun*. (7 May 1905).

Loughnan, William. "A Brace of Anti-Jesuit Novels". *The Month*. No. 215 (May 1882), 49-60.

Lukács, Georg. *The Historical Novel*. London: Merlin, 1962.

Macdonough, Rev. T.M., ed. *Brief Memoirs of Nicholas Ferrar, M.A.: Chiefly Collected from a Narrative by the Right Rev. Dr. Turner* (1837).

Madden, John Lionel. *Joseph Henry Shorthouse and Charlotte May Yonge: Bibliographical and Critical Studies* (1964).

Maison, Margaret Mary. *Search Your Soul, Eustace: A Survey of the Religious Novel in the Victorian Age* (1961), 287-306.

Martin, P. W. *Experiment in Depth: A Study of the Work of Jung, Eliot, and Toynbee* (1955).

Masterman, Charles Frederick Gurney. "J. Henry Shorthouse". *Independent Review*. Vol. 6 (July--August 1905), 109-115.

Masterman, Lucy, ed. *Mary Gladstone (Mrs. Drew): Her Diaries and Letters* (1930).

Marshall, Emma. *A Haunt of Ancient Peace* (1897).

Marshall, Beatrice. *Emma Marshall: A Biographical Sketch* (1901).

Mason, A. J. *The Church of England and Episcopacy*. Cambridge, 1914.

Matthews, Honor. *The Hard Journey: The Myth of Man's Rebirth* (1968).

Maurice, Frederick Denison. *The Kingdom of Christ, or Hints to a Quaker*. 2nd ed. (1842).

——. *The Religions of the World and Their Relations to Christianity* (1877).

Maycock, Alan. *Chronicles of Little Gidding* (1938).

————. *Nicholas Ferrar of Little Gidding* (1938).

Mayor, J.E.B., ed. "Nicholas Ferrar: Two Lives by his Brother John and by Doctor Jebb". *Cambridge in the Seventeenth Century* (1855).

McMurtry, Jo. *Victorian Life and Victorian Fiction: A Companion for the American Reader*. Hamden, Conn., 1979.

Meredith, Gertrude E. "*Sir Percival* and Mr. Shorthouse". *Church Review*. No. 49 (June 1887), 608-619.

Messenger, Ernest C. *The Reformation, the Mass, and the Priesthood: A Documentary History with Special Reference to the Question of Anglican Orders* (1936).

Miller, James E., Jr. *T. S. Eliot's Personal Waste Land: Exorcism of the Demons*. Pennsylvania State University Press, 1977.

Montgomery, Jessie Douglas. "Personal Recollections of Mr. Shorthouse". *Temple Bar*. Vol. 127, 1903, 664-670.

Montgomery, Marion. *Eliot's Reflective Journey to the Garden*. Troy, New York, 1979.

Moorman, J. R. *A History of the Church of England* (1953).

More, Paul Elmer. "J. Henry Shorthouse". *Shelburne Essays*. Third Series. Boston, 1905, 213-224.

More, Paul Elmer and Frank Leslie Cross. *Anglicanism: The Thought and Practice of the Church of England, Illustrated from the Religious Literature of the Seventeenth Century*. Milwaukee, 1935.

Morgan, Charles. *The House of Macmillan: 1843-1943* (1944).

Mortimer, C. G. and S. C. Barber. *The English Bishops and the Reformation, 1530-1560, with a Table of Descent* (1936).

"Mr. John Henry Shorthouse". Obit. *The Academy*. vol. 64, no. 1609 (7 March 1903), 215.

Neill, Stephen. *Anglicanism* (1958).

Newbolt, Henry. Obit. "J. Henry Shorthouse". *The Monthly Review.* XI (April 1903), 1-9.

Newman, John Henry. *Loss and Gain: The Story of a Convert* (1904).

Nichol Smith, David. *Characters from the Histories and Memoirs of the Seventeenth Century.* Oxford, 1918.

Norse, James Ashcroft. "*Blanche, Lady Falaise*". *The Academy.* Vol. 40, no. 1020 (21 November 1891), 452.

"Notes on J. Henry Shorthouse's Prefaces to Herbert, Molinos, Morse, and Galton". *The Academy.* Vol. 64, no. 1610 (14 March 1903), 242.

Nourse, Robert. "A Rare Romance". *Dial.* III (May 1882), 7-9.

Nowell-Smith, Simon. *Letters to Macmillan.* New York, 1967.

O'Day, Rosemary. *The English Clergy: The Emergence and Consolidation of a Profession, 1558-1647.* Leicester, 1979.

Oliphant, Margaret O.W. "Recent Novels". *Blackwood's Magazine.* CXXXI (March 1882), 365-391.

Ollard, Richard and Pamela Tudor-Craig. "Charles I and Little Gidding". *For Veronica Wedgwood These: Studies in Seventeenth-Century History* (1986), 175-187.

Ollard, S. L. *A Short History of the Oxford Movement* (1915).

Olney, James. *Metaphors of Self: The Meaning of Autobiography.* Princeton, 1972.

Olney, James, ed. *T. S. Eliot: Essays from The Southern Review.* Oxford, 1988.

Orel, Harold. *Victorian Literary Critics* (1984).

Pater, Walter. *Marius the Epicurean: His Sensations and Ideas* (1885).

Paul, Herbert, ed. *Letters of Lord Acton to Mary, Daughter of the Right Hon. W. E. Gladstone* (1904).

Paull, H. M. *Literary Ethics: A Study in the Growth of the Literary Conscience* (1928).

Pawley, Bernard and Margaret. *Rome and Canterbury Through Four Centuries: 1530-1973*. New York, 1985.

Peacock, Edward. Review of *John Inglesant*. *The Academy*. Vol. 20, no. 480 (16 July 1881), 45-46.

Pen, Pelican. "J. Henry Shorthouse". *The Central Literary Magazine* (Birmingham). Vol. 17, no. 4 (1905-06), 117- 126.

Peterson, William S. *Victorian Heretic: Mrs.Humphry Ward's "Robert Elsmere"*. Leicester, 1976.

Philipson, Morris. *Outline of Jungian Aesthetics*. Chicago: Northwestern University Press, 1963.

Pickering, W.S.F. *Anglo-Catholicism: A Study in Ambiguity* (1989).

Pinion, F. B. *T. S. Eliot: A Companion* (1986).

Polak, Meier. *The Historical, Philosophical, and Religious Aspects of John Inglesant*. Diss. Amsterdam: Purmerand, 1933.

Progoff, Ira. *Jung, Synchronicity, and Human Destiny*. New York, 1933.

Pulvermacher, Gunter. "Carl Gustav Jung and Musical Art", *Jung in Modern Perspective* (Bridport, Dorset: Prism Press, 1991).

Ratcliffe, S. K. Letter to the Editor. *The New Statesman and Nation*. Vol. 32, no. 308 (17 August 1946), 117-118.

___. "Shorthouse and *John Inglesant*". *Spectator*. CLIII (7 September 1934), 319-320.

Reay, Barry. *The Quakers and the English Revolution* (1985).

Rees, Thomas R. *The Technique of T. S. Eliot: A Study of the Orchestration of Meaning in Eliot's Poetry.* The Hague: Mouton, 1974.

Reinau, Peter. *Recurring Patterns in T. S. Eliot's Prose and Poetry: A Stylistic Analysis.* Basel, Switzerland: The Cooper Monographs, 28, n.d.

Relton, Frederic, ed. *A Relation of the Conference Between William Laud and Mr. Fisher the Jesuit* (1901).

Reresby, John. *The Memoirs of Sir John Reresby, 1634-1689* (1895).

Richardson, Caroline Francis. *English Preachers and Preaching, 1640-1670.* New York, 1928.

Richter, Jean Paul. *Museum.* Stuttgart and Tubingen, 1814.

Rieger, Elfriede. *Joseph Henry Shorthouse und sein John Inglesant: Ein Beitrag zur Geschichte des englishchen Romans im 19. Jahrhundert.* Diss. Georg-August Universitat, 1927. Gottingen: Tageblatt, 1927.

Robbins, Rossell Hope. *The T. S. Eliot Myth.* New York, 1951.

Roberts, R. Ellis. "John Inglesant: Centenary of Henry Shorthouse". *Observer.* (2 September 1934).

Rockey, Denyse. *Speech Disorder in Nineteenth Century Britain* (1980).

Rowell, Geoffrey. *The Vision Glorious: Themes and Personalities of the Catholic Revival in Anglicanism.* Oxford, 1983.

Russell, Elbert. *The History of the Quakers.* New York, 1942.

Russell, George William Erskine. *"John Inglesant".* *Selected Essays on Literary Subjects* (1914?), 268-274.

Sackton, Alexander. *The T. S. Eliot Collection of the University of Texas at Austin.* University of Texas, 1975.

Saintsbury, George. *The English Novel* (1913).

Salmon, Arthur L. "Joseph Henry Shorthouse". *Bristol Observer*.
(2 May 1903).

Samuels, Andrew. *Jung and the Post-Jungians* (1985).

Sanders, Andrew. *The Victorian Historical Novel, 1840-1880*. New York,
1977.

Schimmelpennick, Mary Ann. Original, untitled poem on the flyleaf of
Peckard's *Memorials of Nicholas Ferrar* (1790).

[S.D.R.] "Edgbastonians, Past and Present: No. 14, Joseph Henry
Shorthouse, Author of *John Inglesant*". *Edgbastonia*
(Birmingham). II (15 August 1882), 124-126.

Seeley, J. R. *Natural Religion* (1882).

Segaller, Stephen and Merrill Berger. *The Wisdom of the Dream:
The World of C. G. Jung*. Boston, 1990.

Sencourt, Robert. *T. S. Eliot: A Memoir*. New York, 1971.

Seth-Smith, E. K. *The Way of Little Gidding*.
London: H. R. Allenson, n.d.

Sharland, E. Cruwys. *The Story Books of Little Gidding: Being   the
Religious Dialogues Recited in the Great Room, 1631-1632*
(1899).

Sharma, Jitendra Kumar. *Time and T. S. Eliot: His Poetry, Plays, and
Philosophy*. New York, 1985.

Shorthouse, Edmund. *A Present to Youths and Young Men*.
Privately printed,1864.

Shorthouse, Joseph Henry. *John Inglesant: A Romance*. Birmingham,
1880. (First edition, 100 copies. The author's proof copy with his
manuscript notes is in the Rare Book Room, University of
Illinois.)

__. *John Inglesant: A Philosophical Romance* (1881).

313

___. *The Little Schoolmaster Mark: A Spiritual Romance* (1885).

___. *Sir Percival: A Story of the Past and of the Present* (1886).

___. *The Countess Eve: A Novel* (1888).

___. *Blanche, Lady Falaise: A Tale* (1891).

Other Writings of J. Henry Shorthouse in chronology of publication:

___. "On the Platonism of Wordsworth". Birmingham, 1881.

___. "The Agnostic at Church". *Nineteenth Century.* XI (April 1882), 650-652.

___. "Introductory Essay". George Herbert's *The Temple* (1882). \ (Facsimile reprint.)

___. "An Apologue". *Nineteenth Century.* XII (July 1882), 51-53.

___. "The Marquis Jeanne Hyacinthe de St. Palaye". *Macmillan's Magazine.* XLVI (July 1882), 177-191.

___. "The Baroness Helena von Saarfeld". *Macmillan's Magazine.* XLVI (August 1882), 256-278.

___. "The Humourous in Literature". *Macmillan's Magazine.* LXVII (March 1883), 248-280.

___. "Preface". *The Golden Thoughts from the Spiritual Guide of Miguel Molinos, the Quietist.* Glasgow, 1883.

___. "Ellie: A Story of a Boy and Girl". Birmingham, 1883.

___. "Frederick Denison Maurice". *Nineteenth Century.* XV (May 1884), 849-866.

___. "Preface". Francis Morse, *Peace, the Voice of the Church to Her Sick* (1888).

___. "Of Self-Restraining Self-Denial in Art". *Century Guild Hobby*

Horse. II (1888), 3-7.

___. "A Sunday Afternoon". *English Illustrated Magazine.* XIII (June 1895), 257-265.

___. "Preface on the Royal Supremacy". Arthur Galton, *The Message and Position of the Church of England* (1899).

Letters of J. Henry Shorthouse:

___. Miss Beale (1886-1887). Cheltenham Ladies' College Archives, Autograph Collection: E, vol.3, p.48.

___. William Boyd Carpenter. British Library Add. Mss. 46,723, ff.8-176.

___. T. H. S. Escott (1885). British Library Add. Mss. 58792.

___. "Michael Field" (1884). British Library Add. Mss. 45851, f.64.

___. William Ewart Gladstone (1881-1882). British Library Add. Mss. 44472-44475.

___. Edmund Gosse. (3 April 1883--5 March 1902), Leeds University: Brotherton Library.

___. Henry Harbour (1889-1892). Cambridge, Fitzwilliam Museum.

___. Mr. Harding (1883). University of Oxford, Taylor Institution Library: MS.8.E18/19.

___. G. J. Holyoake (1859). Manchester, Co-operative Union Library: Holyoake 1130.

___. Lord Houghton (1881-1884). Trinity College Library (Cambridge): Houghton 22:195-200.

___. J. Winter Jones (1872). British Library Add. Mss. 48341, f.17.

___. Sidney Lee (1889). Oxford, Bodleian Library: MS. Eng. misc.d.180, fols. 185-186.

___. Alexander, George, and Frederic Macmillan. (20 January 1881--22

January 1903), British Museum MS. 54933 and 54934.

___. Mr. Peyton (1888). University of Oxford, Taylor Institution Library: MS.8.E18/18.

___. Charles Rowley (1883). Manchester Central Library: M38/4/2/30.

___. Clement Shorter (1899). Leeds, Brotherton Library: Shorther Correspondence.

___. James Sime (1883). University of Edinburgh Library: Dk.6.23/2, fols.33-47.

___. William Smith (1889-1892). Cambridge, Fitzwilliam Museum.

___. Dr. Westcott (1890). London: Society of Friends Library, MS Box10(6)8.

"Shorthouse the Quietist". *The Guardian*. (9 September 1903).

Shorthouse, Sarah. *Life, Letters, and Literary Remains of Joseph Henry Shorthouse*. 2 vols. (1905).

___. Letters to George Macmillan. (25 March 1903--28 November 1907), British Museum MS. 54934.

Sidgwick, Arthur and Eleanor Mildred Sidgwick. *Henry Sidgwick: A Memoir* (1906).

Simmons, James C. *The Novelist as Historian: Essays on the Victorian Novel*. The Hague, 1973.

Simpkinson, C. H. *Life and Times of William Laud* (1894).

Singer, June. *Boundaries of the Soul: The Practice of Jung's Psychology*. New York, 1973.

Sinha, Krishna. *On "Four Quartets" of T. S. Eliot*. Alfracombe, 1963.

Skipton, H.P.K. *The Life and Times of Nicholas Ferrar* (1907).

Smidt, Kristian. *Poetry and Belief in the Work of T. S. Eliot*. Oslo,

1949.

Smith, Grover. *T. S. Eliot's Poetry and Plays: A Study in Sources and Meaning*. Chicago, 1956.

Smith, Janet Adam. "Anglican Romantic". Review of *John Inglesant*. *New Statesman*. Vol. 63, no. 1611 (26 January 1962), 128-130.

Smyth, Charles. Review of Bernard Blackstone's *The Ferrar Papers*. *The Criterion*. Vol. XVIII, no. LXXI, January 1939, 366-371.

Soldo, John J. *The Tempering of T. S. Eliot*. Michigan: UMI Research Press, 1983.

Southey, Robert. "St. Gualberto", *Poems of Robert Southey*. Oxford, 1909, 636-641.

Spinks, G. Stephens. *Religion in Britain Since 1900* (1952).

Spurr, David. *Conflicts in Consciousness: T. S. Eliot*. University of Illinois, 1984.

Sri, P. S. *T. S. Eliot, Vedanta and Buddhism*. University of British Columbia, 1985.

Stone, J. M. "Jesuits at Court" and "Charles the First and the Popish Plot". *Studies from Court and Cloister: Essays...Relating to the XVIth and XVIIth Centuries* (1905), 131-157, 178-210.

___. *Reformation and Renaissance: Circa 1377-1610* (1904).

Strange, Rev. Canon Creswell. "In Memoriam: J.H.S". *Parish Magazine*. (April 1903). St. John's Church, Ladywood, Birmingham.

Strelka, Joseph P. *Literary Criticism and Philosophy*. Pennsylvania State University Press, 1983.

Suddard, Sarah Jilie Mary. *Keats, Shelley, and Shakespeare Studies in English Literature*. Part 2, 279-301. Cambridge, 1912.

Summers, Montague. "Molinos and 'John Inglesant'". *Times Literary Supplement* (1 July 1926) 448 and (15 July 1926) 480.

__. "Man of One Book". *Everybody's Weekly*. (2 February 1946) 11.

Sutherland, J. A. *Victorian Novelists and Publishers*. Chicago, 1976.

__. *The Stanford Companion to Victorian Fiction*. Stanford, 1989.

Sutton, Max Keith. "*John Inglesant* and 'Little Gidding'".
    Yeats/Eliot Review. Vol. 8, nos. 1 and 2 (1986), 119-122.

Terry, R. C. *Victorian Popular Fiction, 1860-1880*. New Jersey, 1983.

The Times (London). "The Sale of J. H. Shorthouse's Library".
    (18 November 1909), p. 15, col. 4, and (22 December 1909),
    p. 17, col. 6.

Thwaite, Ann. *Edmund Gosse: A Literary Landscape, 1849-1928*.
    Chicago, 1984.

Van der Post, Laurens. *Jung and the Story of Our Time*. New York,
    1975.

Van der Weyer, Robert. "Nicholas Ferrar and Little Gidding:
    A Reappraisal". *For Veronica Wedgwood These...* (1986),
    152-172.

Van Meurs, Jos with John Kidd. *Jungian Literary Criticism, 1920-1980:
    An Annotated, Critical Bibliography of Works in English*.
    New Jersey, 1988.

Vargish, Thomas. *The Providential Aesthetic in Victorian Literature*.
    University of Virginia, 1925.

Vidler, Alec. *The Theology of F. D. Maurice* (1948).

von Franz, Marie-Louise. *C. G. Jung: His Myth in Our Time*.
    New York, 1975.

Wagner, F. J. *J. H. Shorthouse*. Boston, 1979.

Wagstaff, William R. *A History of the Society of Friends: Compiled from
    its Standard Records and Other Authentic Sources* (1845).

Walsh, Walter. *The Secret History of the Oxford Movement* (1898).

Ward, David. *T. S. Eliot: Between Two Worlds* (1973).

Ward, Mrs. Humphry. *Robert Elsmere* (1888).

Watson, Thomas. *The Fight of Faith Crowned*. Oxford, 1678.

Weby-Gregory, Victoria A.M.L. (Stuart-Wortley). *Links and Clues* (1883).

___. *The Witness of Science to Linguistic Anarchy*. Grantham: W. Clark, 1898.

Wheeler, Michael. *English Fiction of the Victorian Period: 1830-1890* (1985).

Whitmont, Edward C. *The Symbolic Quest: Basic Concepts of Analytical Psychology*. New York, 1969.

Widdowes, Giles. "The Schysmatical Puritan: A Sermon Preached at Witney". Oxford, 1630.

Williams, Raymond. *Culture and Society, 1780-1950*. New York, 1958.

Williamson, George. *A Reader's Guide to T. S. Eliot*. 2nd ed. New York, 1966.

Wilmer, Harry A. *Practical Jung: Nuts and Bolts of Jungian Psychotherapy*. Wilmette, Illinois: 1987.

Wilson, Frank. *Six Essays on the Development of T. S. Eliot* (1948).

Winston, Richard and Clara, trans. Erich Kahler, *The Inward Turn of Narrative*. Princeton, 1973.

Wolff, Robert Lee. *Gains and Losses: Novels of Faith and Doubt in Victorian England*. New York, 1977.

Woodgate, Mildred Violet. "J. Henry Shorthouse and his Work". *The Treasury*. (October 1912), 37-42.

Wordsworth, William. *The Poetical Works of Wordsworth*. Boston, 1904.